cp 92   35—
                         —
                         60

U. C. PRESS
FILE COPY

D1617285

U. C. PRESS
FILE COPY

The Center for South and Southeast Asia Studies of the University of California is the coordinating center for research, teaching programs, and special projects relating to the South and Southeast Asia areas on the nine campuses of the University. The Center is the largest such research and teaching organization in the United States, with more than 150 related faculty representing all disciplines within the social sciences, languages, and humanities.

The Center publishes a Monograph Series, an Occasional Papers Series, and sponsors a series published by the University of California Press. Manuscripts for these publications have been selected with the highest standards of academic excellence, with emphasis on those studies and literary works that are pioneers in their fields, and that provide fresh insights into the life and culture of the great civilizations of South and Southeast Asia.

RECENT PUBLICATIONS OF THE CENTER FOR SOUTH AND SOUTHEAST ASIA STUDIES:

Surinder Mohan Bhardwaj
> *Hindu Places of Pilgrimage in India:*
> *A Study in Cultural Geography*

Richard I. Cashman
> *The Myth of the* LOKAMANYA:
> *Tilak and Mass Politics in Maharashtra*

Edward Conze
> *The Large Sutra on Perfect Wisdom*

Tom G. Kessinger
> *Vilyatpur, 1848–1968:*
> *Social and Economic Change in a North Indian Village*

Robert Lingat
> *The Classical Law of India* (translated by J. Duncan M. Derrett)

URBAN POLITICS IN INDIA

Area, Power, and Policy in a Penetrated System

This volume is sponsored by the
CENTER FOR SOUTH AND SOUTHEAST ASIA STUDIES,
University of California, Berkeley

RODNEY W. JONES

Urban Politics in India

Area, Power, and Policy in a Penetrated System

JS
7065
.I52
J65
West

UNIVERSITY OF CALIFORNIA PRESS

Berkeley • Los Angeles • London

University of California Press
Berkeley and Los Angeles, California
University of California Press, Ltd.
London, England
Copyright © 1974 by
The Regents of the University of California
ISBN: 0-520-02545-8
Library of Congress Catalog Card Number: 73-83052
Printed in the United States of America

In Memory of

SHARAD CHANDRA DUBE

CONTENTS

    Politics, and the Struggle for Power   263
    Section I: Organizing Labor Power   265
    Section II: Unions and Electoral Competition   290
    Section III: Union Bosses and the Struggle for Machine
        Power   300
11. Other Political Arenas: The Fragmentation of Urban Politics   330
12. Area, Power, and Policy in a Penetrated System   347

    Appendix A   381
    Appendix B   387
    Bibliography   391
    Index   407

TABLES, FIGURES, AND MAPS

MAPS

PREFACE

Research on local community affairs is always a delicate task. This is especially true when the investigator is a foreign citizen. Because Indian hospitality does not leave one a stranger long, the foreign scholar must remind himself that doing his work is a privilege, and the doing should be handled with great care. When the research includes matters of government and politics, where feelings run deep, he should anticipate and take precautions against injury to the community or its members that might result, however unintentionally, from his findings or the way in which they are presented. Some authors who have studied small or intimate communities, in the United States as well as abroad, have chosen to give anonymity to the community and actors observed. Such a solution may be required when by publication the subjects of study would lose their accustomed privacy, but it carries with it certain disadvantages for scholarship: it makes the task of verification more difficult for other observers who would tread the same ground, and it requires treating the community in question as if it were isolated—an artificial assumption in most circumstances.

An attempt to disguise the city and people of Indore would have been ineffectual and probably counterproductive. Readers who are at all familiar with the city would easily recognize the characters in the cast. And the tasks of scholarship, particularly that of linking Indore with its larger state and national contexts, would only be impeded by the use of pseudonyms. In this study, therefore, I have followed the practice most common in political science of using the real names of people and places. But I have kept other safeguards. First, this work is confined to public affairs. The actors recognized are public figures, officially or reputationally. Virtually all of the information used about issues and events could readily be gathered from the press or by discussion with knowledgable citizens or officials of Indore. Second, informants, accounts of political events and motives have been treated with caution and checked as much as possible with other sources of information. Where reasonable doubt has remained, statements are qualified accordingly. And finally, the desires of certain informants that attribution be withheld has been respected.

The research for this book was carried out primarily on location in Indore, over a period of fourteen months ending in January 1969. During this time, no elections took place in the city. There was, therefore, no opportunity to observe at firsthand strategies of campaign, nomination processes, or the peak operations of political parties and leaders—all of which would have greatly enriched a study of this kind. On the other hand, the municipal government was superseded by the state government while research was in progress, affording an opportunity to examine at close hand the direct intervention of state authorities in local politics. Partly because of this vivid experience, I was able to describe the vulnerability of local politics to external forces with a degree of detail not always available to foreign observers.

Several factors contributed to my choice of Indore city as a research site. First, Indore had experienced substantial industrialization, thereby permitting an opportunity to study the industrial concomitants of urban politics, particularly the role of labor unions. Second, the city's population was the product of regional immigration, a promising setting for the study of ethnic competition and adaptation. Third, the historical background of the city as a princely state capital was intriguing, for it meant that the continuities of princely influence in urban and regional politics could be explored. Fourth, because Indore has been prominent in the politics and administration of Madhya Bharat and Madhya Pradesh, it appeared to be a fruitful location for the tracing of state–urban political linkages. Fifth, most of the political literature on India has been focused on rural or metropolis-based and national politics, so that the study of a medium-sized hinterland city would help fill a gap in scholarship. And finally, Indore lies in a Hindi-speaking region, enabling me to use my Hindustani language skills extensively.

For sources of information, I relied primarily on public documents and maps; a reading of daily Hindi newspapers—mainly *Nai Duniya, Indore Samachar,* and *Swadesh;* extensive interviewing; and observation. Political, sociological, and economic studies of Indore, except for the *Gazetteers* and other official sources, are practically nonexistent. Consequently, information about the social and economic structure of the population was drawn from a combination of census publications (the *Census of Central India, 1931* is the last in which a sociological breakdown and detailed information about Indore city itself, in contrast to the District as a whole, was available), *Gazetteers,* other published statistics, and interviews with community leaders and officials who were judged to know something about the size and occupational distribution of their respective communities. Time and resources did not permit a city-wide sample social survey. Some data useful for the analysis of electoral processes, and of party and factional competition, were obtained from private collections of newspaper clippings, documents, and other papers. I am indebted in particular in this respect to Niranjan C. Zamindar and to the *Nai Duniya* editorial staff for assistance in tracing down reports of earlier political events. Until the supersession of the Municipal Corporation a few months after my arrival in Indore, direct observation of council and committee meetings provided a further source of information.

My political analysis was informed by in-depth interviewing, in many cases with multiple extended sittings. Formal questionnaires were not administered to respondents. Probing for explanations of political outcomes was instead structured informally through my intuitive response to the personality and apparent experience of the respondent. New avenues of inquiry frequently emerged, and I was able to explore them quite readily under these circumstances. At the same time, however, I maintained a list of social background questions to which answers were sought, successfully in many cases but not in all; the social background queries were usually introduced when they appeared to fit naturally into the development of the interview, with the result that in some cases they did not arise at all. In a very few cases such questions were turned aside altogether.

I selected informants on the basis of reputational and positional (formal) criteria. This selection was a continuous process. Clues about who might be important political participants or otherwise knowledgable persons emerged from successive interviews. I obtained interviews with acknowledged leaders of the major political parties (Congress, Jan Sangh, Communist, Samyukta Socialist), labor unions, and organized groups; with elected politicians (as well as some unsuccessful electoral candidates)—the sitting and former members of the state legislative assembly and of parliament from the city, and nearly half of the sitting Municipal Councillors as well as many former Councillors who had held official positions in the municipal government; and a variety of informed professionals, including small and large businessmen, lawyers, educators, journalists, and a few student leaders. My ability to use colloquial Hindi was frequently a surprise to informants and usually a basis of rapport with them, particularly with those who found the use of English uncomfortable.

It quickly became apparent that bureaucratic officials were often primary and well-informed participants in the local political process. Consequently, about one fourth of those interviewed were administrators, particularly in the Improvement Trust, the Labour Department, the Public Health Department, the Directorate of Small-Scale Industries, the state and central departments of taxation, the Department of Cooperatives, the Collectorate, and the municipal administration. Retired administrative officers of the Holkar (princely) government were also interviewed, for the light they could throw on the pre-independence political affairs of the princely state and its capital city.

Despite the great debt I owe them in making this study possible, most of my interview respondents must go unnamed. The citizens with whom my wife and I became acquainted, from various communities and in different settings, were invariably more courteous, generous, and tolerant of our strange ways and curiosity than we could possibly have expected or deserved. My hope is that the results of this work, in which they may recognize their varied contributions, will provide intellectual satisfaction and a measure of my gratitude, however inadequate a form of recompense it may be.

Of those in Indore who can be acknowledged, I would like to express my special appreciation to Dr. O. P. Nagpal and Dr. Reuben Moses of Indore Christian College; Professors J. P. Dubey and S. K. Dubey, formerly of Sanskrit College in Indore; Surendranath Dube, Captain

H. C. Dhanda, and Captain Jagdale of the former Holkar state administration; His Highness, Richard Holkar, for access to the Manik Bagh Palace Reference Library; "Tatya" V. S. Sarvate and V. V. Sarvate; Bhanwar Singh Bhandari; B. M. Joshi; Niranjan C. Zamindar; Rahul Barpute, editor of *Nai Duniya*; Purshottam Vijay and Ajit-prasad Jain, the present and former editor, respectively, of *Indore Samachar*; Ishwar Chand Jain, editor of *Jagran*; Dr. S. N. Nagu; Vaidya Ram Narain Shastri; and Shri Satyabhan Singhal. Mahendra Trivedi, public relations officer of the Municipal Corporation, cheerfully provided access to public Corporation records and acted as a guide to their contents. Collector P. K. Lahri and Deputy Collector Shri Bobate courteously made available unpublished returns for general and municipal elections by polling station. And finally, Sharad Chandra Dube, former Chairman of the Improvement Trust and Municipal Commissioner in Indore, took a special interest in my work and was an enormous source of inspiration even while suffering from terminal leukemia. As a small tribute to his personal qualities as a citizen and administrator, this volume is dedicated to his memory.

The research was done originally for a doctoral dissertation under the supervision of Professors Wayne A. Wilcox and W. Howard Wriggins at Columbia University; their guidance was invaluable. I am indebted also to Dean Ainslie T. Embree of Columbia University, Dr. Bhabani Sen Gupta of the Southern Asian Institute at Columbia University, Professor S. P. Verma of the University of Rajasthan, Professor Ved Pratap Vaidik of Delhi University, and Professor John A. Vieg, my colleague and *guru* at Pomona College, for reading parts or all of the manuscript and sharing with me their judgments.

Field research in India was under the auspices of the American Institute of Indian Studies in 1967–68 and extended by a grant from the Southern Asian Institute of Columbia University. A Danforth Fellowship in the normal course of study enabled me to complete much of the task of compiling data and writing the original version prior to my initial teaching appointment at Kansas State University in 1969. And Pomona College has been generous in its provision of clerical assistance so this book might go to press.

My wife was a major participant at every stage, criticizing, cajoling, and stiffening my resolve, all the while cheerily maintaining her own professional progress under a no less demanding schedule. She deserves not merely gratitude but admiration as well.

Many have shared in making this book better. But the responsibility for the final product, its point of view, and any errors that remain, are mine alone.

R.W.J.

August, 1973
Claremont, California

PART ONE

THE SETTING

1

THE CITY IN INDIAN POLITICS

Cities have traditionally been centers of civilization and power, the abodes of gods and men. Their glories inspired awe and endowed their chieftains with command. They were the vehicles of recorded history, the repositories of learning and conservators of law and custom. Cities have nurtured most of man's creations, social and technical, and witnessed their elaboration on ambitious scales. Cities have sustained variety and specialty by promoting intramural harmony, and yet they have also served as launching pads for imperial conquest and territorial domination. Once cities were for the privileged; today they are as much for the destitute. Once cities were the focus of imperial communities; today they are submerged in nations. Once cities commanded their hinterlands, but today they are commonly besieged from without. Cities used to monopolize technology, knowledge, and power, yet today they are more often mere shareholders in massive corporations. In a world of accelerating modernization, the city remains important, but not always exclusively so. Cities are still centers of technology, but technology penetrates the non-urban peripheries and exerts autonomous effects. Cities multiply and compete. Their impact today is less as individual units and more as aggregations; it is profound but complex, seldom subject to purposive control, often frightful, and always fascinating.

The special significance of cities for politics in developing countries stems from their strategic contribution to processes of economic development and modernization and from their potential for political

disruption. Both in turn are functions of the growth of cities in size
and number, and of the increasing proportion of a country's population they embrace. Urbanization is seldom an unmixed blessing; it
offers grounds for both hope and despair. In the more familiar Western
experience, while urbanization has had ambivalent consequences, it
has led on the whole to favorable social, economic, and political results, both because the growth of individual cities was usually moderate in scale and because it proceeded concurrently with industrial
growth, bureaucratic and associational development, and increases in
political participation.

But this pattern does not fit neatly with the facts of urbanization
in the less developed countries today.[1] Although the rate of urbanization—that is, of the upward shift of the ratio of urban to total population—is only slightly greater in the developing countries today than
it was in Europe and North America during the last two centuries,[2]
there are several ways in which recent patterns depart from those of
the past. First, the sheer scale of urban populations is far greater;
spectacularly large numbers of people reside in cities today.[3] Second,
while the rate of urbanization has been nearly constant, the growth
rate of the urban population taken by itself has jumped recently, from
an average of 26 percent per decade from 1900 to 1950 to nearly 41
percent per decade between 1950 and 1970. Moreover, the rate of

[1] Gerald Breese, *Urbanization in Newly Developing Countries*; Breese, ed., *The City in Newly Developing Countries*; Scott Greer et al., eds., *The New Urbanization*; Philip M. Hauser and Leo F. Schnore, eds., *The Study of Urbanization*; Kingsley Davis, "The Origin and Growth of Urbanization in the World"; Glenn H. Beyer, ed., *The Urban Explosion in Latin America*; Philip M. Hauser, ed., *Urbanization in Latin America*; Francine F. Rabinovitz and Felicity M. Trueblood, eds., *Latin American Urban Research*; UNESCO, *Social Implications of Industrialization and Urbanization in Africa South of the Sahara*; Leo Jakobsen and Ved Prakash, eds., *Urbanization and National Development*; Jal F. Bulsara, *Problems of Rapid Urbanization in India*.

[2] Kingsley Davis, *World Urbanization 1950–1970, Vol. II: Analysis of Trends, Relationships, and Development*, pp. 49ff.

[3] This is understandable when one considers how massively the population base as a whole has expanded. A continuation of historically constant rates of urbanization produces ever larger absolute numbers of urban dwellers. The number of new urban residents, about 670 million, added to the world's urban population in just the two decades after 1950 is by itself nearly equal to the entire world urban population of about 706 million in 1950. Most of the recent added urban population is in developing countries. Davis, *World Urbanization, Vol. II*, p. 56, Table 14.

growth of the world's population in larger cities, those of 100,000 or more residents, has been even higher, reaching nearly 46 percent in each of the last two decades.[4] Third, all too often in the developing regions of Asia, Africa, and Latin America, urbanization is unevenly dispersed and huge numbers concentrate in "primate" cities.[5] And finally, urbanization today frequently lags far behind industrialization, so that the proportion of industrial workers in the urban centers of developing countries is about half that found in the West at comparable levels of urbanization.[6] Massive, rapidly growing urban populations, the primate city phenomenon, and the discontinuity between industrial and urban growth are what constitute the "urban explosion" experienced today. What are its consequences?

Two interrelated controversies permeate the literature on urbanization. The first concerns the effects of urbanization on economic development. Are cities, to use McGee's terms, "catalysts" or "cancers" in society?[7] The issue arises because expansion of industrial and other modern economic opportunities lags behind urbanization in developing countries. Rural migrants frequently flood into the cities, even when, objectively speaking, economic opportunities would appear to be too scarce to sustain the flow. The rural influx, it is argued, becomes parasitic. It drains inadequate urban and national resources and diverts the investment needed for economic growth. Those who call these trends "overurbanization," therefore, advocate demographic and in-

---

[4] *Ibid.*

[5] The concept of "primate" city refers to an "unbalanced" pattern of urbanization in which a single city so surpasses the others of a particular country in size, and exerts so powerful an attraction for population and investment, that it stunts the growth of other cities and distorts the economy, with adverse effects on development as a whole. The term originates with Mark Jefferson, "The Law of the Primate Cities," *Geographical Review*, Vol. 29, April 1939, pp. 226–232; and it has been expanded upon by many others. See, for example, the works cited in Breese, *Urbanization*, pp. 48–49; in Brian J. L. Berry, "City Size and Economic Development," in Jakobsen and Prakash, eds., *Urbanization and National Development*, pp. 111–155; and in Beyer, ed., *Urban Explosion*, p. 68, and especially Harley L. Browning's article, "Urbanization and Modernization in Latin America: The Demographic Perspective," in the same volume, pp. 71–92.

[6] Barbara Ward, "The Poor World's Cities," p. 57.

[7] T. G. McGee, "Catalysts or Cancers? The Role of Cities in Asian Society," in Jakobsen and Prakash, eds., *Urbanization and National Development*, pp. 157–181. In the same volume, see also Ashish Bose, "The Urbanization Process in South and Southeast Asia," pp. 81–109.

vestment policies designed to curtail the flow of migrants into the large established cities or to divert them to smaller centers.[8]

The second debate follows from the first, for it is concerned with the potentials for political radicalization thought to be present when urbanization outstrips economic growth.[9] Whether the inspiration lies in classical sociological theories of urbanism and alienation, Marxist categories of class conflict, or psychological theories of relative deprivation amidst rising expectations, the outcomes anticipated are much the same.[10] Rapidly growing urban populations are politically volatile, the breeding grounds of revolutionary violence and reaction. Rural migrants to the city are uprooted; their imported traditional way of life does not provide them with the means for coping with the unfamiliar signals and routines of urban life. The effort to adapt is stressful. There is little in the way of family, friendship groups, or other sources of personal warmth and sympathy to cushion failures or restore self-esteem. In the absence of economic rewards, migrants are presumed to be susceptible to radical appeals, easily moved to aggression against those held responsible for their plight. So goes the interpretation. Despite the plausibility of the radicalization model, there is growing evidence that it is not generally valid under present conditions.[11]

Part of the significance of this study lies in its contention that the radicalization model is not very compelling in the Indian urban set-

[8] This point of view is considered in a critical manner in N. V. Sovani's *Urbanization and Urban India,* especially in the chapter entitled "The Analysis of 'Over-urbanization,'" pp. 1–13; and also in Jakobsen and Prakash.

[9] See the excellent review in Joan Nelson, "The Urban Poor; Disruption or Political Integration in Third World Cities?" Also see James F. Guyot, "Creeping Urbanism and Political Development in Malaysia," in Robert T. Daland, ed., *Comparative Urban Research,* pp. 124–161.

[10] Louis Wirth's "Urbanism as a Way of Life" has influenced the first view, which is treated critically in William Kornhauser, *The Politics of Mass Society.* For an approach influenced by Marxist sociology, see Irving Louis Horowitz, "Electoral Politics, Urbanization and Social Development in Latin America," in Beyer, ed., *Urban Explosion,* pp. 215–254. And for psychological theories, consult Ted Robert Gurr, *Why Men Rebel.*

[11] See, for example, Wayne A. Cornelius, "The Political Sociology of Cityward Migration in Latin America: Toward Empirical Theory," in Rabinovitz and Trueblood, eds., *Latin American Urban Research,* pp. 95–125; Alejandro Portes, "Urbanization and Politics in Latin America"; Francine F. Rabinovitz, "Urban Development and Political Development in Latin America," in Daland, ed., *Comparative Urban Research,* pp. 88–123; Nelson, "The Urban Poor"; and Aprodicio A. Laquian, "Slums and Squatters in South and Southeast Asia," in Jakobsen and Prakash, pp. 183–203.

ting. For example, it supports the findings of others that, however necessary the analytical distinctions between rural and urban, or traditional and modern, the social and political realities are not as sharply divided.[12] Migrants to the city are not necessarily uprooted psychologically or socially. The traditional values and behaviors they import often have strong resonance and relevance in the city. Despite their appearance of extreme poverty, their move to the city is often the basis for economic improvement.[13] On the level of political behavior, this study strengthens the view that extremist tendencies, while not unknown in Indian cities, seem to draw their support less from migrants than from more established groups in the city.[14] Migrants are generally politically quiescent. Furthermore, the radicalization tendencies in Indian cities seem to be effectively defused by the political apparatus through mechanisms of cooptation. The system is highly sensitive to political violence and disruption, but also highly effective in eroding the immediate sources of discontent with distributive and regulative actions. Thus something more complex in the way of models about politics and cities in India would seem to be in order, and this study takes a step in that direction.

It is a paradox of Indian public life that cities are both profoundly influential and politically weak. Urban forces pervade modern Indian politics, but cities as corporate actors are not, as a rule, individually powerful. Much of the political energy contained in Indian cities is not expended on their behalf as communities but is instead absorbed in national competition or on behalf of more specific interests. Part of the explanation of this paradox may be found in the imperatives of colonial rule and the upsurge of nationalism. By relinquishing control in stages, and last of all at the center, the British centralized the important stakes of politics at the outset for several generations of indigenous leaders. Cities and towns were the cradle of administrative professionals and the nationalist political leadership—the personnel who inherited the mantle of power. In assuming responsibility for the nation, these leaders were diverted from pleading the special claims of cities, but much of the style and content of their rule reflected their urban background and proclivities.

---

[12] Lloyd I. and Susanne Hoeber Rudolph, *The Modernity of Tradition.*
[13] Sovani, *Urbanization.*
[14] Myron Weiner, "Violence and Politics in Calcutta."

While urbanites swept up most of the high positions of power and status after independence, there has been a steady growth in rural claims for power and recognition. The ruralization of politics or, as Rosenthal ironically puts it, the *"deurbanization* of the Indian political system," has been marked by increasing attention to rural development policies by government and the mobilization of rural leadership in parties.[15] This process had its roots in the Gandhian movement which made the rural areas the focus of the rhetoric of nationalism, but it came to fruition with community development programs and the new *panchayati raj* system of district local government.[16] Universal suffrage, the fact that nearly four-fifths of the population is rural, and the electoral reach of the Congress party have combined to promote a shift in the balance of power from urban to rural sectors.

But this shift should not obscure the importance of cities in Indian politics. The urban sector of India's population is large in absolute terms, more than a hundred million people, and much of this population is concentrated in larger towns and intermediate-sized cities.[17] Opposition parties appear to be more strongly based in cities than elsewhere. Their power will probably expand with urbanization, which is proceeding slowly but surely in the subcontinent. The cities and towns are still the places where social, economic, and political change are greatest. They are still the nerve centers of Congress as well as opposition politics. They are the locus of most of India's high-caste, educational, professional, and business elites, and the physical base for its growing middle and industrial working classes. They are the centers of capital and wealth, technological change, communications, manufacturing, and marketing.

The strategic centrality of the cities in the networks of communication and exchange confirms their function as headquarters for district and regional units of political parties and other political organiza-

---

[15] Donald B. Rosenthal, "Deurbanization, Elite Displacement, and Political Change in India"; Myron Weiner, *Party-Building in a New Nation: The Indian National Congress*; George Rosen, *Democracy and Economic Change in India*; Roy Turner, "The Future of Indian Cities"; and Robert T. Norman, "Urban Political Development: India."

[16] Weiner, *Party-Building*; D. C. Potter, *Government in Rural India*.

[17] Roy Turner, ed., *India's Urban Future*; and Bose, "The Urbanization Process," in Jakobsen and Prakash.

tions. As growing competition makes the tasks of parties and organizations more crucial and complicated, the roles of urban specialists in fund-raising, accounting, and publicity become indispensable, guaranteeing their continued access to decisions about recruitment, the selection of candidates for elective offices, and the formation of government ministries. The city's inhabitants are favored in recruitment to the bureaucracies, and the urban orientation of bureaucrats remains a constraint on policy planning and implementation.[18] Because of their common social upbringing, urban political leaders have easier access to bureaucrats than their rural counterparts. Consequently, as rural leaders are mobilized into state and national politics, they are usually engaged through party organization channels in unequal partnerships with urban leaders.[19] Rural leaders become increasingly sophisticated in dealing with their urban partners, to be sure, but the medium of their sophistication is their internalization of methods, skills, and styles drawn from the urban setting. Their politicization, in short, depends largely on their urbanization.

The guiding purposes of this study are related both to the comparative and American urban political studies and to the literature on Indian politics generally.[20] While certain focal concerns have been fairly sharply defined in the former, the research on politics and urbanism in India is still meager and mostly exploratory.[21] Little is

---

[18] Richard Taub, *Bureaucrats Under Stress.*

[19] Adrian C. Mayer, "Rural Leaders and the Indian General Election."

[20] For surveys of comparative work, see Terry N. Clark, ed., *Community Structure and Decision-Making: Comparative Analyses*; Daland, ed., *Comparative Urban Research*; Leo F. Schnore and Henry Fagin, eds., *Urban Research and Policy Planning*; Horace Miner, ed., *The City in Modern Africa*; and Nelson W. Polsby and Wallace S. Sayre, "American Political Science and the Study of Urbanization," in Hauser and Schnore, eds., *The Study of Urbanization.* For India, see Ashish Bose, *Urbanization in India: An Inventory of Source Materials.*

[21] When this study was begun in 1967, the first book-length treatment of municipal politics in India—Donald B. Rosenthal's *The Limited Elite: Politics and Government in Two Indian Cities* (1970)—had yet to appear; I was fortunate to see and to comment on parts of the unpublished manuscript in an earlier form. Several ground-breaking articles had appeared: Milton Singer, ed., "Urban Politics in a Plural Society: A Symposium" (1961)—which included Henry Hart, "Bombay Politics: Pluralism or Polarization?," Myron Weiner, "Violence and Politics in Calcutta," and Lloyd Rudolph, "Urban Life and Populist Radicalism: Dravidian Politics in Madras"; Donald B. Rosenthal, "Administrative Politics in Two Indian Cities" and "Factions and Alliances in Indian City Politics" (both 1966); and the urban contributions in Myron Weiner and Rajni Kothari, eds., *Indian Voting Behaviour* (1965).

Several other urban political contributions, rather specific in focus, were also

known about the most basic features of urban politics in India, either about its internal structure or its external relations with state and national politics. Who are the major actors in Indian city politics? What are their goals and aspirations? How is political power distributed? On whose behalf is it used? What roles do organizations and elections play in urban political life? How do they affect decision-making patterns and the content of policy? How is urban government organized institutionally, and how do its institutions work? To what extent is urban government autonomous from, or penetrated by, other levels of authority? What, in short, characterizes the anatomy and functions, the behavior and policy processes, of Indian city government and politics? [22]

These are the questions at the heart of this investigation. But something more must be said to establish its terms of reference. The first

---

available: the sections on Kanpur and Aligarh in Paul Brass, *Factional Politics in an Indian State* (1965); studies of the Congress party in Madurai and Calcutta in Myron Weiner, *Party-Building in a New Nation* (1967); a study then in dissertation form of Chamars and Yadavs in Agra politics by Owen Lynch, *The Politics of Untouchability* (1969); V. M. Sirsikar's study of Poona electoral politics, *Political Behaviour in India* (1965); Myron Weiner's essays in *Political Change in South Asia* (1963); and the Indian Institute of Public Administration's Calcutta Research Studies, including M. Bhattacharya, M. M. Singh, and Frank J. Tysen, *Government in Metropolitan Calcutta: A Manual* (1965); Ali Ashraf, *The City Government of Calcutta: A Study of Inertia* (1966); and Frank J. Tysen, *District Administration in Metropolitan Calcutta* (1965). The standard historical survey of the evolution of local self-government for the area is Hugh Tinker, *The Foundations of Local Self-Government in India, Pakistan and Burma* (1954).

Contemporaneous with this research are studies of Jabalpur and Tiruchirapalli by Peter Mayer; of urban villages and Dravidian politics by Steven and Marguerite Barnett; of urban associational politics by Robert Wirsing in his doctoral dissertation, "Socialist Society and Free Enterprise Politics: A Study of the Urban Political Process in Nagpur, India"; of municipal politics in Lucknow by Roderick Church; and of municipal councillors and ward politics in Delhi by Philip Oldenburg.

For the most recent contributions, see Donald B. Rosenthal, "Symposium on Indian Urban Politics," in the April 1973 issue of *Asian Survey*, including Mary F. Katzenstein, "Origins of Nativism: The Emergence of the Shiv Sena in Bombay," Peter B. Mayer, "Patterns of Urban Political Culture in India," Robert G. Wirsing, "Associational 'Micro-Arenas' in Indian Urban Politics," and Roderick Church, "Authority and Influence in Indian Municipal Politics: Administrators and Councillors in Lucknow."

[22] Books which have influenced this study greatly, and which express these concerns, include Robert A. Dahl, *Who Governs? Democracy and Power in an American City*; Wallace S. Sayre and Herbert Kaufman, *Governing New York City*; Edward C. Banfield, *Political Influence: A New Theory of Urban Politics*; Edward C. Banfield and James Q. Wilson, *City Politics*; E. E. Schattschneider, *The Semi-Sovereign People: A Realist's View of Democracy in America*; and Arthur Maas, ed., *Area and Power: A Theory of Local Government*.

problem to be considered is that of the unit of analysis, for it dictates criteria for inclusion and exclusion. The guiding questions point to "city politics" as the subject, but what are the boundaries of city politics? Does city hall or the Mayor's office serve as the focal point? Does city politics correspond to what happens within the municipal boundaries? Or should city politics be defined more abstractly as, for example, community decision-making? The answers to these questions are not self-evident in the Indian setting.

If we look at precedents, the most prominent approach assumes that city politics consists mainly of municipal politics and that the boundaries of the latter may serve, for analytic purposes, as the boundaries of the former. Rosenthal's study of Agra and Poona employed this approach, but with qualifications—particularly his inclusion of extra-municipal party and electoral politics.[23] The choice of the municipality as the unit of analysis for Indian urban politics might appear appropriate at first glance because it offers an analogy at the formal level with the familiar city hall-centered models of American urban politics. But this is an unsatisfactory choice. In any study of urban politics there are two basic concerns. Who exercises power in the city? And what does he do with it? It is on the answers to these questions that our understanding of urban governance in modern as well as developing societies hinges. Yet the keys to these questions do not lie in Indian municipal politics.[24] Municipal government in India is far from sovereign in its own juridical domain, and its functional scope is severely limited. In Indore the scope of municipal action is restricted primarily to such services as maintenance of roads, sanitation, distribution of water, and administration of building regulations.[25] Such functions are

---

[23] Rosenthal, *The Limited Elite.*

[24] Although Rosenthal recognizes this explicitly, he contents himself with a study of the distributive functions of municipal administrators and councillors, and the real and perceived incentive system of municipal actors, instead of expanding the scope of his work to embrace the centers of decision-making. See his "Functions of Urban Political Systems: Comparative Analysis and the Indian Case," in Clark, ed., *Community Structure,* pp. 269–303; and *The Limited Elite,* p. 4.

[25] It is possible that in some Indian cities, particularly those housing the state capital, municipal politics assumes a greater importance in urban and even state politics than is granted by this study of Indore. Roderick Church has some evidence in this connection about Lucknow, the capital of Uttar Pradesh, in his unpublished paper, "The Municipal Administrative Process in Lucknow, India." In the case of Calcutta, which is not only the state capital but a "primate city" in its region, Myron Weiner found that, in the period when he dominated Bengal politics an

but a small part of what urban government is all about. To determine who exercises power in Indian city politics, one must look outside the framework of municipal politics. Where then does one turn?

There is a structural model which captures the outstanding features of city politics in Indore and also suggests a solution to the unit-of-analysis problem. The dominant structure in Indore politics consists of dual sets of cooptive hierarchies, one representative and embedded in electoral politics and the other bureaucratic and governmental. Decision-making crucial to the city is primarily centralized at the summits of the two vertical structures, usually outside the city at the state level of politics. Within the city, the hierarchies are interlocked with multiple centers, or arenas, of political activity. These dual hierarchies serve to integrate the urban political system with that of the state. Thus the political weakness of the city alluded to earlier is but an expression of its dependency on these state-dominated vertical hierarchies. The urban political system is open and penetrated from above; it consists not merely of the urban community and local municipal institutions but also of the interaction of individuals and groups in the city with the lower levels of the representative and bureaucratic hierarchies. The unit of analysis, in Adrian Mayer's terms, is "town outward," rather than city hall-centered.[26] It consists of a multi-centered political system dominated by vertical decision-making hierarchies.

To clarify this model, it may be useful to distinguish three levels of analysis of urban politics, "the city as an actor in state politics," "the politics of the city as a whole," and "the politics of urban subsystems." The first level of the *city as an actor* refers to its corporate competition with other cities or with rural communities for advantage in state and regional politics. Indore city, for example, manifested some degree of corporate unity on several occasions, but perhaps most

---

important component of Atulya Ghosh's power base was the Calcutta municipal Congress party machine. But Weiner also shows, and it corroborates the argument in this study, that Ghosh's control of the district and state Congress party organizations were indispensable to the grip of his machine on the city in the long run. Weiner, "The Politics of Patronage: Calcutta," in *Party-Building*, pp. 321–370. See also Chapter 13 in this book.

[26] Adrian C. Mayer, "System and Network: An Approach to the Study of Political Process in Dewas." A similar approach is used by Richard G. Fox, *From Zamindar to Ballot Box: Community Change in a North Indian Town.*

clearly when it was under consideration as one of the possible sites for the state capital. The *politics of the city as a whole* refers to city-wide political competition, and it coincides with the boundaries of the urban community at large. It does not correspond to what is conventionally known as "city politics," however, because that term usually refers to politics centering on a strong city government. And it is precisely this condition of a strong city government which is absent in Indore; the repository of political power in the city is not city hall (or the Municipal Corporation). In fact, there is no central institutional repository of power in the city at all. Nevertheless, there is a unifying feature of urban politics; it consists of the city-wide contest of political parties for state legislative assembly seats and for influence over bureaucratic agencies that operate in the city, and it is to this process that we refer when we speak of the politics of the city as a whole. The usually dominant City Congress party has been the chief agent of urban political integration at this level of analysis in Indore. Finally, the *politics of urban sub-systems* refers to the fragmentation of urban politics, to subsets of political competition, and to what takes place in various distinct arenas or centers of political activity. The third level of analysis constitutes the less visible substratum of urban politics, and it deserves further discussion.

"Political arenas" can be thought of as constellations of political activity, "islands of power" in the urban political system. For analytical purposes, a *political arena* consists of the recurrent competition for the same resources by a specific set of political actors. Political arenas in Indore tend to be functionally defined dependencies of bureaucratic and government agencies. Around each major agency revolve clusters of political actors and constituencies seeking to shape the implementation of policy and share in the distribution of benefits within that agency's jurisdiction. Just as there is some overlap among bureaucratic jurisdictions, so is there interpenetration of political arenas. Many political actors, whether individuals, factions, or interest groups, operate in more than one arena concurrently, but some actors are also specialists in a particular arena or function. One such arena is that of municipal politics, but Indore city politics also contains the political arenas of industry and labor, education, town planning and improvement, public health and water resources, cooperatives, agricultural markets, and the underworld of proscribed enterprises such as gambling, smuggling, and vice. The vitality of these islands of power is what makes Indore politics multi-centered at the base.[27]

Thus the horizontal boundaries of Indore politics are defined by the reach of city-wide party and electoral competition. The vertical boundaries are defined by the reach of the dual hierarchies from their state-level summits to their multi-centered bases. This way of conceptualizing urban politics in the Indian context does not exclude from the scope of analysis those decisional inputs outside the city that have a bearing on its internal fate. It draws attention to the centralized structure of policy-making and control over the Indian city. In the case of Indore, centralized policy-making has taken the form of a symbiotic relationship between prominent politicians and bureaucrats at the state level, allowing them to intervene in Indore city politics to manipulate the levers of government power on behalf of their own interests or the interests of their allies. In short, this conceptualization permits what the more limited focus of municipal politics does not: an explanation of major political outcomes in the city.

Because the urban political system contains different levels of politics which are penetrated by the state system of politics, their interrelationships must be explored. Part of the penetration, of course, is formal—that of government agencies and jurisdictions—but more of it is informal. To trace the informal structures and determine how they condition the urban political process, the concept of "political linkage" is useful. This concept has been delineated most clearly in the context of international relations theory as a means of expressing the interdependence between national politics and the international system.[28] Its use grew out of the conviction that contemporary study of the international system as if it were autonomous from national influences, or vice versa, introduces distortions and misconceptions about what actually goes on. A similar argument is made here about the relations between the state and urban systems of politics in India, as it might be made more or less forcefully for state–urban relations in

---

[27] Robert Wirsing's findings, in "Socialist Society and Free Enterprise Politics" and "Urban Politics in Nagpur, India," are similar in this respect.

[28] James N. Rosenau, ed., *Linkage Politics: Essays on the Convergence of National and International Systems.*

other countries.[29] Rosenau defines linkage as "any recurrent sequence of behavior that originates in one system and is reacted to in another," a definition which is compatible with even remote analytic relationships between abstract variables.[30] In the related research, however, some of the more intriguing findings concern *penetrative* linkage processes, where members of one polity serve as political participants in the political processes of another.[31] Chalmers, for example, identifies as "linkage elites" Latin American leaders who play dual roles at the nexus of national and international politics.[32]

Such linkages of personnel and groups, more concrete than abstract, are of central concern to this study. It traces "linkage elites" at the interface of the state and urban political systems, but it is equally concerned with linkages at the local level of politics in the city. With this in mind, *political linkages* are defined as structured transactions of influence, support, claims, and information between political participants. They can be regarded as transmission channels established between individuals and groups who share some basis for mutual identification or seek common goals.[33] Political linkages can be ascertained between political leaders and followings, between individuals and groups constituting a faction, and between allied factions in party and labor union organizations. Linkages may consist of sustained ties between politicians and bureaucrats, as well as among bureaucrats themselves, cutting across different branches or levels of administration and quite apart from the prescribed chains of command. Political linkages may be horizontal or vertical. The dominant structure of vertical hierarchies in Indore politics consists of horizontal and vertical linkages binding high-level political chieftains and bureaucrats with each other and with clients in the city for mutual gain. Mapping po-

---

[29] See Mark Kesselman, *The Ambiguous Consensus: A Study of Local Government in France*; William J. and Judith L. Hanna, "The Political Structure of Urban-Centered African Communities," in Miner, ed., *The City in Modern Africa*; and Morton Grodzins, *The American System*.

[30] Rosenau, ed., *Linkage Politics*, p. 45.

[31] *Ibid.*, p. 46.

[32] Douglas A. Chalmers, "Developing on the Periphery: External Factors in Latin American Politics," in Rosenau, pp. 67–93.

[33] For an interesting illustration of linkage mapping among community leaders, which was used to obtain a reputational index of influence, see Floyd Hunter, *Community Power Structure: A Study of Decision-Makers*.

litical linkages provides a way not only of revealing the interpenetration of systems of politics but of illuminating much of the informal fabric of politics. Underpinnings of this kind are all too often overlooked in research confined exclusively to formal group, organizational, or institutional categories of analysis.[34]

Power and incentive comprise the energy of politics—entirely palpable to the participant, but elusive for the observer. Patterns of power and influence can only be detected indirectly. They must be inferred from a variety of possible manifestations—from who participates in the making of, or has access to, authoritative decisions; from who gains or loses by virtue of decisions as well as "nondecisions"; from who occupies official positions in institutions or organizations; and from the possession of private resources such as money, information, and skills, or control over jobs and publicity.[35] Power and influence may even, under some circumstances, be inferred from reputations; for believing "X has power" may make it so. This study of Indore is not preoccupied with any debate over "community power structure" such as has been waged between elitists and pluralists in American social science in recent years, but it is sensitive to the issues that have been raised by them.[36] The sharp inequalities in wealth and status that characterize Indian society at large and Indore city in particular might lead one to expect to find a power elite. The evidence gathered in this work, however, tends to support a more pluralistic model, akin

---

[34] A broader but related concept in use by social anthropologists is that of "network." See the contributions in Marc J. Swartz, ed., *Local-Level Politics: Social and Cultural Perspectives*; and Adrian C. Mayer, "System and Network."

[35] Harold Lasswell and Abraham Kaplan, *Power and Society: A Framework for Political Inquiry*; Lasswell, *Politics: Who Gets What, When, How*; Robert A. Dahl, *Modern Political Analysis*; Peter Bachrach and Morton S. Baratz, "Two Faces of Power"; Bachrach and Baratz, "Decisions and Nondecisions: An Analytic Framework."

[36] Hunter's *Community Power Structure* touched off the debate; Dahl's *Who Governs?* made an impressive rejoinder; and Robert Agger, Daniel Goldrich, and Bert Swanson, *The Rulers and the Ruled*, provided a synthesis and considerable refinement of the issues. There were, of course, antecedents and descendants, too numerous to mention here. For an extensive bibliography as well as compilation of recent articles, see Charles M. Bonjean, Terry N. Clark, and Robert L. Lineberry, eds., *Community Politics: A Behavioral Approach*. Nelson W. Polsby's *Community Power and Political Theory* provides a survey of the earlier literature from the pluralists' perspective, and Willis D. Hawley and Frederick M. Wirt, eds., *The Search for Community Power*, is a balanced anthology. For the international perspective, see Clark's *Community Structure* and Delbert C. Miller, *International Community Power Structures: Comparative Studies of Four World Cities*.

to what Dahl calls "polyarchy." [37] Political resources in Indore today are unequally distributed from the standpoint of urban society as a whole, but they are more dispersed than cumulative—partly because such ascriptive factors as caste divide elites vertically, and partly because electoral politics effectively chastens aspirants to official power.

One of the special features of this study, with respect to elite and power structure questions, is what it does to uncover princely politics and contemporary change in India. Indore city was the capital of the Holkar state from 1818 to 1948, and its administrative role during that period left imprints on modern politics after Indian independence. The princely power structure consisted of a class of nobles—rural land-owning chieftains, commercial and industrial magnates, palace officials, and the chief bureaucrats. Government was autocratic and bureaucratic, with distinct patterns of selective administrative recruitment. This study records the decline of the princely nobility, the emergence of new elites based on popular power, and shifts in the social origins of bureaucratic elites in the city after princely rule ended in 1948.

Perhaps the most stimulating paradigm in the urbanization literature has been that of the role of the city as an agent of social and cultural change.[38] Western studies have usually argued that the close-knit family and group relations of traditional or rural society give way in the modern city to far more impersonal, transitory, and functionally specific relationships. Great size and density of population, specialization and differentiation of occupational roles, mobility, and the complexity of urban transactions are supposed to foster new bases for intimacy and obligation, new norms for recruitment and performance, and new opportunities for self-definition and achievement. Urban living is thought to promote the replacement of primordial attachments to groups of blood and birth with functional and voluntary attachments to modern associations and organizations. Whether this occurs can be of importance to such socially heterogeneous societies as India,

---

[37] Dahl, *Who Governs?* and *A Preface to Democratic Theory*.
[38] Wirth, "Urbanism as a Way of Life"; Max Weber, *The City*; Gideon Sjoberg, *The Preindustrial City, Past and Present*; Robert Redfield and Milton B. Singer, "The Cultural Role of Cities"; and Singer, "The Great Tradition in a Metropolitan Center: Madras," in *Traditional India: Structure and Change*.

for the survival of traditional cleavages can threaten the emerging nation with fragmentation. It is also important in India because of the great inequalities inherent in the traditional caste system. If the city dissolves the structures of caste, status may be redefined in accordance with modern criteria and subjected to the outcomes of competitive representative politics—thereby opening within the system prospects for reallocation of societal resources, greater individual and group mobility, and a narrowing of traditional inequalities.

But empirical studies of urban society and politics have produced a more conditional and accurate picture of social change in the modern city. Ethnic studies in the United States have drawn attention to the extraordinary resilience of immigrant communities and to the durability of the "urban village" in even the greatest and most modern of cities.[39] Research on Latin America, Africa, and Asia has displayed yet more vividly the imprints of rural and traditional social formations in urban society.[40] Moreover, what seems to emerge as a common theme among these studies is the finding that traditional attachments, values, and associations are often adaptable and functional in modern settings.[41] Clearly the city does promote social change, but it is not always as rapid or as thorough as classical theories would suggest. Thus what is appropriate for comparative urban research is not a sharp conceptual dichotomy between rural and urban, but rather a continuum along which segments of urban society can be arranged.

Indore city is a mixture of the traditional and the modern, the rural and the urban. It is a city of immigrants from quite distinct linguistic and regional backgrounds. Ascriptive bases of identification —caste, religion, language, and region—are salient in defining the lines of political cleavage, criteria of affiliation, and stakes of political

---

[39] For example, Nathan Glazer and Daniel P. Moynihan, *Beyond the Melting Pot*; Herbert J. Gans, *The Urban Villagers*; Edgar Litt, *Ethnic Politics in America*; Edward C. Banfield and James Q. Wilson, "Public-Regardingness as a Value Premise in Voting Behavior"; Raymond Wolfinger, "The Development and Persistence of Ethnic Voting."

[40] Rabinovitz, "Urban Development in Latin America," in Daland, ed., *Comparative Urban Research*; Abner Cohen, *Custom and Politics in Urban Africa*; Kenneth Little, *West African Urbanization*; Clifford Geertz, *Peddlers and Princes: Social Development and Economic Modernization in Two Indonesian Towns;* Lynch, *The Politics of Untouchability.*

[41] Rudolph and Rudolph, *The Modernity of Tradition.*

competition. In some cases, traditional patron-client relationships originating in rural regions have been imported into Indore, though the specific purposes they once served have usually been redefined. Yet ascriptive factors do not operate in Indore inflexibly. They do not usually pose insurmountable barriers to political mobility or success, nor do they govern behavior unilaterally. Caste, in particular, remains important in Indore society and politics, especially as a basis of group identification and mobilization, but no longer as a closed or con-sensual system.[42] Although participants in politics are aware of and attach status significance to caste, there is in the city no central mech-anism such as an authoritative caste *panchayat* (adjudicative council of elders) to question or confirm that status. Consequently in public life, especially for intermediate castes, there is considerable ambiguity and fluidity in the relationship between caste membership and status. Modern politics often intensifies caste group identification, but it also obscures the once-clear hierarchical relations among castes.

Ascriptive politics in Indore bears a resemblance to American urban ethnic politics. The combination of ethnic with modern repre-sentative politics tends to induce a distributive rather than issue-oriented process.[43] Caste and religious groups exchange votes and or-ganizational support for political benefits, material and psychic. Some benefits are for individuals and immediate consumption, but others are shared by the group as a whole, elevating its position in the com-munity at large. Where avenues of economic mobility are relatively scarce or inaccessible, politics becomes the principal alternative. Be-cause the number of ethnic groups actively seeking recognition and material progress in Indore is large, electoral coalitions and campaign strategies are complex and there is a considerable premium on machine-like organizational capabilities. Distributive politics has, moreover, an inhibiting effect on the formulation of political issues or of a clear conception of the public interest. Issues clearly stated risk alienating portions of a coalition, and the aggregation of many competing group

---

[42] Mark Holmstrom, "Caste and Status in an Indian City."

[43] James C. Scott, "Corruption, Machine Politics, and Political Change" and "Patron-Client Politics and Political Change in Southeast Asia." See also the Amer-ican classic, Harold F. Gosnell, *Machine Politics: Chicago Model*; and Banfield, *Political Influence*.

interests into a definition of "the public interest" is a thankless task.

What effect do ethnic and distributive politics have on the policy and governmental processes of the city? Fundamentally, they reinforce the vertical hierarchies that link Indore with state politics. The prevalence of particularistic claims in Indore is at the expense of expressions of interest on behalf of the city as a whole, and undermines its potential autonomy. The initiative for urban policy formulation is therefore preempted by politicians and bureaucrats in state government, at the top of the representative and bureaucratic hierarchies. The agencies through which policy is administered in the city, however, are divided along functional lines, with separate responsibilities for labor, welfare, housing, industries, law and order, and so on. It would be difficult, even if there were the will to do so, to promote general policies that would have a coherent impact on the city as a whole through this maze of bureaucratic agencies. The more typical pattern is one of policy-making along specific functional lines relating to specialized clienteles in the various arenas of politics in the city.

Once policy proceeds to implementation, particularistic interests make themselves felt in its administration at the city level. Local leaders, the clients and protégés of political chieftains at the state level, intervene, bargain, and massage the administrative process. They seek administrative decisions that can be converted into patronage, real or apparent, and use them for the creation of constituency support. At this level the effects are of two kinds. First, the administrative process is diffused; it loses coherence, but at the same time it becomes more responsive to local interests. Thus although command over policy in the general sense is centralized, there is a form of autonomy established by the administrative impact of government on the city. Second, the process becomes cooptive. By satisfying particularistic claims, political and bureaucratic actors earn the loyalty and support of their constituents. As new participants are mobilized, they are naturally incorporated into the process. The result is that frustrations are forestalled and the danger of radical politics is minimized.

City politics in India, insofar as Indore is typical, functions in ameliorative fashion to dampen discontent and to integrate urban society into a larger political system. What this study demonstrates concretely is how integration is achieved through governmental and political processes. While integration is obtained at the expense of corporate local autonomy over policy and development choices, given the conditions of slow economic growth and the great heterogeneity of urban society it is no mean feat. In a developing nation, integration must have high priority. Moreover, the pattern of centralization of urban policy-making that has been established may become advantageous for centrally directed planning of urban development, when the will and resources to undertake it ultimately become available.

2

URBAN ECOLOGY AND
DEVELOPMENTAL PATTERN

Indore first became important as the capital of a princely state and is today an industrial city of moderate size, with a diverse population of about half a million.[1] By Indian standards it is comparatively new, dating back only two and a half centuries to 1715. The neighboring city of Ujjain, by contrast, has existed for over two thousand years; the Emperor Asoka began his career as a provincial governor there in the third century B.C. Yet within the last century Indore has become the principal city of the region, outstripping Ujjain as a commercial, industrial, and administrative center. Situated in the historic region of Malwa, Indore lies about 300 miles directly south of Jaipur and 200 miles east of Ahmedabad amidst fertile agricultural lands. It is a transitional city with both traditional and modern features of culture, society, and economy. The contrasts between old and new are less sharp than one is accustomed to seeing in India's coastal metropolises. Perhaps because it was sheltered somewhat in a princely state, Indore's physical and socioeconomic changes have been more

---

[1] There is little secondary source material on Indore or the Holkar state, and the account here relies primarily on Sir John Malcolm's *A Memoir of Central India Including Malwa and Adjoining Provinces* (1832); Lt. Col. C. E. Luard, *Central India Census Series, 1921, Vol. I: Holkar State*; Mashir Bahadur M. A. Rashid, *Census of Central India, 1931, Vol. XVI:* Holkar State; L. C. Dhariwal, *The Indore State Gazetteer* (1931); and Sharad Kumari Dube's doctoral dissertation, *Municipal Administration at Indore—Evolution and Present Set-Up.*

fitful and hesitant than dynamic and compelling, and its residents have managed to blend the past with the present.

Its architecture reflects the vitality of religious, political, and mercantile traditions in Indore. No single feature dominates the gently undulating landscape, but Hindu temples stand along the now almost dry river channels, and Jain temples and Muslim mosques and cemeteries dot the city. Old palaces in Maratha rampart style, new palaces reflecting Versailles and the French tastes of recent rulers, gardens, forts, cantonments, and other public buildings serve as reminders of the city's princely past. The streets, with but a few exceptions, are narrow labyrinths encroached upon by shops and stalls and opening abruptly into squares and markets. Most older buildings are of wood and plaster, three or four stories, sometimes ornately carved or decoratively painted, with porticos and elegant façades, intricate screens to conceal the ladies, and usually complete with verandahs and courtyards. Most shops are open, without glass fronts or modern furniture, and they are usually concentrated on streets, or sections of streets: cloth goods on one, silver and gold on another, and produce or grain on a third. The traffic is heavy and vibrant with cars, buses, lorries, motorized rickshaws and jitneys, horse-drawn *tongas,* bullock carts, *telas* (pushcarts), bicyclists, pedestrians, and wandering animals. Costumes are traditional for the most part, and religious styles are often plainly evident. Society is a complex mosaic of religions, castes, languages, and occupations, and the residential patterns of *mohalla* (subcommunity) and neighborhood reflect this social differentiation quite visibly.

Some features of the city are plainly modern: the railroad, bus transport, the telephone exchange, the cinemas, government buildings, the textile industries, the electric generating plant, the public hospital and medical school, the colleges and engineering institute, and those newer shops which sell everything from watches and fountain pens to electrical appliances and dry-cleaning. Banking, transportation, communications, public administration, and professional life are increasingly prominent, well-organized, and modern in practice or orientation in city life. People are more mobile physically and psychically. Yet the old is still very much in evidence and crowds in on the new in every walk of life.

The ingredients of urban life in Indore have several sources, and it is the task of this chapter to separate out the historical, social, and economic strands. The early political identity and social and organizational characteristics of the community were shaped by the city's historical experience as the princely capital of Maratha military rulers, governing in a Hindi-speaking and therefore alien environment. After the British pacified the warring states of central India, Indore became a center of rapid commercial growth, benefiting from its prosperous agricultural hinterland and from its role as the distribution center for trade between western and central India. Commercial fortunes, especially from trade in opium, provided the capital for industrialization and the manufacture of cloth from the abundant sources of cotton in the vicinity. Economic growth attracted a variety of entrepreneurial and working-class groups from distant regions, diversifying the city's population.

After 1948 Indore ceased to be a princely capital, and the city's political and administrative activities tended to shift away from the city and to refocus around new centers of government in Madhya Bharat and Madhya Pradesh. Despite the change in administrative focus, however, Indore continues today to be an important administrative center in Madhya Pradesh. It is the seat of the state's Labour and Sales Tax Commissioners, the Public Service Commission, and a major branch of the High Court, headquarters of the Indore Division, and the base of the Collector, who is responsible for law and order, revenue, and development activities in the district. And today the city also has a vigorous service sector, with expanding residential, entertainment, and consumer amenities. Blessed with a moderate climate and pleasant surroundings, Indore's *"shab e Malwa"* (romantic nights of Malwa) have attracted many former princely families and retired government servants to make the city their home, and their purchasing power has stimulated the construction and retailing trades.

Early History

Indore's founding as a village settlement is usually attributed to a patrician family of Malwi (Shrigaur) Brahmans by the name of Rao. The Raos acquired very large tracts of land in and around what is today the city of Indore, and they became vassals of the Mughal

Empire with the title of *zamindar*. That title has since become part of the family name, and today they are often referred to as the Zamindars of Indore.[2] The Zamindar family settled in an attractive location just south of the junction of the Khan and Saraswati rivers, on a slight elevation, and built a sprawling fortress-like mansion known as Bada Raola. Around them in what is now Juni (old) Indore congregated other Malwi Brahmans and groups of lower, client castes, artisans and cultivators. Their settlement was called Indreshwar, and Indore is probably a shortened version of that name. (See map, p. 40.)

Before the arrival of the Marathas, central India was under the fluctuating control of Rajput and Muslim vassals of the Mughal Empire, but its foundations were deteriorating in the seventeenth and early eighteenth century. As imperial control weakened, the Marathas expanded in shock waves over the Deccan and into central and northern India. Malhar Rao Holkar, the founder of the Indore dynasty, made an alliance with the Zamindar of Indore and succeeded in defeating Daya Bahadur, the Mughal military chieftain, putting the Malwa region under the control of the Holkar army. Malhar Rao's jurisdiction over the district of Indore was confirmed by a decree from the Peshwa of Poona in 1733 as a reward for his services and as a means of supporting his troops.

It is worth noting here that Malhar Rao Holkar was unique among Maratha military chieftains in that he was neither a Brahman nor a true Maratha by caste, but rather a *Dhangar*. Dhangars are a Marathi-speaking shepherd caste, comparable in status to the *Ahirs* (cattle-breeders) of north India. Just as Ahirs are regarded as inferior to Rajputs—the former stemming from the Sudra *varna* and the latter from Kshatriya—so are the Dhangars ranked below Marathas, a cultivator turned "martial caste" of western India. Malhar Rao rose to prominence because of his military talents and the good fortune of having them recognized by superiors. Because the ruling family in Indore has been Dhangar, the caste locally is accorded a status on a par with Marathas. Indeed, to non-Marathi-speakers, the two castes in the city are now virtually indistinguishable.

The Maratha invasion of Malwa has left its mark on modern regional and local politics in two ways. Within the city, it created a

---

[2] *The Mandlik Papers and the Family*, pp. 11ff; and Patrick Geddes, *Town Planning Towards City Development: A Report to the Durbar of Indore* (1918).

deep political rift. The invasion and rule by Marathi-speaking "foreigners" over Hindi-speaking peoples produced primordial political competition and tension between the two linguistic groups, and the cleavage persists in Indore politics today, affecting the composition of factions within the Congress party organization as well as differences between the Congress and opposition parties. The Maratha impact has also had subtle effects on regional competition within Madhya Bharat politics, and is manifested in the rivalry between Indore and Gwalior. The Marathas were a fragmented military force under several chieftains. Just as Malhar Rao set up a dynasty in Indore, Bhonsle and Scindia established Maratha dynasties in Nagpur and Gwalior respectively. Although they were formally allies under the Peshwas, the Holkars and Scindias fought each other over several generations, seeking to extend their respective domains. Territorial control was fluid, alternately expanding and contracting according to the varying skills or disabilities of successive rulers or the balance of power based on subsidiary alignments. The contemporary result of traditional princely state rivalry has been the competition between groups of politicians, bureaucrats, and clienteles from Indore and Gwalior after the merger of the princely states in 1948. Even under the conditions of modern electoral politics, these groups have continued to identify with the princely state areas in which they were born.

Indore was the nominal but not the official capital of the Holkar state until 1818, following the Treaty of Mandsaur, which marked the beginning of British supremacy in central India and brought an end to the wars between princely states in the region. Political boundaries were frozen by the terms of the treaty at a time when Holkar power was at an ebb, and their territories contracted. Gwalior's territories, by contrast, were extensive and included the district of Ujjain neighboring Indore. As part of the settlement, the British assumed control of the external policies of the princely regimes but, formally at least, left them in charge of internal affairs. In 1818 Indore was also made the headquarters of the Resident, or Agent to the Governor-General for Central India.[3] The Resident, backed by British military

---

[3] The Resident was the main representative of British power in Central India. A large area called the "Residency," outside the heavily inhabited sections of Indore city, was ceded to the British for use as their headquarters. Part of this area today remains only lightly inhabited. Another part, adjacent to the city, grew into a

power, came to enjoy substantial influence in princely states, particularly in Indore where his immediate presence was a contributing
factor. Consequently, Indore became the center of radiating British
imperial influence in the area and a magnet for princely emissaries
whose job it was to detect such shifts in British policy as might affect
the interests of their states. Thus the presence of the Resident added
glamour and regional political importance to Indore, and also ensured
that political developments in the Holkar state would be followed
closely by the British. Above all, it strengthened the "imperial city"
configuration that the Holkar princes had begun.

Urban Growth and Economic Change

The British did their share in fostering modernization in Indore.
They used their leverage over external affairs to induce the Holkar
rulers to invest in railways, to build roads, and to accept the introduction of the imperial postal system (in 1908). British influence contributed to the introduction of modern education and medicine. Moreover, the British exploited personal and factional differences within
the Holkar administration, playing rival ministers off against each
other and against the rulers. Periods of regency between the death or
abdication of one ruler and the investment of his successor gave the
British opportunities to induce and supervise the reorganization of
the administrative, police, and judicial systems in accordance with
models and codes from British India.

Yet the impulses toward modernization were not exclusively British
in origin. The rulers and indigenous entrepreneurs played major
roles too. A good deal of imagination and initiative in this respect is
attributed to Tukoji Rao Holkar II (1852–1886), the first great
"booster" of the city.[4] Tukoji Rao officially established a practice of
giving cash incentives to farmers to market their produce in Indore,
thereby promoting Indore's commercial importance at the expense of
other major markets nearby in Dewas, Dhar, and Ujjain—each of

---

busy bazaar and mercantile area serving the needs of the Residency. Known as Choti
Chowni (or Sanyogitaganj), this area was retroceded to the Holkar state in 1931,
adding an area of 1.5 square miles and a population of about 15,000 to Indore.
In 1951, the remainder of the Residency area, now largely owned by the state
government, was included within municipal limits. See map of Indore, p. 40.

The first A.G.G. for Central India was Sir John Malcolm; see his *Memoir of
Central India*.

[4] Y. H. Godbole, "Indreshwar Nagar Ka Itihas."

which was in a different princely state. A more impressive economic
contribution—for which he is fondly remembered as a *"baniya"*
(moneylender)—was his loan in 1864 of ten million rupees at 4.5
percent interest to the Bombay-Baroda and Central Indian Railway.[5]
By 1877 Indore was linked to the south by rail with Bombay (via
Khandwa), and by 1891 to the north with Ajmer, Agra, and Delhi
(via Ratlam). The Bombay connection was most significant economically, as it provided the main channel by which Bombay's manu-
factures and industrial machinery could be marketed in princely
Central India. Indore merchants became the middlemen in this distribution, and as a result the city outstripped its regional competitors
(the main one being Ujjain city) in commercial volume and profit.
Rail connections had political consequences too, for before independence the local branch of the Indian National Congress had its strongest links with and support from the Congress organizations in Ajmer
(to the north) and Khandwa (to the south), both British-held territories outside the princely states.

A third economic advance attributed to Tukoji Rao II was industrial. The Holkar government, between 1864 and 1866, installed
the first textile factory, known as the State Mills, in Indore. The
achievement was the greater for the fact that though it was a small,
steam-operated plant (the parts being hauled overland, it is said, on
the backs of elephants), it provided an example to the traditional business communities in Indore of the potential profits of investment in an
industry capable of exploiting the locally abundant agricultural resource of raw cotton. Indore's private entrepreneurs were not quick
to move into the textile industry, but the financial success of the State
Mills established grounds for the confidence displayed by a later generation of businessmen.

Encouraged by the growth in demand stemming from World War
One, Indore entrepreneurs between 1915 and 1922 established six
larger textile plants.[6] The industry was dominated almost from the

---

[5] The actual initiative was British. The Government of India after the meeting
desired to strengthen military communication with the garrison at Mhow (Military
Headquarters of the West), the cantonment fifteen miles southwest of Indore.
Dhariwal, *Gazetteer*, Vol. I, p. 41.

[6] The capital base for industrialization in Indore was derived in part from the
production and smuggling of opium bound for China. Indore and Ujjain were
major centers of speculation in this locally grown commodity. See David E. Owen,
British Opium Policy in China and India, pp. 8off.

start by "Marwari" Jains. While Muslim Bohras founded the Malwa Mills and Hindu Baniyas the Swadeshi Mills, three others—the Hukumchand, Kalyanmal, and Rajkumar Mills—belonged to the joint family of Seth Swarupchand Hukumchand, a Rajasthani Jain and the most prominent businessman in Indore. The Bhandari Mills, moreover, were set up by another leading Marwari Jain family. A measure of the growth of the textile industry lies in the combined expansion of machinery, output, and the labor force.[7] By 1928 the industry operated 5,126 looms and 167,239 spindles and produced about 22.6 million pounds of yarn and 22.9 million pounds of cloth. Cloth output had more than doubled, rising to nearly 47 million pounds, in 1939.

The expansion of industry after World War One was paralleled by a sharp rise in population growth. By 1901 Indore already had a population of nearly 98,000, but in the next decade several plague epidemics caused severe depopulation so that by 1911 the population level stood at just over 54,000. By 1921, however, the population had rebounded to a new high of 105,317, and it has continued to rise steadily since then. The growth rate for the 1941–1951 decade, reflecting the industrial boom conditions of the World War Two period, was 52.6 percent, bringing the population up to 310,859. Population growth since 1951 has been slower, about 27 percent for each of the next two decades. The 1961 census figure was 394,941,[8] and the estimate for 1968 put the city at the half million mark.[9]

The development of modern education in Indore, supported by

---

[7] The figures that follow are drawn from Dhariwal, *Gazetteer*, Vol. III, p. 114, and Dinanath, *A Glimpse into Holkar State Administration* (1931), p. 18.

[8] *Census of India, 1961, Madhya Pradesh*, p. 24.

[9] The density of the urban population of Indore is very high, at least in the heart of the city, but the most recent sources do not contain sufficient information to show density by ward. In 1960, the city boundaries enclosed 21.5 square miles, much of which is semi-rural; in terms of the 1961 population, this gives a density of about 18,000 persons per square mile. A still unsatisfactory but better indicator is the density of population in the municipal ward area. That area was 9.27 square miles with 348,000 persons in 1961, producing a density of 37,541 per square mile. *Census, 1961, Madhya Pradesh*, p. 6. According to the *Census of Central India, 1931*, ward densities ranged as high as 119,000 people per square mile in the Sarafa (financial) section of the city. Rashid, Vol. XVI, Part I; calculations based on data on pp. 54ff. Ward boundaries have changed, and the areas of new wards are not given, so recent comparisons are not possible. But it seems probable that density has increased rather than decreased in the older sections of the city since 1931.

the growth of communications, commerce, and industry, kept well
ahead of population increases and gave the city by 1948 the most
numerous and advanced schools and the highest literacy rate of any
city or district of the Central Indian princely states. The level of literacy in Indore city rose dramatically from 22 percent in 1921 to 50.7
percent in 1961.[10] This put Indore significantly ahead of its regional
competitor, Gwalior city, which in 1961 had a literacy level of 42.4
percent. The high level in Indore helps to account for the disproportionate influence and representation the city had in the state government of Madhya Bharat after 1948.[11] Literacy in the vernaculars as
well as in English was politically significant, for it had a differential
impact on the various caste, religious, and linguistic communities in
the city, affecting their access and recruitment to positions of administrative and political power, especially under the Holkar regime.
More generally, educational development in Indore fostered the
emergence in the city of the educated professions of law, medicine,
engineering, and teaching. And it contributed to the appearance of
nationalist impulses, modern political attitudes, and popular political
organizations.

Indore's occupational profile (see Table 1) reflects the levels of
industrial, commercial, and administrative manpower in the city.
The census categories, unfortunately, are not easily rearranged in
terms of social class, for they are too broad. But they provide a rough
idea of the social contours of the city (or, more precisely, the urban
areas of the district). Slightly more than one-third of the working
population was engaged in "manufacturing" of all kinds, and nearly
one-fourth was involved in the textile industry alone. The bulk of
this industrial manpower, of course, falls into the class of skilled and
unskilled blue-collar laborers. (When manpower is counted only for

[10] Luard, *Census, 1921,* Part I, p. 109; and *Census, 1961, Madhya Pradesh.* In
the Indore district by 1961 there were 749 schools of all kinds with a total of
120,402 students, about 70 percent male. The heaviest enrollments were in the 630
pre-primary, primary, and middle schools which together accounted for 90,965 students. The 41 high schools contained 21,111 students, and the 5 degree colleges enrolled 3,607 students. Teacher training and specialized vocational schools accounted
for the remainder. Although these are district figures, the city contained most of
the high school and all of the college students. The growth between 1947 and 1961
varied from one category to another, but was overall about threefold.

[11] See Chapter 5.

TABLE 1. Occupational Distribution in Selected
Sectors, Urban Areas, Indore District, 1961

Occupation	Earners	Percentage of Total
Manufacturing	*41,799*	*35.1*
Textile	27,081	22.7
Foodstuffs	2,093	1.8
Wood Products	1,725	1.4
Publishing	1,040	0.9
Leather	709	0.6
Mineral Products	1,526	1.3
Basic Metal Fabrication	2,296	1.9
Transport Equipment	2,254	1.9
Trade and Commerce	*24,853*	*20.9*
Construction	*5,341*	*4.5*
Transport, Storage, Communications	*8,185*	*6.9*
Services	*38,893*	*32.7*
Utilities	9,399	7.9
Public Administration	11,964	10.0
Educational and Scientific	5,373	4.5
Medical and Health	2,736	2.3
Welfare	1,006	0.8
Legal	534	0.4
Personal and Domestic	7,881	6.6
Total	119,071	100.0

Source: Directorate of Economics and Statistics, *Pocket Compendium of District Statistics*, Indore, 1963.

Certain numerically small subcategories have been omitted, so that totals within the major categories are larger than the sum of their components as presented. While these are urban figures for the district, the Indore share is so large that they can safely be used as indicators for the city itself.

establishments employing ten or more persons, as in the data of Table 2, the share of manufacturing in the work force, 44 percent in 1961, becomes even larger.) That the city has a very sizable middle and lower middle class is indicated by the fact that nearly one-third of the 1961 manpower was engaged in "services," and another fifth in "trade and commerce." These categories, of course, conceal enormous disparities—between the *bidi* or *paan* (cigarette and betel nut) vendors and the wealthy cloth merchants or money-lenders in the "trade" category, and between the upper levels of the civil service and the *chaprasis* (office-attendants) and menials at the bottom of the "serv-

ice" category. In both cases, the proportions of those on the lowest
rungs are certainly far greater than those at the top, but the proportion of those at intermediate levels is also substantial.

TABLE 2. Employment in Private and Public Establishments,
Indore District, 1961–1966[a]

Sector/Industry	Total Employees		Percentage of Total Employees		Net Change of Proportion to Total Employees	Net Change within Categories
	1961	1966	1961	1966		
Total Public Sector	28,369	31,465	48	51	+03	+11
Total Private Sector	31,241	30,565	52	49	−03	−03
Total	(59,610)	(62,028)				
Agriculture and Forestry	1,029	528	02	01	−01	−51
Mining and Quarrying	00	32	00	00	00	00
Manufacturing	26,014	25,983	44	42	−02	00
Construction	1,598	2,459	03	04	+01	+54
Public Utilities and Sanitation	1,188	1,833	02	03	+01	+54
Trade and Commerce	3,519	2,887	06	05	−01	−18
Transport, Storage, and Communication	2,903	3,150	05	05	00	+09
Services	23,359	25,156	39	41	+02	+08

Source: Directorate of Employment and Training, *Indore Employment Review,
March 1961 to March 1966*, Government of Madhya Pradesh (Jabalpur), 1967. Table
is derived from data on pp. 4–5.
[a] Establishments counted employ 10 or more workers.

As to the balance of "public" versus "private" employment (see
Table 2), in establishments employing ten or more persons the sectors
are about equal in size, although the "public" sector had gained a
marginal edge over the private between 1961 and 1966. These figures
are, of course, structurally biased in that they exaggerate the importance of organized establishments, skewing the figures in favor of
"public" employment. Even discounting the bias, however, the stakes
of jobs in the public sector are clearly of very great importance in the
city.

In recent years long shadows have appeared on Indore's economic
horizon, for the city's economic growth has been sharply curtailed,

especially in the private sector. Table 2 provides some indication of the trends (remembering once again that the figures are for establishments with ten or more employees). While public employment expanded at slightly more than 2 percent per year between 1961 and 1966, private employment fell 3 percent over that period. A very slight decline occurred in manufacturing; but the figures conceal a definite decline in textile industry employment, because it was counterbalanced by growth in small-scale industries. In trade and commerce, moreover, the decline was a sharp 18 percent for the period, though this sector constituted only 6 percent of the establishment manpower in 1961. In Indore district, overall employment rose only 4.1 percent in the five-year period, clearly far behind the rate of natural population increase.

Unfortunately there are no reliable unemployment data for the city or district. A state government report in 1961 gave the Indore city unemployment figure as 2,077, an impossibly low figure.[12] By 1966 there were 10,819 persons registered at the Indore Employment Exchange; while this figure (about 2 percent of the city population) probably represents just the tip of the iceberg, it is perhaps significant that it also represented a 160 percent increase over five years in those registered as searching for jobs.[13] More important, the proportion of those seeking jobs who had at least a high school education was high (39.4 percent in 1961) and rising (49 percent in 1966). Nearly one-fifth of the educated job-seekers by 1966 were college graduates.[14] Not only have job opportunities in Indore been contracting relative to demand, but the city is showing serious signs of "educated unemployment," a condition that has, of course, been a severe problem in larger cities in India for a much longer period of time. Indore city has had its share of violent protests, demonstrations, and police repressions, though not with such frequency as the large metropolitan centers such as Bombay and Calcutta. Yet there has been evidence of a deterioration of public order in Indore, in the colleges with language riots dating from 1967, with labor strikes rising in intensity since 1963, and with the first serious outbreaks of communal violence in

[12] *Indore Employment Review, March 1961 to March 1966*, p. 6.
[13] *Ibid.*, p. 8.
[14] *Ibid.*, pp. 9–10.

two decades breaking out in 1968 and 1969. Economic stagnation has curtailed the opportunities both of the working class and the educated middle class, and is probably the single most important factor underlying the intensification of conflict in the city.

Traditional Social Cleavages and Stratification

Apart from formal organizations such as political parties or government bureaucracies, there are three broad types of political forces in Indore. The first consists of heirs to princely power—those groups which exercise residual influence in the city because of special ties or privileges obtained under the former Holkar regime. Second, there are six economic elements which have a long-term impact on city politics —textile industry magnates, bazaar merchants, industrial laborers, white-collar workers, professionals, and urban property or building owners. It would not be accurate, however, to regard these economic groups as coherent political forces, for they are divided internally by primordial rivalries arising from the third type of political force. For a city of its size, Indore has a remarkably diverse population. It contains not only the usual religious minorities, and the usual array of castes ranked hierarchically by traditional status, but several sets of each distinguished by language and regional origin. When economic and occupational differences are compounded by those of religion, caste, and regional background, the society becomes highly segmented indeed. These traditional factors of religious and caste identity, and regional origin, remain highly salient in conditioning the political affiliations and orientations of social groups in Indore.

Historically, Indore has been a city of immigrants. Although migration into the city has not been a major factor in its growth over the last two decades, it was a primary factor in the century and a half before. The newcomers to Indore have been on the whole from quite distant regions, not from the rural environs of the city. Census data on place of origin reveal that fully half of the 1931 population of the city identified their birthplace as outside the Holkar state.[15] Of the immigrants at that time, 13 percent were from western India (Ma-

---

[15] Rashid, *Census, 1931,* Holkar State, Part II, pp. 16–17. The data have been reconstructed in Table 3.8 of my "Area, Power and Linkage in Indore: A Political Map of an Indian City," Columbia University doctoral dissertation, 1970, p. 112.

harashtra and Gujarat), 26 percent from the princely area of Rajputana, 18.5 percent from Uttar Pradesh, 31 percent from Gwalior or other Central Indian states, 7 percent from the Central Provinces (which then included Nagpur), and 4.5 percent from more distant areas such as Punjab, Bengal, Kashmir, and parts of southern India. Many of those who in 1931 gave their birthplace as the Holkar state were of course sons and daughters of earlier immigrants. Only a small part of the city's population has descended from groups that are indigenous to Malwa. The immigration was conditioned by the historical and economic pattern of growth. The Maratha invasion brought Marathi-speakers, most of whom were rulers, soldiers, or bureaucrats. Commercial and service opportunities in Indore attracted merchant castes and a few Brahmans from Gujarat and Rajasthan. And much of the immigration from Uttar Pradesh and Rajasthan was of intermediate and lower castes, attracted by the growing industrial job opportunities of the city.

A more recent profile of groups of language, religion, and caste (in broad categories) for Indore shows that nearly two-thirds of the city is Hindi-speaking, but that there are substantial minorities of those who use Marathi (nearly 15 percent), Urdu (10.6 percent), Sindhi, Gujarati, and Punjabi (see Table 3). The category of Hindi, of course, conceals a variety of different dialects that prevail in central India, Rajasthan, and Uttar Pradesh. Sindhi-speakers are recent immigrants, refugees of partition, from Pakistan. With respect to religion, the city is predominantly Hindu but contains a substantial minority of Muslims (about 12 percent), a sizable proportion of Jains (nearly 4 percent) primarily from Rajasthan and Gujarat, and tiny minorities of Sikhs, Christians, and tribals.

Using the category of *jati* (endogamous unit or subcaste), there are literally dozens of castes in Indore of varying political importance. According to the Census of 1931, Indore was predominantly composed of "high" (30 percent) and "intermediate" (56 percent) castes. The "high castes" consisted primarily of Brahmans and Baniyas, with a few Kayasthas, Khatris, and Muslim Bohras, and the "intermediate" category ranged from Rajputs, Marathas, and Dhangars to Ahirs, Malis, and numerous others, including also most Muslims. The rest consisted of "depressed (or scheduled) castes" (13 percent), or "tribals"

TABLE 3. PROFILE OF MAJOR LANGUAGE, RELIGION, AND CASTE
GROUPS OF INDORE CITY, 1961

Social Grouping	Percentage of Caste and Religion	Percentage of Language and Region
Marathi-speakers		14.7
Maharashtrian Brahman	8.0	
Maratha	3.8	
Dhangar	2.2	
Other	0.7	
Hindi-speakers		63.9
Brahman	8.8	
Jain Baniya	3.9	
Hindu Baniya	6.6	
Scheduled caste	10.2	
Other	34.4	
Urdu-speakers[a]		10.6
Muslim	12.0	
Sindhi-speakers		5.5
Gujarati-speakers		2.2
Punjabi-speakers		2.0
South Indians		0.2
Others		0.9
Total		100.0

SOURCES: The latest caste survey of Indore city, although it is an excellent one,
goes back to 1931. See Rashid, *Census, 1931*, Holkar State, *op. cit.*, Vol. I, pp. 244,
256–257, 280–281; Vol. II, pp. 16ff. *Census, 1961, op. cit.*, p. 127. Directorate of Economics and Statistics, *Pocket Compendium of District Statistics*, Indore, 1963, table of
"Mother Tongues in Indore City."

[a] The Muslims of Indore are not all Urdu-speakers. The Bohras, in particular,
are from Gujarat and use the language of that region.

(1 percent).[16] Among the "depressed castes," Chamars (4.5 percent)
and Koris (2.7 percent) were most important numerically.

When regional and linguistic differences are taken into account,
there is no "dominant caste" in Indore—no single caste which com-
bines great numerical strength with preponderant political and eco-

---

[16] See Appendix A, Table 1, at the end of the book. Unfortunately, the most
recent detailed data on caste for Indore city is from 1931 and now very much out
of date. The figures used here and in Table 3 are based on Rashid, *Census, 1931*,
supplemented by interview information, and should be regarded as estimates.

The terms "depressed castes" and "scheduled castes" are synonymous and refer
principally to the so-called "untouchables," whom Mahatma Gandhi dignified with
the name *Harijan* ("children of God"). The terms preferred in this study are *Harijan*
and "scheduled caste," and they are used interchangeably.

nomic influence—but there are, to use Rajni Kothari's terms, "entrenched" and "ascendant" castes.[17] *Entrenched castes* may be numerically small but are usually high in ritual status and exercise economic and political power. *Ascendant castes* are also normally high in ritual status but have either been excluded or responded less quickly to new educational and political opportunities, and become challengers to those already in power. Indore's chief entrenched castes were those that exercised or gained political and economic power under the princely regime or in the limited politics of constitutional reform which altered the composition of the government in the 1930's and 1940's. Chief among them were the Dhangars and Marathas of the ruling class, the Maharashtrian Brahmans who administered the government, and the Jain Baniyas, who not only dominated business and industry in Indore but had highly placed executive officials in the government attending to their interests.[18] Except for the Jains, the principal entrenched castes were all of Marathi-speaking origin, a function of selective recruitment under a Maharashtrian regime.

After the abolition of the princely state, the Dhangars and Marathas rapidly declined in political influence, and the Maharashtrian Brahmans did so more slowly, but the Jains have continued to be preeminent in Indore politics since 1948, especially at the highest levels. Two Indore Jains were ministers, one the Chief Minister, for several years, of the Madhya Bharat government, and he continued but with lesser portfolios in the Madhya Pradesh Cabinet until 1967. Also indicative of their prominence is the fact that of the 20 major electoral opportunities in Indore (four state legislative assembly seats and one parliamentary seat, over four general elections), Jains have won six times in legislative assembly seats and once in the parliamentary seat, a remarkable record given the fact that they represent less than 4 percent of the city's population.

Maharashtrian Brahmans, though they are divided by four main subcastes in Indore, are a relatively compact and cohesive community, and as such are the largest single group (about 8 percent) in the city. Marathas and Dhangars are smaller (3.8 and 2.2 percent, respectively),

---

[17] Rajni Kothari, *Politics in India*, pp. 234ff.

[18] A more detailed analysis of the social bases of political and administrative prominence is provided in the next chapter. For background on Maharashtrian Brahmans, see D. D. Karve, *The New Brahmans: Five Maharashtrian Families*.

but fairly compact also. And the Jains, though they are divided into sects (Digambar and Schwetambar) as well as by *jati* (Saraogi, Oswal, and Porwal) are perhaps the most cohesive community of all.

The ascendant castes, which consist mainly of Hindi-speaking Brahmans and Hindu Baniyas (8.8 and 6.6 percent, respectively) have a small numerical edge over Maharashtrian Brahmans and Jains, but are far more heterogeneous and less cohesive as a result. Hindi-speaking Brahmans have been the principal challengers of Maharashtrian predominance in administration, the professions, and politics more generally. But Hindi-speaking Brahmans have also had a tendency to compete among themselves as well as with the numerically few but relatively successful Nagar Brahmans from Gujarat. Hindi-speaking Brahmans in Indore consist of groups from three regions: the Malwi natives (Shrigaur and Naramdeo), those from Uttar Pradesh (Kanyakubja and Sanadya), and others from Rajasthan or northern regions (Bundelkhandi, Jodhpuria, and Palliwal). The Hindu Baniya castes similarly have been the chief rivals of the Jains in trade, industry and finance, as well as in the political arena, but are, unlike the Jains, more sharply divided along *jati* and regional lines. These cleavages reflect themselves in party affiliations and voting patterns too, for Hindu Baniyas compete for control of the Congress party but, unlike the Jains, some Hindu Baniyas are disposed to support the Jan Sangh party as well. Moreover, the Maheshwaris, a Hindu Baniya group important in the rural areas surrounding Indore, tend to be allied not with other Hindu Baniyas but with the Jains. The two Hindu Baniya groups that compete strongly with the Jains are the Agarwals and Khandelwals, and of lesser importance are the Neemas and Modis.

Comparative data on caste, literacy, and occupational distribution from 1931 reveals considerable differentiation among these groups, and helps to account for the political, administrative, and professional prominence, particularly of Maharashtrian Brahmans, at an earlier stage in the city's development.[19] Maharashtrian Brahmans had a very much higher rate of general literacy (nearly 62 percent) than Hindi-speaking Brahmans (ranging from 26 to 39 percent), and with respect to literacy in English, a key language for administrative and pro-

---

[19] The source is Rashid, *Census, 1931*, Part I, pp. 195, 200–201; Part II, pp. 70–99; and the calculations are mine. For more detail, see Tables 2.4 and 2.7 of my "Area, Power and Linkage in Indore," pp. 56–57, 64.

fessional purposes, the discrepancy was even greater (28 percent as compared with a range of 6 to 9 percent). Maharashtrian Brahmans were not only three to four times more often literate in English than Hindi-speaking Brahmans, but their proportion of the total population that was literate in English was 38 percent. The comparable proportion of Hindi-speaking Brahmans, though an equally large group in the city population, was only 11 percent. Differences in vernacular and English literacy, though not as sharp, similarly favor Jains over Hindu Baniyas; both of these groups, in fact, were proportionally more literate in the vernacular than Hindi-speaking Brahmans, and on a par with them in English, just the reverse of what might have been expected.

Highly educated by tradition, and employed as administrators by Marathi-speaking rulers, Maharashtrian Brahmans were strategically situated to absorb English, perpetuate their hold over the administrative services, and move into the modern professions. For them power was the key to education, and education the key to power. For the Jains, wealth was the key to both education and power, and both paid dividends. Recognition of this fact led to challenges by ascendant elites, the initial results of which we shall see in the next chapter. The rivalry between the entrenched and ascendant caste coalitions was complicated by the introduction of electoral procedures, for while this introduced new possibilities for winning power, it required the rival coalitions to reach down among intermediate and lower castes for popular support, greatly pluralizing political participation. Eventually this was to shift the balance among the rival coalitions, especially as external allies joined the fray; but even as participation became broader, the interplay continued to be, to a large extent, among shifting coalitions of traditional groups. Before turning to explore this process in the next two chapters, however, something more should be said about the physical and sociological contours of the city.

The Physical Community

The major physical landmarks of Indore city are the river channels (which flow only during the monsoon), the railway, and the axis roads. The Khan and Saraswati rivers divide the city triagonally. The Khan river flows from the southeast until it joins the Saraswati in the center of Indore, and then flows north; the Saraswati winds irregularly

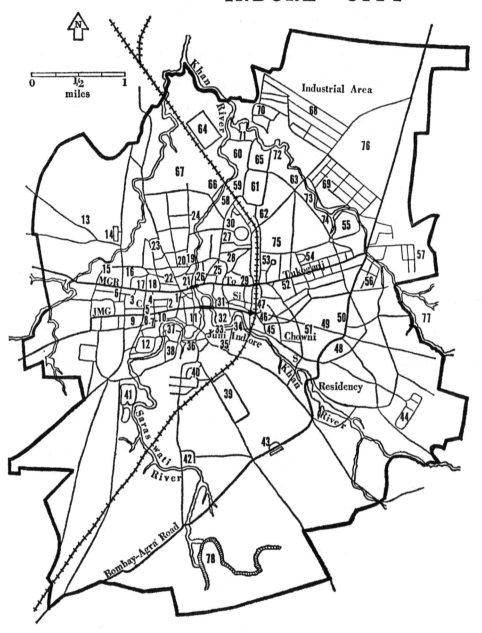

INDORE CITY

N

0 ½ 1
miles

Khan River

Industrial Area

70
68
64
71
76
60
65
72
67
66
59
63
69
58
61
73
24
30
62
74
55
14
27
75
23
54
13
20 19
28
53
57
15
16
25
52
56
MGR
17 18
22
21 26
To 29
Tukoganj
6
Si
3 C
4
2
47
JMG
5
31
46
77
9
8 10
11
32 34
45
49 50
12
37
33
51
38
36
35
48
Juni Indore
Chowni
40
Si
Khan
Residency
41
39
River
44
Saraswati
43
River
42
Bombay-Agra Road
78

To   Topkhana
Si   Siaganj
S   Sanyogitaganj

C   Central Commercial Area
JMG   Jawaharmarg
MGR   Mahatma Gandhi Road

1. Rajbada
2. Sarafa; Ram Laxman Bazaar
3. Maharaja Tukojirao Cloth Market
4. Bohra Bazaar; Bohra Bakhl
5. Santa Bazaar; Kasera Bazaar
6. Malharganj; Yeshwantganj
7. Bombay Bazaar
8. Pinjara Bakhl
9. Lodhipura; Tatpatti Bakhl; Mochi Mohalla; Biabani
10. Deswalipura; Nehalpura
11. Reshimwale Compound; Kabuter Khana; Koila Bakhl; Gautampura
12. Chhatribagh
13. Laxmibainagar Market
14. Fort
15. Karabin; Jinsi
16. Malhar Paltan; Tamboli Bakhl
17. Chhipa Bakhl; Khajuri Bazaar
18. Juna Pitha; Subhash Chowk
19. Rambagh
20. Martand Chowk
21. Krishnapura; Imli Bazaar
22. Gafur Khan ki Bajariya; Manik Chowk; Kamatipura
23. Marathi Mohalla
24. Pant Vaidya Colony
25. Jail Road, Mewati Mohalla
26. Municipal Corporation
27. Shram Shivir (INTUC headquarters)
28. Nayapura; Kacchi Mohalla
29. Labour Commission; Sikh Mohalla
30. Sneheletaganj
31. Ranipura
32. Daulatganj
33. Raoji Bazaar; Shanigali; Toda
34. Murai Mohalla; Champabagh
35. Mominpura; Kumawatpura
36. Pagnis Paga; Alapur
37. Harsiddhi
38. Moti Tabela (Collectorate)
39. Sindhi Colony

40. Palshikar, Dube, and Javery Colonies
41. Lalbagh Palace
42. Manik Bagh Palace
43. Holkar College, Government Arts and Commerce College
44. Daly College
45. Indore Christian College; Gujarati College
46. Choti Gwaltoli
47. Railway Station
48. Stadium
49. Maharaja Yeshwant Rao Hospital
50. Mahatma Gandhi Medical College
51. Jaora Compound
52. High Court
53. Nehru Park
54. Yeshwant Club
55. New Palasia; Palasia
56. Manoramaganj
57. Saket Colony
58. Bhandari Mills
59. Swadeshi Mills
60. Kalyanmal Mills
61. Hukamchand Mills
62. Rajkumar Mills
63. Malwa Mills
64. Malwa Vanaspati
65. Metal Works
66. Power Station
67. New Industrial Estate
68. Nandanagar
69. Nehrunagar
70. Pardesipura
71. Kulkarni Bhatta
72. Jivan ki Phail
73. Gomah ki Phail
74. Pancham ki Phail
75. Vallabhnagar
76. Khajrani
77. Pipliahana
78. Piplia Reservoir (Pipliarao)

from the south and southwest to the central junction. The railway line from Bombay and Mhow enters the city in the southwest and angles eastward until it crosses the Khan river, and then runs north through the railway station (situated between the major east-west roads, Ja-

waharmarg and Mahatma Gandhi road) to the industrial area, where
it swings northwest out of the city before forking in different directions to Dewas in the east and Ratlam to the north. Cutting across the
railway, what is now the Mahatma Gandhi road runs from the Bombay-Agra trunk road, through Tukoganj, across the railway overpass
into what has been known since Holkar days as Topkhana (artillery
depot), over the Khan river (on the Krishnapura bridge, just north
of the junction of the rivers), past Junta Chowk (public square) and
the Rajbada or old palace, through Khajuri Bazaar and Malharganj,
and leaves the city in the direction of the airport and Depalpur to the
west.

The Mahatma Gandhi road is one main traffic artery. It is paralleled about a quarter of a mile to the south by Jawaharmarg, the
second main conduit for cross-city traffic. Jawaharmarg is a new road
that was constructed by the Improvement Trust. It runs almost due
west from the railway crossing in Choti Gwaltoli, through the iron
trade and construction material markets of Siaganj, to cross the two
rivers just south of their junction, and passes between the very densely
inhabited mohallas of Bombay Bazaar and Lodhipura (south) and
the old commercial heart of the city in Bada Sarafa, Santa Bazaar,
Bohra Bakhl, and the Cloth Market (north), past what used to be
military lines in the direction of Dhar to the southwest. On the outskirts of the city in the south and east, the Bombay-Agra trunk road
traverses through the Residency area, linking Indore with Dewas and
eventually Agra in the northeast, and Mhow and Bombay in the
southwest.

Indore had 138 distinct *mohallas* and neighborhoods in 1931, and
there are probably twice that number today. But the principal social
and economic features of the city can be more simply described by
dividing it into six large sections: the industrial area, Tukoganj, the
Residency, Juni Indore, the old commercial heart of the city, and the
newer commercial centers of Siaganj and Topkhana. *The industrial
area* forms a northeastern segment extending from Nayapura up along
the Khan river and to the west where the old Malwa Mills are located.
Today labor colonies, irregular slums as well as the planned developments of Nehrunagar and Nandanagar, are arranged around and between the six major textile plants. Workers of Uttar Pradesh origin
are heavily concentrated in Pardesipura, next to Nandanagar, and

Marathi-speaking workers cluster in Kulkarni Bhatta and Bhindiko, adjacent to the Kalyan Mills and the Hukamchand Mills. Bairwas, Chamars, and Yadavs from Rajasthan congregate in Gomah ki Phail and Pancham ki Phail. The social composition of Nandanagar and Nehrunagar colonies is mixed except for the fact that it consists of the more affluent elite among workers—clerical employees in the mills, INTUC union officials, and skilled workers. On the internal periphery of the industrial area, south of the Rajkumar Mills, there is the Vallabhnagar middle-class colony of Gujarati civil servants and small businessmen. Just to the west of the main industrial area, across the railroad, lies Indore's new Industrial Estate of small-scale enterprises. The industrial area is predominantly inhabited by laboring-class people, but there are admixtures of shopkeepers, small business-men, and rentiers who provide services to the area.

Tukoganj, to the south of the industrial area, falls north and south of Mahatma Gandhi road. Along that road are several very large estates owned by leading Marwari businessmen. Their opulent mansions were built there early in the century, it is said, to escape the dangers of plague in the old city. Further north and south, as well as to the east of the Bombay-Agra road, there are a series of new housing developments, with fine upper-middle-class homes in New Palasia, Palasia, Saket Colony, and Manoramaganj, and middle- to lower-middle-class homes in Tilaknagar and Rabindranagar. Tukoganj also contains the once elegant Yeshwant Club, the city's one western-style hotel, the monumental High Court building, and Nehru Park. The population density of Tukoganj is very low, even though it is mainly residential. It was probably the first suburban area of the city.

South of Tukoganj lies the *Residency* area, the former site of the British establishment of the Agent to the Governor-General; fine old Victorian buildings stand there still. Daly College, once a well-known finishing school for sons of princes and nobles, the St. Raphael school and other buildings of the Roman Catholic mission, the Post Office, and the telegraph office are situated east of the Bombay-Agra road. In more recent years, a large modern hospital, a medical college, and the municipal stadium have been built on sprawling sites, and new residential construction has expanded into Jaora compound. The western section of the old Residency area known as Chowni (or Sanyogitaganj) merges with the city near the railway station. It is a

heavily populated area of shops and older residences and contains one
of the two major grain markets of the city, as well as Indore Christian
College, the Canadian Mission hospital, and the Gujarati College.
Agarwal and Khandelwal merchants dominate Chowni's retailing and
marketing, but many other groups, including mill laborers, reside
there.

Juni Indore, the oldest settlement of the city, is located south and
east of the fork in the rivers. Most of the Malwi Brahman population
of the city resides in and around Raoji Bazaar. Around them are
distributed dense concentrations of low castes, artisans, laborers, and
servants, in Gadi Ada, Murai Mohalla, Shanigali, Mominpura, Kumawatpura and Luniapura. A little further to the west in Pagnis Paga
and Harsiddhi, around the present site of the Collectorate (in what
used to be the princely stables), there are sizable Maharashtrian Brahman, Maratha, and Dhangar settlements. South of Juni Indore there
are a series of newer suburban developments in what once were
princely preserves, including the isolated Sindhi colony, Palshikar,
Dube, and Javery colonies, to name a few. Even further south along
the Saraswati river stand the old Lalbagh Palace, once surrounded by
beautiful gardens but now left untended, and the well-kept Manik
Bagh palace, which is still used by the Holkar heirs during their
infrequent visits. And on the southern periphery of the city are
situated the two public degree colleges, the Holkar College and the
Government Arts and Commerce College.

West of the Saraswati river is the *old commercial heart* of Indore.
The most densely populated and congested part of the city lies between Jawaharmarg and the Mahatma Gandhi road, to the west of
the Rajbada (old palace). It centers on the bazaars and markets of
Sarafa (gold, silver, jewelry, money-lending, and traditional banking),
the Maharaja Tukoji Rao Cloth Market, Bohra Bazaar, Santa Bazaar,
and Malharganj. Malharganj contains the second major grain and
agricultural produce market of the city. Jain merchants dominate
wholesaling and the most lucrative retail trades, but the other merchant communities of Bohras, Agarwals, Neemas, Modis, Sonars, and
Telis do well too. South of Jawaharmarg, the population is less mercantile and more artisan or laborer in composition, but highly diversi-
fied among Hindi-speaking Brahmans, Muslims, and a large array of
other intermediate and lower castes. Muslims are numerous in Pinjara

Bakhl and Bombay Bazaar, and Brahmans in Lodhipura. These are centers of underworld activity as well, and there has been recurrent friction between the strong-arm men of the Muslim and Brahman neighborhoods. To the north of Mahatma Gandhi road, the population is also diverse. The market activity of Malharganj has its satellite to the north in the Laxmibainagar grain market. South of the fort, where the Holkar Army was once housed in barracks, the descendants of officers and soldiers still live, including Kanyakubja Brahmans in Jinsi and Karabin, Dhangars and Marathas in Malhar Paltan, and Rajputs and assorted lower castes distributed throughout the area. The traditional dyers and printers of cloth still survive in Chhipa-bakhl, and timber is still important in Juna Pitha. Closer to the Khan river, Maharashtrian white-collar and middle-class communities are numerically dominant in Rambagh, Martand Chowk, and Pant Vaidya colony.

Finally, the *somewhat newer area* north and east of the big bend in the Khan river has a mixed commercial, administrative, and labor character. It includes along Jawaharmarg the market area of Siaganj, which first thrived as a customs-free corn market and distribution center. It also became a major center of iron-workers, and from that have evolved construction businesses from timber to cement and paint. Partly because of its proximity to the railroad station, it is also an important trucking and warehousing center. Like Topkhana, it contains some of the more modern shops and indigenous-style hotels. Topkhana, however, is primarily an area of retail merchandising and professional offices. Jail road, which goes north from Topkhana, is where the lawyers hang out their shingles. In the vicinity lie several administrative centers, the Municipal Corporation, the district courts, and the Labour Commissioner's headquarters, as well as the Maharaja Sivaji Rao High School, once an important focus of nationalist intellectual settlement. In Ranipura, just south of Siaganj, is the largest Muslim settlement, with butchers, tanners, and a variety of laborers. North of Topkhana, in Nayapura, there are substantial numbers of mill workers, as well as Mewatis, Kacchis, and other lower castes.

Indore is multifunctional and heterogeneous. There are many occupations, both traditional and modern, but dominant among them are trade and commerce, industrial manufacturing, and administrative services. The social groups of the city do cluster by mohalla and neighborhood, but not in a uniform or even sharply segregated fashion. A few neighborhoods are homogeneous, but most are mixtures of people stratified and divided by occupation, religion, language, and caste. The mixture still varies from area to area, conditioned by history, physical features, immigration phases, and changing economic opportunities. Indore's social contours will become better understood as we proceed to examine the politics to which they give rise in the city as a whole and in special arenas in Part Two, which deals with city-wide political competition. Before analyzing city-wide electoral competition and the state-urban political and bureaucratic hierarchies, the subjects of chapters 4 and 5, the princely state background of modern politics in Indore is discussed first in chapter 3, in order to examine more directly the effects of primordial group competition as it was structured under princely conditions, particularly in patterns of elite administrative recruitment.

PART TWO

THE CITY ARENA

3

THE PRINCELY HERITAGE:
SOCIAL BASES OF POLITICAL
AND ADMINISTRATIVE PROMINENCE

The princely state heritage, viewed as an independent variable, is among the most important factors affecting post-independence politics in Indore. Although its importance tends to diminish over time, it shaped early patterns of political and administrative recruitment that have persisted in the decades since independence. There are other factors too that have had a bearing on recruitment patterns: the British presence, the growth of the business and entrepreneurial class, the rise of nationalist and popular political organizations, and the development of the working-class or labor movement in Indore. This chapter deals with the recruitment patterns of political and administrative elites in Indore under princely conditions, with reference to the social composition of the city. Along with the factors of princely preference, education, and wealth, the relation of numbers—or the proportion of given groups in the population—to political and administrative success will be explored. By focusing on social differences and variations in recruitment we get a preview of the interests and aspirations of social groups and their leaders, of the issues their competition generates, and of the stakes and rewards of political competition in Indore.

Continuity and Diminution of Princely Power

While the heritage of princely politics in Indore had a pronounced effect after independence, the form it took was limited in important ways. First, the influence of the princely house in Indore ceased to be direct. Unlike the ruling family of Gwalior, which has transformed traditional loyalties into electoral support as the basis for active princely leadership in Madhya Bharat and Madhya Pradesh politics, the Holkar heirs have attempted neither to find new sources of power nor to use their residual influence much in the era of representative politics. Second, and even more surprisingly, the *sardars* (titled nobles) of the Holkar state have apparently disappeared from the political scene, their former power has evaporated, by contrast with Sardars Bal Angre, Jadhav, and others of Gwalior, who have remained politically active as allies or opponents of the late Maharaja, Jiwajirao Scindia, and the Rajmata of Gwalior, Vijaya Raje Scindia.

The dissolution of the direct influence of the Holkar ruling family may be explained in part by the fact that the British interfered with and undermined their control early in the game.[1] When the Holkar ruler, Khande Rao, died childless in 1844, the British selected and retained considerable control over his successor, Tukoji Rao II.[2] Subsequently the British intervened to bring the abdication of Sivaji Rao II in 1903, and a Council of Regency governed under British supervision until 1911. The Prime Minister during this period was Nanakchand Agarwal, an official responsive to the British presence.[3] After Tukoji Rao III succeeded in 1911, Siremal Bapna, a Jain, was elevated to Prime Minister, holding the position until just before the Second World War began. Tukoji Rao III was also induced by the British to abdicate, in 1926, after his alleged involvement in a crime.[4]

---

[1] K. L. Srivastava, *The Revolt of 1857 in Central India—Malwa*, p. 37.

[2] *Ibid.*, pp. 39–40; Dhariwal, *Indore State Gazetteer*, Vol. I, pp. 58–59. See also Godbole, "Indreshwar."

[3] Dhariwal, *Gazetteer*, Vol. I, pp. 58–59.

[4] "Early in 1926 the Maharaja Tukeji Rao of Indore was offered a Commission of Enquiry to investigate the question of his connection with the conspiracy by certain officials of the State to kidnap Mumtaz Begum, His Highness' favourite dancing girl, culminating in the murder of Sheikh Abdul Qadir Bawla in Bombay. His Highness, however, declined the offer and proposed to abdicate provided the enquiry was abandoned. This was accepted by the Government of India." Urmila Phadnis, *Towards the Integration of the Princely States*, Appendix VI.

His son, Yeshwant Rao II, was then a minor undergoing his education at Oxford. Yeshwant Rao assumed ruling powers in 1930, but his presence in Indore embarrassed the British,[5] and consequently they encouraged him to spend most of his time away from Indore, in Kashmir or traveling on the continent and in the United States.

The cumulative results of British interference were to detach the Holkar rulers from their control over appointments, patronage, and policy in the Holkar state administration, especially in the twentieth century, and to elevate Hindu Baniya and Jain officials who, like Siremal Bapna, strengthened the position of the Prime Minister in the administration, making it autonomous from the Holkar throne, though not from the British. Divorced from control over the administration, the Holkar rulers had little in the way of patronage to dispose of and few opportunities to build constituencies that could later be transformed into political support when the new conditions of electoral politics were introduced. The grip of the Gwalior ruling family over the rival state administration did not appear to be weakened so severely.

The political weakness of the Holkars was furthered by the fact that Yeshwant Rao II was largely the product of Western upbringing, education, and culture. He could not, as a result, claim the full emotional loyalty of the Dhangar community. Moreover, there was a pretender to the throne, a Dhangar relative by the name of Malhar Rao.[6] As to who would succeed him, Yeshwant Rao at first seemed to lean in favor of his son, Richard, born of an American wife and educated at Stanford University. But opposition to this led Yeshwant Rao and the Ministry of Home Affairs of the Government of India to agree that Ushadevi Holkar, his daughter by an Indian wife from the Dhangar community, would be the recognized heir. But about two years before her father's death, in 1958, Usha married a Punjabi named Malhotra, which had the effect of separating her from Dhangar caste affiliation. She inherited the Holkar privy purse when Yeshwant Rao died, but her husband, to put it mildly, did not receive a warm reception among the Dhangars of Indore. Consequently, neither Usha

---

[5] V. P. Menon, *The Story of the Integration of the Princely States*, p. 216.

[6] Malhar Rao founded the *Ahilya Gaddi Rakshan Samiti*, or "Committee for the Protection of Ahilya's Throne." Ahilyabai Devi Holkar, a popularly revered queen, ruled the state from 1766 to 1796 from the previous capital at Maheshwar.

—who knows little Hindi in any case—nor Malhotra saw any possibility of using Indore as an electoral base for political activity. Instead, both spend their time investing the residual Holkar wealth in industrial enterprises in Bombay. By marrying a "foreigner," Usha cut herself off from political opportunities in Indore and apparently ended the possibility of the ruling family's becoming a political force in Indore.

The Holkar state titled nobility, consisting of leading Dhangar, Maratha, Maharashtrian Brahman, and other families, may have retained limited influence, not as a class but as individuals or families linked personally to emerging popular political leaders. Yet on the whole their influence appears to have greatly declined. None have stood for popular elections since 1948, as have Sardar Angre and the Rajmata of Gwalior, and the properties of many appear to have been dissipated.[7] It is possible that one or another member of former noble families will enter the political arena successfully in the future, and that their influence remains important in less visible and public forms, but the evidence now points in the other direction and suggests that the nobles have passed from the scene, superseded by electoral and popular politics, at least in the city of Indore.

Although the Holkar heritage has not in recent years been manifested through the agency of the ruling family or the nobles, it has still been important indirectly in other forms, in shaping the composition of the administrative services generally, in awarding initial political advantages to leaders of the so-called "Praja Mandal group" over the "Congress group" and in influencing the composition of the state-patronized legal, educational, and medical professions. The most prominent social groups in this connection are Marathi-speakers. Their special role in the Holkar government establishments and their continuing influence as a minority make them as important as their language makes them visible.[8]

---

[7] For example, when Surendranath Dube died in 1968, the property of a once-wealthy family of army commanders had diminished to the equivalent of two or three substantial dwellings. Sardar Bolia lost a fortune on ill-advised investments in the cinema industry of Bombay. The heirs of Seth Hukumchand have lost their dominance of capital and industry in Indore to more aggressive entrepreneurs.

[8] Language groups identified here are those using a particular language in the home, though they may be conversant with and use other languages, particularly Hindi, outside the home.

Maharashtrian Brahmans, though only 8 percent of the total population, constituted the core of the administrative services in the Holkar state and were otherwise attracted to the professions of law, medicine, and education or were employed as office workers in the industrial and banking establishments.[9] Most Maharashtrian Brahmans were salaried with modest incomes, but an elite minority among them were *sardars* (titled nobles) with income from land (*jagirs*) or large government salaries. Representative of this elite were the Bhuskute, Khasgiwale, Kibe, Mulye, Palshikar, Phadnis, and Reshimwale (Nigoskar) families.[10] Maharashtrian Brahmans are most noticeably absent from large-scale business ownership; Kibe, the financier, was the only important exception in Indore.

The connection of Maharashtrian Brahmans with the government establishment, their prominence in the professions of law, medicine, and teaching, and their leadership of political movements has led to the view quite common in Indore that they have been and even now are the intellectual, political, and administrative elite of the city. Because there is an element of truth in this reputational stereotype, it is worth examining some of the supporting and contrary evidence. In doing so it will become clear that political competition amidst a socially heterogeneous environment has produced in the city plural and competitive elites. Marathi-speakers, and Maharashtrian Brahmans in particular, as components of princely power, did indeed possess intellectual, professional, and administrative primacy under the old regime. They were, moreover, leading figures in nationalist and radical political movements in the city before the abolition of the princely state in 1948. But their privileged exclusiveness has been eroded over time by competitors from the business and Hindi-speaking Brahman communities, and by leaders from the intermediate caste strata of the city. British influences and nationalist forces began this erosion under the princely regime, but its abolition and the subsequent popularization of politics through the franchise accelerated the

---

[9] The main Maharashtrian Brahman subcastes found in Indore are Chitpavan (Konkanastha), Deshastha, and Karhade. Saraswat Brahmans from Kanara as well as Maharashtra are sometimes included. In this case, subcaste distinctions are more relevant for marriage and social obligations than for politics in Indore. To non-Maharashtrians in Indore, the Brahmans from western India appear as a single group. See Table 2 above, and Appendix A, Table 1.

[10] Dhariwal, *Gazetteer*, Vol. I, pp. 47–61.

process. As one prominent Maharashtrian informant put it, "whereas Maharashtrians were at the head of political revolutionary movements, they were always replaced by others when it came to exercising power. Maharashtrians were in the vanguard, but they were not so good at establishing broad mass contacts and in delivering the goods. They provided intellectual leadership." Consequently, political mobilization has displaced Maharashtrian Brahmans from political leadership, and it has diminished—though by no means ended—their importance in professional circles and the bureaucracies.

Patterns of Princely Administrative Recruitment

Empirical evidence of the pluralization of elites was obtained from "positional" indicators, through an analysis of the community composition of Holkar state government officials and the "gazetted" levels of the administration, and is presented in the accompanying tables.[11] It is assumed that, under the formally autocratic conditions of the princely state, official and bureaucratic positions are adequate indicators of political power, especially in this case where representatives of economic elites openly held high-level government positions and had no need to operate covertly. There were several structural points of access in the later years of the regime. First, there was the Personal Staff of the ruler (see Table 4). Second, there were the executive and policy-making organs: the Privy Council, the Cabinet, the Judicial Committee, the Cabinet Committee of Appeals, and the Legislative Committee. Represented here as the "Official Elite," these officials were the major internal decision-makers in the unreformed regime that lasted until 1947 (see Table 5). In 1947, pressures for constitutional reform produced a more representative Cabinet and a Legislative Council partly elected under a property-qualified franchise or from special constituencies, but mostly nominated by the govern-

---

[11] "Gazetted officers" is a term commonly used in India to refer to those permanent civil servants of high rank who exercise executive responsibilities and whose names are published in the government *gazettes*. The *gazettes* have been issued periodically to record acts of state and other official items of public interest. The ordinary clerical and menial employees of government, who are far more numerous, are not so listed.

The sources were the *List of Officers of the Holkar State*, corrected up to July 1, 1931, and up to October 1, 1947. I gratefully acknowledge help from G. S. Tamhankar and N. C. Zamindar in analyzing the lists of officers by community affiliation.

TABLE 4. ANALYSIS BY COMMUNITY
OF GAZETTED OFFICERS OF HOLKAR
STATE, 1931 AND 1947: PERSONAL
STAFF OF THE MAHARAJA

Social Grouping	1931	1947
Maharashtrians	(4)	(12)
Brahman	1	2
CKP[a]	0	0
Maratha	2	6
Dhangar	1	4
Non-Maharashtrians	(4)	(13)
Brahman	0	2
European	1	1
Baniya	0	1
Rajput	2	0
Muslim	1	4
Other	0	5[b]
Total	(8)	(25)

SOURCES: *List of Officers of the Holkar State*, Indore: Holkar Government Press, 1931 (corrected up to July 1, 1931); *ibid.*, 1947 (corrected up to October 1, 1947).
[a] Chandraseni Kayasth Prabhu (Marathi-speaking writer caste).
[b] Includes 1 Punjabi, 2 South Indians, and 2 Indian Christians.

ment (see Tables 7 and 8).[12] Finally, for an index of bureaucratic representation, there are the departments of administration (Table 6).[13]

In general the representation of communities in these structures is disproportionately skewed toward Marathi-speakers and Maharashtrian Brahmans—and probably would be even more so below the "gazetted" levels of the administration—but there is also a high degree of community pluralism among non-Maharashtrian representatives. The tendency over time is for the proportion of Maharashtrians to decline and for others to take their place, diversifying the composition of government. Community patterns among newcomers provide evidence as to which groups benefit from the early popularization of politics, and are indicators of the penetration and pluralization of elite levels in the city.

The information on the ruler's Personal Staff (Table 4) suggests

[12] See pp. 64, 65.
[13] See p. 58.

an equal balance between Maharashtrians and non-Maharashtrians, both in 1931 and 1947. Among Maharashtrians, as might be expected, the ruler relied for personal service more on Dhangars and Marathas than on Brahmans. Non-Maharashtrians were quite diverse, especially in 1947 when they included two Brahmans, a European, a Baniya, four Muslims, a Punjabi, two South Indians and two Indian Christians. But more important are the patterns among policy-makers of the Official Elite.

TABLE 5. ANALYSIS BY COMMUNITY OF GAZETTED OFFICERS
OF HOLKAR STATE, 1931 AND 1947: THE OFFICIAL ELITE

Social Grouping	1931[a]		1947[b]	
	Number	Percentage	Number	Percentage
Maharashtrians	(18)	(41.8)	(20)	(28.9)
Brahman	13	30.2	14	20.3
CKP	0	0.0	0	0.0
Maratha	0	0.0	1	1.4
Dhangar	5	11.6	5	7.2
Non-Maharashtrians	(25)	(58.1)	(49)	(71.0)
Brahman	1	2.3	11[c]	15.9
European	2	4.8	1	1.4
Jain	6	13.9	10	14.5
Hindu Baniya	8	18.6	6	8.7
Rajput	2	4.7	3	4.3
Muslim	2	4.7	8	11.6
Punjabi	1	2.3	5	7.2
Kayastha	2	4.6	1	1.4
Other	1	2.3	4	5.8
Total	(43)	(100.0)	(69)	(100.0)

[a] The 1931 column includes members of the Privy Council, Cabinet, Judicial Committee, Cabinet Committee of Appeals, and Legislative Committee.
[b] The 1947 column includes members of the Privy Council, Cabinet, Public Service Commission, and Indore Legislative Council. It corresponds to the same part of the *List of Officers of the Holkar State* as the 1931 column. The Legislative Council of 30 members included 10 members elected from the city and special constituencies.
[c] Includes 2 Malwi, 4 Naramdeo, 2 Gujarati, 1 South Indian, and 2 Kashmiri Brahmans.

The Official Elite data (Table 5) reveals interesting changes over time. Although 42 percent of the Official Elite in 1931 were Maharashtrians, and although their absolute number increased slightly, expansion of the Official Elite to 69 persons by 1947 reduced the proportion of Maharashtrians to 29 percent. Nearly three-fourths of the Maharashtrians were Brahmans in each case, and the rest were Dhangars, individuals closely related to the ruling family. In 1931 the non-Maharashtrian component (58 percent) of the Official Elite was quite diverse, but of these 25 persons, 14 were either Jains or Hindu Baniyas. Thus as early as 1931 these representatives of the business communities numerically balanced Maharashtrian Brahmans at the highest levels of decision-making, reflecting the patronage of such prominent Agarwal officials as Munshi Ramchand, Nanakchand, and Shriman Singh, and the unofficial influence of Seth Hukumchand, the leading Jain notable.

Perhaps the most striking result of the expansion of the Official Elite is the influx of non-Maharashtrian Brahmans, growing from a base of 1 in 1931 to 11 in 1947, with 6 of them Hindi-speaking Brahmans from Malwa or the nearby Narmada region. The shift reveals the extent to which local Hindi-speaking Brahmans were formerly excluded from the regime and how they were later coopted by the regime, as political pressures for constitutional reform and representation of nonprincely elites mounted. Also worth noting is the substantial increase in numbers of Jains, the protégés of Prime Minister Siremal Bapna, and the decline in proportion of Hindu Baniyas by 10 percent. The inclusion of Europeans, Rajputs, Muslims, Punjabis, Kayasthas, and others is further indication of the extent to which the uppermost elite level of the princely regime was pluralistic, but confined to the higher castes and upper strata of certain intermediate castes.

The analysis of bureaucratic departments (Table 6) reveals similar patterns, but with greater detail. Here the concentration of Maharashtrians is even more pronounced, though the patterns vary somewhat from one department to another; and, just as in the Official Elite, there is a tendency toward the dilution of Maharashtrian predominance over time. With the exception of the Police department, Maharashtrian proportions ranged in 1931 from a high of 64.2 percent in Revenue to a low of 44 percent in the Secretariat. Almost half (48.6 percent) of the gazetted departmental bureaucrats in 1931 were Maharashtrians, a figure that becomes more meaningful when it is recalled that only about 18 percent of the population in that year were Marathi-speakers. By 1947 the proportions of Maharashtrians in most

TABLE 6. Analysis by Community of Gazetted Officers

	Percentages of							
	Secretariat[a]		Revenue		Police		Home	
Community	1931	1947	1931	1947	1931	1947	1931	1947
Maharashtrians	(44.0)	(31.3)	(64.2)	(55.7)	(5.3)	(35.0)	(52.2)	(31.8)
Brahman[b]	33.3	18.8	46.3	36.7	0.0	22.5	43.3	25.0
CKP	0.0	3.0	0.0	0.0	5.3	2.5	1.5	2.3
Maratha	0.0	6.3	1.5	3.8	0.0	2.5	4.5	2.3
Dhangar	11.1	3.0	16.4	15.2	0.0	7.5	3.0	2.3
Non-Maharashtrians	(56.0)	(68.7)	(35.8)	(44.3)	(94.8)	(65.0)	(47.8)	(68.2)
Brahman	11.1	43.8	9.0	16.5	21.1	40.0	11.9	31.8
Uttar Pradesh[c]	11.1	6.3	3.0	5.1	21.1	20.0	6.0	9.1
Malwi[d]	0.0	9.4	4.5	5.1	0.0	10.0	1.5	6.8
Naramdeo	0.0	0.0	0.0	0.0	0.0	2.5	1.5	2.3
Rajasthan	0.0	0.0	0.0	2.5	0.0	2.5	1.5	6.8
Gujarati	0.0	12.5	0.0	1.3	0.0	0.0	1.5	4.5
Other	0.0	15.6	1.5	2.5	0.0	5.0	0.0	2.3
European	0.0	0.0	0.0	0.0	5.3	2.5	0.0	0.0
Jain	11.1	0.0	1.5	7.6	0.0	0.0	3.0	4.5
Hindu Baniya	0.0	0.0	4.5	6.3	0.0	2.5	13.4	9.1
Rajput	11.1	0.0	14.9	1.3	21.1	12.5	4.5	0.0
Muslim	0.0	6.3	6.0	5.1	31.6	2.5	4.5	6.8
Kayastha	0.0	3.0	0.0	5.1	0.0	5.0	0.0	9.1
Gujarati	0.0	0.0	0.0	0.0	0.0	0.0	0.0	0.0
Sudra	0.0	0.0	0.0	2.5	0.0	0.0	0.0	0.0
Punjabi	11.1	3.0	0.0	0.0	0.0	0.0	1.5	0.0
Other	11.1	12.5	0.0	0.0	15.8	0.0	9.0	2.3
Total	100.0	100.0	100.0	100.0	100.0	100.0	100.0	100.0
Total Number	9	32	67	79	19	40	67	44

[a] Secretariat: Prime Minister, Secretariat, and Foreign department.
Finance: for 1931 includes Finance, Customs, and Audits and Accounts departments; and for 1947 includes the Customs and Excise and the Audits and Accounts departments.
General: for 1931 includes General, Commerce and Industries, Public Works,

departments had declined—from 44 to 31.3 percent in the Secretariat, 64.2 to 55.7 percent in Revenue, and 52.2 to 31.8 percent in Home Affairs—but the average for all departments declined only marginally because of compensating *increases* in the Police (from 5.3 to 35.0 percent) and in the numerically large General category (from 45.9 to 51.7 percent). Still, the data substantiate the gradual erosion of Maharashtrian predominance and the pluralization of the bureaucracies.

OF HOLKAR STATE, 1931 AND 1947: DEPARTMENTS

Percentages of						Total, All Depts.		All Depts. except Army	
Finance[a]		Army		General[a]					
1931	1947	1931	1947	1931	1947	1931	1947	1931	1947
(45.5)	(42.1)	(50.9)	(43.9)	(45.9)	(51.7)	(48.6)	(46.7)	(48.0)	(47.4)
29.5	39.5	5.2	10.1	38.7	44.0	30.4	31.9	37.8	37.8
2.3	0.0	0.9	0.0	3.1	1.4	1.9	1.1	2.3	1.3
4.5	2.6	12.1	15.1	2.6	1.7	4.8	5.2	2.8	2.5
9.1	0.0	32.8	18.7	1.5	4.5	11.4	8.5	5.3	5.8
(54.5)	(57.9)	(49.1)	(56.1)	(44.1)	(48.3)	(51.4)	(53.3)	(52.0)	(52.6)
15.9	28.9	9.5	7.9	17.0	20.6	13.6	21.0	14.8	24.5
2.3	7.9	7.8	4.3	10.8	6.3	8.1	6.8	8.3	7.5
6.8	15.8	1.7	2.2	1.5	7.7	2.3	6.8	2.5	8.1
0.0	0.0	0.0	0.0	0.5	0.7	0.4	0.6	0.5	0.8
0.0	5.3	0.0	0.0	0.5	1.7	0.4	0.5	0.5	2.5
2.3	0.0	0.0	0.0	2.1	0.3	1.2	1.2	1.5	1.5
4.5	0.0	0.0	1.4	1.5	3.8	1.2	3.5	1.5	4.0
0.0	0.0	0.9	3.6	3.1	0.3	1.6	1.2	1.8	0.4
2.3	2.6	0.0	0.0	1.5	3.1	1.6	2.7	2.0	3.5
13.6	5.3	4.3	1.4	7.7	2.8	7.4	3.3	8.3	3.9
9.1	2.6	21.6	23.0	2.6	3.1	10.1	7.3	6.8	3.1
4.5	7.9	8.6	9.4	5.2	3.5	6.8	5.5	6.3	4.4
2.3	2.6	0.0	0.7	3.6	2.8	1.6	3.2	2.0	3.9
0.0	0.0	0.0	0.0	1.0	0.0	0.4	0.0	0.5	0.0
0.0	0.0	1.7	0.7	0.0	2.1	0.4	1.4	0.0	1.5
2.3	2.6	0.0	2.2	2.6	4.5	1.6	3.0	2.0	3.3
4.5	5.3	2.6	7.2	9.8	5.2	6.6	4.9	7.8	4.2
100.0	100.0	100.0	100.0	100.0	100.0	100.0	100.0	100.0	100.0
44	38	116	139	194	286	516	658	400	519

Excise, and Forests departments; and for 1947 includes the new Medical, Education and Municipal departments in addition to the others or their equivalents.

  b Includes Chitpavan, Deshasta, Karhade, and Saraswat.

  c Includes Bundelkhandi as well.

  d Includes Shrigaur, Gaur, and Dasora Brahmans.

When the distributions of the several Maharashtrian castes are individually examined, differentiating clustering tendencies among departments are discernible. Maharashtrian Brahmans are most heavily concentrated in the civil departments—and, if the Army is excluded, they maintained an average proportion of 37.8 percent in the departments. This figure correlates very closely with the proportion of Maharashtrian Brahmans of the city's population that was literate in

English,[14] which helps account for their disproportionate recruitment into the bureaucracy by a factor of five times their group size. Among the departments in 1931, Maharashtrian Brahmans clustered most heavily in Revenue (46.3 percent), Home (43.3 percent), and General (38.7 percent). Their proportions declined between 1931 and 1947 in the Secretariat, Revenue, and Home—usually due more to expansion of personnel than actual attrition—but their proportions increased in the Police, Finance, the Army, and the General departments. On balance, the erosion of their strength was only slight.

Dhangars were heavily represented in the Revenue department— much more so than one would expect from their community rates of literacy[15]—and to a lesser but still significant extent in other departments as well, a result of princely patronage in the community. Like the Marathas, however, the Dhangars were most concentrated in the Army, a product of the military histories of the two communities. In general (excluding the Army), Dhangars were about twice as numerous and Marathas were somewhat less numerous in the bureaucracies than might be expected from their group sizes in the population at large, if proportional representation were the norm.

Slightly over half of the gazetted officials were non-Maharashtrians in both years. But these were almost exclusively from "higher" and "higher intermediate" castes. In 1931 there were no representatives of Sudra castes (cultivators and artisans), let alone scheduled castes, and by 1947 Sudras had secured only 1.5 percent of the gazetted posts. Again it is Brahmans who predominate, though not to the same extent as among Maharashtrians, and there is, moreover, considerable pluralism among non-Maharashtrian Brahmans.

Non-Maharashtrian Brahmans in 1931 ranged from a low of 9 percent in Revenue to a high of 21.1 percent in the Police, and averaged just under 14 percent in all the departments combined. But these Brahmans registered in the aggregate a more substantial increase over time than any other major group—their proportions rising markedly and their absolute numbers even more so. Their proportions nearly quadrupled in the Secretariat, tripled in Home, almost doubled in the Police and Finance departments, and increased everywhere else

---

[14] The actual figure in 1931 was 38.3 percent. See Table 2.7 in my "Area, Power and Linkage in Indore," p. 57; and Appendix A, Table 1, in this work.

[15] *Ibid.*, Table 2.7; Appendix A, Table 1.

except the Army—bringing their average for all departments in 1947 up to 21 percent, twice their strength in the city population at large.

The key to this increase was the relaxation of princely ascriptive recruitment for the merit system, combined with the spread of education in the city. After the Maharashtrian Brahmans and modernizing business communities, it was the Hindi-speaking Brahmans who most early saw and appropriated educational opportunities and converted them into administrative position and political power. In particular, the Malwi and Rajasthani Brahmans advanced rapidly between 1931 and 1947. The proportion of Malwi Brahmans in the departments as a whole more than tripled, rising from 2.5 to 8.1 percent, about three times their group size in the population. In 1931 they were unrepresented in the Secretariat and the Police, but by 1947 they had obtained one-tenth of the gazetted positions in those departments. Similarly, the average proportion of Rajasthani Brahmans rose from 0.5 to 2.5 percent, and by 1947 they claimed 6.8 percent of the gazetted positions in Home and 5.3 percent of those in the Finance department.

The local Hindi-speaking Brahmans of Malwa and the Narmada region were late modernizers by comparison with their caste fellows from Rajasthan, Uttar Pradesh, and Kashmir. The Uttar Pradeshi Brahmans, most of whom were Kanyakubja (or Kanaujia) Brahmans, were attracted to Indore by the opportunity of serving in the Holkar Army, some as early as the late eighteenth century. Although most of the Kanyakubja remain in the central and western districts of Uttar Pradesh, many of their families have emigrated in search of new opportunities. They have moved as far south as Bangalore and Bombay, and as far east as Calcutta and even Assam, but retain marriage and social networks with their caste-fellows in the north. They have been remarkably adaptive to modern occupational stimuli and have distinguished themselves as administrators, politicians, jurists, and professionals.[16] In Indore, once entrenched in the Army—to which one of their families contributed several commanders-in-chief—they moved into the Police and the civil administration. In 1931 about two-thirds of the non-Maharashtrian Brahmans in the Holkar gazetted services were Kanyakubjas. By 1947 their proportion, though not absolute

---

[16] For an excellent study of their urbanized organization and behavior, see R. S. Khare, *The Changing Brahmans: Associations and Elites among the Kanya-Kubjas of North India.*

numbers, had declined to less than one-third as a result of bureaucratic expansion and the influx of other Hindi-speaking Brahmans. Because of their early and well-established representation in the princely regime, Kanyakubjas, unlike most other Hindi-speaking Brahmans in Indore, tended after independence to be allied with the political heirs of the princely state and saw other Hindi-speaking Brahmans as rivals. In recent Madhya Pradesh politics, as will be shown in later chapters, Kanyakubja Brahmans have been the state's most prominent single source of political leaders.

Jain and Hindu Baniya bureaucratic representation in the departments was less notable than at the Official Elite level and, except for Hindu Baniyas in 1931, much less than their group size or literacy rates in the population at large would lead one to expect. Their stakes were primarily in business, and it was at the highest levels of the administration, where license and tax policies were made, that they generally sought access; and as we have seen, they had representatives of high standing there.

There are certain other cluster patterns of interest. Muslims were not proportionally represented, but given that most of their number were artisans or laborers, they were stronger in the gazetted bureaucracies than might be expected. But their affinity for the Police and Army stand out. A similar pattern holds for Rajputs, though their presence in the administration is most notable for its sharp decline between 1931 and 1947, an indication that their community was falling behind in the competition for education and that they could no longer rely on princely patronage. Their large share (14.9 percent) of the posts in Revenue in 1931 seems to reflect their former importance as intermediaries between the princely regime and the rural population of the state.

And finally, of some interest with respect to the pluralization of the bureaucratic elites are the growing proportions of such small but adaptive groups from the north as Punjabis (mainly Khatris) and Kayasthas—both traditionally urban in their orientation. Under the rule of the last prince, Yeshwant Rao, the prominence of Punjabis at the highest levels of the administration was indicated by the succession of Dinanath as Prime Minister, following S. M. Bapna, and by the appointment of H. C. Dhanda as Deputy Prime Minister in 1947.

As the momentum of popular political movements in the city

gained force during World War Two, and as India approached self-rule, the pressure for political reform and representative institutions in the princely state became irresistible. Dilute forms of representative government had been introduced earlier, in stages, at the municipal level, and in 1947 elections on a narrow franchise were held for the Legislative Council. Popular representation was coopted in the Cabinet in 1947, and in 1948 the Cabinet was given over almost entirely to popular political leadership (see Tables 7 and 8). The community composition of these leadership groups provides a further positional index to the prominence and influence in politics of social groups in the city.

The two outstanding groups represented in the Cabinets of 1947 and 1948 are Maharashtrian Brahmans and Jains, and next in importance are Hindi-speaking Brahmans—groups that had succeeded in organizing political support through the property-qualified franchise. As individual leaders, however, these cabinet ministers had delicately avoided antagonizing the regime and were, by contrast with some of their more radical colleagues, the beneficiaries of tacit support from the *sardars* (titular nobility) and official underpinnings of the regime. Similarly, with the addition of Hindu Baniyas and a Parsi, the elected leaders in the Legislative Council are from the same social groups. It is the nominated members of the Council who add some diversity, though even among them over one-third are Jains or Hindu Baniyas.

The data thus far firmly support the view that the Maharashtrian Brahmans were important in the administration and early popular politics quite out of proportion to their numbers in the local population, but that their earlier leads in education and avenues of recruitment were increasingly under challenge by rival Brahmans from the locality and neighboring Hindi-speaking regions. The analysis of gazetted officials of the state also shows that the princely bureaucracies were quite pluralistic, and increasingly so over time.

Post-Independence Shifts in Administrative Composition

Some additional data from post-independence administration in Indore city is indicative of how the popularization of politics and the enlarged arenas of state politics have made inroads on the erstwhile predominance of the Maharashtrians, and particularly Maharashtrian Brahmans, in the administration. It is worth noting that

TABLE 7. HOLKAR CABINETS, 1947–1948

Office	Person	Background[b]	Community
Cabinet of 1947[a]			
Prime Minister	M. V. Bhide	official	Maharashtrian Brahman
Deputy Prime Min.	H. C. Dhanda	official	Punjabi, Khatri
Revenue Min.	C. G. Matkar	official	Dhangar
General Min.	Masood Quli Khan	official	Muslim
Education Min.	V. S. Sarvate	representative	Maharashtrian Brahman
Agriculture Min.	Vaijnath Mahodaya	representative	Hindi-speaking Brahman
Food Min.	Mishrilal Gangwal	representative	Jain
Labour Min.	V. V. Dravid	representative	South Indian Brahman

Office	Person	Background	Community
Cabinet of 1948[c]			
Prime Minister[d]	M. V. Bhide	official	Maharashtrian Brahman
Revenue Min.	V. S. Khode	representative	Hindi-speaking Brahman
Commerce and Finance Min.	K. A. Chitale	semi-representative[e]	Maharashtrian Brahman
General Min.	Manoharsingh Mehta	representative	Jain
Education Min.	V. S. Sarvate	representative	Maharashtrian Brahman
Labour Min.	V. V. Dravid	representative	South Indian Brahman
Food Min.	Mishrilal Gangwal	representative	Jain
Agriculture Min.	Vaijnath Mahodaya	representative	Hindi-speaking Brahman

[a] This was the first cabinet to contain a substantial number of people with a popular following. It lasted until January 26, 1948.

[b] Background refers to whether the person's career was administrative exclusively (official), or political in the sense of having a popular base or following (representative).

[c] This cabinet was transitional, lasting from January 26, 1948 until June 1, 1948, when merger into Madhya Bharat took place.

[d] Bhide was nominally Prime Minister, but the powers were actually exercised by Khode.

[e] K. A. Chitale, a prominent barrister, was not a politician in the popular sense, but neither was he an ordinary administrative official. His energies were largely exerted professionally, but his temperament was more "official" than "representative."
He has maintained very good relations with those in power through the years, but his professional reputation and integrity have never been questioned.

TABLE 8. ANALYSIS BY COMMUNITY OF GAZETTED OFFICERS OF HOLKAR STATE: THE LEGISLATIVE COUNCIL OF 1947

A. *Officers*	*Person*	*Community*
President	C. G. Matkar	Dhangar
Deputy-Pres.	N. H. Dravid	South Indian Brahman
Secretary	F. R. Tankariwala	Parsi
Joint Sec'y	Shambhunath Chaturvedi	Hindi-speaking Brahman
B. *Nominated Members*		
2		Dhangar
2		Hindi-speaking Brahman
1		Gujarati Brahman
1		South Indian Brahman
1		European
4		Jain
2		Hindu Baniya
1		Muslim
1		Kayastha
1		Khatri
C. *Elected from Indore City*		
	N. G. Kothari	Maharashtrian Brahman
	V. V. Sarvate	Maharashtrian Brahman
	Mishrilal Gangwal	Jain
	M. A. Khan	Muslim
D. *Special Constituencies*		
Graduates	N. H. Dravid	South Indian Brahman
Jagirdars	M. V. Kibe	Maharashtrian Brahman
Jagirdars	K. K. Agnihotri	Maharashtrian Brahman
Textile Industry	R. C. Jall	Parsi
Other Industries	Chhaganlal Mittal	Hindu Baniya
Trade, Commerce	B. Ganpatbhai	Hindu Baniya
Women	Kamalabai Kibe	Maharashtrian Brahman
Women	S. Parulkar	Maharashtrian Brahman
Women	Pukhrajbai Jain	Jain

although the proportions of Maharashtrian Brahmans at the gazetted levels were generally balanced by others, at *intermediate* levels—where line, clerical, and bookkeeping functions rather than executive or supervisory responsibility are the rule—Maharashtrian Brahmans were literally predominant in many branches of the administration. This fact was of considerable political importance after 1948. When the Holkar state was merged into Madhya Bharat, most of the Holkar civil servants were absorbed wholesale into the bureaucracies of the new state government and continued to operate in line agencies in the city. Their former princely state acculturation and parochialism posed control problems for state governments once the state capital was located away from Indore. Two cases, the first drawn from the Indore Premier Cooperative Bank and the second from the state Public Health Department (Engineering section) offices for Indore district, are illustrative.

The Indore Premier Cooperative Bank is the central bank for rural cooperative societies in Indore district, and is subordinate today to the apex bank and Department of Cooperatives at the state government level. The I.P.C.B. was founded early in the century by Maharashtrian Brahmans with princely support, and has been managed for many years by its sponsors in the interests of urban residents and cooperatives. The Kibes, a notable family of bankers of central India, were central in the organization and capitalization of the I.P.C.B.[17] Not surprisingly, the employees of the Bank in its earlier years were almost exclusively Maharashtrians. Unfortunately, only figures for 1947, 1951, and 1967 were available, but the story they tell is clear (see Table 9).

Maharashtrians (almost entirely Brahmans) remained at the same relative strength (54.8 percent) on the Executive level of the Bank between 1947 and 1951, and probably for about five years after. On the Clerical level the proportion of Maharashtrians even increased from 62.5 to 72.4 percent in those same years. A major change was soon underway, however. In 1954 a Rural Credit Committee was set up, under the auspices of the Reserve Bank of India, to study the needs of agricultural interests for credit to underwrite increased agricultural productivity. The stimulus may have been Congress party interest in increasing its share of the rural vote. The Committee recommended in its report that the governments of the states become major shareholders in cooperative banks. Legislation was accordingly prepared, and in 1958 the government of Madhya Pradesh acquired one-third of the shares in the Indore Premier Cooperative Bank, enlarged the Bank's assets, and increased the potential credit base for farmers in the district.

The government then exerted its leverage to ensure that the

---

[17] Maharashtrian Brahmans traditionally have avoided large-scale business and finance. In those days, the Kibe family was a remarkable exception. They had a central Indian banking network so extensive that it is memorialized in the couplet "Holkar ka raj, Kibe ka biaj," which freely translated means "Kibe's interest from loans equals the revenues of the Holkar state." It could also be taken to mean that the two were interdependent.

TABLE 9. INDORE PREMIER COOPERATIVE BANK STAFF, 1947–1967

Year	Level of Staff	Maharash-trian	Non-Mahar-ashtrian	Jain	Hindi-speaking Brahman	Muslim	Percentage of Maharash-trians
1947	Executive	23	19	2	17	0	54.8
	Clerical	10	6	2	4	0	62.5
	Peon[a]	2	11	0	6	5	15.4
	Total	35	36	4	27	5	(49.3)
1951	Executive	6	5	1	5	0	54.5
	Clerical	22	8	0	8	0	72.4
	Peon	1	26	0	24	2	3.7
	Total	29	39	1	37	2	(41.8)
1967	Executive	5	35	3	32	0	12.5
	Clerical	9	26	0	25	1	25.7
	Peon	3	43	1	42	0	6.5
	Total	17	104	4	99	1	(14.0)

SOURCE: Indore Premier Cooperative Bank.

[a] Peons, or *chaprasis*, are messengers or office boys with low salaries and low status.

Between 1967 and 1968 two more Jains were added to the Executive level, increasing the Jain proportion slightly. They were given key positions.

Apparently between 1947 and 1951 a major reorganization of the Executive level took place, reducing the number of top-level staff from 42 to 11. Such a drastic change, perhaps an amputation, suggests political causes, probably linked to efforts by the new government of Madhya Bharat to bring this institution under government control. Similarly, the Executive level was vastly enlarged somewhere between 1951 and 1967 in what may have been a packing of the Executive with non-Maharashtrians.

Bank's resources would be channeled primarily to rural interests, altering the Bank's earlier urban orientation. In 1958 agricultural forces allied with Congress party leaders from outside the city attempted to win control of the Bank's Board of Directors from its Maharashtrian patrons. The agricultural bloc won the Board elections, gained control of internal administrative policy, and introduced recruitment favoring non-Maharashtrians.

The last Maharashtrian Manager of the Bank was W. T. Karambelkar, who retired in 1960. His immediate successor was a government appointee and career civil servant who presided while the Bank's elected body was temporarily under supersession, the response to a deadlock between the Working Committee on one side and the Chairman and Secretary on the other. The Chairman and Secretary had been elected by the controlling faction of the Working Committee, but subsequently one person had changed sides and shifted the Committee's balance in favor of the opposing faction, which now demanded the resignation of the two officials. Supersession by the government was followed by fresh elections in 1962, after which Mr. Gyani (Gujarati) was appointed Manager of the Bank by the Board of Directors.

The question of control of the Bank has become very important. Today it has assets of over ten million rupees. This sum, revolving in the form of small, short-term loans to farmers, obviously provides enormous political resources and influence to those who control Bank policy, and those today are notably not Maharashtrian Brahmans nor are they people of Indore city.

The second example is that of the Division Office of the state Public Health Department (Engineering section) in the city,[18] as illustrated in Table 10. The figures consist of a breakdown simply in

TABLE 10. Public Health Department Staff, 1968

Level of Staff	Maharashtrian	Non-Maharashtrian	Percentage of Maharashtrians
Executive[a]	10	3	76.9
Clerical	12	8	60.0
Peon	0	8	0.0
Total	22	19	(53.6)

Source: The City Office, Public Health (Engineering) Department, Indore.
[a] The Executive Engineer, Assistant Engineers, etc.

terms of Maharashtrians (again, mainly Brahmans) and non-Maharashtrians in 1968. Not including the *peons*, Maharashtrians again are clearly dominant with a ratio of 2 to 1, a clear case of selective community recruitment. The balance has still not been radically altered, even twenty years after merger. The reason appears to be that the Executive Engineers posted in the Indore office have themselves been Maharashtrians for most of the period since 1948 and that they have

[18] Figures were not available for the subdivisional staff of the Indore waterworks (maintenance personnel, machine operators, linemen, etc.) or the staffs of the other subdivisional offices in Indore division. The impression was received, however, that in mechanical as opposed to clerical jobs Maharashtrians were less numerous, though by no means unrepresented.

exercised a preference for members of their own community, keeping this office a Maharashtrian enclave. This means they have probably influenced the recruitment process even on appointments on the Executive level, where state Public Service Commission approval is required. The first Executive Engineer in this period was V. G. Apte (a Maharashtrian Brahman), a former official of the Holkar state, who held the post from 1948 to 1956. In the next decade there were three Executive Engineers, Pushkarnath Kazi (a Kashmiri Brahman), Baput (a Maharashtrian Brahman) and Sharma (a Sanadya Brahman). Only one of these three was Maharashtrian, but the other two were from communities numerically unimportant in Indore. Finally, in 1966 the current Executive Engineer, Gavande, was appointed. Though he is a Shimpi (a lower Maharashtrian caste), he protects most Maharashtrian Brahmans on his staff as a *quid pro quo* for their administrative loyalty.

While Maharashtrian Brahmans have tenaciously resisted penetration of their bureaucratic strongholds—their concentrations have been attenuated less by expulsion than by expansion to accommodate newcomers—they have been more rapidly displaced in the arenas of electoral politics and party competition. Their challenges have sprung from those social groups with more durable and extensive organizational resources—money and manpower. Intellect and ideology in the genteel fencing with the princely autocracy have given way to muscle and interest in the rough-and-tumble cannonading of electoral politics. It is Jain and Hindu merchants and Hindi-speaking Brahman leaders who have usurped the primacy of Marathi-speakers, oiled the machinery, broadened the base of competition, and cultivated the voter.

But the transition took time, and as is usually the case with gradual change, elements of the old have been accommodated by the new. While princely participants faded from visible politics, they left their imprint on the system. The new political actors who were acculturated in princely politics before 1948 found that the bonds they had established, and the enduring bureaucratic structures they had become accustomed to, were serviceable assets in the wider arenas of Madhya Bharat and Madhya Pradesh politics. The focus now shifts from the social foundations of recruitment in the princely regime and its bureaucratic structures to the social composition of popular political organizations and leaderships, and the background of competition among them, in Indore city politics.

4

CONGRESS FACTIONS IN INDORE: ORIGINS AND ELECTION OUTCOMES

The highly differentiated and pluralistic character of society in India seems ineluctably reflected within political parties and other modern political organizations in the form of "factions." And factions are prominent in the politics of Indore city. One cannot hope to understand them without knowing something of their social origins and structural characteristics, their city-wide electoral roles and competition, and their effects on the Indore City Congress party. The social background of these factions can best be delineated in the context of princely politics. Ascriptive, economic, and historical factors combine to explain the continuation of factional rivalry after the merger of the princely state. Finally, a survey of outcomes in Congress party nominations and general elections, in the context of multi-faction and multi-party competition, is needed to provide a backdrop of landmark events in the politics of the city against which more specialized forms of political competition can be measured. City-wide party and factional competition in general elections, where the stakes are elected offices in the state and national governments, is the principal matrix for the integration of city politics, more important even than the municipal arena upon which it impinges.

The utility of the term "faction" lies first in its convenience as a means of referring to unofficial but identifiable groups that operate competitively within a given political organization or institution, but include only a portion of its whole membership. Where the formal organization is the primary unit of analysis but informal group divisions do exist, "faction" may be employed to point out such internal groups as political actors of secondary importance. Because of the high visibility and vitality of factions in Indian political organizations, there is a tendency to regard the faction as the key unit of analysis in explaining political outcomes.[1] There is consequently need for a clear definition of the concept, not merely as an informal division within a formal organization but as a discrete entity with its own empirical characteristics. One must further distinguish between types of factions according to the kinds of ties that hold faction members together.

For the purposes of this study, a *faction* is a collection of individuals within an organization or institution who operate together in politics long enough, or with sufficient regularity, to become recognized as a discrete group.[2] The limiting case would be a group emerging for a single contest, and would preferably be called a "factional tendency," but typically factions are more durable, operating for months and years. A faction may coalesce regularly among members of a certain type when salient issues surface, and the faction may for all practical purposes disappear as the issue fades. For example, within a political party organization, laborers united by a common occupational tie may act as a faction when labor interests are at stake, but may divide up in joining conflicting factions when communal, but not labor, issues are involved. Thus factions can have overlapping boundaries (an individual may be a member of two or more factions simultaneously); factional affiliations can be multiple just as various political goals and social characteristics (ascribed and achieved) can inhere in a single individual. In a given political setting, of course, there are limits to factional affiliation. Some factions tend to be more strictly exclusive and demanding of their members than others, and factions seldom cross political party or labor union organizational boundaries. But fluidity of factions, coalescing and disappearing, gaining and los-

---

[1] Paul Brass, *Factional Politics in an Indian State: The Congress Party in Uttar Pradesh*.

[2] Myron Weiner has defined a faction as "a group with an articulated set of goals, operating within a larger organization, but not created by or with the approval of the parent body." Weiner, *Party Politics in India: The Development of a Multi-Party System*, p. 237. A broader definition is employed here because factions in Indore *qua* factions do not necessarily have "articulated" goals.

ing members, is sufficiently pronounced in Indore politics that the limits of factional eligibility and the durability and scope of individual factions must be specified in each organizatonal or institutional context.

A typology of factions developed by Donald Rosenthal,[3] with some modification, is used here for exposition. The first type is the *personal following,* where an individual leader offers sufficient personal attraction, prestige, or private rewards to establish his own clientele or faction.[4] The second type of faction is the *machine,* where organized distribution of benefits, particularly material benefits, takes precedence; loyalty is relatively institutionalized, and leaders can be interchanged with little or no disruption of support. The third type of faction is *primordial,* where the bond of unity emerges from ascriptive identifications such as family, caste, religion, language, and so on. Building political support in a heterogeneous society is usually easiest where ascriptive characteristics of leaders and followers coincide. Communication is easier to establish and maintain, and the grounds for mutual confidence are stronger. The fourth type of faction is *ideational,* where a bond between members is established by common acceptance of a set of principles, abstractly defined goals, or a general intellectual orientation to the political environment. Such types rarely if ever exist in pure form as actual factions. Factions usually contain characteristics of two or more types simultaneously. But to the extent that actual factions approximate types, or typical characteristics stand out, reference to this typology provides a basis for clearer analytical differentiation of factions in terms of origin, basis of cohesion, patterned behavior, and fate under changing political conditions.

The delineation of factions in Indore politics is necessary because they are often the primary political actors that determine political outcomes. The delineation of factions and factional linkages is useful because, like political parties, the major factions penetrate different arenas of politics in the city, providing some degree of horizontal political integration. Factional linkages also constitute vertical relationships between political and bureaucratic actors on different levels of politics, from a given arena within the city, to the city level as a whole,

[3] Rosenthal, "Factions and Alliances in Indian City Politics," pp. 324ff.
[4] According to Paul Brass, this is the chief defining characteristic of Congress party factions in Uttar Pradesh politics. *Factional Politics,* pp. 54–55.

and upward to the levels of state and central government. Thus a map of the political linkage structure in the city is in part a map of factions.

Congress Party Factionalism in Indore: Social and Political Origins

Factions in Indore, though by no means confined to the Congress party, have nevertheless been most visibly a Congress party phenomenon. Because the Congress party and its internal politics have been the dominant feature of post-independence politics in the city, a knowledge of Congress factionalism holds the keys to explaining the more significant political outcomes in the city. Consequently, for the purposes of this study, opposition factionalism will be bypassed except in later sections on labor and municipal politics, where closer analysis requires otherwise. This chapter is concerned, therefore, with the origins and characteristics of factions in the local Congress party organization, their external linkages to regional and state-wide party factions, factional outcomes in Congress party nominations, and general election outcomes in Indore.

The principal Congress factions in Indore go by the names "Nai Duniya," "Khadiwala" and "INTUC." The Nai Duniya (New World) faction—so-called because of its association with the local Hindi newspaper by that name—is successor to the organizational heritage and political orientation of the Praja Mandal in Holkar state politics. The Khadiwala faction is the major heir of Congress organizational activity in the Holkar state, and has had for its spokesman the rival Hindi newspaper, *Indore Samachar* (Indore News). Finally, the INTUC (Indian National Trade Union Congress), or "labor," faction was the product of pro-Congress efforts to seize control of organizational movements among the city's textile industry workers. The INTUC faction has had its own newspaper, *Jagran* (Vigilant), as a mouthpiece of labor interests. Each of these factions has varied in its relative strength within the party organization, in internal cohesion, and to some extent in the sources from which support has been drawn. Yet each faction has maintained a durable identity in Indore city politics, partly because the loyalty of the social constituencies on which each faction was based has largely been retained.

The Khadiwala and Nai Duniya factions—or more precisely, their antecedents—are the oldest rivals in modern Indore politics. The rivalry has traditional roots, first in the primordial reaction of the "indigenous," Hindi-speaking inhabitants of Malwa to the rule of Marathi-speaking "foreigners," and second in the competition among merchant communities differentiated by religion, caste, and regional origin. The basic cleavages in each case were ascriptive. The Hindi-speaking locals, led by Malwi and Naramdeo Brahmans, were largely isolated from the Holkar administrative apparatus, a condition that they attributed less to their handicaps in education and literacy than to deliberate discrimination by "foreign" Brahmans in the Maharashtrian regime.

Among the business communities, the Jains had the most intimate access to the Holkar regime, a factor that contributed to Jain dominance of the textile industry, finance, and trade in Indore. Jain business allies in the surrounding rural areas—the dealers in raw cotton and marketers of finished cloth—were the "indigenous" Maheshwari Baniyas, themselves in competition with Rajput, Malwi Brahman, and other landlords for control of agricultural land. On the other side, the main business rivals of the Jain–Maheshwari Baniya coalition were Hindu Baniyas, Agarwals and Khandelwals from Rajasthan and the north. Given Jain proximity to Holkar patronage, particularly under Prime Minister Siremal Bapna, it was tactically sensible for the Agarwals and Khandelwals to join the other side as allies of the Brahman opponents of the princely government, forming the "Hindi-speaking Brahman" or Khadiwala faction.[5]

---

[5] Kanhaiyalal Vyas "Khadiwala" is today the best-known leader of this group in Indore and, although his organizational grip has deteriorated greatly since 1963, he was a powerful figure in the state Congress party in the preceding decade and a half. The appellation "Khadiwala" is a nickname affectionately recalling that he once made a living by hawking *khadi* cloth.

"Hindi-speaking Brahman" is an artificial and somewhat awkward term encompassing Brahmans from the Hindi-speaking heartland of north and central India. It is used because Maharashtrian Brahmans generally view the Hindi-speakers as rivals, producing a fundamental cleavage between the two in Indore. Hindi-speaking Brahmans are by no means a unified, compact group; they are, in fact, differentiated in a variety of ways by subcaste and region of origin. While Hindi-speaking Brahmans are not all supporters of the Khadiwala faction, many have been, and the faction is commonly identified with them. Representative of its Hindi-speaking Brahman leaders were such pioneers as Ram Narain Arya and Aryadutt Jugran and, more recently, V. S. Khode, Nandlal Joshi, Ambikaprasad, Krishnakant Vyas, Rukhmanibai Sharma, and Saraswatidevi Sharma.

There have also been important exceptions. Mishrilal Gangwal, a Jain leader, has been highly sensitive to changing political currents. He was closely associated with both the local Congress organization (Khadiwala faction) and the Praja Mandal

External influences interacted with primordial and business rival-ries to condition the social composition of political factions. The tendency within Indore of Hindi-speaking Brahmans and Hindu Baniyas to form a coalition was reinforced and given organizational form by the joint participation of these groups in the Indian National Congress meetings held on British-Indian territory, both in Ajmer to the north and Khandwa to the south. The organizational connection reinforced regional and ascriptive linkages between elites in Ajmer (Rajasthan) and the leaders in Indore whose families had migrated from Rajasthan. The Indore political leaders who participated in the Ajmer and Khandwa units of the Congress established a branch of the organization in Indore city in 1921, about a decade after "na-tionalist" stirrings had first appeared in the city. Because the Congress organization was illegal in the Holkar state, the local branch func-tioned *sub rosa,* except in the areas of the Residency and Chowni where British extraterritorial jurisdiction made its open activities per-missible. It was this branch of the Congress, however, which gave organizational cohesion to the coalition of Hindi-speaking Brahman and Hindu Baniya leaders, and which was the forerunner of the Khadiwala faction.

The Hindu Baniya components of the faction were based both in the Cloth Market area—in the heart of the city's main financial and commercial district—and in Sanyogitaganj-Chowni, the commer-cial area in the Residency. Sitaram Parasrampuria in the Cloth Market area, and Seth Badrilal Bholaram, Chotilal Gupta, and Gappulal Gupta of Chowni (known as the "Chowni group"), were the chief Agarwal leaders and financiers of the local Congress and the main allies of the Hindi-speaking Brahman leaders. The Khandelwal Baniya component was represented by two brothers, Naneria and Purshottam Vijay, who in 1946 established *Indore Samachar,* the first daily ver-nacular newspaper in Indore to become financially profitable. *Samachar* was from its inception the public mouthpiece of the local Congress (Khadiwala) faction, and since 1963 has been supportive of the state-wide Hindi-speaking Brahman faction of D. P. Mishra. It has con-

---

(Nai Duniya), but never became exclusively identified with either. Gangwal exem-plifies in Indore what Myron Weiner has described as "the unique role of the party leader as a unifier. What makes the party leader a unifying force is his 'detachment' from the various factions." Weiner, *Party Politics,* p. 241.

sistently opposed the Jain (Nai Duniya) interests in Indore and state politics, and has been the main business competitor of the *Nai Duniya* daily, an indication of the summation of ascriptive, commercial, and political competition.

As "nationalists," the local Hindi-speaking Brahman leaders were in principle opposed to the princely state, but in practice they were hamstrung by the law so that they could not directly or openly attack the regime. Support from the National Congress was dilatory both because of factional divisions at higher levels and because its primary concern was to win control from the British and to enlist the tacit support of princely rulers for this purpose. In an internal struggle over the official policy of the National Congress toward the princely states, the Gandhian view had prevailed, and it was not sympathetic to nationalist agitation within the princely states.

Gandhi urged that different strategies be used against the British and the princes. The British were to be firmly driven from India by noncooperation and mounting *satyagraha* (non-violent) pressure, but the princes were Indian and could be accommodated for the time being, using milder pressures to bring about the constitutional reform of their governments—which in most cases would effectively undermine them in the long run anyway. The instrument favored by Gandhi for the application of mild pressure on the princes was the *Rajya Praja Mandal* (States' Peoples' Conference). The Indore Praja Mandal was founded in 1934 but did not become particularly active until 1939, when political events in British India and the outbreak of the Second World War generated considerable unrest in the city. At that point, both the Praja Mandal and the local Congress—the latter ostensibly in the Residency, but in actuality throughout the city— sought to capture the mobilized political forces, and their rivalry for the same popular constituencies and public attention bred conflict and appeals to the National Congress.

Gandhi reaffirmed his policy with respect to Indore by supporting the Praja Mandal as the "political arm" of the National Congress and restricting the local Congress to "social work." In theory this meant that the Praja Mandal would be exclusively in charge of mobilization tasks—demonstrations, *satyagrahas,* and political agitation—while the local Congress would confine itself to constructive work in education, the uplift of the "depressed classes," the demonstration of *khadi* manufacture, and the propagation of Gandhian ideas. But in practice the distinction between "political" and "social" responsibilities was impossible to maintain, and there were running disputes over primacy and jurisdiction between the two organizations. The local Congress sought to avoid the restrictions placed on it by organizing its own protest movement and political agitation—though its illegality outside the Residency continued to be a handicap—and its attempts to outflank the Praja Mandal not only intensified competition but forced a degree of radicalization on this otherwise staid organization. Until merger, however, the legality of the Praja Mandal, and its competence to sponsor candidates for the new positions created by postwar reforms, gave it advantages over the local Congress compensating for the latter's much earlier arrival on the organizational scene.

Thus while the Khadiwala faction received its organizational stimulus from the Indian National Congress and the support of Brahman and Baniya elites in Ajmer, it was neither the sole claimant to the Congress mantle nor of support from the north. The Jains, too, had their social, economic, and political ties with Ajmer, Jaipur, and Mewar, as well as allies within the leadership of the National Congress. Moreover, the antecedents of both the Nai Duniya and INTUC factions had strong supportive linkages with textile capitalists and labor forces respectively in Ahmedabad and Gujarat, to the west of Indore—a factor that will be amplified later. The effect of these linkages with Gujarat was to reinforce the alignment of both the Nai Duniya and INTUC factions in Indore with the "Gandhian wing" and Gujarati elites in the National Congress.

The Indore Praja Mandal, forerunner of the Nai Duniya group, was dominated at the outset by Maharashtrian Brahman, Jain, and Maheshwari Baniya political leaders. Because of the stakes their communities had in the Holkar regime, Maharashtrian Brahman and Jain politicians were ambivalent in their attitudes toward the princely establishment. Their association with the regime, directly and indirectly, had bred certain threads of sympathy and loyalty—not so much to the prince himself, but to the favorable *status quo* now besieged by outsiders. But they were also restless at the prospect of being caught on the wrong (i.e., anti-nationalist) side in the event of the termination of princely rule, a prospect that appeared ever more probable. Though much more closely identified with the princely regime than the local Congress leaders, therefore, the Praja Mandal leaders gravitated leftward warily but deliberately in order to build popular support and protect their flank from the local Congress. The maneuver was on the whole adeptly executed, though the Jain more than the Maharashtrian Brahman leaders entered the era of popular politics with their leadership intact.

The most highly esteemed political leader of Indore before independence, and the "grand old man" of the Indore Praja Mandal, was a Maharashtrian Brahman named Vinayak Sitaram Sarvate. Born in 1884, "Tatya" Sarvate was a curiously complex personality, the author of the first analysis (a sympathetic one) of Socialism in the Marathi language,[6] but also reputed to have once had seemingly contrary affinities for the Hindu Mahasabha. Also known locally as the "Gandhi of Indore," Sarvate led the *satyagraha* demonstrations of 1941–47 for constitutional reform of the Holkar government, and he was coopted into the Holkar Cabinet in 1947 as Education Minister. His mentors and predecessors in Indore were Trimbakrao Gogate and S. K. Datey, and his colleagues and closest supporters in the Praja Mandal were D. M. Parulkar, Dr. N. G. Kothari, and his own son, Vishnu Vinayak Sarvate—all Maharashtrian Brahmans. The Jain element of the Praja Mandal was led by Mishrilal Gangwal and his close friend, Hastimal Jain, as well as by Manoharsingh Mehta and Babulal Patodi, a prominent merchant of the Cloth Market area of Indore. Two Maheshwari Baniyas, Rameshwardayal Totla and Bhagwat Sabu, were also among the Mandal's key leaders.

The Praja Mandal organization ceased to exist not long before the merger of the Holkar state into Madhya Bharat in June 1948. Praja Mandal official goals had been partially realized in 1947 when the ruler conceded a measure of representative government. But the Praja Mandal *faction* did not cease to exist. Instead it merged with the local Congress organization and continued to operate within the party, competing with the rival Khadiwala faction for dominance.

About one year after the *Indore Samachar* began publication, in June 1947, Labchand Chajlani, Vasanthilal Sethiya (both Jains), and Narendra Tiwari (a Kanyakubja Brahman) formed a business partnership to produce the *Nai Duniya* newspaper. At the outset the paper

---

[6] *Samajik-vade*, published in 1919. The title was coined by Sarvate to convey "socialism."

was published at the Modern Printery, a press managed by Maharash-trian Brahmans with Jain and Gujarati capital. After a brief but un-successful experiment with a senior journalist, a young Maharashtrian Brahman intellectual named Rahul Barpute was hired as chief editor. Barpute employed his literary talents to build *Nai Duniya* into one of the leading Hindi dailies in the country. But the central figure and political inspiration of *Nai Duniya* was Labchand Chajlani. Though publicly self-effacing, Chajlani has an unparalleled reputation in Indore as a skillful behind-the-scenes operator, a reputation that has diminished recently only because of age and ill health. Aware of the political power of a widely circulated Hindi daily newspaper, he gathered around him the younger leaders of the Praja Mandal faction and assembled the strategies for organizational and electoral participa-tion of the faction after 1948. Chajlani's influence was paramount in Indore within this faction; he was the nucleus around which it gravi-tated, while the senior Maharashtrian Brahman leaders of Praja Man-dal vintage dropped by the wayside and young Jain politicians in Indore came to the fore.

The team leadership consisted of Manoharsingh Mehta and Babulal Patodi (both Jains), Laxmansingh Chauhan (Rajput), and Madhavrao Khutal (Maratha), operating in Indore city with some help from Mishrilal Gangwal and Hastimal Jain. Bhagwat Sabu and Ramesh-wardayal Totla (Maheshwari Baniyas) extended Nai Duniya influence in the rural areas nearby Indore city. Mehta, Patodi, Gangwal, Sabu, and Totla were the high-status leaders or "chieftains" of the faction. Laxmansingh Chauhan, a *pahlwan* (wrestler) of humble origins but expansive ambitions, combined great organizational talents and ora-torical gifts. His ability to mobilize and organize popular support made him the key link between the faction chieftains and the urban electorate, and gave him the role of a machine boss and the rewards of the municipality. The municipality came to be regarded for some time as Chauhan's domain, and he held key positions as President (1959–60) and Secretary (1947–55, 1961–67) of the Indore City Congress committee.

Chajlani's key role behind the chieftains of this faction in Indore was based in part on the newspaper but also on other factors. First, the Jain capitalist and mill-owning families, in supporting or in-fluencing the Congress party in Indore and the state, have often operated through the agency of Chajlani. Second, Chajlani, the newspaper, and the Nai Duniya faction all inherited from the Praja Mandal its close connections with Holkar officials such as H. C. Dhanda and K. A. Chitale. In addition, Chajlani's personality was important. Intelligent, with great political insight, shrewd in his calculations, and persuasive, Chajlani's primacy in setting political strategy was unquestioned. His disinterest in public office or personal recognition forestalled jealousy and rivalry. Chajlani's cumulative influence became so great, like that of Seth Govind Das in Jabalpur, that he was regarded as the "kingmaker" or "minister-maker" of Indore. There is no doubt that his influence contributed to the central Jain role in Madhya Bharat Cabinets after 1950. The faction of which Chajlani was the nucleus, consisting primarily of Praja Mandal functionaries, was popularly known after merger as the "Modern Printery group" or the "Nai Duniya group."

In terms of the faction typology introduced earlier, the evidence shows that both the Nai Duniya and Khadiwala factions contained a mixture of typical characteristics. Both factions contained ideational elements, nationalism being more pronounced in the local Congress faction, and demands for constitutional reform characterizing the Praja Mandal faction. But the ideational elements were of no great importance in distinguishing the Khadiwala and Nai Duniya factions after 1948. The most important characteristic of both factions has been primordial, the recruitment of leaders from and representation of different ascriptive groups. In the case of the local Congress or Khadiwala faction, leadership recruitment was primarily from among Hindi-speaking Brahmans alienated by the privileged position of Marathi-speakers, and from among Hindu Baniya communities resentful of Jain commercial and industrial dominance. The Praja Mandal or Nai Duniya faction drew its leadership and support primarily from among the Marathi-speaking and Jain communities, both intimately involved with princely rule, as well as from among Maheshwari Baniyas and Gujaratis. These ascriptive bases of the two factions have continued as differentiating factors since merger, except for the fact that Maharashtrian Brahmans have lost their leading role in the Nai Duniya group.

Second in importance have been machine and personal characteristics. Personal followings have been of considerable importance in the Khadiwala faction. But personal followings were overshadowed in the local Congress faction by machine characteristics. Khadiwala's primacy was accounted for by his fund-raising and organizational abilities, not by charisma. Furthermore the local Congress branch, dating from 1921, was institutionalized over a long period—much longer, for example, than the Praja Mandal, which did not become active until 1939.

Personal followings were probably of greater initial importance in the Praja Mandal organization than machine characteristics. Tatya Sarvate was regarded as the "Gandhi of Indore" because of the spontaneous support he was capable of generating between 1939 and 1946, and he was indispensable to the Praja Mandal for that reason. (He was never, however, given a state public office that included any significant degree of power but was instead shunted off to the Rajya Sabha, where he held a seat until 1955.) After 1947, Labchand Chajlani's role gave him a personal following of chieftains, but his role was never public and he had no popular following. Also, after 1947, through the diligence of Laxmansingh Chauhan, Madhavrao Khutal, and lesser-known lieutenants, the Nai Duniya faction increasingly acquired machine characteristics. Increasing access to patronage after 1948, and competition for control of the existing party machinery by both factions, reinforced the tendencies toward the machine type, though the merging of the two factions in a common organization made faction machinery difficult to distinguish from party machinery.

The INTUC or labor faction had a distinctive background, as will be shown in more detail in the chapters on labor politics. Suffice it to say here that in the interwar period the textile labor force in Indore fell under Communist control. In response to urgings from Holkar officials, the Ahmedabad labor organization delegated V. V. Dravid and Ramsingh Verma to organize an alternative, pro-Congress union in the city. Cooperation between Dravid and Ramsingh Verma, on one side, with the millowners and government authorities on the other, guaranteed the success of this venture. Though linked with the Praja Mandal and local Congress organization through personal ties, the Indore Mill Mazdoor Sangh with its distinctive textile labor following became an autonomous, albeit imperialistic, organization.

More than the Nai Duniya and Khadiwala factions, because its clientele was occupationally homogeneous (though ascriptively plural) and because of the primacy of patronage from both government and the millowners, the INTUC faction developed machine characteristics. Ramsingh Verma, in his heyday, was the very epitome of a machine boss. After 1952, when control of the labor arena had been consolidated, the INTUC faction leaders sought to extend their organizational power for electoral and patronage purposes throughout the city. Drawing on the intermixture of textile workers scattered in settlements throughout the population, the INTUC faction leaders organized a party substructure parallel to that of the regular Congress organization in order to capture control of the key offices and decision-making bodies of the party. By 1954, as the accounts of municipal politics will demonstrate, the efforts were quite successful until finally reversed by the intervention of the Congress high command (central leadership) in 1963.

Ideational characteristics were of no practical significance in distinguishing INTUC from the other Congress factions. But personal characteristics were of some importance. In the interwar period, when Dravid and Ramsingh were imprisoned and underwent real sacrifices, both drew large popular followings. But after 1948 the tendency was to institutionalize the union's labor following. The advent of machine control almost entirely eroded the personal appeal of Ramsingh Verma, and Dravid's popularity suffered too, but to a lesser extent. Following the defeat and expulsion of Ramsingh in a power struggle in 1963, and the subsequent polarization of the remaining INTUC forces between Dravid and Gangaram Tiwari, a former lieutenant, the once proud INTUC faction has been crippled by fission.

The cohesion and relative influence of each of the factions in Indore has been conditioned by vertical and external linkages with regional and state-wide factions, as well as with factions in the Congress party and INTUC high commands at the center. Within Madhya Bharat, the Nai Duniya faction of Indore aligned with Takhtmal Jain and the corresponding group in Gwalior, and the Khadiwala faction in Indore aligned with Liladhar Joshi and the Hindi-speaking Brahman group in Gwalior. Within the new Madhya Pradesh, the Nai Duniya and Takhtmal Jain factions linked up with the Deshlehra group of Mahakoshal and Chhattisgarh as a state-wide Baniya faction. The Khadiwala and Hindi-speaking Brahman groups linked themselves with the Kanyakubja Brahman groups of Ravi Shanker Shukla

(Chhattisgarh) and Dwarka Prasad Mishra (Mahakoshal), constituting a state-wide Brahman faction. While the INTUC factional linkages are dealt with in detail in chapter 10, it may be noted here that Gangaram Tiwari's challenge to Dravid's leadership of Indore laborers after 1963 was dependent on support from the Hindi-speaking Brahman (Mishra) group of Mahakoshal. (See map, p. 119.)

The Urban Electoral Arena: Party and Factional Competition in General Elections[7]

A distinction was made at the beginning of this work between the "politics of the city as a whole" and "politics of urban sub-systems," the first referring to the city as a single arena and the second referring to politics decentralized in a number of separate arenas within the city. Much of this study consists of microanalysis of politics in separate arenas within the city. But the "politics of the city as a whole" cannot be ignored, because its outcomes condition local politics within the various local arenas. The "politics of the city as a whole" consists of party (or organizational) and electoral politics oriented toward higher levels of politics, and especially toward state-level politics. The *external* orientation of party and electoral competition in Indore is uppermost, because the keys to most government benefits do not lie in capturing control of a strong or autonomous local government but rather in asserting influence in state government decisions that may subsequently have an impact within various bureaucratic jurisdictions in the city. The critical elections in Indore are not municipal but rather general elections, contests for membership in the legislative assembly. At this level of Indore politics, the competition among political parties, and among rival factions within the dominant Congress party, occupies the center of attention. Party organizational and electoral competition—centered more in internal factional competition within the dominant Congress party than among parties as such—has some areally integrative effect on the city, and to that extent provides a surrogate, albeit a weak one, for the relatively autonomous city hall-centered politics characteristic of the larger American cities.

The dominance of the Congress party in general elections before 1967 draws our attention not only to the efforts by opposition parties

---

[7] The account presented here is a condensed version of what appears in Chapter Four of my "Area, Power and Linkage in Indore," pp. 135–164.

to defeat Congress candidates and weaken the hold of Congress on the city, but also to the competition within the Congress party by faction leaders to maximize their respective shares of nominations and to deny nominations to rival factions. The outcome of factional contests in the awarding of Congress party "tickets" (nominations) gives some indication of the relative strengths of each faction at given points in time and makes it possible to show in certain cases how factors external to the city have strengthened or weakened individual factions. The election outcomes, too, are important as clues to future conditioners of local politics. Those who win election as members of the legislative assembly (MLA's), or Parliament, usually become if they are not already party and factional "chieftains" (key leaders) of the city. When "chieftains" belong to the ruling party or coalition, or to the dominant faction, in state and central politics, their local influence is magnified through the instruments of government—a theme that will be explored further in the next chapter on state–urban political and bureaucratic linkages. The electoral competition is significant as it contributes to the membership and composition of state government —where the governance of Indore city is by and large controlled.

A noteworthy characteristic of Congress party dominance of general electoral competition in Indore is the persistence and durability of the major Congress factions, even in the face of defeats in nomination and electoral contests and despite unfavorable shifts in the factional balance in the state capital. Factions and chieftains in the dominant party have a remarkable capacity to survive. The explanation probably lies in the fact that factions have alternative social, organizational, and patronage resources, derived from earlier established positions in the patronage-rich social service auxiliary organizations of the Congress party (true of the Khadiwala group) or from the accumulated wealth and private resources of the business communities. There is also the fact that state-wide factional linkages make factions less vulnerable to losses in a given locality, for support can usually be counted on from victorious allies in other localities. The implication is that the political system is comparatively weak in the sense that political (electoral) outcomes do not have an authoritative impact on the fate of chieftains or factions, and in the long run alternative (nongovernmental) sources of power and sanctions require accommodation among factions.

Outcomes here are restricted to the elite level of analysis because of the unavailability of areal social survey data on the city. Despite this limitation, elite analysis reveals patterns that substantiate what has been said earlier about the social origins of the three major Congress factions. It discloses the striking prominence of Jains among election winners—one-third of the cumulative (1952 through 1967) general election seats in Indore—despite their small numerical strength of under 4 percent in the city population. The pattern of declining electoral success of Maharashtrian Brahmans is clearly evident, as is their gravitation away from the Congress toward the Jan Sangh party. Of general import is the fact that when Congress has been defeated in Indore, it has almost invariably been by left-wing candidates (Socialists, Communists, Independents), not by the leaders of the Jan Sangh, even though the Jan Sangh has made dramatic gains elsewhere in the Madhya Bharat region. And finally, the outcomes show a strong correlation between declining Congress party cohesion—the product of increasingly bitter internal factional competition—and Congress electoral failure, just as one would expect.

After the abolition of the Holkar state, the Nai Duniya faction, heir to the Praja Mandal movement, stood out as the leading faction in the Congress party until at least 1956. In 1948, as one of its final acts, the Holkar state sent a delegation of fifteen representatives to the Constituent Assembly of Madhya Bharat. All but two of these delegates were from Indore city. Two others, who were *sardars* (nobles), declined to continue in politics after 1951 when the franchise was extended for the first general election. The social background and factional loyalties of the delegates reflects Nai Duniya (Praja Mandal) preeminence in the early years after independence. Eight of the fifteen delegates were tied to Nai Duniya, constituting a Jain–Maharashtrian Brahman coalition, while the remaining seven were divided among the two other factions and independents.[8]

Prior to the general elections of 1951–52, the Indore City Congress

---

[8] The Nai Duniya coalition consisted of two Jains, four Maharashtrian Brahmans, a Parsi, and a Maheshwari Baniya. The three Khadiwala faction delegates included two Hindi-speaking Brahmans and a Harijan. The INTUC faction had two South Indian representatives. Of the remaining two delegates, the first, a Jain, was neutral, and the other, a Muslim, was not placed.

For the composition of the Legislative Council, from which this delegation was selected, see Table 8 above.

party presented a unified appearance; interfactional accommodation was more effective than it was to be in later elections. Factional conflict was concealed, but beneath the surface the Nai Duniya and INTUC factions formed a coalition to secure control of the party nomination process in the city. The four legislative assembly nominations in the city were divided equally by this coalition. V. V. Sarvate (Maharashtrian Brahman) and Manoharsingh Mehta (Jain) got the Nai Duniya "tickets," while the INTUC chieftains, V. V. Dravid and Ramsingh Verma, took two nominations on behalf of labor interests. The Khadiwala faction, however, was compensated with the Indore parliamentary nomination, which went to Nandlal Joshi, a Hindi-speaking Brahman.[9] The election results were indicative of the relative Congress party unity. Each of the Congress nominees won his contest.[10] Within Indore city, the Congress candidates ran strongly. Their average poll was nearly 61 percent of the votes, despite the comparatively poor showing of Ramsingh Verma (49 percent in the labor seat)[11] and the fact that the vote for the four city MLA seats was divided among 24 separate candidates. The results were auspicious for Indore. Not only were all four of its MLA's part of the governing party, but two were destined to become Cabinet ministers in the state government, assuring the city's interests direct access at the higher level.

Before the next election of 1957, however, important changes in the structure of state politics had occurred, changes that would influence election outcomes in Indore. The transition in October 1956 by which Madhya Bharat was merged with a much larger Madhya Pradesh was also marked by a shift in power from Jain to Hindi-speaking Brahman leadership at the state level, bolstering the local power of the Khadiwala faction. Within Indore city, the Nai Duniya-INTUC partnership had become strained. The precipitating factor had been the INTUC takeover of control of the chief offices of the

---

[9] Approximately half of the electorate for the Lok Sabha constituency was rural. The Khadiwala faction had an edge over the other two factions in the rural areas of the erstwhile Holkar state, and secured the two Depalpur nominations (one being a reserved scheduled caste seat) for Kanhaiyalal Khadiwala himself and Sajjan Singh Vishnar. Even so, R.C. Jall (Parsi) and Rameshwar Dayal Totla (Maheshwari Baniya) of the Nai Duniya faction obtained the two predominantly rural assembly nominations for Mhow and Mahidpur.

[10] See Appendix B, Tables 1–4, for electoral returns and the opposition candidates for this and subsequent general elections.

[11] The labor contests are examined more closely in Chapter 10, Section II.

City Congress organization in 1955, dominated since 1949 by Nai Duniya leaders (see Table 11). This INTUC coup, which reflected encroachment at the membership level of the organization on the domain of the Nai Duniya faction in the heart of the city, provoked a more intense factional rivalry within the party and pushed the Nai Duniya faction into a cautious alliance with the Khadiwala faction.

TABLE 11. Indore City Congress Executive Officers, 1947–1969

Year	President	Faction	Secretary	Faction
1947	Kanhaiyalal Khadiwala	K[a]	L. S. Chauhan	ND
1948	Kanhaiyalal Khadiwala	K	L. S. Chauhan	ND
1949	Babulal Patodi	ND[a]	L. S. Chauhan	ND
1950	Babulal Patodi	ND	L. S. Chauhan	ND
1951	Manoharsingh Mehta	ND	L. S. Chauhan	ND
1952	Manoharsingh Mehta	ND	L. S. Chauhan	ND
1953	Babulal Patodi	ND	L. S. Chauhan	ND
1954	Babulal Patodi	ND	L. S. Chauhan	ND
1955	Gangaram Tiwari	INTUC	Chhaganlal Katariya	INTUC
1956	Gangaram Tiwari	INTUC	Chhaganlal Katariya	INTUC
1957	Natwarlalbhai Shah	INTUC	Chhaganlal Katariya	INTUC
1958	Natwarlalbhai Shah	INTUC	Chhaganlal Katariya	INTUC
1959	L. S. Chauhan	ND	Madhavrao Khutal	ND
1960	L. S. Chauhan	ND	Madhavrao Khutal	ND
1961	Kantilal Patel	K	L. S. Chauhan, M. Khutal	ND
1962	Kantilal Patel	K	L. S. Chauhan, M. Khutal	ND
1963	Mathuralal Sharma	INTUC	L. S. Chauhan, M. Khutal	ND
1964	Mathuralal Sharma	INTUC	L. S. Chauhan, M. Khutal	ND
1965	Joharilal Jhanjhariya	K	L. S. Chauhan	ND
1966	Joharilal Jhanjhariya	K	L. S. Chauhan	ND
1967	Chaudhuri Faizullah[b]	Mishra	(No Secretary)	
1968	Gangaram Tiwari	INTUC-Mishra	Suresh Seth	Mishra
1969	Gangaram Tiwari	INTUC-Mishra	Suresh Seth	Mishra

[a] Abbreviations: K = Khadiwala faction; ND = Nai Duniya faction.

[b] Chaudhuri Faizullah was installed by D. P. Mishra as President of an *ad hoc* City Congress Committee, following the dissolution of the regular executive positions by the Pradesh Congress Committee. The normal term of office of elected officers is two years. Faizullah's term ended soon after the fall of the Mishra regime in Bhopal, in the summer of 1967.

Indore city was favored in January and February 1957 as the location of the annual all-India Congress Session, a major asset for all the local Congress chieftains in the campaign build-up. Kanhaiyalal Khadiwala and Babulal Patodi, both holding state-wide offices in the Congress party organization, were the key figures in planning and organization of the convention in the city. Costly arrangements had to be made for housing, feeding, and entertaining the Congress high command, secondary leaders, delegates, and numerous camp-followers. Khadiwala and Patodi supervised the expenditures of large sums of money for these purposes. The patronage thus at their disposal and the symbolic impact of the convention were contributing factors to the Congress electoral strength in the city and its environs in 1957.[12]

Holding the Congress Session in Indore meant that the local nominations process would be supervised even more closely than usual by the party high command. From its new vantage point in the Indore City Congress, the INTUC group demanded three Indore "tickets," two for MLA seats to be contested by V. V. Dravid (then state Minister of Labor) and Gangaram Tiwari, and the third for the Indore

---

[12] Khadiwala's personal prestige and organizational influence were at their peak from about 1957 to 1962, but declined thereafter. Khadiwala's popular appeal in the urban area and in the party organization was weakened by the widespread belief that he had personally enriched himself through the manipulation of funds and resources in the 1957 session, by buying corrugated iron sheets at controlled government prices for the 1957 convention shelters, selling them after the session on the black market at much higher prices, and pocketing the money himself—a belief that was strengthened by Khadiwala'a inability to produce satisfactory accounts in court as to how the iron sheets had been disposed of and where the proceeds had gone. (The amount of money involved was estimated in the High Court to be about 1.2 million rupees.)

The case arose, ironically, by Khadiwala's own avoidable legal initiative. In January 1960, *Sarita*, a magazine published in Delhi, printed an article entitled "Sansad Sadasya Shri Chadarwala—ek vyanga" ("Mr. Sheetseller, Member of Parliament—a satire"). The resemblance between Khadiwala and "Chadarwala" was unmistakable, as was the allusion to iron "sheets" in the satirical name. The article clearly alluded to the sale of iron sheets; the resale of new jeeps, purchased for the party convention, at low prices to relatives; and a variety of other apparently corrupt practices attributed to Chadarwala. Although advised against doing so, Khadiwala took the editor (Viswanath) of *Sarita* to court on charges of libel. Khadiwala won in the lower court, but Viswanath naturally appealed. The case finally came before Judge Krishnan of the High Court, a man known for hard-headed integrity. The case turned on Khadiwala's inability to produce evidence to show that the charges of profiting from irregular sale of the iron sheets were unfounded. Krishnan overturned Viswanath's earlier conviction and chastised Khadiwala verbally for the corrupt practices to which the evidence pointed. The judge's admonition had the effect of strictures on Khadiwala's political career, and since 1963 Khadiwala has never been able to fully reassert his leading role in the region. "High Court Judgment of the Khadiwala Case," Criminal Revision Nos. 151 and 153 of 1963, *Viswanath vs. Khadiwala*, and *Khadiwala vs. Viswanath*, July 29, 1964, the High Court Bar Association Library, Indore.

parliamentary constituency to be contested by Ramsingh Verma. While the INTUC group did obtain three nominations, only the two MLA ones were in Indore. The Nai Duniya and Khadiwala coalition blocked Ramsingh Verma's demand and persuaded the high command to extend the Indore parliamentary nomination to Khadiwala. By way of consolation, Ramsingh was given the Nimar (Khargone) parliamentary ticket, and thus INTUC got its chance to send a man to Delhi. The remaining MLA nominations in Indore city went to Babulal Patodi, of the Nai Duniya group, and Mishrilal Gangwal, the neutral chieftain. In the nearby rural areas, the Nai Duniya group secured three MLA nominations and the Khadiwala group two. On the whole, then, the factional balance in nominations in the Indore area was similar to that of 1952, and the party went into the campaign with confidence, spurred by the Congress Session.

All the Congress candidates in the Indore area except Gangaram Tiwari, who attracted only 39.5 percent of the vote in the labor seat, were successful in the 1957 election. The other three city candidates ran even more strongly than in 1952.[13] The strong Congress showing was in part probably due to fewer contestants dividing the total vote —only 10 in the four MLA seats, by contrast with the 24 in 1952—but this worked against Congress in the labor seat, where the key to a clear victory for the Communist labor leader, Homi Daji, was the unity of the opposition effort and the absence of alternative opposition candidates.[14] Daji's victory surprised and shocked the self-assured chieftains of INTUC, indicating that Congress electoral success in the labor seat could no longer be taken for granted. The loss of this one seat, however, did not by itself much affect the access of Indore interests to the state government, nor did it significantly weaken the INTUC faction in Indore.

But in the larger state system of Madhya Pradesh, as the next chapter shows, the share in state-level influence possessed by Indore representatives was greatly diminished, and the patronage at their disposal shrank correspondingly. Within Indore city other changes were under way. Following short-lived INTUC control of the municipal arena, the Congress municipal party was defeated by a coali-

---

[13] See Appendix B, Tables 1–4.
[14] See Chapter 10 for details.

tion of opposition elements (the *Nagrik Samiti*) in the 1958 municipal elections. Generational changes became visible as Holkar college students who had gained notoriety in the police-suppressed violent agitation of 1954 sought political entry. N. K. Shukla, Suresh Seth, and Yugydutt Sharma tried to establish a foothold in the municipal arena, Shukla and Sharma both riding opposition currents. And by 1959 the Nai Duniya faction had reasserted a measure of control of the City Congress party, which was shared from 1961 by the Khadiwala group.[15]

Despite Nai Duniya–Khadiwala joint control of the local organization, the allocation of nominations in the city prior to the 1962 elections reflected the organizational strength of the INTUC chieftains, not only in Indore but also at the center. Just as in 1957, the INTUC faction demanded two MLA tickets in Indore and the Indore parliamentary seat. The local INTUC boss, Ramsingh Verma, had declined to cultivate his Nimar constituency and insisted that he be granted the Indore parliamentary seat in exchange. This time the high command's intervention went in his favor; and Khadiwala, against his wishes, was told to take the Nimar seat. Within Indore, Dravid, Tiwari, Gangwal, and Patodi retained the MLA nominations for essentially the same seats (slight boundary adjustments were made) as in 1957. In the nearby rural areas, the incumbents were re-nominated. Thus the nominations of 1962 were less balanced than before, for the INTUC faction had gained the local parliamentary seat at the expense of the Khadiwala faction.

The 1962 election was a curious one in that seven of the eight MLA contests within the Indore parliamentary district were won by Congress candidates, but the parliamentary contest was taken by the Communist leader, Homi Daji, running as an Independent and without the benefit of fully unified opposition support. Ramsingh Verma, who was regarded as virtually invulnerable at the polls, went down to defeat.[16] Within the city, each of the four MLA seats went to Congress, making Gangaram Tiwari a winner in his second attempt. Yet there were ominous signs in the general erosion of Congress polling strength. The average Congress returns for the four MLA constituencies dropped from 59 percent in 1957 to 47.2 percent in 1962, and

---

[15] See Table 11 above.
[16] See Chapter 10 for an analysis of this outcome.

whereas Khadiwala had polled 62.6 percent of the Indore parliamentary vote in 1957, Ramsingh managed to capture only 38.9 percent in 1962. The number of candidates competing for the four MLA seats increased from 10 in 1957 to 21 in 1962, but still did not equal the 1952 figure. The main factor in 1962 contributing to the decline in Congress electoral strength was not the number of opposition candidates but rather the intensified factional rivalry within the local Congress.

By 1967 the picture had changed further. On the state level, D. P. Mishra's accession as Chief Minister in 1963 heralded a period of constituency-building in Indore through the state administrative machinery and the Congress party organization. The development of a severe water shortage in the city in 1965 made it possible for Mishra —through the assistance of a protégé-Mayor who was newly converted to the Congress party—to use large quantities of state and local resources to ameliorate the effects of water scarcity in the eighteen months before the general election of 1967.[17] Mishra's efforts were only partially successful. They gained him favorable nominees, but did not win him electoral control over Indore.

The upheaval within INTUC also had its effects. Ramsingh's defeat in 1962 revealed the extent to which INTUC encroachment on the Nai Duniya domain in the City Congress and municipal arena had cost him the support of the Jain chieftains. To compensate, Ramsingh had tried to consolidate his control over the labor organization, but succeeded only in precipitating the 1963 power struggle in which he ultimately was dethroned altogether. Early in 1964, Dravid, the state Labor Minister, resigned from the cabinet and returned to Indore to restore labor unity under his own command. But Chief Minister Mishra extended his support in Indore labor politics to Gangaram Tiwari, thereby bypassing Dravid and producing a new division in the once-proud INTUC organization of Indore.

The selection of nominees in 1967 reflected the diminished power of INTUC, for the organization received only one nomination, and that went to Mishra's new protégé, Gangaram Tiwari. Two other MLA nominations went to new Mishra allies, N. K. Shukla (Malwi Brahman) and Suresh Seth (Khatri), both from the 1954 student gen-

---

[17] For the case study, see Chapter 8.

eration. Only one Nai Duniya chieftain, Babulal Patodi, was nominated in Indore. The parliamentary ticket was given to Prakash Chand Sethi, a Jain from Ujjain, who had been careful to accommodate himself to the Chief Minister.

Of the Congress MLA candidates, only Gangaram Tiwari won his seat, narrowly defeating a Communist labor leader. Babulal Patodi was defeated by Arif Beg, a young Muslim Samyukta Socialist party candidate.[18] Suresh Seth was trounced by a former business partner, Kalyan Jain, who ran as an SSP candidate. Suresh Seth's 28.9 percent of the vote was the lowest ever scored by any Congress candidate in the city. N. K. Shukla was defeated by Yugydutt Sharma, an Independent, by a narrow margin of 0.27 percent of the votes. Thus two of Mishra's MLA nominees were rejected by the electorate. P. C. Sethi, the Congress parliamentary nominee, won with 43.6 percent of the vote, but depended for his victory on rural support, for Homi Daji (the incumbent) outpolled him in the city by 4.4 percent. Congress voting strength in the city fell to an all-time low average in the MLA seats of 36.2 percent, down by more than 10 percent over 1962.

On the surface, the city in 1967 appeared to have given a verdict against the Congress, but the outcome by no means suggested a coherent alternative. The election results were probably indicative not so much of an anti-Congress electorate as of bitter factional infighting within the Congress organization, so that segments of the organization were working at cross purposes and undermining each other's efforts. With respect to the victors, there was no clear ascriptive, ideological, or partisan pattern, except that none were Jan Sangh or Communist. Ostensibly the three non-Congress MLA's were "leftists." Homi Daji, Harisingh (Tiwari's Communist opponent), Kalyan Jain, Arif Beg, and Yugydutt Sharma had banded together in a joint opposition front. Kalyan Jain and Arif Beg ran on SSP tickets, while the others labeled themselves Independents. Aside from Daji and Harisingh, who are openly Communist party members, the others fit no clear ideological

---

[18] Patodi's defeat was attributed by some to the covert opposition of Ramsingh Verma, who may have found this a way to get revenge for Nai Duniya defection from his own campaign in 1962. But other factors were probably of greater importance. The constituency boundaries had been altered prior to the election, excluding some of the Marathi-speakers who would have leaned toward Patodi; a Jan Sangh Jain candidate drew away a share of the Jain voters; and Arif Beg drew heavily on the Muslim voters who previously had supported Congress.

pattern. Yugydutt Sharma strikes most observers as conservative in spite of his Socialist rhetoric, no surprise when it is noted that his father was an ardent Arya Samajist. The one common trait of the non-Congress MLA winners was their comparative youth and political socialization as college students in the mid-1950s. They were members of a generation in whom memories of nationalist agitation were never deeply-rooted, and they were preoccupied instead with the performance of Congress governments and frustrated by the preemption of political opportunities by the "old guard." Yet the generational factor does not distinguish them from two of the Congress nominees they defeated, so it does not account for their election. Congress intramural factional rivalry was the critical factor.

In 1967, opposition candidates for the first time captured a majority of the legislative assembly seats in Indore. The defeat of Congress nominees in that year did not signify an erosion of the major Congress factions in Indore but merely the breakdown, and possibly only a temporary one at that, in their earlier accommodation and cooperation. The city electorate appeared to be unreceptive to the purposeful integration of the electoral arena from above by the Chief Minister, who was, after all, an outsider to the region of Madhya Bharat. The Sanyukta Vidhayak Dal regime of Govind Narain Singh, a coalition of Congress "defectors," followers of the Rajmata of Gwalior, and opposition parties in Madhya Pradesh, was formed following the collapse of the Mishra regime in mid-1967. The Nai Duniya faction's antipathy for D. P. Mishra led to its covert support of the SVD government, and even Khadiwala fell out with Mishra over regional interests. After the fall of G. N. Singh's SVD regime in March 1969, most of the Congress defectors returned to the Congress party, but only to support the party.[19] Shyam Charan Shukla, the son of Ravi Shanker Shukla, formed a compromise Congress ministry, balancing the major regional interests and accommodating representatives of the major factions. The new Shukla regime appeared to make possible a restoration of the old factional balance within the Indore City Congress, but the split in the all-India Congress organization that emerged

---

[19] D. P. Mishra was disqualified from legislative leadership at about the same time by the High Court of Madhya Pradesh under the Representation of the People's Act, on the grounds that his 1963 by-election from Kasdol had involved corrupt practices. *Hindustan Times*, March 12, 1969. The six-year interval between the election and the court decision is noteworthy.

in November and December of 1969 introduced a new factor, making the future shape of factional politics in Indore uncertain.[20]

In summary, this chapter reconstructs the politics of Indore city as it is defined by city-wide competition among political parties and factions in general elections. The arena of city politics centers on the effects of the interaction between the electoral process and the representative hierarchy. That interaction is integrative in effect, both as it draws urban participants vertically into the arena of state politics and as it provides locally, in the absence of a strong local government, a substitute focus for the areal integration of city politics. Because the Congress party has been dominant both in the city arena and in the representative hierarchy, and because factionalism within the Congress is as important to electoral outcomes as interparty competition, attention has been focused on the origins and makeup of those factions and on their respective fates in winning nominations and elections.

These Congress factions arose out of the popularization of princely politics and the development of the labor movement. Primordial competition between elites of different regional origins and castes, conditioned by differential privilege and access under the Holkar regime, gave rise to two competing popular movements, the Praja Mandal and the Indore branch of the Indian National Congress. Maharashtrian Brahmans and Jains—the entrenched castes of the city, with close ties to the Holkar regime—dominated the Praja Mandal and emerged after 1948 within the Congress party as the Nai Duniya faction. The Congress group, led by ascendant castes of Hindi-speaking Brahmans and Hindu Baniyas, emerged within the Congress party as the Khadiwala faction. Both factions were primarily primordial in character, with some personalist attributes and machine overtones, but they did not reflect deep differences over matters of principle or ideas. The INTUC faction developed as a separate organization with an occupationally distinctive clientele; though it had some strong personalist qualities because of the earlier charisma of Dravid and Ramsingh, it evolved into a classical machine in the labor area and subsequently vied for control of the Congress party in the city.

---

[20] Field work for this book was discontinued in January, 1969.

Nomination and electoral outcomes reflect the shifting strengths of these factions, as well as of coalitions among them, and their relative strength very often depends on what allies or opponents they have at the state level of politics. In the 1952 elections, the INTUC and Nai Duniya factions, both well-placed in the Madhya Bharat government, shared equally the four MLA nominations, and a single Khadiwala faction candidate stood from the parliamentary seat. This pattern continued in 1957, except for the fact that one of the MLA nominees was Mishrilal Gangwal, the Chief Minister of Madhya Bharat until 1955. Though Gangwal is a Jain and accessible to the Nai Duniya faction, he is not a partisan of it, but rather a neutral. Consequently, Congress nominations in the city in 1957 were balanced among the three factions. In 1962, however, the INTUC faction challenged the balance, claiming not just two MLA nominations but the parliamentary one as well. INTUC was granted these claims, but at the cost of embittering the Nai Duniya faction. The result was that the Nai Duniya group gave only perfunctory support to Ramsingh Verma's parliamentary campaign, indirectly contributing to his defeat by Homi Daji. The 1967 Congress nominations for Indore reflected the shift in power at the state level, for D. P. Mishra was now Chief Minister, and he strengthened the position of the Khadiwala faction in the city. Two of his protégés and one labor ally got Congress MLA tickets, and Nai Duniya was left with only one. A Jain who was from outside Indore district and more responsive to Mishra's interests got the parliamentary nomination. Thus, between 1952 and 1967, the INTUC and Nai Duniya factions each dropped from the two nominations they counted on in the Madhya Bharat period to only one apiece in 1967, and even the INTUC nominee in this case was a Mishra ally.

Until 1967, Congress party supremacy at the hustings was clear. Though the opposition did count two key victories in 1957 (Daji defeated Gangaram Tiwari in the labor seat) and 1962 (Daji defeated Ramsingh Verma in the parliamentary seat), the Congress party won eleven out of twelve MLA contests and two out of three parliamentary ones. But in 1967 the picture was abruptly changed, for the opposition took three MLA seats, severely battering the Congress for the first time. In retrospect there appears to be a very strong inverse correlation between the intensity of intraparty rivalry in the Congress and its success at the polls. A factor of nearly equal importance, however, is the degree of unity among the opposition parties. The growing tendency for the leftist opposition (Communists, PSP, and SSP) to act in concert has paid off in both Daji victories and in the 1967 triumphs of Yagydutt Sharma, Kalyan Jain, and Arif Beg. In municipal elections the Jan Sangh has also joined united-front efforts with the leftists, but in the general elections Jan Sangh leaders have preferred to make their own showing, even though their electoral strength has grown only slowly.

Nominations as a whole are predominantly high-caste in composition, and those who win are even more so. One of the most striking features of Indore city politics is the prominence of Jains in electoral politics. Though they constitute less than 4 percent of the city's population, Jains have held seven out of twenty of the MLA or parliamentary seats representing Indore between 1952 and 1967. Hindi-speaking Brahmans follow closely with six of these seats, but they are more than twice as numerous in the city. It is interesting that not a single Hindu Baniya has been elected from these seats in Indore, though quite a few have been nominated. The nominations also reflect the shift of Marathi-speaking leaders and support to the Jan Sangh and away from Congress. Of the fifteen Jan Sangh or Hindu Mahasabha nominations identifiable in terms of caste affiliation, four went to Maharashtrian Brahmans and two to Marathi-speaking Kayasthas (CKP, or Chandraseni Kayasth Prabhu). Another four of these nominations were to Hindu Baniyas, and two to Hindi-speaking Brahmans.

The key stakes in city politics lie in capturing power in the representative hierarchy and at the state level of politics. Congress factional chieftains have usually been the most successful players at this game. But to exert power in the city, through policy and the various forms of patronage, it is equally crucial to have control over the bureaucratic hierarchies that penetrate urban politics. It is to that subject—to the peculiar way in which politicians and bureaucrats reared in the Holkar state functioned together in a mutually supportive relationship, and to an explanation of how that relationship has been altered by shifts in power in state politics—that we turn in the next chapter.

5

INDORE'S CHANGING AUTHORITY
STRUCTURE: VERTICAL LINKAGES
AND INTEGRATION

The abolition of the princely states in 1948 thrust India's encapsulated political systems into broader arenas of competition, subjected local politics to new and penetrating forces that eroded the autonomy of established elites, and generated deeper and more pluralistic patterns of participation. These changes were part and parcel of broader processes of political modernization and national integration unleashed by independence and the assertion of power by nationalist leaders at the center. Their effects on the politics of Indore were both traumatic and invigorating—traumatic because the abrupt creation of state–urban relationships left much uncertainty about their long-term consequences, and invigorating because the changes expanded the scope, and enlarged the stakes, of competition. The concern of this chapter is with the formation and changes in state–urban relationships, and how they have affected the influence and autonomy of the urban political system in the larger environment of state politics.

Supporting data assembled in this chapter—much of which is based on positional analysis of state-level politicians and bureaucrats from Indore—indicate several interesting patterns. First, in Madhya Bharat politics, politicians and bureaucrats from Indore itself secured a disproportionately large share of the key positions in the government. The subsequent merger of Madhya Bharat into the larger state of Madhya Pradesh, however, robbed the chieftains from Indore of much of their state-level power and diminished the impact of the city on state politics. Second, the initial preeminence of the chieftains from Indore was based on symbiotic relationships with senior bureaucrats from Indore: the perpetuation and cultivation of cohort ties and a common identification shaped before 1948 in Holkar princely politics, ties that acquired new meaning in a wider arena of competition. Working together, Indore state-level politicians and bureaucrats were able to use the instruments of government vertically to exert influence and cultivate their constituencies in the city. Third, as chieftains and bureaucrats from Indore lost their grip at the state level, their places were taken by newcomers (or "outsiders") from other parts of Madhya Pradesh, who in turn used the instruments of government to exert influence vertically in the city, reducing its autonomy from external forces and contributing to political integration within the state.

Integration and Princely State Attachments

The union of Madhya Bharat[1] was formed in May 1948 by the territorial integration of 24 princely states[2] in the Malwa region, enclosing an area of 47,000 square miles (slightly larger than Pennsylvania). The two major constituent states, Indore and Gwalior, were competitors. Together they made up approximately 77 percent of the area and population of the new state, the other smaller states comprising the balance. The area and population of Gwalior state at merger were more than twice that of Holkar.[3] Consequently, Gwalior's territorial and population contribution to Madhya Bharat came to over 55 percent, whereas the Holkar share was only slightly more than 21 percent, or about one-fifth. These proportions become significant

---

[1] Known officially as the "United States of Gwalior, Indore, and Malwa (Madhya Bharat)." For background, see V. P. Menon, *The Story of the Integration of the Indian States*, and Urmila Phadnis, *Towards the Integration of Indian States, 1919–1947.*

[2] Of the constituent states, 2 were ruled by "Marathas" (Gwalior and Indore), 3 by "Rajput-Maratha" dynasties (Dewas Senior, Dewas Junior, and Dhar), 15 by Rajput princes (Ratlam, Alirajpur, Barwani, Jhabua, Kilchipur, Narsingarh, Sailana, Sitamau, Jobat, Kathiwara, Mathwar, Rajgarh, Nimkhera, Jamnia, and Piploda), and 4 by Muslim princes (Jaora, Kurwai, Muhammadgarh, and Pathari).

[3] Gwalior state included an area of approximately 26,000 square miles (a little larger than the state of West Virginia) against 9,731 in the Holkar state (about the size of Vermont).

when compared with the Holkar share of high-level positions in the Madhya Bharat government.

Prior to formation of the Union, the rulers of Indore and Gwalior had bargained with the States Ministry (Sardar Vallabhbhai Patel) for conditions that would preserve a measure of continuing identity, status, and influence for their state peoples in the new framework. Both rulers competed for the symbolic preeminence of their state areas in the Union, contested the location of the new state capital— each hoping to have it in his princely capital [4]—and vied for the position of Rajpramukh (Governor). Each sought, moreover, to maximize the political representation of his princely state area in the Madhya Bharat legislative assembly and to get maximal inclusion of bureaucrats from his princely apparatus in the administrative structure of the Union, especially at the highest levels and in key positions. The configuration of political and bureaucratic representation changed over time, however, for the outcomes negotiated by the princely rulers and cohorts set the stage for a constant process of adjustment and readjustment.

For the leading princes, Holkar and Scindia, the first considerations were of their personal status in the new government. Each hoped to become the titular ruler of the planned union. The central States Ministry, anxious to win the accession of the princes and their future cooperation in the new regime, conceded the demand in a form that recognized the greater political resources (territory, population, and historical precedence since the early nineteenth century), of the Gwalior prince: the positions of *Rajpramukh* (Governor) and *Uprajpramukh* (Deputy-Governor) were given to the rulers of Gwalior and Indore respectively, with no provision for rotation. These acquired positions were formally circumscribed, but provided the rulers of Indore and Gwalior with vantage points at the apex of the Union's internal bureaucratic communication channels and close to if not astride the vertical communication channels between the center and

---

[4] The contention was over whether Gwalior or Indore would become the seat of state government. The issue was finally settled by the Congress High Command with a compromise. The (provisional) Nehru Award gave a share in the capital status to each city. Indore became the "summer capital" for five and a half months, and Gwalior the "winter capital" for the remainder of each year. In 1956 the capital issue arose again, the competition being mainly among the cities of Jabalpur (Mahakoshal), Indore, and Gwalior, but the Congress High Command settled the issue by selecting the city of Bhopal as the permanent capital of Madhya Pradesh.

the Madhya Bharat secretariat. The positions of Rajpramukh and Uprajpramukh did not guarantee the rulers firm control over policy or appointment, but did guarantee them information and the opportunity to compete with other participants for influence in most high-level decisional processes.

Aware that their constitutional supremacy would be meaningless, in practice, without embodiment in the new government of a substantial number of allies, the rulers insisted in return for their co-operation that the bulk of the union's administrative services be formed at the outset from the service cadres of the princely states and that the Indore and Gwalior rulers have a virtually decisive role in determining who would be coopted from their respective cadres, and at what levels and even in which positions they would serve in the new government. The States Ministry was obliged by circumstances to agree to the substance of this demand, with certain qualifications that will become apparent. The independent Government of India was notably short of indigenous administrative personnel, particularly at the highest levels of administration. Some of the princely states— and in this respect Indore was outstanding among the Central Indian states—had produced a substantial number of well-educated and experienced administrators, many of whom compared favorably with British Indian administrators at similar levels of responsibility. The States Ministry readily acknowledged this fact, but it really had no choice in the matter. Accordingly, most of the administrative cadres of the princely states were incorporated into the Madhya Bharat services. Some of the highest officers of the Indore and Gwalior states were integrated into the elite Indian Administrative Service by fiat.[5]

Many, perhaps most, of the newly merged administrative personnel merited their inclusion by virtue of competence and ability, but the quality was uneven, the inputs of individual states varying on this dimension. Some administrative personnel were included and strategically position by their princely patrons, with loyalty being the paramount consideration. But the crucial fact bearing on administrative merger and subsequent positioning was that basic loyalties cor-

---

[5] They thus entered laterally, without being subject to the entrance examinations or lower rungs of experience of the I.A.S., and were regarded informally by their peers of British Indian cadres as an inferior administrative class within the structure.

responded in the new Union largely to former princely state attachments, whether to the prince himself, the members (and colleagues) of the former state establishment, or the political movements and leaders whose former sphere of activity had largely been defined by the former state area. The point is admitted clearly by Menon:

> The new Unions [including Madhya Bharat] lacked internal strength and stability. The impulse for integration came mainly from the Government of India, and the personalities of Nehru and Sardar furnished the main cohesive force. There were practically no political organizations to kindle or sustain the spirit of national patriotism. The Congress organizations composed of old Prajamandals had not taken deep roots in the soil. They were driven by factions centering on personalities and deriving sustenance, surprisingly enough, from traditional feuds. *The top servants of the States lacked even the opportunity to work together for any common purpose, and the majority of them were inevitably steeped in old jealousies and intrigues. Some found it both profitable and congenial to hitch their wagons to the new political leaders from their respective regions, thus exposing the new administration at its very birth to the strain and stresses of regional pulls and factious intervention.*[6]

Thrown together with strangers in a larger political environment, administrators clung to and supported familiar faces, bureaucratic or political, from their home state. In the new administrative structure —where the criteria of performance were no longer authoritatively prescribed by a single ruler, but were in flux and subject to competitive alteration by a variety of competitors; where former status and achievement were no longer authoritative measures of relative ability, and bureaucrats from different states carried differing standards of interpersonal estimation—bureaucrats felt relatively insecure, and frequently compensated by seeking political support individually and collectively. The search for support was typically directed toward the bureaucrats, politicians, and princely rulers with whom a working relationship, however uneasy, had been established before merger. Support from the princely ruler, politicians, and other bureaucrats from the home state was generally forthcoming on a *quid pro quo* basis. Politicians and the princely rulers also had stakes that could be realized only through bureaucratic collaboration. Consequently,

---

[6] Menon, *Integration,* p. 422 (emphasis added).

among the fundamental cleavages that worked their way through the new regime were those based on princely state acculturation and the parochial identifications that had been established before merger, products of the princely state heritage.[7]

For the Government of India, the princely state cleavages were an invidious obstacle to rational integration—or to central bureaucratic control, which was of greater importance to the States Ministry. The center's response was to establish control, or at least supervisory influence, in key administrative positions from which the internal provincial rivalries might be exploited by adroit maneuvers. The instruments for this purpose were I.A.S. (Indian Administrative Service) officers, usually from the Bombay cadre but in any case individuals without personal roots in Madhya Bharat:

> If there was one element in the new set-up which served the Unions with single-minded devotion, it was the band of officers contributed by the States Ministry who, by their zeal and labour, laid the foundations of a stable administration. . . .
>
> By means of rules and regulations; by the organization of service cadres; by the constitution of Public Service Commissions; by precept as well as by example, every effort was made to reorientate the outlook of these State servants and thus to lay the foundations of organized public services in the new Unions. It was, however, soon realized that if the parochial outlook and regional loyalties inherited from the erstwhile states were to be exorcized from the administrative services, it could be done only by extending the senior cadre of the all-India services to the Unions.[8]

Accordingly, the center "loaned" Indian Civil Service, Indian Administrative Service, and Indian Police Service officers to Madhya Bharat to fill key positions such as those of Chief Secretary, Secretary of Finance, Inspector-General of Police, the Advisor to the Rajpramukh, and frequently the Senior Member of the Board of Revenue. Similarly, the Chief Justice and the Chairman of the Public Service Commission were usually men from the center. Central control was further reinforced by the stipulation that all new legislation, budgets, and appointments to the posts of Chief Justice of the High Court and Members of the Board of Revenue and the Public Service Commission be

---

[7] There were factional divisions that potentially cut across the princely state cleavages; but factions were more pronounced within the state cleavages, and their cross-cutting tendencies remained subordinate in the Madhya Bharat period.

[8] Menon, pp. 422–423.

approved by the States Ministry.[9] But within these restraints, themselves subject in practice to bargaining between the constituents of the Union and the center, there remained considerable scope for action. The representatives of the center were political actors in their own right, complicating the main lines of princely state competition but not obviating them.

Indore's Political and Bureaucratic Representation in Madhya Bharat

In the initial bargain over "bureaucratic representation" at the highest levels (the Secretariat, Heads of Departments, and Public Service Commission), Indore came off well, with a larger share than might have been expected strictly in terms of the numerical proportions of former state population or area in relation to the whole of Madhya Bharat. The Holkar state constituted approximately one-fifth of the population and territory of the merged area. But as will be seen from Table 12, Indore's share of higher-level administrative posts was significantly higher. In 1949, the year that most closely reflects the princely bargain at the outset, Indore bureaucrats held 4 out of 10 of the Secretariat posts, 6 out of 24 of the Heads of Departments, 5 out of 8 of the High Court judgeships, and 1 out of 3 of the positions on the State Public Service Commission. In total, Indore's share of the "bureaucratic" positions was 16 out of 45, or *more than one-third*. By 1951 Indore's share of "bureaucratic" positions had declined somewhat to about one-fourth, more closely in line with the degree of representation that might have been expected, but it expanded again in 1952.

The "political" positions include both the membership of the Legislative Assembly and the Council of Ministers. The Madhya Bharat Legislative Assembly from 1948 to February 1952 was a provisional and constituent assembly. The members from the former Holkar state were largely selected by its legislative assembly from among its own membership.[10] The Holkar assembly, because of its restricted franchise base, was composed primarily of high-status politicians, or social and economic notables of the princely regime, and those who were selected by this body to sit in the Madhya Bharat assembly were

---

[9] *Ibid.*, p. 421.
[10] See Table 8, page 65.

TABLE 12. INDORE'S SHARE OF HIGHER-LEVEL ADMINISTRATIVE POSITIONS, MADHYA BHARAT AND MADHYA PRADESH

| | Administrative Level | | | | |
| | Proportions | | | | |
Year	Secretariat	Heads of Departments	High Court	Public Service Commission	Total
		MADHYA BHARAT			
1949	4/10	6/24	5/8	1/3	16/45
1950	5/14	7/25	2/6	1/3	15/48
1951	3/12	5/22	2/6	1/3	11/43
1952	2/11	6/22	2/5	1/3	11/41
1954	8/19	12/25	4/8	1/3	25/55
1955	9/20	14/28	4/8	1/3	28/59
1956	5/12	13/27	5/8	1/3	24/50
		MADHYA PRADESH			
1957	2/12	5/38	2/10	1/6	10/66
1958	2/14	5/39	1/12	0/4	8/69
1959	1/15	5/39	1/13	0/3	7/70
1960	1/17	4/32	1/12	0/3	6/64
1962	1/15	2/44	1/15	0/3	4/77
1963	1/15	2/41	1/12	0/2	3/70
1964	1/14	1/41	1/12	1/4	3/71
1965	1/15	1/35	1/12	1/3	4/65
1967[a]	0/14	1/25	1/14	1/3	3/56

SOURCES: Times of India, *The Indian and Pakistan Yearbook and Who's Who, 1949–53* and *Yearbook and Directory, 1955–1967*, Bombay. Former Holkar state officers were identified by comparison with *List of Officers of the Holkar State, 1947*, Indore: Holkar Government Press.

[a] Mishra Regime, after 1967.

similarly high in status. The first Madhya Bharat assembly contained 75 members divided among three blocs representing the constituent princely areas. Gwalior's delegation of 40 MLA's was the largest, reflecting its 55 percent proportion of area and population, and giving it an absolute but narrow majority of seats in the house. The numerous small states together were represented by a delegation of 20 members, and Indore had a delegation of 15 members, in each case again reflecting the size of the merged states. Similarly, Indore was equitably represented on the Cabinet from 1948 to 1951, with the exception of a period in 1950. As Table 13 shows, in 1949 Indore politicians held 3 of 16 Cabinet posts. In 1950, for at least part of the year, Indore

TABLE 13. INDORE'S SHARE OF CABINET AND LEGISLATIVE ASSEMBLY,
1949–1967

Year	Cabinet Ministers	Deputy Ministers or Ministers of State	Members, Legislative Assembly
		Levels of Government	
	MADHYA BHARAT		
1949	3/16		15/75
1950	0/13		15/75
1951	2/12		15/75
1952	3/6		9/99
1954	3/8	1/3	9/99
1955	3/9	1/3	9/99
1956	3/11	1/2	9/99
	MADHYA PRADESH		
1957	2/12	1/9	10/289
1958	2/12	1/9	10/289
1959	2/11	1/8	10/289
1960	2/11	1/8	10/289
1962	2/11	1/4	8/289
1963	2/12	1/7	8/289
1964	1/11	1/9	8/289
1965	1/11	1/8	8/289
March 1967	1/12	1/8	6/297
August 1967[a]	0/14	0/14	6/297

SOURCES: Same as Table 12.
[a] Sanyukta Vidhayak Dal government.

politicians were absent from the Cabinet, but returned to hold 2 of 12 positions in 1951.

Thus far bureaucratic and political representation has been viewed in relation to the total area of the former Holkar state, but even more important is where the representatives come from *within* the state. At the Cabinet level, all the Ministers from the Indore delegation— in this period, V. S. Khode, Rameshwardayal Totla, Mishrilal Gangwal, D. M. Parulkar, and Manoharsingh Mehta—were from Indore city itself. Similarly, the Holkar administrative officers at the top levels, and all but two members of the Indore assembly delegation, were from the city. If Indore city is viewed as a constituency, it becomes apparent that an urban population of about 300,000 was disproportionately well represented in the extreme, in this period. Since the phenomenon was similar for Gwalior and Ujjain, it is fair to say that Madhya Bharat politics was dominated by urban elites, giving the cities in this period excellent access to rewards dispensed at the state level of politics. But subsequent constitutional and electoral changes, especially universal adult suffrage, have tended to draw the rural areas into participation as rival claimants for state largesse, and a gradual but steady erosion of urban dominance set in after 1952.

The political changes that took place at the Cabinet level between 1948 and 1951 were significant for Indore city. Madhya Bharat state politics was characterized primarily by two cleavages. The first and more important consisted of a struggle between the Gwalior state delegation on one side and the Indore delegation, usually allied with the small states delegation, on the other. This cleavage was reflected in the Cabinet. But complicating the interstate rivalry was a factional cleavage that ran throughout the three delegations. The faction that tended to dominate Madhya Bharat politics, particularly at the Cabinet level, was the Nai Duniya (or Takhtmal Jain) faction, which consisted of an alliance between Maharashtrian Brahman and Jain politicians drawn almost exclusively from the urban centers. The other was the Khadiwala faction, led by Hindi-speaking Brahmans of local origin, which drew additional support from some Hindu Baniyas and Rajput leaders—still heavily urban in composition, but less exclusively so.

From 1948 to 1949, the Cabinet was briefly dominated by the Hindi-speaking Brahman faction, Liladhar Joshi of Gwalior becoming the first Chief Minister. Other Hindi-speaking Brahmans on the Cabinet in this period were V. S. Khode (Indore), Radhelal Vyas (Gwalior), and Ramkrishna Dixit (Gwalior). The faction was supported by Yeshwantsingh Kushwah (Rajput of Gwalior), Jagmohanlal Srivastava (Kayastha of Gwalior), Syed Hamid Ali (Muslim of the small states delegation), and Mishrilal Gangwal (Jain of Indore)—the last being a neutral bridge between the rival factions. The alternate faction was represented by Rameshwardayal Totla (Maheshwari Baniya of Indore), D. M. Parulkar (Maharashtrian Brahman of Indore), and Kaluram Virulkar (Maharashtrian Brahman of the small states).

In 1950, when Indore was briefly unrepresented, the balance began to shift. The Hindi-speaking Brahman faction was still represented on the Cabinet through Liladhar Joshi, Jagmohanlal Srivastava, and

Syed Hamid Ali, but the new Chief Minister was Gopikrishnan Vijay-vargiya (Jain of Gwalior), and the Jain-dominated faction was represented also by Shyamlal Pandviya (Jain of Gwalior), Dr. Prem Singh Rathor (Jain of the small-states delegation) and Kaluram Virulkar. By 1951 the key Jain faction leader of Gwalior, Takhtmal Jain, had become Chief Minister, supported by Shyamlal Pandviya, Dr. Prem Singh Rathor, Mishrilal Gangwal and Manoharsingh Mehta (all Jains). Thus five of the six senior Cabinet positions were occupied by Jains, two from Gwalior, two from Indore, and one from the small states. The sixth was Raghunandan Saran Sharma, a Hindi-speaking Brahman from the small states. Syed Hamid Ali of the Hindi-speaking Brahman faction had been demoted to a Deputy Ministership. A second Deputy Ministership was held by Sannulal of Gwalior.

From 1948 through 1951 Gwalior politicians had a slight edge in the Cabinet and, when the Indore–Gwalior rivalry became pertinent on policy issues, the Gwalior politicians, regardless of faction, favored their former state area. Because they were not vigorously opposed on these issues by the chief Indore politician, Mishrilal Gangwal, government policy was often biased slightly, though by no means exclusively, in favor of Gwalior. For example, when the question of establishing a university in Madhya Bharat arose, representatives of both states lobbied for their areas as the proper location. Indore was the most suitable location from the point of view of the number and standing of higher educational facilities. Gwalior, however, would also have been an appropriate place. The final decision, an apparent compromise, was to establish the Vikram University in Ujjain city, a less attractive spot in terms of existing educational infrastructure, but favored by its location in the former Gwalior state area, and acquiesced in by Indore representatives because Ujjain is much closer to Indore than to Gwalior city. Gwalior opposition to a university in Indore was not overcome until May 1964, when the Indore University was finally established. Similarly, Takhtmal Jain and the Gwalior representatives delayed for a number of years final state approval of Govindram Sakseria Technical Institute (G.S.T.I.), Indore's modern engineering institution. It was eventually established with state guarantees of long-term support through the lobbying efforts of Chandan Singh Bharkatiya (the Jain Managing Director of the Malwa Mills), who had excellent contacts at the central level with Maulana Abul Kalam

Azad, the Minister of Education, and the support at the state level of
Manoharsingh Mehta and the Nai Duniya politicians from Indore.

Following promulgation of the Constitution of India, the appor-
tioning of constituencies roughly according to population, and the
first general elections, the distribution of "bureaucratic" and "political" posts in the state government changed significantly in favor
of the Indore state delegation and, accordingly, in favor of Indore
city. In 1952 Indore bureaucrats held only 2 of 11 Secretariat positions
and 6 out of 22 Heads of Departments, and a total of only 11 out of
41 of the top administrative positions (see Table 12), a proportion
continuing from before the 1952 general election. But by 1954 Indore
bureaucrats occupied 8 of 19 Secretariat posts, 12 out of 25 Heads of
Departments, 4 of 8 High Court judgeships, and 1 of 3 Public Service
Commission posts. The proportion of the total, 25 out of 55, had increased by nearly twice, from about one-fourth to *nearly one-half* of
the higher-level administrative positions. The change was not a mere
aberration, for this proportion held virtually constant until 1956,
when Madhya Bharat was superseded by the new Madhya Pradesh.
With only one-fifth of the territory and population, the Holkar state
area and the city of Indore in particular came to hold almost half of
the key state-level bureaucratic positions.

Indore bureaucrats were ambitious, but the phenomenal gain in
high-level positions appears to have been due to a corresponding gain
in high political positions by Indore city politicians (see Table 13).
As a result of apportionment of constituencies, the number of seats
in the Legislative Assembly increased to 99. The former Holkar state
area retained an equivalence in seats, but of these seats only 9, or less
than half, were filled by Congress politicians whose careers had begun
in the capital of the princely state.[11] Thus the Indore city portion of
the MLA's from the former Holkar state area decreased absolutely
from 13 to 9, and decreased as a proportion of the assembly from about
20 percent in 1948 to only 10 percent in 1952. Elections based on
universal adult franchise thus partly circumscribed the explicit urban
dominance of the princely capital over the rural portions of the former

---

[11] Most stood from constituencies falling outside the Indore city boundaries.
The 9 were Mishrilal Gangwal (Bagli), Kanhaiyalal Khadiwala (Depalpur), Sajjan-
singh Vishnar (S.C., Depalpur), R. C. Jall (Mhow), Rameshwardayal Totla (Tarana),
Ramsinghbhai Verma (Indore City A), V. V. Dravid (Indore City B, mostly rural),
Manoharsingh Mehta (Indore City C), and V .V. Sarvate (Indore City D).

state area and increased the opportunities for participation at the state level by rural politicians.[12] But although the city's reach in the rural areas was limited, its hold on the Cabinet in this period was not.

The 1952 Cabinet was small. Takhtmal Jain, who would otherwise certainly have headed the Cabinet, was disqualified by his failure to win reelection as an MLA. He failed again in a by-election in 1953, and did not finally return to the Cabinet and the position of Prime Minister until 1955. In the meantime, the chief Jain politician of Indore, Mishrilal Gangwal, held the position with Takhtmal's consent. Gangwal's role was viewed as that of a caretaker for the Jain faction and for Takhtmal himself in particular. Gangwal did not hesitate to relinquish the position in favor of Takhtmal in 1955 when the latter finally won reelection. In the meantime, however, Gangwal appears to have used his position shrewdly to pack the high levels of the administration with bureaucratic allies from Indore. He was assisted in this by two other key Indore politicians, Manoharsingh Mehta (Jain and Nai Duniya group) and V. V. Dravid, the high-status labor leader who had close ties to the Nai Duniya group and the former princely bureaucratic apparatus. The three from Indore dominated the Cabinet; there were only two Ministers from Gwalior and one from the small states. Four of the six were Jains, and all were either partisans of the Jain (Nai Duniya) group or acceptable to it. Thus Indore had acquired half of the Cabinet posts, whereas the much larger former state of Gwalior held only one-third.

The Jain (Nai Duniya) dominance continued for the duration of Madhya Bharat—a remarkable phenomenon when one considers the tiny proportions this religious group makes up in the urban areas (under 4 percent in Indore, and less in Gwalior) not to speak of the rural areas—but the dominance of the Indore trio in the Cabinet did not hold firm, and the proportion of Gwalior leaders increased. By 1954 Indore still had a slight advantage, with Gangwal as Chief Minister and Mehta and Dravid present; but Gwalior now occupied four

---

[12] Paralleling the decline of urban influence in state politics was the loss of representation by Maharashtrian Brahmans in the Cabinet. Though still a significant proportion of the MLA's between 1952 and 1957, Maharashtrian Brahmans went unrepresented in the Cabinet under the Katju, Mandloi, and Mishra regimes as well. Maharashtrian Brahmans remained important in the administration, however, though their fate in political leadership may be a sign that their positions in the bureaucracies are embattled too.

positions, with Shyamlal Pandviya (Jain), Sobhagmal Jain, Sitaram
Jajoo (Maheshwari), and Narsinghrao Dixit (Hindi-speaking Brahman). Only Dixit represented the Hindi-speaking Brahman group. Jain
dominance was reinforced by Dr. Prem Singh Rathor as before. In 1955
the only changes were the absence of Jajoo and the return of Takhtmal
Jain to the head of the Cabinet, reasserting the initiative of Gwalior.
In 1956 Radhavallabh Vijayvargiya (a Jain from Narsingarh, of the
small states) and Sawai Singh Sisodia (a Rajput operating in the rural
area of the former Holkar state) were moved up into the Cabinet from
their former positions as Deputy-Ministers.

Practically as important as the proportion of positions held by
bureaucrats and politicians from Indore was the nature of the positions, insofar as they had a bearing on policy or patronage affecting
Indore. The portfolios of Ministers and the jurisdictions of Secretaries
and Heads of Department become salient when they have a bearing
on Indore city, especially when there is a linkage of common identification with the former Holkar state between a Minister and a
bureaucrat who preside over the same policy-area and functional jurisdiction impinging on the city. When the Minister in turn is linked
by electoral constituency or organizational and factional affiliation
with interest and community groupings, the channels, formally at
least, form a continuous chain for transmission of demands, formulation and implementation of policy, and subsequent reaction and feed-
back.

The predominance of certain elite groups in their respective
spheres has already been brought out in chapter 3, especially that
of Maharashtrian Brahmans in the civil services and the Jains in
industry and commerce. The Maharashtrian Brahmans survived as a
disproportionately large part of the administrative structures in Indore
city after merger, especially in the middle ranks as clerks, researchers,
and recorders, a level of the services that was not greatly affected by
interregional transfers of personnel characteristic of I.A.S. and Class
I officer levels. The middle levels of the state government bureaucracies with establishments located in Indore city were affected more
by augmentation, which did not so much disestablish Maharashtrian
Brahmans but rather over time diluted their collective influence in
the administrative structures. Even so, the middle-level bureaucrats,
Maharashtrian Brahmans as well as others, who had been recruited

under the Holkar regime remained especially susceptible to influence from superiors in their departments and Cabinet Ministers who themselves were formerly administrators or political actors in the city under the Holkar regime, establishing continuous linkages in many cases from the Cabinet through to the lower reaches of the state administration in the city.

The Jain community of Indore traditionally held a superior though by no means exclusive position in both the textile industry and commercial enterprise (raw cotton, wholesale marketing of manufactured cloth, opium, precious metals, jewelry, old-fashioned commercial banking and credit, and brokerage firms, handling speculation). Most of the largest and most successful businessmen in Indore have been Rajasthani Jains. Second to them came Hindu Marwaris (Agarwals), a number of whom have become leading businessmen in recent years. There are large numbers of small businessmen, especially retailers, shopkeepers, brokers, and owners of small-scale industries from other communities (Khandelwals, Gujaratis, Bohras, Sindhis, and Punjabi Khatris and Aroras)—but the business elite, if one can describe it as such, is Jain. Jains have also been leaders in the professions and in the upper ranks of the administration, far out of proportion to their numbers in the population.

Maharashtrian Brahmans, together with Jains, have played a key role in maintaining bureaucratic channels of political influence linking state-level politicians from Indore with policy and patronage outputs in Indore, thereby assisting the maintenance or building of urban political constituencies and electoral, party organizational, and factional supports.[13] Outside the labor area, most of Indore's state-level politicians, and from 1952 until 1967 those who became Cabinet Ministers, were Jains. Consequently Indore's representation in the Cabinet has closely reflected the economic superiority of Jains in the city.

In the Congress party organization, dominated since the 1920's by Hindi-speaking Brahmans and Hindu Baniyas, the picture was less clear. In the organization after 1948 and at least until 1963, the Hindi-

---

[13] In Table 15, p. 113, of the 22 former Holkar civil servants with high-level bureaucratic positions in the Madhya Bharat government, 9 were Maharashtrian Brahmans and 4 were Jains, comprising more than half the total. Moreover, these Maharashtrian Brahmans and Jains were heavily distributed at the bureaucratic apex—that is, the Secretariat.

speaking Brahman faction leader, Kanhaiyalal Khadiwala, supported
by Sajjan Singh Vishnar among others, was the major figure. But even
in the organization, Babulal Patodi (Jain)—supported by Rameshwardayal Totla and Bhagwat Sabu (Maheshwari Baniyas)—was a rival
to be reckoned with, again reflecting Jain economic power in Indore,
as well as in Gwalior and Ujjain. Prior to 1950, when Liladhar Joshi
and the Hindi-speaking Brahman faction dominated the Cabinet, the
Khadiwala faction of Indore had good state-level access. But from
1950 to 1956, and even from 1957 to 1963, the primary political linkages between Indore city (excepting the labor area) and the state
Cabinet were those between local and state-level Jain political leaders,
both personal ties and the channels of party organization.

By combining the information concerning ministerial portfolios,
bureaucratic jurisdictions, and coincident tenure of Indore political
and bureaucratic actors contained in Tables 14 and 15, it is possible
to sketch in some of the major outlines of political-bureaucratic linkages between the state government of Madhya Bharat and Indore city.
The portfolios held by Mishrilal Gangwal and V. V. Dravid are par-

TABLE 14. Indore Cabinet Politicians and Portfolios, 1949–1956

V. S. Khode	Home Affairs (1948)
Rameshwardayal Totla	N.A. (1948)
D. M. Parulkar	Development and Labour (1949)
Mishrilal Gangwal	Industries, Commerce, Civil Supplies (1949–50)
	Finance, Customs, Excise and Sales Tax (1951)
	General Administration, Appointments, Finance, Separate Revenue (1952–53)
	General Administration, Planning (1954–55)
	Finance, Separate Revenue (1955–56)
Manoharsingh Mehta	Education, Labour (1951)
	Home, Education (1952–53)
	Home, Public Works (1954)
	Education, Law (1955–56)
V. V. Dravid	Development, Labour, Local Self-Government (1952)
	Development, Labour, Public Health (Engineering) including Town Improvement and Housing (1953–55)
	Labour, Public Health (Engineering), Housing, Agriculture (1956)
Sajjan Singh Vishnar	(Deputy-Minister)—Harijan and Tribes, Revenue (1955)
	Public Works, Tribal Welfare (1956)

TABLE 15. INDORE'S HIGH-LEVEL BUREAUCRATS[a] AND JURISDICTIONS,
1949–1956

H. C. Dhanda	Advisor to Senior Uprajpramukh (1948–49)
K. V. Kalewar	Secretary of Customs (1949–50)
	Secretary of Public Works (1951–52)
	Joint Secretary of General Administration (1953–55)
K. B. Wagle	Secretary of Communications and Education (1949–50)
A. S. Banawalikar	Labour Commissioner (1949–54)
S. P. Mehta	Health Secretary (1949–51)
G. Cornelius	Secretary of Food and Civil Supplies (1949–50)
	Deputy-Secretary of General Administration (1949–50)
Masood Quli Khan	Commissioner for Customs and Excise (1949–50)
	Inspector-General of Municipalities (1953–54)
	Director of Rural Development, Registrar of Cooperative Societies (1955–56)
S. N. Dube	Development Commissioner (1949–53)
V. N. Singh	Accountant-General (1949–54)
G. N. Swami Iyer	Director of Industries (1949–56)
J. K. Kaul	Director of Food (1949–50)
	Secretary of Development (1951–53)
	Secretary of Commerce and Industries (1954–56)
S. V. Kanungo	Member, Public Service Commission (1949–53)
L. O. Joshi	Deputy-Secretary of Development (1950)
	Secretary of Development (1954–56)
P. S. Bapna	Food Production Commissioner (1950–53)
	Development Commissioner (1954–56)
	Planning Secretary (1955–56)
M. G. Karnikar	Director of Agriculture (1954–56)
K. M. Bapna	Commissioner for Customs and Excise (1951–56)
C. G. Matkar	Commissioner, Jagirs and Land Reform (1952–53)
K. M. Ranade	Deputy-Secretary of Home Affairs (1954–55)
V. N. Sherlekar	Chief Inspector of Factories (1954–55)
K. A. Chitale	Advocate General (1954–56)
G. S. Sondhi	Chief Conservator of Forests (1954–56)
S. S. Joshi	Deputy Secretary of Labour (1954)
	Labour Commissioner (1955–56)
B. S. Sibbal	Chief Engineer (Electrical) (1954)
K. R. Gawade	Commissioner, Southern Division (1954–55)
Darshan Singh	Inspector-General of Prisons (1954–56)
N. Padmanabhan	Member, Public Service Commission (1954–56)
W. V. Oke	Home Secretary (1955–56)
R. S. Date	Transport Commissioner (1955–56)
K. B. Kher	President, Industrial Court (1955–56)
M. R. Sarmandal	Director, Harijan and Tribal Welfare (1955–56)
R. N. Bhandari	Director of Health Services (1956)
B. K. Dube	Secretary of Board of Revenue (1956)
B. M. Joshi	Inspector-General of Municipalities (1956)
P. N. Bhalla	Superintending Engineer (1956)

[a] Not including judicial positions.

ticularly important in this respect. The evidence suggests that between 1951 and late 1956 Gangwal and Dravid virtually monopolized the formal and informal power stemming from Cabinet positions that were of continuing significance for Indore city.

In 1949 and 1950 Mishrilal Gangwal held the portfolios of Industries, Commerce, and Civil Supplies. At the same time Indore bureaucrats G. Cornelius and G. Narayan Swami Iyer were Secretary of Food and Civil Supplies and Director of Industries, respectively. The most important linkage here was that of Industries. On the one hand, state governments have concurrent powers over non-defense and non-strategic industries, particularly in the areas of enforcement of labor regulations (wages, working conditions), the social side-effects of industrial location, the supply of electric power and water, the supply of scarce materials, excise taxation, and the provision of government or government-guaranteed private capital loans—all of which have a direct bearing on the textile industries of Indore. On the other hand, the Directorate of Industries has primary responsibility for the stimulation of small-scale industries in the state. This has taken the form of development of so-called "Industrial Estates," where the Directorate of Industries appropriates land in or around urban areas and develops the land—installing roads, water and electric power connections, drainage—and even in many cases provides buildings, workshops for machinery repair, and other services.[14] It is significant that Indore has acquired the largest such Industrial Estate in the state, at a government investment of approximately 20 million rupees, and that the foundation for this development was laid in the Madhya Bharat period. This Estate is the most visible contribution to Indore with which Gangwal was intimately associated. It also indicates something of the potential magnitude of state policy expenditures and operations in the urban arena.[15]

---

[14] The development is expensive, but the rationale is that capital-short entrepreneurs will be attracted to such locations by the already-installed infrastructure and will concentrate their energies on production and marketing. The concentration of small industries in a given location also has the decided advantage of discouraging the installation of factories and workshops—with the concomitant noise, smells, and dirt—in residential areas of the town or city.

[15] Although this work does not deal with the politics surrounding the regulation of and investment in small-scale industries in Indore, it is worth pointing out that here is another arena of political activity that might well be singled out for detailed treatment as a part of urban politics. Even without going into detail, how-

In 1951 Gangwal took over the Finance, Customs, Excise, and Sales Tax portfolios. His administrative counterpart in this case was K. M. Bapna, a leading Jain bureaucrat from Indore, who was Commissioner for Customs, Excise, and Sales Tax from 1951 to 1956. As the leading commercial center of Madhya Bharat, Indore made the largest sales tax contribution to state government revenues. The tax portfolios were, therefore, of great importance to the businessmen of Indore, and the manner in which excise and sales taxes were collected (the state government also collects central excise taxes on behalf of the government in Delhi) provided opportunities for Gangwal and Bapna to build constituencies and obligations among Indore business communities. When Gangwal became Chief Minister in 1952, he acquired much wider powers through the portfolios of General Administration and Appointments, Finance, and Separate Revenue. Though the use of these powers must in practice have been checked to some degree by his obligations to Takhtmal Jain of Gwalior, Gangwal shrewdly used his appointment powers to greatly increase the proportion of Indore bureaucrats directly responsible to the Cabinet. Gangwal's immediate connections in his tenure as Chief Minister were enhanced by the presence in positions of high responsibility of such Indore bureaucrats as K. M. Bapna, Commissioner for Customs and Excise; K. V. Kalewar, Joint Secretary of General Administration; V. N. Singh, Accountant-General; P. S. Bapna, Planning Secretary; and C. G. Matkar, Additional Secretary of Revenue.

In the field of labor, more than any other, the supremacy of Indore politicians and bureaucrats was unrivaled. Indore's labor preeminence was due largely to the greater size and strength of the Congress labor movement in Indore, by contrast with those in Gwalior and Ujjain, and to the collaboration of the Holkar government, textile magnates, and national Congress labor leaders in attempting to capture the organizational initiative from Communist leadership in Indore between 1942 and 1947. Furthermore, Indore city was made the head-

---

ever, enough has been said to suggest the importance of vertical, state-urban linkages in the arena of small-scale industrial enterprise. In this connection it should be noted that the Directorate of Industries obtains a jurisdiction in the town or city that entirely by-passes the local (municipal) government. Land appropriated for Estate developments falls outside municipal jurisdiction, and in establishing water and electricity service the Directorate of Industries deals with other state bureaucratic agencies.

quarters of the office and establishment of the state's Labour Commissioner, and the personnel inherited in this office were chiefly of
Holkar state origin. The key figure in state labor politics for many
years was V. V. Dravid, who began his official career as Labour Minister of the Holkar government in 1947.[16] A key functionary at that
time had been the Holkar Labour Commissioner, A. S. Banawalikar,
whose *Banawalikar Report* drawn up under Dravid's supervision became the prescriptive basis of labor legislation for Madhya Bharat
and Madhya Pradesh. Although Dravid himself did not immediately
enter the Madhya Bharat government as Minister of Labour, his
predecessors in that position, D. M. Parulkar and Manoharsingh
Mehta, were both from Indore and allies of INTUC. Their collaboration with Banawalikar, who had been coopted as the Madhya Bharat
Labour Commissioner, was picked up by Dravid in 1952.

In 1952 Dravid acquired not only the Labour portfolio but also
those of Development and Local Self-Government. He could count
not only on Banawalikar's support but also that of S. N. Dube as
Development Commissioner; G. Narayan Swami Iyer, then Director
of Industries; and J. K. Kaul, who was Secretary of Development from
1951–53—all former officials of the Holkar state. Between 1953 and
1955 Dravid dropped Local Self-Government, but added to Labour
and Development the portfolios of Public Health (Engineering), Town
Improvement, and Housing, all peculiarly relevant to the development and improvement of the labor area and living conditions of
laborers in Indore. In addition to access to Banawalikar, Dube, Iyer,
and Kaul in this period, Dravid was able to work through such high-
level Indore bureaucrats as V. N. Sherlekar, Chief Inspector of Factories; P. S. Bapna, Development Commissioner; Masood Quli Khan,
Inspector-General of Municipalities; J. K. Kaul as Secretary of Commerce and Industries; L. O. Joshi, Secretary of Development; S. S.
Joshi, Deputy-Secretary of Labour and Labour Commissioner; and
K. B. Kher, President of the Industrial Court.

In 1956 Dravid added the Agriculture portfolio to his repertoire,
still holding the others, and acquired special access to other Indore
bureaucrats M. G. Karnikar, Director of Agriculture, and Masood
Quli Khan, Director of Rural Development and Registrar of Co-

---

[16] See Table 7, p. 64.

operative Societies. The extension of Dravid's interests to agriculture and the rural areas in this period reflected the elusive objective of organizing agricultural labor along the same lines as industrial labor, and an attempt to capture panchayat and cooperative organizations in an effort to influence the selection of Congress MLA candidates in the rural areas, particularly around Indore. In 1956 Indore bureaucrats B. M. Joshi, Inspector-General of Municipalities, and P. N. Bhalla, Superintending Engineer, besides others noted earlier, were in positions linked directly or indirectly with improvements under way in Dravid's labor constituency in Indore.

With the exception of Chief Ministers, there does not seem to have been any other political leader in Madhya Bharat or Madhya Pradesh politics who successfully combined and utilized so large an array of interrelated and mutually supportive portfolios and strategically situated bureaucrats for the concentrated satisfaction of a large urban constituency as Dravid did for textile labor.[17] Dravid's concentration of relevant powers at this point, and the resultant opportunities, depended to a significant extent on the fact that the Chief Minister's office was in the hands of an Indore politician and that the Cabinet was still small. After 1956 Dravid never had such extensive opportunities to use state government powers and patronage, though he by no means became helpless, at least not until 1964, when he left the Cabinet. The success of Congress and INTUC in controlling the labor movement in Indore has been to a considerable extent due to the success of this labor leader in turning the relevant government administrative structures into supporters of INTUC political and organizational interests in this early period.

Manoharsingh Mehta, though Minister of Education and Home Affairs in 1952–53, Home Affairs and Public Works in 1954, and Education and Law in 1955–56, held portfolios relevant to Indore city, particularly that of Education. But he did not have subordinate to him a clear assemblage of Indore bureaucrats, by contrast with Gangwal and Dravid. There were exceptions such as K. M. Ranade, Deputy Secretary of Home Affairs (1954–55) and K. A. Chitale, the Advocate-General (1954–56). Where Mehta succeeded in using the Education portfolio in favor of Indore interests, it was to a large ex-

---

[17] Cases illustrating the use of this combination of powers are provided in Chapters 9 and 10, on the politics of town planning and the labor arena.

tent with central support and in spite of the absence of Indore bureaucrats in the strategic positions of the Department of Education. The
absence of bureaucratic support complemented and may have been a
further reflection of the rivalry between Gwalior and Indore politicians for educational benefits such as the first university and the
locations of agriculture and engineering colleges. Nevertheless, Mehta
was supportive of Gangwal and Dravid in their virtual dominance of
the Cabinet from 1952 to 1955.

Indore's Diminishing Representation in Madhya Pradesh

The new state of Madhya Pradesh came into existence in November 1956, a few months prior to the general election of February
1957. The new state, comprising an area of about 170,000 square miles
(larger than California) with a population of about 26 million (1951
Census), was formed by the merger of the 14 Hindi-speaking districts
of old Madhya Pradesh (an area of 93,392 square miles with a population of 13.64 million) with the previously formed princely states union
of Vindhya Pradesh (an area of 23,600 square miles with a population
of 3.57 million), Madhya Bharat (about 47,000 square miles with 8
million population) and the state of Bhopal (6,878 square miles with
840,000 population). The Sironj subdivision of Rajasthan was also
added to the new state. The politics of the new state of Madhya
Pradesh has been generally characterized by regional competition;
and the dominant region, with more than half the area and population, has been that of old Madhya Pradesh, or Mahakoshal-Chhattisgarh.[18]

In the old Madhya Pradesh, which formerly included the Marathi-
speaking districts around Nagpur and Berar, the major cleavage of
political competition was regional-cum-linguistic. In the Marathi-
speaking districts the dominant leadership was Maharashtrian Brahman. In the Hindi-speaking districts of the eastern area, divided into
the Mahakoshal subregion centered on Jabalpur and the subregion of
Chhattisgarh to the southeast (including Raipur and Bastar), the
dominant leaders were Kanyakubja Brahmans, originally of Uttar
Pradesh, but now domesticated in central India and increasingly a
landholding caste. The rivalry between Maharashtrian and Kan-

---

[18] For background, see Wayne Wilcox, "Madhya Pradesh," in Myron Weiner,
ed., *State Politics in India.*

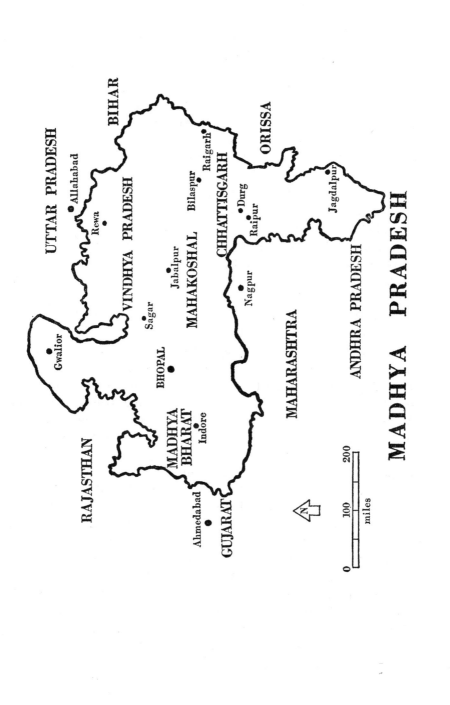

MADHYA PRADESH

UTTAR PRADESH

BIHAR

ORISSA

VINDHYA PRADESH

Allahabad

Rewa

Raigarh

CHHATTISGARH

Bilaspur

MAHAKOSHAL

Jagdalpur

Durg

Raipur

Jabalpur

Sagar

Nagpur

Gwalior

MAHARASHTRA

BHOPAL

ANDHRA PRADESH

RAJASTHAN

MADHYA
BHARAT

Indore

Ahmedabad

GUJARAT

N

0   100   200

miles

yakubja Brahman leaders set the tone of old Madhya Pradesh politics
with its implications for administrative recruitment and distribution
of revenue. The Hindi-speaking leaders of the relatively poor east
sought to maximize a share of state revenue to which the larger con-
tributor was the relatively prosperous Marathi-speaking western area.
A similar relationship came to exist in the new Madhya Pradesh,
where the relatively poor districts of Mahakoshal profited from the
more prosperous area and larger revenue contributions (particularly
of Sales and Excise Taxes and Land Revenues) of the Madhya Bharat
region.

Within the Mahakoshal-Chhattisgarh region, there tended to be
two competitive alignments that weakened the thrust for control of
new Madhya Pradesh politics. The first was competition between the
subregions so that the Kanyakubja Brahmans of Chhattisgarh, led by
Ravi Shanker Shukla and family, have sought to dominate the leaders
of the same community from Mahakoshal, including Dwarka Prasad
Mishra and Kunjilal Dube. A second source of cleavage, paralleling
that in Madhya Bharat, has been the rivalry between Baniyas and
Brahmans, the Baniya network being headed by Mulchand Deshlehra
in Chhattisgarh and formerly represented in Mahakoshal by "Raja"
Seth Govind Das. The overriding tendency in the new Madhya
Pradesh politics has been for the Takhtmal Jain–Nai Duniya faction
of Madhya Bharat to align with the Deshlehra Baniya faction of
Mahakoshal–Chhattisgarh, and the Hindi-speaking Brahman faction
of Mahakoshal–Chhattisgarh to link up with the Hindi-speaking
Brahmans of Madhya Bharat (Narsinghrao Dixit in Gwalior, Kanhaiyalal Khadiwala in Indore, and Shanker Dayal Sharma in Bhopal).

On the whole the Baniya faction of new Madhya Pradesh has
been put on the defensive by the Brahman faction, particularly in
the state Congress party organization and in the state Cabinet, but
the Baniya factions leaders have retained their economic power in
the cities. Hence part of the explanation of the inability of D. P.
Mishra to win electoral control of Madhya Bharat in 1967, and part
of the explanation of defections from the Congress party which
undermined the Mishra regime later that summer, lies in the reasser-
tion of a measure of power by the Baniya (Deshlehra–Takhtmal Jain)
faction outside the Mishra-dominated spheres of government and
party organization.

When the new Madhya Pradesh was first formed, the government was headed briefly by Ravi Shanker Shukla. Following his death, the Congress high command in 1957 delegated Kailash Nath Katju, a Kashmiri Brahman from Uttar Pradesh, to lead the government and assert the influence of the center against the pulls of regional and factional competition. Katju's regime characterized the first phase of Madhya Pradesh politics, during which competitive interests were fairly successfully balanced and no major component of Congress was permanently alienated. Following Katju's death in 1961, Bhagwantrao Mandloi (a Hindi-speaking Brahman) came to power briefly but was discredited in the 1962 elections, giving D. P. Mishra, who had been building up support in the Congress organization and at the center, an opportunity to become Chief Minister in September 1963.

Mishra's accession marks the second phase of Madhya Pradesh politics. Under Mishra's leadership, the penetration of Mahakoshal influence throughout the other regions, previously gradual and tolerable, now became pronounced, and friction increased so much that observers were greatly surprised when in the 1967 general election the Mishra-dominated Congress not only managed to hold its previously narrow majority in the Legislative Assembly, but actually managed to increase it. The unexpected success was ascribed by some observers to bureaucratic influence in the electoral process on behalf of Congress nominees.

Mishra's victory was pyrrhic. Within five months defections brought his reorganized ministry down. The coalition government (Sanyukta Vidhayak Dal) which was then set up consisted of alienated Congressmen from Mahakoshal and Vindhya Pradesh, the Jan Sangh party delegation and the followers of the Rajmata of Gwalior, both strong in Madhya Bharat, and scattered members of leftist parties and independents. The SVD coalition government, united mainly by opposition to the former Chief Minister, was unstable and finally collapsed in the spring of 1969. But during its twenty-month tenure it was tacitly supported by the Baniya faction of Madhya Bharat, reflecting the bitter reaction against Mishra's and Mahakoshal's administrative and electoral penetration of the Madhya Bharat region. In 1969, as D. P. Mishra was disqualified by the High Court from holding elected office as a result of a judicial finding of corrupt practices in his by-election of 1963,[19] the other major Brahman contender,

---

[19] It is noteworthy that this case was decided only after Mishra's fall from power.

Shyam Charan Shukla, son of Ravi Shanker Shukla, found his way
clear to becoming leader of the Congress legislative party and the
sixth Chief Minister of the new Madhya Pradesh. Initial appearances
suggest that he is most gingerly representing all major interests of
the party to secure maximum loyalty, but at the cost of an unwieldy
Cabinet.

The formation of the new Madhya Pradesh introduced a new
element of bureaucratic competition. In Madhya Bharat, I.C.S. and
I.A.S. officers who had served under the British regime were delegates
of the center and, though strategically situated, still relatively few
in number. Most of the old Madhya Pradesh (Central Provinces and
Berar) had been under British-Indian direct rule and contained an
established component of I.C.S. and I.A.S. officers. When merged into
a new state administration in which many of the officers had first
served under princely regimes, those with British-Indian experience
tended to regard their princely colleagues as inferior, or at least from
a different bureaucratic caste. Moreover, just as bureaucrats who had
grown up in Indore or Gwalior relied on politicians from their respective princely state areas as allies in the process of bureaucratic
rivalry and competition that developed, the bureaucratic cadres of
Mahakoshal and Chhattisgarh tended to act as the allies of the dominant Brahman political leaders from their region. Mahakoshal bureaucratic competition for the best government positions neatly complemented the Mahakoshal political objectives of penetrating the
other regions for some semblance of factional, electoral, and administrative control.

What is surprising in this light is how much residual "bureaucratic" and "political representation" Madhya Bharat and, in particular, Indore retained at the outset. Although the Holkar state area
contributed less than 5 percent of the area, and a slightly larger proportion of the population, of the new Madhya Pradesh, Indore bureaucrats still held about one-seventh (slightly more than 14 percent)
of the highest bureaucratic positions (see Table 12).[20] Of twelve Ministers in the Cabinet and nine Deputy Ministers, Indore contributed
two Ministers and one Deputy Minister, giving the former princely

---

[20] The positions of Rajpramukh and Uprajpramukh ceased to exist with the
termination of Madhya Bharat. As a Class A state, the new Madhya Pradesh now
had a nonprincely Governor, formally appointed by the President.

state area a highly disproportionate political representation. (Gwalior's representation was inferior to that of Indore: one Minister, Takhtmal Jain, and one Deputy Minister, Narsinghrao Dixit.)

In the process of Cabinet formation, it was difficult for Ravi Shanker Shukla to resist the claims of former Chief Ministers, Mishrilal Gangwal and Takhtmal Jain, to places in the Cabinet. Indore's special advantage was that it was equally difficult to ignore the claim of V. V. Dravid, the outstanding labor leader, to the Labour portfolio. Thus Indore secured two senior Cabinet positions because of the high political status of its two foremost leaders. On the other hand, politicians from the old Madhya Pradesh had a distinct edge in the Cabinet, holding seven senior Cabinet positions[21] and three Deputy Ministerships.[22] Once Ravi Shanker Shukla died and Katju succeeded, however, the situation was almost balanced evenly between Mahakoshal–Chhattisgarh and the other regions.[23] At the same time, Mahakoshal–Chhattisgarh leaders were more cohesive than those from the other regions, putting the latter on the defensive.

Though relatively well represented at the highest levels in 1957, there was a steady erosion of Indore's "bureaucratic" and "political" representation and influence. As Tables 13 and 16 show, Indore's high-level administrative representation fell from one-seventh in 1957 to one-tenth in 1959, and declined to about one-twentieth in 1962. Thereafter the proportion tended to stabilize, partly because the absolute numbers of high-level positions were reduced by Mishra (in an effort to centralize bureaucratic control). From 1959 to 1965 only one Secretary was from Indore, and by 1967 there were none. After 1963, only one Head of Department was from Indore, as against five in 1957. The decline in Cabinet representation occurred at specific points. V. V. Dravid resigned from the Cabinet early in 1964 as part of the conditions for resolving a power struggle in the labor arena in Indore,

---

[21] They included Bhagwantrao Mandloi, Shankerlal Tiwari, Raja Naresh Chandra Singh, A. Q. Siddiqi, Ganesh Ram Anant, and Rani Padmavati Devi, in addition to the position of Chief Minister held by Ravi Shanker Shukla.

[22] Mathura Prasad Dube, Kesholal Gomashta, and Jagmohan Das.

[23] Besides Mishrilal Gangwal, Dravid, and Deputy Minister Vishnar from Indore, and Takhtmal Jain and Narsinghrao Dixit from Gwalior, Bhopal contributed one Minister (Shanker Dayal Sharma) and one Deputy Minister (Maulana Inayatullah Khan Mashriqi). Shambunath Shukla and Dasrath Jain, a Deputy Minister, represented Vindhya Pradesh. The small states of Madhya Bharat were represented by a Deputy Minister, Shivbhanu Solanki.

and Mishrilal Gangwal was defeated in his constituency in the 1967 general elections.

Until 1964, at least, Indore's "political representation" in the Cabinet, with two full Ministers and one Deputy Minister, was clearly overrepresentation when considered together with the area, population, and MLA representation of the city (from 1957 to 1962, only 10 out of a Legislative Assembly of 289 members, and with the proportion declining after 1962) (see Table 13). Yet the unusually large share in political power for Indore was in absolute decline. Whereas before, government power in Madhya Bharat had been contested mainly by Gwalior, and Indore had managed to establish a high proportion of bureaucratic and political posts, the new Madhya Pradesh government was dominated by politicians from outside the Madhya Bharat region altogether. Despite some overrepresentation, in this much enlarged government the leading politicians from Indore could not establish so clear or mutually reinforcing a set of bureaucratic channels with their constituencies in Indore. Some linkages did remain clear, while others were attenuated by the positioning of alien bureaucrats (alien to Indore) astride many of the urban-oriented jurisdictions. Fewer portfolios, of course, remained in the hands of Indore representatives (see Tables 16 and 17).

TABLE 16. INDORE CABINET POLITICIANS AND PORTFOLIOS, 1957–1967

Mishrilal Gangwal	Finance, Separate Revenue, Economics and Statistics, Registration (1957–61)
	Finance, Separate Revenue, Economics and Statistics, Registration, Social Welfare (1962)
	Planning and Development Economics and Statistics (1963–66)
V. V. Dravid	Labour, Rehabilitation, Housing, Chambal Project (1957–61)
	Labour, Agriculture, Housing, Chambal Project (1962–64)
Sajjan Singh Vishnar (Deputy Minister)	Forest, Natural Resources, Jails, Food, Civil Supplies (1957–61)
	Civil Supplies, Food, Jails (1962)

Mishrilal Gangwal with the portfolios of Finance and Separate Revenue from 1957–61 could work with and through Masood Quli Khan, the Excise Commissioner and an Indore bureaucrat, in the

TABLE 17. INDORE HIGH-LEVEL BUREAUCRATS AND JURISDICTIONS,
1957-1967

M. G. Karnikar	Commissioner, Bhopal Division (1956–61)
	Secretary, Governor's Personal Staff (1962–66)
W. V. Oke	Labour Commissioner (1957–61)
P. S. Bapna	Secretary, Planning and Development (1957–66)
S. P. Mehta	Commissioner, Gwalior Division (1957–60)
R. M. Bhandari	Inspector-General of Prisons (1957–58)
L. O. Joshi	Secretary of Agriculture (1957)
	Secretary of Education (1958)
B. M. Joshi	Inspector-General of Municipalities (former Madhya Bharat region) (1957)
Masood Quli Khan	Excise Commissioner (1957–62)
N. Padmanabhan	Member, Public Service Commission (1957)
Darshan Singh	Inspector-General of Prisons (1958–61)
G. N. Swami Iyer	Director of Industries (1962)
B. S. Holkar	Superintendent of Stationery and Textbooks (1962–63)
C. H. Sanghvi	Chief Engineer (Irrigation), P.W.D. (1963–66)
Manoharsingh Mehta	Member, Public Service Commission (1964–69)

same period—the jurisdiction being especially pertinent to the industrial and commercial entrepreneurs located in Indore city. Similarly, with the Planning and Development portfolio from 1963–66, Gangwal was able to work closely with P. S. Bapna, the Indore bureaucrat in the Secretariat astride the same jurisdiction. Planning and Development was concerned as much with rural projects as with the city, but within the city it provided patronage opportunities for businessmen, speculators, and contractors involved in public housing developments or town planning. With the Housing portfolio from 1957 to 1964, V. V. Dravid also had access to P. S. Bapna, and the channel had payoffs for the labor constituency in terms of residential improvement in the labor area and slum clearance projects.

As Minister of Labour from 1957–64, Dravid's most important linkages, both political and bureaucratic, were of course with the labor constituency, and it is significant that the Commissioner of Labour from 1957–61 was also an Indore bureaucrat, W. V. Oke. On the whole, however, it is clear that in the Madhya Pradesh period Gangwal and Dravid were less frequently able to rely on Indore bureaucrats or their protegés in bureaucratic jurisdictions affecting the city. This does not mean, of course, that as Ministers their po-

litical influence in the city was blocked, but it does suggest that it
was substantially reduced. Working through bureaucrats recruited
from backgrounds other than the Holkar state was undoubtedly more
time-consuming, costly, and unreliable. The opportunities for Cabinet
politicians from other regions to inject their own influence into the
formal jurisdictions of Gangwal and Dravid were correspondingly
increased.[24]

To summarize, in the Madhya Bharat period, political groups in
Indore city that were identified with the former princely regime—
particularly the Nai Duniya and INTUC factions—successfully placed
a disproportionately large number of leading politicians and bureaucrats in key positions in the state government. The political and
bureaucratic linkages thus established—bearing common characteristics of identification with Indore city and the former princely state
area as well as Jain and Maharashtrian Brahman community identifications—had major political payoffs for the Nai Duniya and
INTUC factions in Indore. Through these urban-based factions and
urban-oriented bureaucrats, the power of Indore city was manifest in
Madhya Bharat state politics. It is no exaggeration to say that the
urban areas of Madhya Bharat, among which Indore was *primus inter
pares,* dominated state politics.

The "big three" from Indore—Mishrilal Gangwal, V. V. Dravid,
and Manoharsingh Mehta—made effective use of their official positions in the Cabinet to direct a large share of government benefits in
the direction of their constituencies in Indore. The capacity to concentrate numerous portfolio jurisdictions in a small state government,
together with the collaboration of strategically placed high-level bureaucrats from Indore, enabled the triumvirate to manage the bureaucratic line agencies in the distribution of patronage and the implementation of policy in a coherent fashion on behalf of their factional,
community, and organized clienteles in the city. The concentration
of portfolios and subordinate bureaucratic agencies relevant to the
labor area in Indore goes a long way in explaining the effective and

---

[24] Evidence that D. P. Mishra in particular, but other Cabinet politicians as
well, attempted to systematically build bureaucratic channels of influence and
corresponding political constituencies in Indore city is introduced at appropriate
places in following chapters.

machine-like control of the textile laborers by Ramsingh Verma and the Congress union. Similarly, the electoral strength and relative unity of the Congress party in Indore through the general elections of 1957 are largely due to the coherent impact through vertical bureaucratic channels of the "big three" state-level political chieftains from Indore.

The formation of the much larger state of Madhya Pradesh introduced a more complex structure of political competition and greatly reduced the cumulative state-level power of Indore city and the Madhya Bharat region. Political chieftains and high-level bureaucrats from the other regions, particularly Mahakoshal–Chhattisgarh, sought to maximize their own cumulative state-level influence. Though still proportionally well represented at the outset, Indore chieftains and bureaucrats were in a position to cultivate their constituencies in Indore, but with diminished force and coherence. Moreover, their influence was progressively eroded over time by the displacement of Indore bureaucrats from the highest levels, the dilution of princely and Nai Duniya influence in the local bureaucracies in Indore by augmentation, and eventually the resignation of Dravid from the Cabinet in 1964 and the electoral defeat of Gangwal in 1967. As the Indore chieftains' grip on the state government instruments weakened, the electoral grip of the City Congress deteriorated, factional rivalries intensified, and Congress' hold on the labor arena suffered.

What was most visible after 1963, with the accession of D. P. Mishra as Chief Minister, was not only the penetration of state-level positions by allies of Mishra from Mahakoshal but the use of the bureaucratic line agencies of the state government in Indore city to undermine Mishra's antagonists in the Nai Duniya and INTUC groups and to build up the subordinate Hindi-speaking Brahman faction and other allies in the city, with the objective of controlling the City Congress organization and party nominations for MLA seats in the city.

The dominance of the Nai Duniya and INTUC chieftains in the Madhya Bharat period, and the attempt by Mishra to subordinate the Congress party and electoral arena in Indore to his control, together bring out the predominance of vertical political and bureaucratic linkages as they shape the urban political process and subordinate it to state-level influences. What emerges from the picture is two sets of formal structures, representative and bureaucratic, linked at the top through symbiotic relationships between allied political chieftains and high-level bureaucrats. The representative structure includes the party organization and the electoral process, but is informally conditioned by factional and ascriptive linkages, binding political chieftains at the state level vertically to local allies and clienteles in the city. Political ties between political chieftains and high-level bureaucrats are similarly a function of ascriptive and cultural identifications based on caste, community, and princely state experiences. The bureaucratic structures provide the vertical institutional channels for influencing political outcomes in the city and building or strengthening local political constituencies, but the process of bureaucratic influences is similarly conditioned by ascriptive factors.

The vertical representative and bureaucratic structures fuse or diverge as a function of levels and symbiotic relationships that are conditioned by ascriptive variables. The interplay between alternative competition "sets"—representative and bureaucratic—is such that the "system" of allocation of decisions and resources in the city is unique to each period and issue, but generally derivative from the intersection patterns of the two formal structures and informal conditioners. The coherence and impact of state-level political action on the city is a function of this process. The process became more complex with the formation of Madhya Pradesh—the widening of the political arena has made coherent rigging exercises more difficult—and now resembles arbitrage or mediation more than authority or power bargaining.

The predominance of vertical political and bureaucratic linkages conditioned by ascriptive variables suggests further considerations. The urban political system is not defined exclusively by processes at the local level, but is drawn vertically through political and bureaucratic linkages into state politics. Thus a process of political integration is taking place through institutional, organizational, and ascriptive channels; but the effect of this is to eliminate the potential autonomy of local politics. Major decisions affecting political outcomes in the city are to a large extent external and located at the state or higher levels of politics. The primacy of external decisions affecting urban politics requires a broad scope of analysis combining local arenas with relevant processes at higher levels of politics. Some of the questions this raises for comparative urban politics research will be considered in the final chapter.

This chapter concludes Part Two. The focal concern of Part Two has been city-wide political competition, rooted in princely and primordial rivalries, and structured since the princely period both by party and factional competition in general elections and by the state-level penetration of representative and bureaucratic hierarchies. While this level of the "politics of the city as a whole" will continue to be pertinent to what follows, the center of attention now shifts to the "politics of urban sub-systems"—to microanalyses of individual political arenas. We turn first, in Part Three, to the municipal arena, where politics is highly visible and city-wide in territorial scope, but severely limited in its functional reach. Chapter 6 describes the formal limits of municipal authority and the effects of state encroachment on municipal functions. Chapter 7 is a detailed analysis of municipal political processes centering on the stakes of municipal politics, the changing social composition of Municipal Councils, the outcomes of party and factional competition, and the effects of state-level political penetration in the municipal arena. And chapter 8 consists of a case study of interagency jurisdictional conflict and policy processes based on the critical water shortage of the late 1960's. Following the three chapters on municipal politics, Part Four covers several other political arenas in the city.

PART THREE

THE MUNICIPAL ARENA

6

STATE PENETRATION OF THE
MUNICIPAL ARENA

The municipal government of Indore is the symbolic focus, but not the center of gravity, of city politics. It is the symbolic focus because only in the municipal arena is there a continuous and public process of politics with a general, city-wide constituency. Politics is continuous elsewhere in other political arenas in the city, but it is only within the municipal institutional nexus (council and committees) that politics is formally open to the public and that elected representatives have general constituencies that collectively coincide with city boundaries. Other arenas (labor, agricultural produce markets, cooperatives) may include representative institutions and electoral processes, and to that extent are publicly visible, but their constituencies are circumscribed functionally, occupationally, and even areally. In most bureaucratic arenas (taxation, law and order, public works) politics is not usually publicly visible, but consists of official and unofficial negotiations among bureaucratic and political actors. The municipal government, formally at least, represents the entire population of the city; there is no other agency, except perhaps the Improvement Trust, which does so explicitly and exclusively.

It is this that has led to the recognition of the President, or Mayor, of the municipal government as the "first citizen" and symbol of the population of the city as a collective, political unit. He is not usually, however, the holder of concentrated political power. The municipal government and its officials wield exceedingly limited power. The

city-wide constituency is broad, but the functional jurisdictions allocated to the municipal government are only a very few of those that
have a bearing on the lives of citizens of the city. Moreover, the state
government has enormous opportunities to intervene vertically in
such limited jurisdictions as remain statutorily under the municipal
government.

This chapter is concerned with the predominance of vertical linkages in the municipal arena; with the statutory powers that constitute
legal channels of state access to the municipal arena; with the tendency toward the continued erosion of residual municipal autonomy,
and its implications for the political roles of municipal officials; and
also with those rare and exceptional instances when municipal political actors have managed to expand the political resources and
scope of the municipal government, not so much to resist vertical
influence from the state as to maximize their own political opportunities within the existing institutional framework. The present
chapter outlines the structural framework within which municipal
political processes (examined in the following chapter) take place.

Limits of Municipal Authority

The municipal government of Indore, until 1956 a Municipality
and since October 1956 a Municipal Corporation,[1] follows the British-
Indian model of subordination to the state government. The Constitution of India allocates powers to the central and state governments, including the power of the state governments to constitute
urban and rural local governments. The urban local governments,
following the imperial pattern, are statutory bodies with provision
for some degree of popular local representation. The statutes prescribe
not only a functionally narrow scope of municipal jurisdiction but
subject virtually all actions of municipal government to supervision
and possible reversal by state authorities. The emphasis, as was the
case under the imperial regime, is on control from above. The municipal representative body is tolerated for the same reason that it was

[1] The legal description here is primarily of the Corporation, based on the *Madhya Pradesh Municipal Corporations Act* (1956) and the *Madhya Pradesh Municipal
Corporations Law (Extension) Act* (1960), contained in Indore City Corporation,
Nagrik, special number, September 15, 1961. For comparative descriptions of
municipal structure, see Hugh Tinker, *The Foundations of Local Self-Government
in India*, and Donald B. Rosenthal, *The Limited Elite*.

useful to the imperial (or princely) authorities—as a convenient means of raising and legitimizing additional revenues in the city for the support of city administration and services.

The statutes prescribe "obligatory duties" and allow for "discretionary functions" of the Municipal Corporation. The major "obligatory duties" include: (1) the sanitation of public streets and spaces; (2) construction and maintenance of public streets, drains, sewers, urinals, and facilities for drinking water; (3) management and maintenance of the municipal water works and distribution system; (4) the establishment and operation of primary schools; and (5) providing street lighting and (6) certain health services. The Corporation is also empowered to administer building regulations; to administer licenses and regulations affecting the production and sale of food products and nonalcoholic beverages in shops and restaurants; to regulate dangerous trades and practices; and—subject to state government consent —to engage in town planning entailing property acquisition.

Similarly the statute prescribes "obligatory" and "discretionary" taxes to be administered by the Corporation. "Obligatory" taxes include: (1) a property tax on buildings and lands, calculated as a percentage of the assessed annual rental value; (2) a conservancy tax; (3) a sanitary cess; (4) a water rate; and (5) *octroi*. (*Octroi* is a local form of customs duty levied on goods transported into the city.) The more important "discretionary" taxes include (1) entertainment taxes on theatres and public amusements and (2) taxes on professions, trades, and occupations.

An indication of the relative importance of functional jurisdictions and tax powers can be obtained from the number of municipal employees in the major departments and sections of the Corporation, expenditures under major heads, and the major sources of income.[2] The most important functional jurisdictions from the point of view of employment and expenditures are those coming under the municipal Public Health and Public Works departments.

The Public Health Department was the largest employer within the Corporation, with nearly 1700 employees in 1967–68, and spent just over 20 percent of the budget, largely on salaries. The Depart-

---

[2] Data about personnel and expenditures were drawn from Corporation publications, but particularly from Indore City Corporation, *Statement of the Budget, 1967–68*. For more detail, see my "Area, Power and Linkage in Indore," pp. 220ff.

ment employed 945 persons solely to sweep the gutters. The political importance of the sanitation jurisdiction lies in its employment patronage, useful for constituency-building among the low and scheduled castes and unemployed laborers of the city. The Public Health Department may also have had opportunities to build constituencies among the food services sector, through the enforcement of health regulations in hotels and restaurants, and among the lower classes, by providing medical care through the rudimentary Corporation hospital; but these were apparently of limited value.

The most patronage-rich municipal department in terms of expenditures is Public Works. It was allocated an estimated 44 percent of the budget in 1967–68. The P.W.D. disposed of a considerable number of jobs (573) and, although a substantial amount went toward salaries, the great bulk of its expenditure was on upkeep of fixed assets and construction of new works, involving purchasing materials and awarding contracts to private suppliers and contractors. The higher-salaried employees of Public Works are engineers by training, the most important being the Municipal Engineer, followed by several assistant engineers. Beneath the engineers in the Buildings Permissions and Construction Works sections are about two dozen "overseers." The engineers and overseers had opportunities to develop working relationships with suppliers and contractors and to advise Councillors in the Public Works and Standing committees to award contracts and purchases to selected contractors, with potential rewards to bureaucratic and political participants. The "technical advice" of engineers with respect to specifications of pipes and building materials can be used to favor some contractors and deprive others in the awarding of contracts.

The engineers and overseers also exploit another rich source of irregular income based on their technical role in interpreting building regulations and passing or withholding permits for new building or alterations in the city. Permits can be delayed indefinitely unless the machinery is oiled at appropriate points. The engineers and overseers are probably the most important bureaucratic participants in municipal administrative politics, their roles and rewards being based on technical expertise, detailed familiarity with complex regulations, and strategic legal power both to spend large amounts of money and enforce building regulations. Primarily because of Public Works Department functionaries, numerous businessmen and building owners are forced to deal with the Corporation, sometimes intermittently but often on a continuous and time-consuming basis.

A second patronage-rich jurisdiction is that of municipal taxation. The *Octroi* Section is the heart of the Income Collection Division. In 1967–68 the *Octroi* Section consisted of some 22 "inspectors" and 110 *nakedars*. The *nakedars* are clerks stationed at *nakas,* or *octroi* posts, on all roads entering the city, to collect taxes from truck drivers and other carriers according to fixed schedules. Trucks passing through without unloading in the city pay only a transit fee, but are subject to inspection on exit from the city. Articles brought into the city for sale are taxed at varying rates under the *octroi* schedule, the heaviest rates falling on machinery, alcoholic beverages, and luxuries. The *nakedars,* most of whom are paid only a little more than 100 rupees a month, supplement their incomes from a variety of irregular procedures, the most typical of which is expediting the paperwork for those drivers in transit who cannot afford long delays and are usually willing to pay a tip to speed their release. There is considerable evasion of *octroi* duty altogether, but this is usually handled at the point of origin through the use of false documents stating the values of machinery or commodities by exporters and importers, and so does not usually implicate the *nakedars.* Employment in the tax collection bureaucracy of the Corporation is one of the most competitively sought-after types of municipal jobs.

When all is said and done, however, what the municipal government does and offers is minimal when contrasted with what it does not do. By contrast with American local government, the police or public safety agencies in India are not under municipal jurisdiction or control but rather are under the joint control of the state and central governments. Public education does not, in practice, come under the municipal authority in any form in Indore.[3] The major medical facilities—hospitals and dispensaries—are preempted by the state Public Health Department. One of the "discretionary" functions permits municipal management of a public transportation system, but

---

[3] Despite the statutory requirement that the Corporation construct and maintain primary schools, the Education Departments of Madhya Bharat and Madhya Pradesh have retained complete control of all levels of public education through high school.

bus service in Indore is under the jurisdiction of the Madhya Pradesh Roadways Transport Corporation. Town planning, as will be seen later, has been largely preempted by the Improvement Trust and the state Town Planning Department. Deprived of so many functions that could conceivably be performed locally in public safety, education, and medicine, the municipal agency is weak and limited.

Limited though the scope of municipal authority is, the state government still retains overriding statutory powers to direct municipal administration. The chief executive officer of the Corporation, known as the Municipal Commissioner, is appointed by the state government from among the state cadre of civil servants. He is usually but not invariably a member of the Indian Administrative Service (I.A.S.). Three-fourths of the members of the Municipal Council may reject an individual appointee, but the Council has no formal role in initial selection. As a civil servant of the state cadre, the Municipal Commissioner is likely to be highly sensitive to directives from the Minister and Secretary of Local Self-Government (Urban), much more so at least than to the locally elected Council. The elected members and officers of the Corporation do not have formal administrative or executive powers, with minor exceptions in the case of the Mayor. It is the Commissioner who has the executive and administrative authority to implement the decisions of the Council.

The Commissioner's powers as the chief executive officer extend to his role as initiator of the budget. He is authorized to prepare the "budget estimate" of income and expenditure in the coming year and to propose changes in taxation that may be required to obtain sufficient income, before the budget goes to the Standing Committee. The Commissioner has the authority to make property surveys and tax assessments; to make contracts (to invite and accept tenders) not exceeding 5,000 rupees in value on behalf of the Corporation; to be present and speak in any meeting of the Council or any committee; and to act as the agent of the Corporation in working with the police in enforcement of municipal regulations. Finally, in emergencies or when disaster is threatened, the Commissioner is authorized to take such action as he believes necessary, but must report such action promptly to the Standing Committee.

The state government holds a variety of other direct powers over the Corporation: the power to remove Councillors; to declare an emergency and have the officials of the Corporation routinely follow state directives; to require the Corporation to undertake new functions; to review the Corporation budget annually (and, if it is in debt, to assume control of it); to approve and regulate loans raised by the Corporation; to audit municipal accounts and order the rectification of defects or irregularities; to prescribe minimum and maximum limits on the amounts and rates of any municipal tax; to exempt persons, groups, or property from municipal taxation; to require the Corporation to undertake a town planning scheme, and to authorize or reject proposed schemes; to extend or restrict municipal jurisdiction anywhere in the city; to require the furnishing of any information or documents; to overrule any act of any municipal official or committee or the Council; to require the Corporation to discipline a negligent official; and the power to supersede the Corporation and administer the city through the Commissioner for up to two years.

The state government not only has these powers formally, but on occasion uses almost all of them. In addition, the state government indirectly shares power with the elected members of the Standing Committee over appointment of administrative officers below the Municipal Commissioner. As all such appointments must be made with the concurrence of the State Public Service Commission, political actors at the state level can influence or block the strategically important selections of Health and Revenue Officers and the Engineers of the Public Works Department.

Thus the workings of the municipal government and the politics of the municipal arena must be viewed in terms of the central importance of state powers of control and intervention, and of the opportunities for state-level political actors to influence outcomes in the municipal arena. When the political groups in power at the state and municipal elected levels correspond, or are mutually supportive, the municipal authority may tend to have the appearance of autonomy; but when the groups at the two levels are in opposition to each other, the appearance of autonomy tends to evaporate, and the predominance of vertical authority and influence becomes clear, as the next chapter shows.

State Encroachment on Municipal Authority

Not only has the scope of municipal government been narrow to start with, there has been a tendency for the state government to appropriate or preempt municipal jurisdictions and to reduce the sources of municipal revenue. The progressive reduction of municipal powers appears to be a result of felt needs by political actors at the state level to take over important patronage resources and to bolster the weak revenue resources of the state government. Whether the reduction of the municipal government's institutional autonomy has been consciously intended is not clear; it is doubtful that the relationship is ever perceived quite so abstractly by political participants, or that a matter of principle is ever seriously considered at stake. But what *is* clear is that the centralization of patronage in the hands of state political actors does have the effect of denying it to local potential rivals; and of the presence of this situational motive there is no doubt.

It has already been noted that the administration of primary education was not transferred to the Indore Municipality. Education Minister Narsinghrao Dixit of Madhya Bharat (1954) once indicated an interest in having this jurisdiction decentralized, but he was unwilling to permit a corresponding decentralization of control over state revenues allocated to primary education. Consequently the demand in Indore was subsequently dropped. In 1954—under the influence of V. V. Dravid, the Labour Minister—administration of the Shops and Establishments Act, which had until then been under the control of the Municipality, was transferred to the office of the Labour Commissioner based in Indore. This took from the hands of the Councillors an important source of influence over the large number of shops, hotels, restaurants, and other similar establishments in the city.

At about the same time, while Mishrilal Gangwal was Chief Minister of Madhya Bharat, the state government took over the motor vehicle tax, which under the Holkar state system had been collected and used by the municipal government. For the state government this was an act of rationalization of the administrative and revenue structure, as it was atypical for a local government to control motor vehicle

taxation. Still, it deprived the local government of a small but growing source of revenue. Similarly, a move was made in the Madhya
Bharat period to transfer the entertainment tax to the state. Although
the move was blocked in the legislature in 1954 and 1955, the succeeding government of Madhya Pradesh obtained the necessary legislation in 1958. The government promised to allocate a major proportion of the revenues derived from this tax in Indore to the Corporation; but the promise was not fulfilled, and the local government was
deprived of an important source of revenue.

Under the Mishra regime of Madhya Pradesh, from about 1965,
the state government imposed a 7 percent house tax on the home-
owners of Indore over and above the existing 7 percent already levied
by the Corporation. The move was challenged in the courts, but the
government action was upheld. Although assessed valuations on
property and houses in Indore are low, a total tax rate of 14 percent
was not an insignificant burden. For the Corporation it meant a dis-
incentive to raise valuations through reassessment, and imposed a
ceiling on Corporation advancement of the house tax rate.

In the face of this encroachment on its revenue resources, the
local government has come to rely more heavily on its most important
source of revenue, *octroi*. The revenue from *octroi* increased from
733,591 to 8,310,000 rupees between 1948 and 1967. Even after discounting for currency devaluation and the natural growth of commerce and consumption in the city, this remains an impressive increase in taxation, tending to negate the often-heard assertion that
municipal governments are unable or unwilling to raise rates or
maximize their existing revenue resources. But even on this important
item, indispensable to the current level of municipal services—or
perhaps because of its importance—the state government has made
noises about the abolition of *octroi*. An *Octroi* Inquiry Committee
has been established in Madhya Pradesh to investigate the advantages
and disadvantages of *octroi* taxation. *Octroi* does appear, on the surface at least, to adversely affect road carriers and road-borne commerce, and the small importers tend to be hit harder by it than the
large importers in the city; but the abolition of *octroi* would further
the dependence of the urban local governments on the state. To compensate for *octroi* abolition, the state presumably would raise excise

tax rates and allocate a commensurate portion to municipal governments. Again, an important source of local patronage would be
destroyed.

Another example of state encroachment on municipal prerogatives
in Indore, again justified by the requirements of rationalized state
administration, has to do with the jurisdiction of *nazul* land in the
city. *Nazul* land is government property that frequently has no building on it because of its proximity to watercourses or roadways (where
building within a certain distance is prohibited). Under the Holkar
and Madhya Bharat governments, *nazul* land in Indore was administered for all practical purposes by the municipal government. The
administration of such land was sometimes a useful source of patronage for those influential in the municipality. For example, when the
influx of Sindhis and other refugees from Pakistan hit Indore, many
were permitted by special regulations to erect small shops (*gumtis*) on
nazul land adjacent to major thoroughfares. They paid taxes to the
municipality for these rights; and the local Congress, especially the
Nai Duniya group (Laxman Singh Chauhan, V. V. Sarvate), obtained
added electoral and political support from the *nazul* beneficiaries. In
old Madhya Pradesh, which had been under British administration,
nazul lands were administered not by municipal governments but by
the state administration instead. Rationalization of *nazul* administration along the old Madhya Pradesh lines was slow in coming, but
appropriate legislation was passed in 1964; its enforcement became
strong in Indore only late in 1967 and in 1968. In Indore, the *Nazul*
Department of the state administration, under the supervision of the
Collector, now collects annual rents from *gumtis* and decides whether
constructions will be removed or permitted to remain in given locations on *nazul* land.

By and large, therefore, despite some increments in substantive
municipal power through increases in the collection of *octroi,* house
tax, and other levies, the picture remains one of progressive erosion
of municipal institutional jurisdictions and power. V. V. Sarvate, a
former President of the Municipality, an MLA from 1952–57, and
the President of the Madhya Bharat Municipal Authorities Federation, sought to block state encroachment on municipal powers—but
with few if any powerful allies, he was unsuccessful, especially after
1956 when the new Madhya Pradesh came into existence. Community

support for municipal institutional autonomy in Indore appears to be negligible if not nonexistent.

Residual Influence of Elective Office

The formal powers of the Mayor are minimal, and his actual powers seldom much greater, except in those cases where an individual who becomes Mayor has additional offices of authority, or political or organizational support *outside* the Corporation. The Mayor has administrative control over the "office of the Corporation and its staff," including the Secretary and Public Relations Officer and some 45 clerks and office employees. The Mayor is empowered to fix the dates of ordinary Council meetings and call special meetings, and exercises a casting vote in case of a tie. He has emergency powers to direct execution or suspension of Corporation actions, but must report his action to the Council at the next meeting. The Mayor is elected by, and usually from among, the elected members and Aldermen of the Council, not by the city population at large. As the executive powers are largely preempted by the Commissioner, and legislative powers rest largely in the Standing Committee or Council (or, as in the case of budget initiative, in the Commissioner), and because the Mayor is indirectly elected, the position bears virtually no inherent power.

The only exception, and it is a partial one, is that the Mayor is automatically the chairman of the five-member Appeals Committee. Most executive actions of the Commissioner or his administrative subordinates, including the granting or refusal of licenses and building permits, may be reviewed by the Appeals Committee if the injured party appeals the action within thirty days. "The Appeals Committee may remand any case for further inquiry or decision, or may pass any other order as may be deemed just and proper; and no appeal or revision shall lie against this decision of the Committee" (Article 403).[4] The Appeals Committee, or the Mayor in case it is not sitting, may order a halt to orders or actions that are being contested in an appeal until the Committee decides the case. As long as the Mayor is supported by two members of the Committee, he and the Committee members become bargaining participants with the municipal bureaucrats in the Public Health, Revenue, and Public Works departments in the bureaucratic regulatory process.

---

[4] *Madhya Pradesh Municipal Corporations Act* (1956).

Wallace Sayre and Herbert Kaufman have identified four roles realized in varying degrees by Mayors of New York City.[5] The roles are those of "Chief of State for the City," "Chief Executive" and "Chief Legislator" of the city government, and "Chief of Party." None of these roles inhere institutionally in the Mayor of the Indore Corporation. The Mayor in Indore may be regarded as the symbolic representative of the city, as the "first citizen," but he is not the focus of expectations of governmental action. The functional division of powers denies that role to anyone in the city. Public expectations for government action usually focus on bureaucratic officials, primarily on the Collector of the district—particularly when law-and-order questions arise, but also in relation to services provided by one or another department of the state government that is locally supervised by the Collector—and to a lesser extent on the Revenue Commissioner of the Division or, within the municipal arena, as much on the Municipal Commissioner as anyone else. The Commissioner rather than the Mayor is the "Chief Executive," and shares the role of "Chief Legislator" with the Chairman of the Standing Committee within the municipal arena. Finally, the Mayor is not by virtue of his position the "Chief of Party" in the city, though on occasion by coincidence he may hold both positions.[6] The criteria for selection of local party chiefs tend to be quite independent of the processes of municipal politics.

The Mayor's role in Indore, then, is circumscribed to minor executive functions and to presiding over the appeals process. An active Mayor's key asset is probably fairly comprehensive information about municipal administrative actions and proceedings in the committees and Council, for such information can be used to bargain with bureaucrats wherever questions of legality and exposure arise. But unless the Mayor, by virtue of strong organizational support or external political assets, has special access to key functionaries, his main role is that of a "master of ceremonies" at municipal functions held for visiting dignitaries and at sports tournaments, the dedication of construction

---

[5] Wallace S. Sayre and Herbert Kaufman, *Governing New York City,* pp. 657 ff.

[6] After 1948 there was no such coincidence. The closest Indore came to this pattern was in 1953 and 1954, when Laxman Singh Chauhan was both President of the municipality and Secretary of the Indore City Congress party.

works, and so on. This role gives him some public status and visibility, but is by no means a measure of political influence.

The Standing Committee (usually ten members) elected by the Council, and its elected Chairman, are the key legislative agents in the Corporation. The Standing Committee's powers include the appointment of municipal employees with salaries exceeding 150 rupees a month, subject to the approval of the State Public Service Commission, and the authority to appoint temporary employees for up to six months without SPSC approval. Similarly, the Standing Committee has the power to discipline municipal employees, provided that severe punishment requires the concurrence of the SPSC. Powers of appointment and discipline enable the Chairman or the Committee to harass and reward key executive officers beneath the Commissioner, giving elected members of the Corporation access to bureaucratic patronage embedded in the administrative and regulatory processes. Furthermore, the Standing Committee is empowered to sanction contracts up to 25,000 rupees in value (those with higher value require government sanction), and to authorize the Commissioner to enter contracts without inviting tenders, provided that the reasons for doing so are recorded in the Committee's proceedings. The Standing Committee may also authorize the Commissioner to acquire immovable property at stipulated rates, subject to state government approval. But the key powers of the Standing Committee, aside from those of appointment and discipline, reside in the budgetary process. The Committee is empowered to deliberate over the "budget estimate," to make modifications and *additions,* and to shift amounts from one budget head to another in the course of the financial year. But Standing Committee actions on the budget require Council ratification.

The Chairman of the Standing Committee holds more formal power than any other elected officer of the Corporation. As the spokesman of the Standing Committee, he has a role in major contracts, bureaucratic appointments and discipline, and Council legislation in the form of the budget. The Chairman, as long as he has adequate support in his own Committee, has far greater institutional opportunities to build influence within the municipal arena than the Mayor, and he can operate with little deference to the Mayor unless the Mayor happens to be an individual with strong external political support apart from his elected position. But the Chairman's role is that of an operative, with low visibility. The Mayor's position is sought after for its status-potential and visibility. The Chairmanship of the Standing Committee is sought after for its comparatively important legal powers and patronage potential.

This chapter has provided the major outlines of the legal setting for politics in the municipal arena, showing the subordination of the municipal institutional nexus to overriding state government power. The legal structure is a setting of constraints and opportunities that vary as political conditions on the state and local levels change. This will become apparent in the following chapter, where the delineation of political structures and processes in the municipal arena makes it possible to show how political actors on the state level have increasingly used the available legal instruments to participate in municipal politics from above, or through allied agents on the local level. This chapter has also shown how the state government has trimmed away some patronage-rich jurisdictions, and continues to threaten to do so on the *octroi* question, further limiting the previously narrow scope of municipal government.

7

THE MUNICIPAL PROCESS: PARTY AND FACTIONAL COMPETITION AND OUTCOMES

The portrayal of political actors competing for power and influence in the municipal arena, though incomplete as a picture of city politics, still provides a setting for the charting of urban political linkages in greater depth and consistency than where politics in the city is less visible. Personal, ascriptive, and factional linkages within the municipal arena are integrated to a degree with other political arenas in the city. But the linkage and factional structure of the municipal arena also bears features of its own, making municipal politics a distinguishable arena in linkage structure as well as formal jurisdiction. A major purpose of this chapter, therefore, is to trace political linkages within the municipal arena between municipal politicians, social constituencies, and factions, and between elected politicians and bureaucrats of the municipal administration. The result will be an account of the ascriptive and economic bases of political factions within the Congress party and of opposition parties in the municipal arena.

Secondly, this chapter illustrates and amplifies the generalizations made in the previous chapter about the predominance of vertical political and bureaucratic linkages that draw the municipal arena into higher levels of political cleavage and competition. The organization of municipal politics is shown to be autocratic in many respects —a continuation, in effect, of the imperial pattern, emphasizing the "control" characteristics of state–municipal relations. And finally, this study of municipal politics highlights the rewards and benefits available to municipal political participants.

The weakness of municipal government would lead one to suppose that city politicians would be indifferent to the municipal arena. Why run for office when it will bring little power, and that only over unimportant matters? The evidence shows that there is indeed a tendency for successful politicians—particularly political chieftains successful at the state level—to regard the municipal arena condescendingly, a playground for small fry.[1] Despite the indifference of state level chieftains, politics in the Indore municipal arena is intense and municipal positions are much sought after, especially by members of the less affluent income classes. The main reason is that the municipal arena affords a variety of tangible and intangible rewards. Many of these are particularistic, and therefore require situational explanation. But some are generalizable in terms of material benefit, political power, and status considerations.

As others have observed, municipal councillors in India are primarily concerned not with policy and legislation, but with administrative outputs.[2] Administration becomes a patronage process, for it is concerned with water, health, and sanitation services, with the issuing of building permits and licenses, the regulation of property tax assessments, and the supervision of contracts awarded for construction or repairs. Influencing who benefits from distributive and regulatory policies as they are applied in individual cases is the chief concern of the councillor. Some make a business out of this, while others do it out of civic pride and duty. The personal interests of the councillor, if he is a property owner or professional, may be directly at stake in some cases, but for the most part he does favors

---

[1] This was, however, not the case before the merger of the Holkar state. As long as the Holkar government was not accessible to popular politicians, and since the Municipal Council was partly elected—albeit from a qualified electorate—popular politicians found the municipal arena useful as a means of developing and demonstrating popular constituencies. But after merger the attention of political chieftains shifted to state politics, and MLA's only rarely stooped to participate directly in municipal politics.

[2] See Roderick Church, "Authority and Influence in Indian Municipal Politics"; Donald B. Rosenthal, *The Limited Elite*; Henry C. Hart, "Bombay Politics: Pluralism or Polarization"; and Myron Weiner, *Party-Building in a New Nation,* especially Part V, "The Politics of Patronage: Calcutta."

for others—for his ward constituents or special interest groups. There are not only material rewards involved, but power considerations as well. The Council can be a steppingstone to higher office if patronage is shrewdly used to build not only public support for the councillor himself but for other candidates of his party in general elections. Strengthening the party and assisting the election of candidates creates obligations that the councillor may cash in on at a later date. Municipal influence may be instrumental for the councillor, and his family and friends, in other bureaucratic arenas as well—for a cousin may need a job, a grandmother's admission to a hospital may need to be expedited, or a neighbor's friend may deserve a medical scholarship. These stakes may seem small, but they loom large when they are scarce, and access to them is facilitated by achieving political influence and prominence.

Finally, status and prestige are significant incentives, especially for those who are already well off in material terms.[3] In the city, because the traditional criteria of caste and ritual status are more ambiguous, political position becomes a more effective and sought-after way of guaranteeing or elevating an individual's status, as well as that of those closely associated with him. Municipal positions are limited in power but highly visible in the urban community, and that official visibility can be a source of considerable satisfaction. A study of the municipal political process makes it possible to identify many of these rewards concretely and to understand in contextual terms why they become objects of strenuous competition. In a politics of scarcity, even the limited jurisdictional scope of the municipal government of Indore offers ample material, patronage, and status rewards to produce vigorous claims for shares in their distribution.

This analysis is organized chronologically according to major turning-points such as the municipal elections of 1950, 1955, 1958, and 1965; the states reorganizations of 1948 and 1956; and shifts in factional or party control at the state level, following general elections. In outline, this chapter shows that from 1945 to 1950—a period that began under Holkar rule but ended after merger into Madhya

---

[3] Rosenthal stresses personal and group "visibility" and "prestige," and discounts "material incentives," as motivations for seeking municipal office in Agra and Poona. *The Limited Elite,* p. 122. In Indore "material incentives" generally take precedence, but status incentives do motivate certain Councillors strongly. They are probably best viewed as interdependent motivations in the Indian context.

Bharat—the Council was dominated by the Nai Duniya faction. Since 1950 there has been a gradual erosion of the dominance of the Nai Duniya group, a result at first of the growing organizational power of the INTUC faction. The INTUC faction acted as a balancing force in the Council of 1950 and became the dominant group in the Council elected in 1955. INTUC dominance in turn was shaken in 1958 through the combined electoral onslaught of opposition parties and Khadiwala group sympathizers who stood against Congress party nominees in the election.

The merger of Madhya Bharat with the new Madhya Pradesh in 1956 strengthened the Hindi-speaking Brahman faction on the state level, and this in turn bolstered the Khadiwala group in Indore. By the time D. P. Mishra became Chief Minister in 1963, the stage was set for him to work through the local Khadiwala forces and other subordinate allies to seek control of the local government. Although this aim was never fully realized, the Khadiwala (Mishra) group emerged as the key municipal faction until supersession overtook the Council in the summer of 1968, and the local elected body was dissolved. The erosion of the municipal hold of the Nai Duniya group, the temporary success of the INTUC group, the bolstering of the Khadiwala group in the Mishra period, and the supersession of the Corporation by the SVD government all reflect the increasing penetration of Indore municipal politics by politicians and factions on the state level—pointing to the overriding importance of vertical political linkages, in this case, between local and state-level factions. The process of state penetration of the municipal arena suggests that a form of political integration was taking place. Local politicians in the municipal arena of Indore were subordinated to and forced to become attentive to not just a princely capital or a comparatively small state area, but to the much more extensive area and government of Madhya Pradesh.

Princely Continuity in Municipal Poltics, 1945–1950

The Municipal Council of 1945 spanned the transition from Holkar state to Madhya Bharat politics. Elements that it inherited from the princely era have endured, affecting Indore municipal politics for years afterward, although they have diminished in importance from one succeeding Council to the next.[4] The elements of continuity that stand out most clearly are the persisting high representation of Maharashtrians and Jains and the power of the Nai Duniya faction, in municipal politics and administration. Formally, the 1945 Council consisted of 22 Councillors elected from wards through a property-qualified franchise, 8 Holkar government officials who were nominated to the Council by the government, and 4 non-officials also nominated by the government. One-third of the 22 elected Councillors were Marathi-speakers (all but one Brahman), as were 6 of the 8 nominated officials (also all but one Brahman), giving the Council a heavily Maharashtrian Brahman complexion.[5] The remaining seats were distributed among other communities, primarily Jains, Hindi-speaking and Gujarati Brahmans, and Baniyas.

The clearly dominant faction among the elected Councillors was the Praja Mandal group, known since 1948 as the Nai Duniya faction and the heir of Holkar princely state political influence. The Nai Duniya group in the Council contained at least 13 (a majority of) elected members. Their position was fortified by the nominated officials who, as representatives of the Holkar regime, exerted a pro-Holkar influence on the Council and generally supported the Nai Duniya group. The control of the Council by the Nai Duniya faction was reflected in its monopoly over the key elected positions of President and Chairman of the Standing Committee, which rotated mainly among Brahmans (V. V. Sarvate, N. G. Kothari, Narendra Tiwari, Tarashankar Pathak) and Jains (Babulal Patodi, and Manoharsingh Mehta).[6]

The Praja Mandal Councillors, supported by the nominated Holkar officials, developed close working relationships with the executive officers of the municipal administration, relationships which survived years later when the power of the Nai Duniya group had

[4] A list of members, with their community and factional affiliations is available in my "Area, Power and Linkage in Indore," p. 245.

[5] All but one of the elected Maharashtrian Brahmans were part of the Praja Mandal group. Maharashtrian Brahmans rarely if ever supported the Khadiwala group.

[6] The representation of Nai Duniya and Indore City politicians in the Madhya Bharat Cabinet and Legislative Assembly helped the Nai Duniya group maintain its dominance after 1948. The relative political stature of some of these municipal leaders was greatly enhanced by their state-level positions. V. V. Sarvate and N. G. Kothari were among the members of the Legislative Assembly from Indore after 1948.

otherwise been considerably eroded in the municipality. Two officers in particular, G. S. Ghatpande (Municipal Engineer) and Murlidhar Chauhan (Accountant), got their municipal posts under the Holkar regime and remained in the municipal administration until very recently. Ghatpande retired in December 1966 and Chauhan retired as late as 1968. Both contributed to the survival of the Nai Duniya group's influence in the municipality beyond the degree warranted by its "power" in the Council after 1955.

Ghatpande and Chauhan were both strategically placed in the municipal bureaucracy. Ghatpande supervised the expenditures on all municipal construction, administered the municipal by-laws regulating buildings, and had charge of municipal distribution of water. The patronage opportunities of the Municipal Engineer are undoubtedly far greater than those of any other municipal officer, except perhaps those of the Commissioner. Ghatpande's long tenure enabled him to establish a singular concentration of bureaucratic and personal power within the municipal administration. Chauhan was for many years in charge of the municipal Revenue Department, giving him influence over the appointment of *nakedars* and ample opportunities for informal rewards when enforcing tax laws with less than maximum rigor.

The Holkar state passed on to the municipal administration, as it did in so many other branches also, a high proportion of Maharashtrians. Interview evidence suggests that, excluding the sanitation employees who were and are largely Harijans, about 90 percent of the remaining clerical and white-collar staff of the municipality in 1948 were Marathi-speakers. The Maharashtrian complexion of the 1945 Council lends support to such a view. Ghatpande in the municipal services, like V. G. Apte in the Public Health Department, helped maintain a high proportion of Maharashtrian Brahmans, now estimated to be still about 50 percent of the clerical and white-collar employees of the Corporation.

Nai Duniya Dominance and the INTUC Challenge
in Municipal Politics, 1950–1955

The Municipal Council of 1950 consisted of 22 members elected from the same number of wards and 12 aldermen nominated by the Madhya Bharat government. The accompanying tables (nos. 18–22)

TABLE 18. FACTIONAL AFFILIATION: MUNICIPAL COUNCIL, 1950–1955

Nai Duniya	Khadiwala	INTUC	Opposition	Independents
V. V. Sarvate	Kantilal Patel	Jhumerlal Verma	Ram Narain Shastri	Ajitprasad Jain
Laxman Singh Chauhan	Kanchanlal Dhruve	Abdul Rup Nishtar	K. S. Meherunkar	P. D. Sharma[c]
———— Tarashankar Pathak ————→	Shrikrishan Khandelwal	Dattatrey S. Patil	(A) S. D. Mulye	Khemraj Joshi
Ratanlal Gupta	Siremal Chajer	(A)[a] Jal D. Patel	(A) V. G. Apte[d]	(A) Balkrishnan Gohar
S. G. Dube	Vimalchander Jhanjhariya	(A) Gopikrishnan Gohar		
J. P. Dube[b]	Babulal Nigam			
Babulal Malu				
———— G. R. Dighe ————→	(A) Ram Gidwani			
	(A) Pukhraj Bahen			
(A) B. M. Bhandari				
(A) Gopaldas Jhalani				
(A) Fakkuruddin				
(A) Malini Harmalkar				
(A) Hirabai Bordiya				

[a] (A) = Alderman, nominated by the government.
[b] Resigned in 1951; Chotilal Gupta, who leaned toward the Khadiwala faction, won the by-election from Dube's vacant seat.
[c] Resigned; M. R. Khutal was nominated to the Council by the government in 1952 to fill Sharma's seat. Khutal has been a supporter of the Nai Duniya group.
[d] V. G. Apte was replaced by D. S. Sarangpani through government appointment in 1953.

TABLE 19. Occupational Distribution by Political Parties: Municipal Councils, 1950, 1955, 1958, 1965

Political Parties	Seats in Council	Percentage of Seats by Party	Business[b]	Law	Medicine	Government Service	Journalism	Education	Industrial Worker (clerical)	Industrial Worker (operative)	Politician or Social Worker	Other
Council, 1950–1955	34	100.0	6 (18)	8 (24)	2 (06)	3 (09)	4 (12)	1 (03)	2 (06)	3 (09)	4 (12)	1 (03)
Congress	26	76.5	6 (23)	6 (23)	1 (04)	1 (04)	3 (12)	—	2 (08)	3 (12)	3 (12)	1 (04)
Jan Sangh and Hindu Mahasabha	3	08.8	—	1	1	1	—	—	—	—	—	—
Communist	1	02.9	—	—	—	1	—	—	—	—	—	—
Socialists	0	00.0	—	—	—	—	—	—	—	—	—	—
Independents	4	11.8	—	1	—	—	1	1	—	—	1	—
Council, 1955–1958	50	100.0	10 (20)	8 (16)	2 (04)	2 (04)	2 (04)	1 (02)	5 (10)	13 (26)	6 (12)	—
Congress	40	80.0	10 (25)	5 (13)	1 (03)	2 (05)	2 (05)	1 (03)	5 (13)	10 (25)	4 (10)	—
Jan Sangh and Hindu Mahasabha	3	06.0	—	1	—	—	—	—	—	—	2	—
Communist	3	06.0	—	1	—	—	—	—	—	2	—	—
Socialists	0	00.0	—	—	—	—	—	—	—	—	—	—
Independents	4	08.0	—	1	1	—	—	—	—	1	1	—
Council, 1958–1965	50	100.0	14 (28)	6 (12)	4 (08)	1 (02)	3 (06)	4 (08)	—	12 (24)	3 (06)	3 (06)
Congress	20	40.0	8 (40)	2 (10)	2 (10)	—	—	3 (15)	—	4 (20)	—	1 (03)
Jan Sangh and Hindu Mahasabha	4	08.0	—	1	1	—	1	—	—	—	1	—
Communist	7	14.0	—	—	—	—	—	—	—	6 (86)	—	1

	N	%											
Socialists	5	10.0	2	1	—	—	—	—	—	—	—	2	—
Independents	14	28.0	4 (29)	2	1	1	2	1	—	—	2	1	
Council, 1965–1968	60	100.0	16 (27)	7 (12)	1 (02)	3 (05)	—	—	6 (10)	11 (18)	5 (08)		
Congress	36	60.0	12 (33)	4 (11)	1 (03)	2 (06)	—	—	6 (17)	4 (11)	5 (14)	2 (06)	
Jan Sangh and Hindu Mahasabha	4	06.7	1	1	—	—	—	—	—	—	—	1	1
Communist	9	15.0	—	1	—	—	—	—	—	6 (67)	—	—	2
Socialists	4	06.7	—	1	—	—	—	—	—	1	3		
Independents	7	11.7	3	1	1	—	1	—	—	—	—	2	—

ª This type of table contains a good deal of information, not all of which can simultaneously be displayed in percentage form. The numbers in parentheses are percentages of the total N for each row, and they are rounded to the nearest whole number. What they show is how the occupational proportions within parties differ from each other and from the Council as a whole, providing cross-sectional comparisons. For certain purposes, however, it may be useful to know how Council members of a given occupational category "bunch up" within one or another party. This can best be seen by percentaging within columns rather than rows. In the 1950–55 and 1955–58 Councils, for example, 100 percent of the "Businessmen" were members of the Congress party, yet their distribution within that party tends to conceal this fact. It should also be apparent that when the numbers within a category are very small, percentages can be misleading and should be cautiously interpreted. To enhance readability, dashes have been substituted for zeros. And for the same reason, some percentage figures have been omitted.

ᵇ Includes landowners and rentiers in the city.

TABLE 20. OCCUPATIONAL DISTRIBUTION BY CONGRESS FACTIONS: MUNICIPAL COUNCILS, 1950, 1955, 1958, 1965

Congress Factions	Congress Seats	Percentage of Seats by Faction	Occupation[a]									
			Business[b]	Law	Medicine	Government Service	Journalism	Education	Industrial Worker (clerical)	Industrial Worker (operative)	Politician or Social Worker	Other
Council, 1950–1955	26	100.0	6 (23)	6 (23)	1 (04)	1 (04)	3 (12)	—	2 (08)	3 (12)	3 (12)	1 (04)
Nai Duniya	13	50.0	2 (15)	4 (31)	1	1	2	—	1	—	2	1
Khadiwala	8	30.8	4 (50)	1	—	—	1	—	1	—	1	1
INTUC	5	19.2	—	1	—	—	—	—	1	3 (60)	—	—
Council, 1955–1958	40	100.0	10 (25)	5 (13)	1 (03)	2 (05)	2 (05)	1 (03)	5 (13)	10 (25)	4 (10)	—
Nai Duniya	11	27.5	4 (36)	2 (18)	—	1	—	1	1	—	2	—
Khadiwala	7	17.5	3 (43)	1	—	1	1	—	—	1	1	—
INTUC	22	55.0	3 (14)	2 (9)	1	1	1	—	4 (18)	9 (41)	1	—
Council, 1958–1965	20	100.0	8 (40)	2 (10)	2 (10)	—	—	3 (15)	—	4 (20)	—	1 (05)
Nai Duniya	9	45.0	5 (56)	1	—	—	—	3 (33)	—	—	—	—
Khadiwala	5	25.0	3 (60)	1	—	—	—	—	—	—	—	1
INTUC	6	30.0	—	1	2 (33)	—	—	—	—	4 (66)	—	—
Council, 1965–1968	36	100.0	12 (33)	4 (11)	1 (03)	—	2 (06)	—	6 (17)	4 (11)	5 (14)	2 (06)
Nai Duniya	10	27.8	4 (40)	2 (20)	—	—	—	—	—	—	2	2
Khadiwala	15	41.7	8 (53)	3 (20)	—	—	2 (13)	—	1	—	2	—
INTUC	11	30.5	—	—	1	—	—	—	5 (45)	4 (36)	1	—

[a] Numbers within parentheses are percentages of totals within rows, rounded to the nearest whole number. See note a in Table 19.
[b] Includes landowners and rentiers in the city.

reveal that the Council was predominantly high-caste and high-status occupational in composition.[7] Brahmans (12) were most heavily represented, equally distributed between Maharashtrians and non-Maharashtrians, a clear movement away from the Maharashtrian dominance that had been maintained by Holkar government preferences in the preceding Council. The next most important groups were from business communities—Jains (7), followed by Hindu Baniyas (4)—and the rest were distributed among other communities, including two members of the scheduled castes. The Council reflected the politically dominant positions of the Brahman, Jain, and Hindu Baniya communities of Indore, particularly in the early years following merger. In the 1950 Council, 70 percent of the seats were held by members of these three groups alone.

The Council was also dominated by high-status "urban" occupations, by the professionals, businessmen, and white-collar workers, who together occupied 78 percent of the seats. There were 8 lawyers, 6 businessmen, 3 journalists, 3 college teachers, 2 medical practitioners, 3 persons with backgrounds in Holkar administration, and 2 textile mill clerical employees, leaving only 7 members from other occupations, including labor and full-time politics or social work. The 1950 distribution of occupations displays two other patterns, that the laborers fall entirely into the Congress party's INTUC group (which becomes meaningful when opposition party laborers are elected in later Councils), and that there was a tendency for "small business" members (Patel, Dhruve, Khandelwal, Gidwani) to support the Khadiwala group in contrast to the "big business" representatives of textile interests (Bhandari, Jhalani), who identified with the Nai Duniya group and who got seats not by election but by nomination as Aldermen (see Table 18).

The Congress party won 17 seats, while only 5 went to members of the opposition or independents.[8] The construction of the tables

---

[7] The factional affiliations of the 1950 Council members are shown in Table 18, and the occupational and caste distribution within political parties and factions in all four Councils are shown in Tables 19, 20, 21, and 22.

[8] Of the 2 partisan opposition members, Ram Narian Shastri was then identified with the Hindu Mahasabha and has since become a prominent city Jan Sangh leader, and Kripashankar Meherunkar had close ties with the left-wing and Communist parties. The 3 Independents each had informal ties with Congress members, and because of internal factional competition, Congress groups frequently sought and obtained support from one or another of them.

TABLE 21. CASTE DISTRIBUTION BY POLITICAL PARTIES: MUNICIPAL COUNCILS, 1950, 1955, 1958, 1965

Political Parties	Seats in Council	Percentage of Seats by Party	Caste or Community Affiliation[a]											
			Hindi-speaking Brahman	Maharashtrian Brahman	Jain	Hindu Baniya	Gujarati	Kayastha	Rajput	Maratha Dhangar	Sindhi	Muslim	Scheduled Castes	Other
Council, 1950–1955	34	100.0	6 (18)	6 (18)	7 (21)	4 (12)	2 (06)	1 (03)	1 (03)	1 (03)	1 (03)	2 (06)	2 (06)	1 (03)
Congress	26	76.5	3 (12)	3 (12)	6 (23)	4 (15)	2 (08)	1 (04)	1 (04)	1 (04)	1 (04)	2 (08)	1 (04)	1 (04)
Jan Sangh and Hindu Mahasabha	3	08.8	1 (33)	2 (67)	—	—	—	—	—	—	—	—	—	—
Communist	1	02.9	—	1	—	—	—	—	—	—	—	—	—	—
Socialists	0	00.0	—	—	1	—	—	—	—	—	—	—	—	—
Independents	4	11.8	2 (50)	—	—	—	—	—	—	—	—	1	1	—
Council, 1955–1958	50	100.0	7 (14)	5 (10)	7 (14)	4 (08)	2 (04)	1 (02)	4 (08)	3 (06)	1 (02)	3 (06)	6 (12)	7 (14)
Congress	40	80.0	5 (13)	2 (05)	7 (18)	4 (10)	2 (05)	1 (03)	3 (08)	3 (08)	1 (03)	3 (08)	4 (10)	5 (13)
Jan Sangh and Hindu Mahasabha	3	06.0	—	2 (67)	—	—	—	—	1	—	—	—	—	1
Communist	3	06.0	—	1	—	—	—	—	—	—	—	—	—	1
Socialists	0	00.0	—	—	—	—	—	—	—	—	—	—	—	—
Independents	4	08.0	2	—	—	—	—	—	—	—	—	—	2	—
Council, 1958–1965	50	100.0	12 (24)	7 (14)	3 (06)	7 (14)	1 (02)	—	2 (04)	1 (02)	1 (02)	2 (04)	6 (12)	8 (16)
Congress	20	40.0	6 (30)	1 (05)	1 (05)	4 (20)	1 (05)	—	1 (05)	1 (05)	—	1 (05)	1 (05)	3 (15)
Jan Sangh and Hindu Mahasabha	4	08.0	—	3 (75)	—	1 (25)	—	—	1	—	—	—	—	—
Communist	7	14.0	—	1	1	—	—	—	1	—	—	—	3 (43)	1
Socialists	5	10.0	—	1	1	—	—	—	—	—	1	—	1	2
Independents	14	28.0	6 (43)	1	1	2 (14)	—	—	—	—	1	1	1	2

Council, 1965–1968	60	100.0	16 (27)	6 (10)	3 (05)	8 (13)	2 (03)	—	3 (05)	3 (05)	3 (05)	4 (07)	8 (13) 4 (07)
Congress	36	60.0	10 (28)	2 (06)	2 (06)	6 (17)	2 (06)	—	3 (08)	2 (06)	3 (08)	2 (06)	2 (06) 2 (06)
Jan Sangh and Hindu Mahasabha	4	06.7	—	3 (75)	—	1 (25)	—	—	—	—	—	—	— —
Communist	9	15.0	1	1	—	—	—	—	—	1	—	—	5 (56) 1
Socialists	4	06.7	—	—	1	—	—	—	—	—	2 (50)	1	1 —
Independents	7	11.7	5 (71)	—	—	1	—	—	—	—	—	—	1 1

a Numbers within parentheses are percentages of totals within rows, rounded to the nearest whole number. See note a in Table 19.

TABLE 22. CASTE DISTRIBUTION BY CONGRESS FACTIONS: MUNICIPAL COUNCILS, 1950, 1955, 1958, 1965

Congress Factions	Congress Seats	Percentage of Congress Seats by Faction	Caste or Community Affiliation[a]											
			Hindi-speaking Brahman	Maharashtrian Brahman	Jain	Hindu Baniya	Gu-jarati	Ka-yastha	Raj-put	Maratha Dhangar	Sindhi	Mus-lim	Scheduled Castes	Other
Council, 1950–1955	26	100.0	3 (12)	3 (12)	6 (23)	4 (15)	2 (06)	1 (03)	1 (03)	1 (03)	1 (03)	2 (06)	1 (06)	1 (06)
Nai Duniya	13	50.0	3 (23)	3 (23)	2 (15)	3 (23)	—	1 (13)	1 (08)	—	1 (13)	1 (08)	—	—
Khadiwala	8	30.8	—	—	4 (50)	1 (13)	1 (13)	1 (13)	—	1 (20)	—	1 (20)	1 (20)	1 (20)
INTUC	5	19.2	—	—	—	—	1 (20)	—	—	—	1 (05)	1 (05)	1 (05)	1 (20)
Council, 1955–1958	40	100.0	5 (13)	2 (05)	7 (18)	4 (10)	2 (05)	1 (03)	3 (08)	3 (08)	1 (03)	3 (08)	4 (10)	5 (13)
Nai Duniya	11	27.5	1 (09)	1 (09)	2 (18)	2 (18)	1 (09)	—	1 (09)	1 (09)	—	2 (18)	1 (10)	1 (14)
Khadiwala	7	17.5	—	—	3 (43)	1 (14)	1 (14)	—	—	—	—	—	1 (14)	1 (14)
INTUC	22	55.0	4 (18)	1 (05)	2 (09)	1 (05)	—	1 (05)	2 (09)	2 (09)	1 (05)	1 (05)	3 (14)	4 (18)
Council, 1958–1965	20	100.0	6 (30)	1 (05)	1 (05)	4 (20)	1 (05)	—	1 (05)	1 (05)	—	1 (05)	3 (15)	3 (15)
Nai Duniya	9	45.0	3 (33)	1 (11)	1 (11)	1 (11)	—	—	—	1 (11)	—	1 (11)	1 (11)	1 (11)
Khadiwala	5	25.0	1 (20)	—	—	2 (40)	1 (20)	—	—	—	—	—	—	1 (20)
INTUC	6	30.0	2 (33)	—	—	1 (17)	—	—	1 (17)	—	—	—	1 (17)	1 (17)
Council, 1965–1968	36	100.0	10 (28)	2 (06)	2 (06)	6 (17)	2 (06)	—	3 (08)	2 (06)	3 (08)	2 (06)	2 (06)	2 (06)
Nai Duniya	10	27.8	3 (30)	1 (10)	—	—	1 (10)	—	1 (10)	1 (10)	—	2 (20)	—	1 (10)
Khadiwala	15	41.7	5 (33)	—	1 (07)	5 (33)	—	—	—	—	3 (20)	—	1 (07)	—
INTUC	11	30.5	2 (18)	1 (09)	1 (09)	1 (09)	1 (09)	—	2 (18)	1 (09)	—	—	1 (09)	1 (09)

[a] Numbers within parentheses are percentages of totals within rows, rounded to the nearest whole number. See this note in Table 19.

suggests that the salient Congress factions in the Council at this time
were Nai Duniya, Khadiwala, and INTUC. This requires qualifica-
tion. Kanhaiyalal Khadiwala was interested in controlling the Congress party organization, particularly on the district and state levels,
and to some extent at the city level. He was personally indifferent to
municipal politics, apparently because the control of the municipality
was not really crucial to determining group control of the City Congress organization and had no measurable effect on the rural sections
of the District Congress organization. He did not as a rule try to make
the supporters of his faction act as a cohesive unit within the Council.
At the same time, the supporters of the Nai Duniya faction did not
act entirely as a cohesive group either. Thus the Council's factions
were, for a time, intramural and distinct from the city-wide factions
described in Chapter 4. The tables are, however, still important at
later stages to show the increasing concern at higher levels of politics
with the municipal government, for a crystallization of these city-wide
and state-wide factions within municipal politics did eventually occur.[9]

Municipal politics between 1950 and 1955 consisted of two inter-
twining patterns of competition. The first pattern was primarily intramural, within the Council itself. Structurally, it consisted of a
rivalry between three Congress personalities and their separate followings. As "personal followings," these three groups included non-
Congress Councillors and were comparatively fluid and unstable in
their memberships.[10] They did not correspond directly to the historic
Congress factions—Nai Duniya, Khadiwala, and INTUC. As a matter
of fact, two of the personalities, V. V. Sarvate and Laxman Singh

---

[9] It is noteworthy that the government nominees were weighted in favor of
the Nai Duniya group; 5 openly identified with the faction (B. M. Bhandari,
Gopaldas Jhalani, Fakkuruddin, Malini Harmalkar, and Hirabai Bordiya), and
2 known to be sympathetic to the Hindu Mahasabha (S. D. Mulye and V. G.
Apte) probably tacitly supported the Nai Duniya group. Furthermore, G. R. Dighe
and Tarashankar Pathak, though reputedly neutral, seemed to have leaned toward
the Nai Duniya group and are so counted in Tables 20 and 22. The Khadiwala
group, by contrast, received support from only 2 government nominees, as did the
INTUC group. The distribution of government nominees in the Council reflected
the weight of respective factions on the Indore delegation in the Madhya Bharat
Legislative Assembly. The Khadiwala group had only 3 members (V. S. Khode,
Sajjansingh Vishnar, Nandlal Joshi) against 6 from the Nai Duniya group and 2
from INTUC.
[10] Memberships are documented in my "Area, Power and Linkage in Indore," p.
263.

Chauhan, belonged to the Nai Duniya faction, and the third leader, Tarashankar Pathak, was sympathetic to the same faction, though formally neutral. The stakes of competition among these groups were the elected municipal offices and concomitant statuses, and the routine exploitation of the substantive powers of the municipality. But because the municipal process is not entirely insulated from the rest of city politics, the triangular, personalist rivalry was subjected to broader organizational forces. The second pattern of competition was bipolar, between a Sarvate–Pathak middle-class coalition on one side and a Chauhan–INTUC–big business coalition on the other. The stakes in this second struggle concerned control of the City Congress organization and the expansion of municipal jurisdiction to embrace the labor area of the city. Sarvate and Pathak were structurally committed to a defense of the intramural status quo, while Chauhan sought to overturn it by expanding it in his search for allies; thus the two patterns of competition became interdependent.

Laxman Singh Chauhan (Rajput) was a protégé of the Jain component of the Nai Duniya group, supported by Babulal Patodi and Manoharsingh Mehta in the foreground and Labchand Chajlani, one of the proprietors of *Nai Duniya,* from behind the scenes. He was also patronized by B. M. Bhandari, one of the Jain industrialists and party financiers—a government nominee on this Council. Chauhan was of humble origins but with uncommon ability to rouse popular support. He was the key link between the lower-class citizens of the city and the Nai Duniya group, filling a role of mundane organizational and mass contact work that the Maharashtrian Brahmans and moneyed Jain businessmen were ill-suited to, if not incapable of performing. He had proved himself as an effective secondary-level leader in the political movements of protest against unrepresentative Holkar rule and the British Raj. Returned to the Municipal Council in 1950, he quickly became Sarvate's chief rival.[11]

V. V. Sarvate (Maharashtrian Brahman) had far higher social status than Chauhan. Sarvate's father had been the outstanding leader of the Praja Mandal, and V. V. Sarvate himself had not only been on the Holkar Legislative Council of 1947 but was currently a member of

[11] Underlying his contest for municipal control, there may also have been a Jain interest in reducing Maharashtrian Brahman influence in the local Congress party.

the Madhya Bharat Assembly, and he was a veteran of municipal politics from 1945. Having worked together and developed a personal friendship with Tarashankar Pathak (Malwi Brahman) on the previous Council, it was possible for Sarvate and Pathak to form an alliance of their two groups, with the support at this time of the INTUC group and some of the Independents, to dominate the Council. Their success is indicated by the fact that for the next two years the two leaders alternated in the positions of President and Chairman of the Standing Committee, monopolizing the two most powerful positions. Only the Vice Presidency as a consolation prize was left to a Chauhan supporter, Pukhraj Bahen. Jhumerlal Verma, a clerical employee in the Kalyanmal Mills and a member of the INTUC group (who usually supported Pathak or Sarvate), was given the key patronage post of Chairman of the Public Works Committee.[12]

In the general election of 1952, V. V. Sarvate was the only sitting Municipal Councillor in Indore to be returned as an MLA. He became the Deputy Speaker of the Assembly, and this new responsibility combined with committee work in the Assembly caused him to be absent more frequently from Indore and diluted his guardianship of municipal affairs. In the same year, V. V. Dravid became the Minister for Labour and Local Self-Government in the Madhya Bharat Cabinet and began to exercise a more deliberate influence in municipal affairs. His objective at this time was to consolidate INTUC power in the labor area following the Malwa Mill disturbances of 1950.[13]

One of the chief instruments for Dravid's purpose was an organizational innovation known as the *Mohalla Sudhar Samiti* (mohalla improvement committee) network formed under the supervision of Ramsingh Verma. This committee network was organized as a parallel City Congress party organizational substructure and served to enlist the support necessary to capture control of the party's decision-making superstructure. It served also to establish INTUC factional dominance

----

[12] This position was of more than casual importance to him because in the early 1950's the Improvement Trust project of Jawaharmarg (west) was in progress, and the clearance and acquisition of land affected his ward of Deshwalipura. As is pointed out in Chapter 9 on the politics of improvement, the Public Works Committee of the municipal government has a potential delaying veto in the transfer of Trust schemes to municipal jurisdiction, and Verma was able to bring influence to bear on the manner in which his constituents were affected.

[13] These are described in Chapter 10 on the politics of the labor arena.

in the municipal government. Dravid and Ramsingh hoped to use the municipality as an instrument for INTUC constituency-building among the textile laborers, by having municipal funds spent on the physical improvement and maintenance of roads, bridges, drainage facilities, lighting, and water supplies in the labor area—much of which was not even within the municipal boundaries in 1952—and by providing secondary labor leaders with greater scope for political advancement in elected local offices and corresponding benefits. Dravid had sought to have the localities of Pardesipura and Nandanagar, in the labor area, incorporated in the municipality, but he initially encountered resistance within the Council. To offset this resistance from the Sarvate–Pathak coalition, the INTUC faction formed a counter-alliance with the Chauhan group. Laxman Singh Chauhan had earlier ties with the local Congress labor organization, the Indore Mill Mazdoor Sangh (IMMS), as well as with those big business leaders who tacitly supported the INTUC-affiliated IMMS as a counterweight to more radical unions.[14] As a result, within the municipal government, it was the Chauhan and INTUC groups in a coalition that supported Dravid's plan to have municipal limits expanded to include most of the labor area, a goal that was finally achieved late in 1954 prior to the next municipal election.[15]

The INTUC group first supported the Chauhan group in 1952, to shift the balance of power in the Council away from the Sarvate–Pathak partnership, and enabled Chauhan to become President of the Municipality and Chairman of the Appeals Committee. He did not, however, immediately dominate the municipal government. The Sarvate–Pathak coalition retained enough support in the Council to control the Standing Committee (the linchpin in the municipal legislative process), to get one of their men into the Vice Presidency, and to keep a majority in the Public Works Committee. But in 1953 the Chauhan–INTUC coalition became stronger, attracting the support

---

[14] The Jain element of the Nai Duniya group cooperated very closely with V. V. Dravid and the INTUC group in the early post-merger years, continuing the close association that had developed between the Praja Mandal and the IMMS between 1941 and 1948. The Nai Duniya group hoped to use growing INTUC strength to cancel out the influence of the Khadiwala group, and they did not foresee that INTUC could challenge the Nai Duniya group itself in the commercial heart of the city.

[15] Other details are given in Chapter 9 on the politics of improvement.

of Independents, and Chauhan was reelected President. The Chauhan–INTUC coalition finally succeeded in getting the Vice-Presidency filled with an INTUC man for the first time in municipal history, and gained control of the Public Works Committee under the Chairmanship of D. S. Patil, another INTUC man.[16]

In 1954 and 1955, first Sarvate and then Pathak again became President of the municipality, but Chauhan gained the key Chairmanship of the Standing Committee. With a majority of his group supporters on the Standing Committee for the remaining life of the Council, Chauhan was able to lead the municipal government in the direction of enacting Dravid's policy of extending municipal limits to include most of the labor area. The Vice-Presidency also remained in the hands of INTUC group members, Jal D. Patel and D. S. Patil. Thus, the emergent Chauhan–INTUC coalition gained supremacy and helped lay the stage for dominance by INTUC Councillors of the succeeding Council and for the state-level policy initiatives of the Labour Minister, V. V. Dravid.

While the main struggles and stakes in the 1950 Council were factional, there were also numerous particularistic aspects of municipal politics stemming from the individual interests and special constituency linkages of Councillors. Some of the more important are mentioned here to help explain why there is such a high degree of competition for seats in so impotent a local government. The representation of minority communities on the Council is one important type of special constituency linkage. The representation of Sindhis, Bohras, and scheduled castes was obtained in 1950 by the method of government nomination. Sindhi refugees in Indore posed a problem for the municipality after 1947, because of their needs for housing and occupational opportunities, but they were not sufficiently concentrated in 1950 to elect a Councillor from among their own ranks. Ram Gidwani was appointed on their behalf, and he did press in the Council for assistance to this special group. Sarvate and Pathak both extended their cooperation to Gidwani. As the Shops and Establishments Act was administered under the municipal government until 1954, Sarvate was able to bend municipal by-laws that restricted

---

[16] The same year Patil was elected by the Council to the Improvement Trust, where he served as a Trustee and an agent of Dravid and INTUC for the next seven years.

the setting up of *gumtis* (small shops or stands) on the edge of main thoroughfares, helping to ameliorate the plight of the numerous Sindhis who had set up makeshift shops along Topkhana and other city streets in an effort to reestablish themselves in small businesses. The Bohras, too, many of whom were shopkeepers, were interested in the administration of the Shops and Establishments Act, and Fakkuruddin, also a supporter of Sarvate, was nominated to represent them.[17]

The two Gohar brothers, Gopikrishnan and Balkrishnan, were nominated to the Council to give some representation to the scheduled castes. As Councillors they also represented the Harijan sanitation employees of the municipality. With Gopikrishnan's support, Chauhan also developed ties with the sanitation workers and encouraged their unionization. Leadership of the sanitation workers was a personal asset to Chauhan in that it reinforced his ties with Ramsingh Verma and other INTUC leaders who came to regard Chauhan as one of their key labor vote mobilizers in the city outside the labor area. The threat of a strike of sanitation workers was a weapon that Chauhan used to good effect after 1958, maintaining a strong influence in municipal politics and administration even when officially out of power in the Corporation.

The Gujarati merchant community was among the smaller minority groups, but effectively represented in the Congress party organization through Natwarlalbhai Shah and Kantilal Patel (both Presidents of the City Congress in the Madhya Bharat period) who were in a position to get themselves Congress municipal tickets. Kantilal Patel was himself a small businessman with part ownership of an iron and steel rolling plant in Indore. As a Chauhan supporter in 1954 and 1955, he was able to secure the Chairmanship of the Public Works Committee of the Municipality, a position that could be used to influence the Improvement Trust on questions affecting Gujarati merchant interests in the Siaganj portion of the Jawaharmarg scheme. (Natwarlal Shah was nominated as a Trustee in 1955, and took up where Patel left off in this role of community representation.)

---

[17] Sarvate's influence in the regulation of shops was facilitated by the fact that D. V. Jhokarkar, a protégé of his in the municipal administration, was in charge of the Shops and Establishments section until 1952, when he was made Assessment Officer and then Assistant Revenue Officer in the Revenue section.

The Public Works Chairmanship may also have been used by Patel to develop ties with contractors and municipal engineers who could reciprocate by patronizing the products from Patel's steel plant.

Reference is made later to the role of INTUC and Gujarati Councillors on the Improvement Trust.[18] Election from the Council was one of the routes to becoming a Trustee, a position of considerable status in the city and a channel of influence for represented interests. Madhavrao Khutal, a veteran of municipal politics from the previous Council, had his own housing interests to protect from the Trust's Jawaharmarg scheme.[19] The owner of considerable property in Indore, he was personally interested in the value at which his buildings were assessed for property tax purposes. Khutal is also a recognized representative of his community of Marathas, and Dhangars as well, and his role is fulfilled in this respect by assisting his community fellows in obtaining municipal employment.

B. M. Bhandari and Gopaldas Jhalani represented the interests of the local textile industry on the Council, for which their support to Chauhan and the INTUC group was instrumental. Laxman Singh Chauhan, without other regular sources of income, was at one time or another on the payroll of Bhandari. Another Councillor, Babulal Malu, was even more openly a client of Bhandari, a regular clerical employee in the Bhandari Mills as well as his *gumashta,* or household affairs manager. Babulal Malu devoted his attention in the municipality mainly to the Revenue Office under which *octroi* was collected. Bhandari and Jhalani were interested in reducing the impact of *octroi* on the raw materials and machinery that they (or the interests they represented) imported in large quantities into the city. Their allies in this respect were L. S. Chauhan and Babulal Malu, in close association with Murlidhar Chauhan of the Revenue section.

Though the powers of the municipal government are narrow in scope, they nevertheless impinge in various ways on the interests of social minorities, shopkeepers and small businessmen, urban property-holders, lower caste laborers, construction contractors, and even, on occasion, big businessmen. A substantial number of the Councillors are elected from or nominated on behalf of these special interests and serve them as agents in the municipality, overseeing and tempering

---

[18] See Chapter 9 on Improvement Trust politics.
[19] Khutal was a member of the Public Works Committee in 1954 and 1955.

the application of administrative rules. The stakes, though seldom impressive and only rarely converted into general policy issues, are still of compelling importance to particular individuals and groups in the city. They help keep the municipal political process competitive and prevent it from sinking into the obscurity of monotonous routine between elections.

Labor Seizure of Power in Municipal Politics, 1955–1957

The major transformation in municipal politics stemming from the 1955 election was the takeover of the Council by the INTUC organization. The INTUC faction had laid their foundation for the coup well, using the *Mohalla Sudhar* Committees to capture control of the City Congress and using their influence with Laxman Singh Chauhan to get an enlargement of municipal boundaries. Dravid and Ramsingh Verma, assisted by Gangaram Tiwari and Mathuralal Sharma, built up a labor organizational nucleus in every *mohalla* independently of the regular Congress organization. The *Mohalla Sudhar* Committees were organized by IMMS members or employees living in each *mohalla*. By registering primary members of the Congress party in sufficient numbers, they succeeded in dominating many of the *Mandal* Committees, and then in electing a majority of the City Congress Committee. As a consequence, in the 1955 municipal election a majority of tickets went either to actual IMMS members or employees or to INTUC sympathizers. The existence of the *Mohalla* Committee network provided the INTUC leaders assurance that they could get most of their nominees elected.

The second factor accounting for INTUC supremacy was the incorporation within municipal boundaries of the labor area, together with a reapportionment and enlargement of the number of wards. Altogether the number of municipal seats was raised from 34 to 50. Nearly one-third of the 16 new seats went directly to labor. In 1950, that portion of the mill area inside city limits fell within a single ward (number one). In 1955, however, the same area plus the newly incorporated labor areas of Pardesipura and Nandanagar were divided among four wards, two of which became double-member constituencies—thereby increasing the number of representatives from the northeast labor sector from 1 to 6 between one election and the next. While the central city area received 11 new seats as well, the six-fold enlargement of direct labor representation implied a substantial potential shift in the group balance of power in the Municipal Council.

Besides increasing the number of labor area seats and dominating the nominations of Congress candidates, INTUC had acquired one other significant weapon in its armory. Again it was the Labour Minister, V. V. Dravid, operating at the state level, who played the key role. The supervision and regulation of shops and hotels under the Shops and Establishments Act was transferred in 1954 from the jurisdiction of the municipal government to that of the Labour Department. The Labour Commissioner and one of his subordinates were put in charge of licensing and regulation. The rationale, of course, was that it was logical to bring the administration of the Act under labor authorities. But the move was as much political as it was a rationalization of authority. To begin with, it was entirely in keeping with the general pattern by which the state government and state-level politicians (including those elected from Indore itself) have progressively pruned away the powers and functions of the municipal government and grafted them onto administrative structures more directly accountable to the state government. The consequence has been to deprive strictly municipal politicians of opportunities to build effective constituency supports within such functional areas, supports that are indispensable for the effective determination and implementation of policy in areas remaining under municipal control.

The other side of the coin is that the separated powers or jurisdictions have been placed under the control of bureaucrats who are not formally responsible to city politicians or local representatives of the constituency concerned.[20] Instead, the bureaucrats are responsible to state-level politicians, and especially the Minister or Ministers in charge of their departments. The bureaucrats in charge of a given functional constituency are induced by the structure of the situation to build their own informal linkages of support and influence among those being regulated and thereby compete, albeit unconsciously, with local politicians and with the municipal government itself—tending to weaken the municipal government progressively. The effect on the

---

[20] As far as Indore was concerned in this period, an Indore man was Minister in control of the Labour Department—a man to whom shopkeepers had informal access, so their interests could still be represented through nonbureaucratic channels. But this remained true only as long as an Indore man held the position, and the relationship did not necessarily hold for shopkeepers in other cities.

competition for power is to make capture of the state-level positions, above the department concerned, the crucial objective—reinforcing the vertical linkages through the bureaucratic chain of command and furthering state political integration.

In the immediate political circumstances, the effect of the transfer of the Shops and Establishments jurisdiction to the Labour Department was to provide the local INTUC leaders with an additional instrument to penetrate the shopkeeper constituency, giving them new opportunities to attract a nucleus of middle-class allies in the commercial areas of the city and to use these allies to help them capture control of the municipal arena. A manifestation of this influence was the distribution of municipal election tickets to shopkeepers or representatives of shop-owners in wards where the distribution of labor population was too small to be able to expect a laborer to win the election, or where middle-class IMMS leaders had no other effective base. In this way, middle-class businessmen such as Santramdas and Balchandra Gokhale were given Congress tickets and INTUC support in their elections, and Kurshid Hassan Khan was nominated to the Council later through INTUC influence. Each supported the INTUC group on the Council.

The main INTUC effort in the city, however, was pressed through white-collar employees of the IMMS and mill-workers (clerical and labor) in wards that were at least partially middle-class. Middle-class IMMS leaders who won their elections are exemplified by Mathuralal Sharma, Ratanlal Vyas, Ishwardatt Mishra, Chhaganlal Katariya, and Ishwar Chand Jain. Similarly, Chandmal Gupta, Vijaysingh Chauhan, Rameshwarsingh Kushwah, and Ratansingh Yadav are examples of mill-workers who won election from wards with significant proportions of middle-class voters. The INTUC group also helped secure tickets for professional middle-class allies such as Nirmalarani Potdar, Dr. Surjikishan Kaul, and Madhavrao Bingle, among others.

The outcome of the 1955 municipal election was that, out of 31 Congress candidates returned, 16 were actual members or employees of the IMMS and 3 were dependent for their nominations and electoral success on INTUC efforts, for a total of 19 firm INTUC supporters. This left only 12 others, who were divided in their primary factional loyalties between the Nai Duniya or Khadiwala groups. There were but 6 Nai Duniya and 5 Khadiwala group elected Coun-

cillors, with the formally neutral (but pro-INTUC) Bhanudas Shah
making the twelfth. (See Table 23.) Even among those in the Nai
Duniya or Khadiwala groups, there were 7 elected Councillors who
were allied with or generally supported the INTUC group on the
Council. The actual INTUC group of 19 combined with their 7 non-
INTUC allies, for a total of 26 elected members, was by itself sufficient to dominate the Council. But the INTUC group was further
strengthened by a government nomination of 2 more firm supporters
(Laxman Dafal and Ramsevak Mama) and 2 allies (Gopaldas Jhalani
and Kurshid Hassan Khan), bringing the operative INTUC-dominated
coalition in the Council up to 30.[21] The strength of the real opposition was only 6, including one nominated member, and there were 4
Independents. Among the Independents, Madanlal Rawal was actually
a supporter of the Nai Duniya group and Khemraj Joshi a supporter
of the Khadiwala group. The final strength of Congress and pro-
Congress Independents, therefore, was 42 out of a total of 50 Council
members.

The information on the Council's social and occupational composition by party and Congress faction reveals striking changes (see
Tables 19–22). The most obvious are the greatly increased proportions
of lower-caste and labor-class representatives, most of whom fall into
the category of INTUC faction supporters. Between 1950 and 1955,
there was a tripling of scheduled castes, raising their Council proportion to 12 percent, an equitable level reflecting their proportion in
the urban community. In addition, the category of "Other" in Tables
21 and 22 conceals the entry of other lower castes, particularly Ahirs,
of whom 5 were added to the Council (all but one by election). With
respect to labor, both "clerical" and "mill operatives," the proportion
was more than doubled from the 15 percent level of 1950 to the 36
percent level of 1955; more than one-third of the Council was composed of members employed in the Indore textile mills. Of the 15
Congress (INTUC) Councillors employed in the mill area, 5 were
white-collar or clerical in occupation, employed either by the mills

---

[21] The addition of Devilal Yadav in 1957, following the death of Bhanudas Shah,
raised the number to 31. In Tables 20 and 22, the figure for the INTUC faction in
the Council of 1955 is given as 22, which includes elected and aldermanic members
of the faction but excludes the pro-INTUC members of other Congress factions.
Thus the INTUC-dominated coalition in the Council is larger than the faction as
such.

TABLE 23. FACTIONAL AFFILIATION: MUNICIPAL COUNCIL, 1955–1957

Nai Duniya	Khadiwala	INTUC	Opposition	Independents
Babulal Patodi	Vimalchander Jhanjhariya	Ishwar Chand Jain (IM)	Dattatriya Vaidya (NM, CPI)	Balkrishnan Gohar
Fakkuruddin	Kantilal Patel	Mathuralal Sharma (IM)	Munnilal (NM, CPI)	Madanlal Rawal (ND)
L. S. Chauhan (I)	Nirmalarani Potdar (I)	ChhaganlalKatariya (IM)	Harisingh (CPI)	Tulsiram Uike
M. R. Khutal (I)	Shrikrishan Khandelwal (I)	Surjikishan Kaul (IM)	Vasudevrao Lokhande (JS)	Khemraj Joshi (K)
Babulal Malu (I)	Kishanlal Chandele (I)	Girjanandan Saksena (IM)	Narayansingh Albela (HMS)	
S .G. Dube (I)		Kanhaiyalal Yadav (IM)		
		Ratanlal Vyas (IM)		
		Ishwardatt Mishra (IM)		
		Morulal Yadav (IM)		
Bhanudas Shah[a] ⟶		Ratansingh Yadav (IM)		
		Gangaram Master (IM)		
		Abdul Rup Nishtar (IM)		
		Gopikrishnan Gohar (IM)		
		Chandmal Gupta (IM)		
		Rameshwarsingh Kushwah (IM)		
		Vijaysingh Chauhan (IM)		
		Devilal Yadav (IM)[a]		
		Santramdas		
		Balchandra Gokhale		
		M. R. Bingle		

(A) Gopaldas Jhalani (I)
(A) Kurshid Hassan Khan (I)
(A) Shalini Moghe   (A) Hastimal Jain   (A) Ratanprabha Dhanda
(A) Hirabai Bordiya   (A) Pukhraj Bahen (A) (A) Ramsevak Mama (IM)
                                                   Laxman Dafal   (A) S. D. Mulye (HMS)

(I)   = Allies of the INTUC group.
(A)   = Alderman.
(IM)   = Actual IMMS members or employees.
(NM)   = Nagrik Morcha.
(CPI) = Communist Party of India.
(HMS) = Hindu Mahasabha.
(JS)   = Jan Sangh.
(K)   = Khadiwala group sympathizer.
(ND)   = Nai Duniya group sympathizer.
a Bhanudas Shah died in 1957 and was replaced by Devilal Yadav.

or as officials in the IMMS organization. Nearly half (47 percent) of the INTUC faction membership in the Council was of high-caste background, primarily Hindi-speaking Brahmans or Jain and Hindu Baniyas.

There was thus both a broadening of the caste and community base of the Council—a reaching down into lower social strata—and an increase in the working-class composition of the Council, changes which to a large extent overlapped. They resulted from the penetration by the INTUC faction of the municipal arena, and of the City Congress too. While this INTUC drive was sponsored by Hindi-speaking Brahman and Jain (high-caste) elites, their mobilization of lower-class and caste supporters harbored the potential for changing both the balance between the elites, where a putative tension existed, and the balance between the elites and their clienteles. Thus municipal electoral recruitment in Indore reflects a traditional democratic dynamic of competitive support-building efforts leading to broadened access and the entry of new participants.

A second noticeable pattern is the exclusion of Maharashtrian Brahmans from the municipal Congress party in this election, the apparent victim of the INTUC monopoly and the declining Holkar leverage over nominations. Just ten years before, Maharashtrian Brahmans held nearly 40 percent of the municipal seats, but their proportion dropped to 18 percent in 1950 and then to 10 percent in 1955, finally bringing them into line with their distribution in the city's population. Of the 5 Maharashtrian Brahmans on the 1955 Council, 4 were elected, but only one of these (Balchandra Gokhale) was in Congress, and even he was clearly an INTUC faction protégé. The 3 others elected were members of the opposition parties, indicating the declining hold of members of this community on the Congress party and their gravitation toward the conservative Jan Sangh party.

The Council was actually short-lived, extending from July 28, 1955 to October 1957, a period of a little over two years. The interruption came as a result of two almost simultaneous changes, the transition from Madhya Bharat to the new Madhya Pradesh on November 1, 1956, and the translation of the Indore "Municipality" into the Indore Municipal Corporation by legislation passed at the end of the final Madhya Bharat Legislative Assembly session. The Act provided that the sitting Council would continue as the Corporation

Council for one year, after which fresh elections would be held. The District Collector (Narayan Singh) was appointed the Administrator, and the Council was dissolved in October 1957. Meanwhile, election preparations were made by bureaucratic authorities and held in March 1958.

The election of officers in July 1955 resulted in the selection of Babulal Patodi (Nai Duniya) as President, Ishwar Chand Jain (INTUC) as Chairman of the Standing Committee, and Nirmalarani Potdar (Khadiwala) as Vice-President. In this way, each major Congress faction was represented at the apex. Patodi, a Jain cloth merchant soon to become an MLA, was on good terms with Ishwar Chand Jain and Chhaganlal Katariya, the key Jain leaders of the INTUC group. But the main committees, the Standing, Appeal, and Public Works committees, were each clearly dominated, if not monopolized, by INTUC group members or sympathizers. In the next election of officers, in March 1956, the Nai Duniya group was denied any of the three positions. Ishwar Chand Jain (INTUC) himself became President, Mathuralal Sharma (INTUC) became Chairman of the Standing Committee, and Mrs. Potdar (Khadiwala) was reelected Vice-President. Each retained his position through the transition to a Corporation, with I. C. Jain and Mrs. Potdar being elected the first Mayor and Deputy-Mayor of Indore respectively. The key committees also remained under INTUC control, with Chhaganlal Katariya the Chairman of the Public Works Committee.

The period of 1955 to 1957 was a golden one for the INTUC organization in Indore as a whole. The control of the municipality was used to supplement development and construction, which were in full swing in the labor area with funds from various sources: IMMS membership dues; the funds of associated INTUC-controlled labor organizations for young men, women, and special purposes; and money from the state and central governments, particularly for the development of housing. There were ambitious projects to clear slums such as that of Bhindiko, the development of Nandanagar and Nehrunagar labor housing colonies, and the construction of the imposing IMMS headquarters, Shram Shivir. In this overall picture, municipal resources added a comparatively small but still significant amount. The rising municipal expenditures for the labor areas were concealed under the budgetary heads of "Other Purposes Grants" and "Public

Works Department," but as Table 24 shows, expenditures under "Other Purposes Grants" almost tripled between 1952–53 and 1955–56, rising from 96,675 rupees to 277,025 in the first year of the INTUC-dominated Council; the figure continued upward to 295,075 for the following year. The increase was not only absolute but also proportional: in 1952–53 the figure was about 2.7 percent of total budgetary expenditures; by 1956–57 it had increased to nearly 5 percent of the total. The proportion of PWD expenditures remained about 24 percent, but the absolute amount increased from 863,683 to 1,531,372 rupees. About 80 percent of PWD expenditures were on construction and maintenance of public works in this period.

TABLE 24. SUMMARY EXPENDITURES OF MUNICIPAL BUDGET, 1952–1958

	1952–53	1954–55	1955–56	1956–57	1957–58
Other Purposes Grants	96,675	241,925	277,025	295,075	295,825
PWD Total Expenditures	863,683	899,290	989,716	1,317,650	1,531,372
Total Budget Expenditure	3,517,400	4,038,257	4,132,277	5,544,800	6,183,900

SOURCE: Summaries in the printed *Statements of the Budget*, 1952–53, 1955–56, Indore: the Municipal Corporation Office.

Most of the funds under "Other Purposes Grants" were designated for the improvement of slum areas. Under the previous Council dominated by Sarvate, Pathak, and Chauhan, most of these funds as a matter of practice had been used in slum areas within the city, with little concern whether they were labor settlements or not. The slum improvement funds were divided among different wards and the representative of the ward had considerable influence over the manner in which the money was used in his ward. As the labor area outside the city originally all fell into a single ward, the division of funds was unsatisfactory to the labor group. The balance may have shifted slightly when the Chauhan–INTUC coalition dominated the Council from 1953, but a major shift took place in 1955 and 1956 when the INTUC group captured virtually complete control of the Council. A substantial share of the slum improvement funds was now channeled into the labor area or into the newly added INTUC-controlled wards where there were pools of labor voters. The PWD expenditures were also increased dramatically, by over 90,000 rupees between 1954 and 1955, by nearly 330,000 rupees the next year, and by another 210,000 in the final year of this Council. A substantial proportion of these new expenditures also went into the improvement of the labor area, into roads, drainage channels, bridges, lighting, water sources, and parks. Even so, municipal expenditures were supplementary to the main resources that were distributed through other labor channels. Control of the municipality was only one of many political objectives of the INTUC leadership, and far from the most important. Yet it was useful also as a means of providing individual secondary leaders with positions of status and minor powers, reinforcing the effects of patronage obtained from other sources.

The INTUC group in this period benefited from municipal administrative constituencies as the Nai Duniya group had in the previous Council, revealing a degree of factionalism among municipal bureaucrats. From before 1948 and up to 1955 the Municipal Commissioner had been a Holkar officer with a rank equivalent to that of a present-day Revenue or Divisional Commissioner. After 1948, Commissioners K. M. Bapna (until 1950) and Hanumant Rao (until 1955), both former Holkar officers, cooperated with the Nai Duniya group leaders on the Council. Before 1954 the Municipal Commissioner was appointed with the consent of the Council, and Hanumant Rao had been appointed accordingly. But the Madhya Bharat Municipalities Act of 1954 permitted an officer of lesser rank, equivalent to that of Collector, to be appointed as Municipal Commissioner. When Hanumant Rao was transferred after a normal term of about five years, he was not replaced immediately by a state official. Instead, in October 1955, G. S. Ghatpande, the chief Municipal Engineer, was made Acting Commissioner, and S. V. Dravid, the First Assistant Engineer—and the brother of the Labour Minister—was moved up to be the Acting Municipal Engineer (in charge of Public Works). This move was designed to put the entire municipal administration as well as the Public Works Department under the real control of the INTUC group and to facilitate the implementation of their development plans in labor constituencies.[22] While Ghatpande had worked closely with

[22] V. V. Dravid was not only Minister of Labour but from 1954 to 1957 also held the portfolios of Housing and Public Health (Engineering) and, from 1954 to 1956, the portfolio of Town Improvement.

the Nai Duniya group, he was not averse to working now for the INTUC group. I. C. Jain, Mathuralal Sharma, and Chhaganlal Katariya, therefore, did not have to contend with any serious bureaucratic obstruction to their projects at any level.

The Council of 1955–57 was important in visible construction projects, not only in the labor areas but also elsewhere within the city. The swimming pool in Nehru Park, an expensive item which had been initiated under the auspices of the previous Council, was completed between 1956 and 1957, and the building of a city stadium for sports, particularly wrestling and Indian games such as *kabadi* and *kho kho*, was begun about the same time. The Council received a large sum from the state government, ostensibly for the convenience of travelers going to the *Simhasta Mela* (religious festival) in Ujjain, but actually for use in preparations for the plenary session of the Congress party held in January 1957 in Indore. Some of this money was used to resurface roads; to build a new route from Laxmibainagar market area to the convention area on the other side of the city; to establish a better connection with the Dhar and Bombay–Agra road for trucks; and to erect a new series of mercury streetlights. As the *Indore Samachar* described it then, "the city was dressed and decorated as if for the reception of a bridegroom," alluding to the impending Congress session. The expenditures helped to temporarily mute factional controversies in the city.

Opposition Seizure of Power and Indirect Rule by Congress in Municipal Politics, 1958–1965[23]

Prior to the municipal elections of February 1958, a number of major changes affecting Indore had taken place. The state of Madhya Bharat had been merged into the new state of Madhya Pradesh, adding the regions of Bhopal, Vindhya Pradesh, Mahakoshal, and Chhattisgarh. The effect on Indore was to dilute the influence of Indore's leading politicians and the bureaucrats of Holkar state origin in the reconstituted government.[24] Furthermore, the addition of Mahakoshal strengthened the Hindi-speaking Brahman (Khadiwala) faction of the

---

[23] The normal term would have terminated in 1962, but the term was extended to the beginning of 1965, ostensibly because of the border problems with China and the national emergency that was declared in October 1962.

[24] See Chapter 5, pp. 123ff.

Madhya Bharat region by bringing it into a supportive alliance with the Kanyakubja Brahman (Shukla) faction of Jabalpur and Raipur. In the general election of 1957 it was Khadiwala himself who ran from the Lok Sabha seat of Indore.

The Khadiwala faction in Indore had also been strengthened somewhat in January 1957 by the holding of the Annual Session of the All-India Congress Party in the city. Khadiwala and Babulal Patodi cooperated to arrange that session, and to some extent the rivalry of the Nai Duniya and Khadiwala groups was subdued. In fact, in 1957 and 1958 the Nai Duniya and Khadiwala factions formed a mutual alliance against the INTUC group and succeeded in reducing the influence of INTUC in the city and the City Congress party. This left a split between the labor leaders and city leaders of the local Congress party that weakened its total electoral effort and gave an opportunity to the municipal opposition in 1958.

The effectiveness of a united opposition against the Congress MLA candidate (Gangaram Tiwari) in the labor seat in 1957, culminating in the victory of a Communist, Homi Daji, encouraged the opposition leaders in the municipal arena to concert their efforts in a united front against Congress nominees. The leftist labor leaders had already united in the Mazdoor Union under the Secretaryship of Prabhakar Adsule, providing an instrument for an electoral drive in the labor areas. For the rest of the city, a new organization was formed, the *Nagrik Samiti,* or Citizens' Committee, under which the municipal leaders of the Communist, Praja Socialist, Hindu Mahasabha, and Jan Sangh parties united together with a number of Independents, some of whom were Congress dissidents. Of the Independents, N. K. Shukla, Khemraj Joshi, Purshottam Vijay, and Baddulal were actually sympathizers with the Khadiwala faction of Congress but were running in opposition to Congress (usually Nai Duniya group nominees) to weaken the Nai Duniya group in the Corporation. In fact, the collaboration of these Congress dissidents was an important factor contributing to the success of the opposition drive to oust Congress in the election.

But the primary factors were that the factional warfare between the Nai Duniya–Khadiwala coalition and the INTUC group weakened the Congress effort while the opposition was, temporarily at least, united for the first time in a municipal campaign. The outcome

TABLE 25. MUNICIPAL ELECTION OUTCOMES, 1958

Congress Party			Nagrik Samiti Coalition				
Nai Duniya	Khadiwala	INTUC	Jan Sangh	Hindu Mahasabha	Commu- nist	Praja Socialist	Independ- ents
6	4	6	2	2	7	5	8
16			24				

was the sound defeat of Congress in the 1958 municipal election. Table 25 summarizes the partisan affiliations of the winners. Although a Congress nominee stood in each ward, only 16 won, while the *Nagrik Samiti* was able to return 24 candidates. The INTUC group, which had been so powerful on the previous Council, was reduced on this Council to only 6 members. The Nai Duniya–Khadiwala coalition had paid off in undermining INTUC candidates, but the intraparty rivalry also weakened the Nai Duniya and Khadiwala candidates so that as separate groups they did no better than the INTUC faction.[25]

Although the Congress party did poorly, the combined opposition parties barely matched Congress returns with 16 members. The other 8 members, or one third of the opposition, were Independents, and 5 of these Independents actually leaned toward one or another Congress faction. (See Tables 26 and 19–22 for the faction, caste, and occupational breakdown.) The Independents constituted a "soft" element in the opposition coalition by contrast with the relatively "hard" opposition of the non-Congress party members. The softness of the opposition provided the Congress members with opportunities to divide the opposition by playing one internal group off against another in the Council and by coopting Independents, so that after 1960 the Congress municipal party actually governed the Council and its committees indirectly.

---

[25] The damage to the Nai Duniya group was reflected specifically in the fact that its municipal arena leader, Laxman Singh Chauhan, was defeated in a prestige contest from Lodhipura, his home constituency, by Yugydutt Sharma. Sharma, the son of Lalaram Arya, was in part waging a personal contest to overthrow Chauhan, who had previously wrested electoral control of the ward from Sharma's family. Before 1950 Lalaram Arya had been regarded as a local boss or strong man of the Arya Samaj in the Lodhipura area, and Nai Duniya had used Chauhan to undermine his influence. This victory of Sharma reflected a restoration of the local power of Lalaram Arya's family and the corresponding erosion of Nai Duniya influence at the mohalla and ward level.

TABLE 26. FACTIONAL AFFILIATION: MUNICIPAL COUNCIL, 1958–1965

Nai Duniya	Khadiwala	INTUC	Jan Sangh and Hindu Mahasabha	Communist	Socialist	Independents
V. V. Sarvate	Shankerlal Joshi	S. N. Nagu	V. R. Lokhande (JS)	Harisingh	Prabhakar Adsule	P. Vijay (K)
Hiralal Dixit	Babulal Mittal	S. K. Kaul	Rajendra Dharkar (JS)	K. S. Meherunkar	Shersingh	N. K. Shukla (K)
Suresh Seth	Ramgopal Agarwal	Chandmal Gupta	Bhallerao Ingle (HM)	Abdul Quddus	Narendra Patodi	Yugydutt Sharma
M. R. Khutal	Ramchandra Verma	Vijaysingh Chauhan	S. N. Gupta (HM)	Kishanlal Chaudhuri	Ramprasad Manoharlal	Khemraj Joshi (K)
Kurshid Hassan Khan	(A) Babubhai Desai	Morulal Yadav		Durgadin Sukhram	Mannulal Sar	B. B. Purohit (ND)
C. W. B. David		Devilal Yadav		Ranchod Ranjan		J. Sethiya (N)
				Ramlal		Balkrishnan Gohar Baddulal (K)
	←—— (A) Tarashankar Pathak ——→					(A) R. N. Zutshi (ND)
(A) B. S. Bhandari						(A) Saraswatidevi Sharma (K)
(A) Vimala Jagdale						(A) A. L. Purohit
						(A) R. M. Bhandari (ND)
						(A) Khushiram Mulchand (K)
						(A) Sardar Jamitsingh (K)

(A) = Alderman, nominated by the government.
(ND) = Nai Duniya group sympathizer.
(JS) = Jan Sangh.
(K) = Khadiwala group sympathizer.
(N) = neutral.
(HM) = Hindu Mahasabha.

The electoral outcomes were not the final factor in determining the Council's composition. In 1958 the ten Aldermen were still to be appointed by the Congress-controlled state government—in which V. V. Dravid (INTUC) and Mishrilal Gangwal (neutral) were both Cabinet Ministers. Purshottam Vijay, the editor of *Indore Samachar* and a leader of the Independents in the *Nagrik Samiti* coalition, began a fast immediately after the election in support of a demand that the government pass an ordinance amending the provisions for selecting Aldermen to allow the elected Councillors to choose them. The existing procedure of government appointment of Aldermen could obviously be used to overcome the *Nagrik Samiti* elected majority and give the Congress municipal party a strength of 26, thereby in effect voiding the results of the popular election. The fast was partly successful in that a compromise was reached. The Aldermen were appointed by the government after all, but four of the Alderman-designates made a commitment to the *Nagrik Samiti* leadership that they would not vote against the *Nagrik Samiti* or upset its majority. If this commitment were kept and the constituent elements of the *Nagrik Samiti* held together, they could expect to govern in the Council. Consequently, Vijay gave up his fast and attention was then focused on the choice of a non-Congress Mayor.[26]

The question of the selection of the first opposition Mayor (or

---

[26] The selection of Aldermen added three members to the Nai Duniya group, one to the Khadiwala group, and one member (T. Pathak), who was neutral. Among the Independent Aldermen, two leaned toward the Nai Duniya group, three toward the Khadiwala group, and one individual (A. L. Purohit) was regarded as "a star without orbit." See Table 26 for the details.

The choice of Aldermen affected the social composition of the Council in a minor but interesting way. Two Kashmiri Brahmans, Dr. S. K. Kaul and Dr. S. N. Nagu, had been elected. Two of the Aldermen chosen were also Kashmiri Brahmans, Vimala (Kaul) Jagdale and R. N. Zutshi, giving a total of 4 Kashmiri Brahmans on a 50-member Council. This marked the most disproportionate representation of any single Indore community on the Council at any time, as there are only a dozen Kashmiri families in the city. Their strength was undoubtedly due in part to the fact that K. N. Katju was Chief Minister and Mushran was a leading figure in the Madhya Pradesh Congress Committee—both of them Kashmiri Brahmans.

Otherwise, the social breakdown of the Council membership reveals a few new significant patterns. Perhaps the most notable was the elimination of Congress Jain Councillors, until the selection of Aldermen. The decline of Maharashtrian Brahman membership in the municipal Congress party was confirmed. There was a tendency for Agarwal Baniyas to be clustered in the Khadiwala group. Pro-Khadiwala Independents tended to be Hindi-speaking Brahmans (N. K. Shukla, Khemraj Joshi, Saraswatidevi Sharma) or Khandelwal Baniya (P. Vijay). The trend seems to have been in the direction of social and occupational diversification of membership of the Council as a whole (see Tables 19–22).

President) was first decided in the 21-member Working Committee of the *Nagrik Samiti*—which included some extramunicipal members (Homi Daji, the Communist MLA, among others) but excluded some of the *Nagrik Samiti* Councillors and the pro-Congress Aldermen. Two names were put up, Purshottam Vijay (Independent conservative) and Prabhakar Adsule (Socialist). Vijay had become somewhat of a temporary hero because of his fast, and was supported by most of the Working Committee members. Adsule was sponsored by Homi Daji and only five or six leftist followers. (Some of the leftist members, K. S. Meherunkar and Shersingh in particular, did not support Adsule but gave their votes to Vijay instead.) Consequently, Vijay was nominated by the *Nagrik Samiti* in the Council and duly elected.

The *Nagrik Samiti* supported by the committed Independents established control of the Standing Committee and the Public Works Committee. As Table 27 shows, K. S. Meherunkar (Communist) and Sardar Shersingh (Socialist) were rewarded for their help in selecting the new Mayor by being appointed Chairmen of the Standing and Public Works committees respectively. Balkrishnan Gohar, a scheduled-caste Independent supporting the *Nagrik Samiti* in 1958, was made Deputy Mayor. For the first time in the Indore municipal arena in post-independence politics, the Congress party lost control of the elected Council, despite Congress rule at the state level, and the city opposition won control.

But opposition control of the Council was tenuous rather than firm because of its reliance on Independents and the agglomeration of opposition parties, and more symbolic than real in any case because of Congress bureaucratic control of the municipal administration as well as statutory control from the state level. The local Congress leadership took advantage of the underlying disputes and differences in the *Nagrik Samiti* to gradually undermine and eventually overthrow *Nagrik Samiti* control of the Council. Laxman Singh Chauhan, following his election defeat in Lodhipura, was made President of the City Congress in 1959, and from 1961, for six more years, he held the position of Secretary. He and V. V. Sarvate, the Leader of the Congress municipal party, and Hiralal Dixit, the acting Leader during Sarvate's prolonged absences to the Rajya Sabha, worked together to divide the opposition by playing one internal group off against another.

The internal differences within the *Nagrik Samiti* began to come

TABLE 27. OFFICERS OF THE MUNICIPAL CORPORATION, 1958–1964

Position	1958	1959	1960
Mayor	Purshottam Vijay (March–July 1958) Babubhai Desai (July 1958–March 1959)	Prabhakar Adsule (March 27–31, 1959) Balkrishnan Gohar (April 1, 1959– March 1960)	Sardar Shersingh
Chairman of Standing Committee	K. S. Meherunkar (Nagrik Samiti dominant)	Narendra Patodi (N. S. dominant)	Narendra Patodi (N. S. Chairman, Congress majority)
Deputy Mayor	Balkrishnan Gohar	Sardar Shersingh	R. N. Zutshi
Chairman of Public Works Committee	Sardar Shersingh (Nagrik Samiti dominant)	Bhallerao Ingle (N. S. dominant)	Bhallerao Ingle (N. S. dominant)
Municipal Commissioner	B. M. Joshi (to June 1959)	A. M. Kadam	Masood Quli Khan

out in the open almost immediately. As a Mayor, Purshottam Vijay made himself unpopular with some of the other Councillors by initiating a drive to reduce municipal expenditures for ceremonial purposes and to abolish the honoraria that Councillors receive for the occasions on which they sit in Council or Committee meetings.[27] As these expenditures form but a trivial part of the Corporation budget, and as the less affluent Councillors had meaningful stakes in them, it was not a shrewd move. Moreover, Councillors believed that Vijay's newspaper business was prospering partly as a result of municipal patronage,[28] implying that Vijay's austerity measures were more sym-

[27] Councillors and other citizens and guests occasionally enjoy good food at civic receptions at municipal expense. According to one informant, while Vijay was Mayor a reception for 250 people was held at which only "lemon water" was served, for a total expense of Rs. 17.

[28] *Indore Samachar* circulation had increased to about 12,000 in the election period as a result of a wave of anti-Congress lower-middle-class feeling, making Vijay's newspaper in a sense the most influential in the city. The circulation of

TABLE 27 (continued)

1961	1962	1963	1964
B. B. Purohit (pro-Congress Independent)	R. N. Zutshi (March–October 1952) N. K. Shukla (October 1962– March 1963)	N. K. Shukla	B. M. Bhandari
Saraswatidevi Sharma (Congress and Vijay groups)	B. B. Purohit (Congress majority)	M. R. Khutal (Congress majority and Vijay group)	M. R. Khutal (Congress majority and Vijay group)
Jagganath Sethiya	N. K. Shukla (March–October 1962) K. S. Meherunkar (October 1962– March 1963)	K. S. Meherunkar	K. S. Meherunkar
N.A.	N.A.	N.A.	N.A.
Masood Quli Khan	B. M. Joshi	B. M. Joshi	G. S. Ghatpande (to March 1965) S. C. Dube (from April 1965)

bolic than effectual. But the real source of tension stemmed from group differences.

Homi Daji, Prabhakar Adsule, and Harisingh (leftists) had hoped to be able to control Vijay, but he declined to become their instrument. Consequently in July 1958, when Vijay had served less than four months of his term as Mayor, Adsule led a "no confidence" motion against Vijay, and the motion received the support of just over

---

Nai Duniya, by comparison, was about 7,000 in the same period. Furthermore, *Indore Samachar* now received a larger share of Corporation advertisements, improving its financial base.

When Vijay's name was put up for Mayor, some Councillors raised questions about a conflict of interests. Ajitprasad Jain had been made chief editor of the paper, and Vijay's name was dropped from the masthead following the municipal election. His share of the ownership was registered in his wife's name and Naneria, his brother and the manager of the press, filed an affidavit in court stating that Vijay was a paid employee of the newspaper and not a share-owner in either the newspaper or Indore Printery where it was published. This removed legal barriers to Vijay's remaining a Councillor.

two-thirds of the Council. Vijay retained the support of pro-Khadiwala group Independents, of three out of four right-wing party members and of those leftists who had made his election possible in the first place, giving Vijay a total of 12 supporting votes. The motion to remove Vijay was supported by Congress party members, the Daji–Adsule group, Bhallerao Ingle (Hindu Mahasabha), and other Independents (including Yugydutt Sharma, who had previously supported Vijay), for a total of 34. (Four members were absent or abstained.) Purshottam Vijay was ousted from the Mayoralty and his group of 12 supporters was temporarily isolated in the Council, though their strength in committees was not substantially affected at this time.[29]

Babubhai Desai, an Alderman who was formally neutral but tacitly a supporter of the Congress (Khadiwala group), was then elected as Mayor to finish out Vijay's term. Desai was elected with the support of most of those who had cooperated to remove Vijay—that is, a coalition of the Congress Councillors, the Daji–Adsule group, and Independents who leaned either toward Congress or the leftist group. From the point of view of the Congress municipal leaders it was they who had toppled Vijay, but it was possible only because of the defection of the hard-core leftist, Daji–Adsule group from among Vijay's supporters. Once the *Nagrik Samiti* had been openly divided in this manner, however, it was difficult to put the pieces back together. There was no doubt that the initiative, if not the Council, had passed back into the hands of the Congress leaders within just months of the Council term's beginning.

When the mayoral election came up again in March 1959, the Socialist Adsule again briefly came into the foreground, much to his later embarrassment. Aspiring to become Mayor, he secured a promise of support from the municipal Congress leaders. But members of his own following, particularly Yugydutt Sharma, were prepared to support Adsule only if he wrote his resignation down on paper in advance and left it with the *Nagrik Samiti* Working Committee. This was a device to ensure that Adsule kept faith with his original supporters, revealing the deep-seated currents of distrust in the opposition. When Adsule had been Mayor for only five days, the *Nagrik Samiti* forwarded Adsule's resignation to the Corporation and he was

---

[29] K. S. Meherunkar, a Vijay supporter, remained Chairman of the Standing Committee.

forced to step down. The move was engineered by Yugydutt Sharma and the Vijay group in the *Nagrik Samiti*. For Vijay personally it was retaliation for the previous defection of the Adsule group.

In Adsule's place, the municipal Congress and the *Nagrik Samiti* finally agreed on Balkrishnan Gohar, an Independent. Gohar is a Harijan, although atypically he has a high level of education and a law degree. His election was almost historic. Had a Harijan Mayor not been elected in Bombay a few days before, Gohar would have been the first Harijan Mayor of a City Corporation in India. Congress support for Gohar was designed to help detach other scheduled-caste Councillors from their loyalty to the *Nagrik Samiti* and to further divide the opposition.

The other key positions in 1959 remained in the hands of *Nagrik Samiti* members. Narendra Patodi became Chairman of the Standing Committee, Sardar Shersingh Deputy Mayor, and Bhallerao Ingle Chairman of the Public Works Committee. But it was clear from the group loyalties of these Councillors, as well as the loyalties of most members selected for the two committees, that both the Adsule and Vijay groups had been shut out. Shersingh, though a Socialist, was personally antagonistic to Homi Daji and Adsule, and had also voted against Vijay. Narendra Patodi and Bhallerao Ingle also voted against Vijay and both tended to support Shersingh personally and to act as another small faction in the Council.

The following year (1960), the Shersingh group was continued in office with the support of Congress. Shersingh himself became Mayor, and his colleagues, Narendra Patodi and Bhallerao Ingle, retained their chairmanships of the Standing and Public Works committees for the second consecutive year. R. N. Zutshi, the Principal of Daly College and an Alderman who usually leaned toward the Congress Nai Duniya group, was elected Deputy Mayor. The Public Works Committee in 1960 still had a *Nagrik Samiti*, though anti-Vijay, majority, but the Standing Committee was clearly controlled by Congress Councillors who were in the majority. From 1960 to 1962 the Congress party indirectly controlled the Council and most of the important committees.

By the time of the mayoral election of March 1961, the *Nagrik Samiti* leadership had given up trying to maintain a united front against the Congress and they did not even propose a candidate. The

Congress put forward B. B. Purohit, an Independent with Congress leanings. The Vijay group supported Purohit too, in a deal through which Saraswatidevi Sharma became Chairman of the Standing Committee. The membership of the Standing Committee included K. S. Meherunkar and N. K. Shukla, who were also part of the Vijay group. The Congress by itself was one short of a majority on the Standing Committee, but the four Congress members could join with either the Vijay group members or with Shersingh and Narendra Patodi, the other two members, to form an operative majority. Shersingh and Patodi were not too deeply estranged from the Vijay group members to collaborate against Congress on the Committee. The position of Deputy Mayor went to Jaggannath Sethiya, an Independent and a genuine neutral.

The Congress party continued to balance off the Vijay and Shersingh groups in 1962, but to use them together to exclude the Adsule group almost entirely from Committee memberships. It was the extreme left-wing members, mainly those of the Communist party, who were out in the cold. In March 1962, R. N. Zutshi was elected Mayor, but he stepped down in October. N. K. Shukla of the Vijay group, who had been Deputy Mayor from March to October, was elected Mayor for the remainder of Zutshi's term. Meherunkar, who had been supporting Vijay, became the new Deputy Mayor. The Chairman of the Standing Committee throughout this year was B. B. Purohit, presiding over a committee in which the Congress held a clear majority.

In 1963, N. K. Shukla was reelected Mayor, but the Chairman of the Standing Committee then elected was explicitly a Congressman, M. R. Khutal. Khutal retained the Chairmanship the following year also, presiding over a Congress majority for two terms. In 1964, Congress control of the Council came directly into the open with the election of B. M. Bhandari as Mayor. In 1963 and 1964, K. S. Meherunkar of the Vijay group held the Deputy Mayorship. Between 1963 and 1964, members of the Vijay group, particularly N. K. Shukla and Vijay himself, were being drawn toward Congress. Vijay rejoined Congress in 1965 and Shukla followed in 1966, each giving as his rationale that they were impressed with the leadership of D. P. Mishra in the Madhya Pradesh Congress.

The *Nagrik Samiti* victory in the municipal election of 1958 was important in symbolic and psychological terms, especially for the combined leftist opposition, but it was a hollow victory as far as establishing effective control of the municipal government. The municipal administration was essentially a product of Holkar state and Congress party (especially Nai Duniya group) patronage, and as a permanent service it could not be significantly altered in the brief period of *Nagrik Samiti* control of the Standing Committee. Moreover, when the Corporation Act came into force it degraded the power of the Council in at least one important way. Under the municipalities statutes, the Municipal Commissioner was appointed with the approval of the Council, so that unfavorable administrators could be rejected by the elected body. The Corporation Act, by contrast, provided for government appointment of the Municipal Commissioner, without the limiting requirement of Council approval. The only remaining limitation was that the elected body, by a three-fourths vote, could remove an objectionable Commissioner. But the unstable group composition of the Council was likely in practical terms to prevent resort to this provision.

A few weeks before Purshottam Vijay became Mayor in March 1958, the Madhya Pradesh government (the Minister in charge of Local Self-Government was B. M. Mandloi, of the state-wide Hindi-speaking Brahman group) appointed B. M. Joshi Municipal Commissioner in Indore. Joshi's administrative career began with the personal patronage of Yeshwant Rao Holkar, who made Joshi his Private Secretary. When the Holkar government services were merged with Madhya Bharat, Joshi was one of those inducted at a high level into the larger state service, due to the former ruler's personal influence. B. M. Joshi maintained his personal standing with the Congress party politicians of Indore, particularly with Mishrilal Gangwal, who had equally good relationships with the Nai Duniya and Khadiwala groups.

When the new Madhya Pradesh was formed, B. M. Joshi was appointed Inspector-General of Municipalities (for the former Madhya Bharat area), a post with "Head of Department" status. From there he was transferred to the Indore Corporation executive post. As Municipal Commissioner he was a supporter of Congress party interests, equally hospitable to the various Congress factions but opposed to the *Nagrik Samiti* coalition, particularly the Daji–Adsule group. B. M.

Joshi was followed as Municipal Commissioner by A. M. Kadam (June 1959 to 1960) and Masood Quli Khan (1960–1962)—also a former Holkar civil servant in a mutually self-supporting relationship with Indore's leading Congress politicians[30]—and in 1962 B. M. Joshi himself was reappointed Municipal Commissioner for the duration of the Council term that expired early in 1965. B. M. Joshi and Masood Quli Khan were responsible for preserving Congress dominance in the composition and outputs of the municipal administration between 1958 and 1965, even when the Council and Standing Committee were under *Nagrik Samiti* control.

It is worth noting that B. P. Jhanjhariya was made Special Assistant to the Municipal Commissioner (B. M. Joshi) in 1958. Jhanjhariya is the brother of Pukhraj Bahen and Joharilal Jhanjhariya. While a Councillor in December 1954, Pukhraj Bahen had succeeded in getting her brother appointed as Assistant Municipal Pleader (in the legal advisory services of the municipality). Joharilal Jhanjhariya and Pukhraj Bahen had both been Jain supporters of the Ajmer Congress (Khadiwala) group in Indore from before 1948, and in 1958 Joharilal Jhanjhariya had become influential in the City Congress as a result of the new influence of his group on the state level under K. N. Katju, B. M. Mandloi, and others. In 1965, Joharilal became President of the City Congress. That his brother was working closely with B. M. Joshi as an advisor in this period draws attention to a specific personal and family linkage between the Municipal Commissioner and the City Congress, giving further support to the argument that the City Congress controlled the municipal administration even when Vijay was Mayor.

B. P. Jhanjhariya was later promoted to Municipal Pleader under the same Council. He thus became the chief legal advisor of the Corporation, giving him personally a certain amount of legal patronage, particularly where municipal property taxation was challenged by local property-owners either through petition or in the courts, and in interpretation of municipal by-laws regulating the construction or

---

[30] Masood Quli Khan, with the title Muntazim-i-Khas Bahadur Sahebzada, had been General Minister in the Holkar Cabinet in 1947, and became Commissioner for Customs and Excise (1948–51), Inspector-General of Municipalities (1954–55), and Director of Rural Development and Registrar of Cooperative Societies (1955–56) in the Madhya Bharat government. In the new Madhya Pradesh government he became Excise Commissioner (1957–60).

modification of buildings. He was in a position to safeguard the interests of his elder brother who owns the Alka Cinema and other buildings in the city, illustrating one of the particularistic benefits of municipal participation. B. P. Jhanjhariya recently left his administrative post for private practice, but he is still retained as a legal advisor of the Corporation and receives special fees. As a consequence, he has been able to expand his activity and income without entirely losing his influence or income in the Corporation.

It is frequently particularistic and personal interests that explain the motives and behavior of individuals who compete intensely for a seat on the Council, the position of Mayor, or the chairmanships of important committees. It has already been suggested, for example, that Purshottam Vijay was anxious to undercut the influence of the Congress Nai Duniya group in the city. In part this ambition derived from the intense business rivalry of the two leading newspapers. As part owner and the main editorial inspiration of the *Indore Samachar,* Vijay had made the paper not only influential politically but the first successful local paper in strictly business terms. By establishing his personal influence on the Corporation he hoped to weaken the financial base of his journalistic competitors, and in 1958 he had some measure of success.

It was later alleged in the 1965 municipal election by Yugydutt Sharma and Bhallerao Ingle, who were bitter over the Vijay group's tacit cooperation with the municipal Congress from 1961 to 1965, that Vijay had used his influence in the Council to avoid the full payment of *octroi*. In 1964 the Indore Printery imported into the city a rotary printing machine that had cost about 80,000 rupees. But it was contended that through forged invoicing or collaboration with the exporter the Indore Printery had only paid *octroi* duty on a stated value of 37,000 rupees. This unfavorable publicity undoubtedly played a part in Vijay's defeat in the Harsiddhi municipal contest in the 1965 election. Vijay promptly abandoned the opposition and rejoined the Congress party. The *Indore Samachar* also suffered for three years (1962–65) when, because of Vijay's personal unpopularity in the Council, enough support developed to blacklist the paper from municipal advertising.

The case illustrates the point that Vijay's aspirations to prominence in the Council also made him and his paper more vulnerable to the vicissitudes of politics or shifting group alliances, but this does not negate the fact that his interest in the Corporation related directly to his business. It rather shows that an entrepreneur whose business depends in part on government patronage is following a high-risk strategy when he seeks a public office as visible as is that of the Mayor. At the same time, part of the attraction of the office to Vijay must have been its status-building potential, for it should have been clear that his business interests could have been served equally well with less risk if he were satisfied with the less visible but potentially more powerful Chairmanship of the Standing Committee.

Mishra Group Penetration of Municipal Politics, 1965–1968

Ever since D. P. Mishra took over the reigns of government in Bhopal in September 1963, he had been maneuvering to build and strengthen a group of supporters in Indore and other areas where he had little original influence. His political penetration of Indore was facilitated by several factors: the presence at strategic levels in the police administration of officers belonging to the same caste as Mishra (Kanyakubja Brahman), the presence of local politicians who were looking for a viable Congress alternative to the Nai Duniya and INTUC groups; and the accidental but politically convenient problem of a serious water shortage in the city.

The last factor was immediately salient for penetration of municipal politics, because the Corporation had jurisdiction over the daily distribution of water. The water shortage had the effect, albeit temporary, of putting the municipal government for the first time into the center of city politics, because the water problem affected most citizens of the city by depriving or threatening to deprive them of a basic, daily requirement. The water shortage also threatened to undermine local industrial production. But the Corporation did not have the resources to do more than manage the available quantity of water. For augmentation of the water supply, the Corporation was dependent technically on the state Public Health Department and financially on the state and central governments. The financial dependence of the Corporation was used to great advantage by the Chief Minister, D. P. Mishra, to build his influence in Indore and the urban level of politics. (See Chapter 8.)

Mishra's influence had not been very pronounced in the Council of 1958, and such as it was, was manifested only after 1963. Nor was it an important factor in the municipal election of 1965. Purshottam Vijay and N. K. Shukla, both of whom later joined the Congress party as Mishra group sympathizers, in this election ran against Congress nominees. The election results returned the Congress to direct power in the Corporation, with 27 out of a total of 48 elected seats.[31] Two other Councillors, though elected as Independents, became for all practical purposes Congress supporters in the new Council.[32]

The opposition still made a significant showing with 19 elected seats.[33] While it was a major setback from the level of 60 percent of the elected seats that the *Nagrik Samiti* coalition commanded in the 1958 election, the 40 percent of elected seats won by the combined opposition in 1965 was substantially better than the roughly 20 percent obtained in the two previous municipal elections. While this trend indicates a considerable reduction in the electoral dominance of the Congress party in the city, it does no more than hint at the electoral disaster the City Congress was to suffer in the 1967 general election, when it lost three out of four city MLA seats to the opposition. The 1965 opposition returns also tend to confirm a trend, already visible in 1958, for the growth in opposition to be primarily "leftist"

[31] The number of wards was increased from 35 (of which 5 were double-member constituencies, one of each reserved for scheduled castes) to 48, and the number of elected Councillors from 40 to 48. INTUC did not benefit disproportionately this time as the number of *seats* in the labor area was increased by only 2, and 6 were distributed elsewhere in the city. In 1965, wards 1–4, 14, and 22 were reserved for scheduled castes, and a member of the opposition won in each.

[32] Morulal Yadav, a Bairwa supporter of Ramsingh Verma, had been denied a Congress ticket because of V. V. Dravid's opposition, so he ran as an Independent in ward no. 3, a scheduled-caste seat, from Gomah ki Phail and Pancham ki Phail. Because of the united support of Bairwa community laborers, Morulal defeated the Congress (Dravid's) nominee and the Communist candidate. But Morulal was not really part of the opposition and generally supported the Congress majority. Secondly, N. K. Shukla ran under the *Nagrik Samiti* with the support of Purshottam Vijay and Yugydutt Sharma. But Shukla was attracted by the gravitational force of Mishra into the Congress Mishra group in 1966.

[33] The opposition would probably have done much better if it had been really united. In the 1955 municipal election there was an average of 2.8 candidates per seat. In the municipal election of 1958, when the opposition was even more strongly united under the *Nagrik Samiti* and bolstered by Congress dissidents, there was an average of only 2.4 candidates per seat, and the *Nagrik Samiti* won a majority. In 1965, however, the opposition was badly divided, despite some formal unity. The Communists (Daji group), Socialists, and Independents (Yugydutt Sharma group) all used separate election symbols. The average number of candidates rose to 4.8 per seat. What is surprising is that the opposition did so well under the circumstances.

in ideological orientation. While the conservative Jan Sangh and Hindu Mahasabha proportions of the Council tended to remain stable at a low level, the combined Communist and Socialist proportions in the Council, most of which resulted from electoral shifts rather than aldermanic appointments, rose from a low of 3 percent in 1950 to 24 percent in 1958, and only slightly declined to 22 percent in 1965. Of the leftists elected in 1965, 8 were Communists (their highest number in the Council thus far), 4 were Socialists, and 4 were Independents. It is also of interest that 5 of the 6 scheduled-caste seats were captured by the Communist party, an indication of considerable penetration by radical organizational forces of a traditionally pro-Congress clientele. This Communist penetration of scheduled-caste communities, moreover, was entirely among textile laborers and a reflection of the weakened condition of the IMMS following its 1964 internal power struggle in the labor arena. (See Chapter 10.)

A look at the factional affiliation of *elected* Congress Councillors at first suggests that the three main factions were almost evenly balanced. The Nai Duniya and Khadiwala–Mishra groups each contained 9 members, and INTUC had 10. But this appearance was slightly deceiving, for 7 of the elected INTUC members tended to sympathize also with the Nai Duniya group, favoring the latter numerically. (See Tables 28 and 19–22.) Even the apparent balance was altered, however, by the selection of Aldermen. In 1958, it will be recalled, the *Nagrik Samiti* denounced the practice of government nomination of Aldermen. Prior to 1965, the procedure had been amended to allow the election of Aldermen in the Council, with each Councillor casting a single nontransferrable vote. By concentrating their votes in a manner agreed upon in advance, the opposition elements were able to elect 4 Aldermen, in proportion to their representation on the Council.[34]

It was in the election of Aldermen that D. P. Mishra's influence was most clearly felt. He worked through both party and government channels to strengthen the faction most sympathetic to his purposes. The first step was to maximize the number of Khadiwala–Mishra

---

[34] Tarachand was elected with Daji group votes, Satyabhan Singhal with Jan Sangh votes, and the Socialists and Independents united to elect Yugydutt Sharma and Saraswatidevi Sharma as Aldermen. Mrs. Sharma was allied with Yugydutt in this period.

group supporters among those whom the municipal Congress could elect as Aldermen. This was achieved through prior deliberation in the City Congress party, where the pro-Mishra President, Joharilal Jhanjhariya, could lean on the nominating committee. The result was that of the 8 aldermanic slots controllable by the municipal Congress, 5 candidates were Mishra supporters, 1 was neutral, and only 2 favored the Nai Duniya faction. In the final tally, the Nai Duniya faction together with its INTUC sympathizers totaled 18 members, while the Khadiwala–Mishra faction with only 2 INTUC allies came to 16. When N. K. Shukla subsequently joined the Mishra group, its membership rose to 17.[35] But this did not complete the picture, for Mishra had the state government issue an ordinance waiving the age restriction that Aldermen be at least thirty years old. The immediate purpose was to have Kailash Agarwal, then only twenty-one years old, elected as an Alderman, and to give the Mishra group parity with the Nai Duniya coalition.[36] The seating of Agarwal in this special manner created something of a stir at the time and signified that Mishra had begun to establish his influence among those of the business elites in Indore who were seeking to reduce the long standing Jain dominance.

The social composition of the 1965 Council membership (see Tables 19 through 22) records Mishra's influence in another fashion. The most interesting feature of caste distribution is the large number of Hindi-speaking Brahmans on the Council, a total of 15, which accounts for over one-fourth of the membership. Although the Hindi-speaking Brahmans are distributed unevenly among the opposition, Independents, and the Nai Duniya group, the largest single cluster (6) was pro-Mishra, revealing clearly on the Council for the first time the Hindi-speaking Brahman complexion of the faction. Mishra's influence at the local level had a marginal effect in strengthening an empathetic ascriptive group that supported his interests at the state level. A second important feature is the clustering of Hindu Baniyas in the

---

[35] Although the Mishra group was slightly smaller than the Nai Duniya–INTUC coalition, the alignments were unstable. But the instability in the long run was greatest in favor of the Mishra group, as is described below.

[36] Kailash Agarwal illustrates the tendency of Agarwal Baniyas in Indore to support the Hindi-speaking Brahman group. The tendency seems to stem in part at least from Jain–Agarwal business rivalries. Kailash's father, Mannalal Agarwal, purchased a majority of the shares of the Hukumchand Mills, formerly Jain, about ten years ago. Kailash was made Managing Director of the Mills in 1964, and was also elected President of the Mill-Owners Association.

TABLE 28. FACTIONAL AFFILIATION: MUNICIPAL COUNCIL, 1965–1968

Nai Duniya	Khadiwala–Mishra	INTUC	Jan Sangh and Hindu Mahasabha	Communist	Socialists	Independents
Hiralal Dixit	Suresh Seth	V. R. Chaukhande (ND)	V. R. Lokhande	Vasant Sanvatsar	Kalyanmal Jain	N. K. Shukla (K-M)
Kurshid Hassan Khan	Chironjilal Gupta	Mahesh Thakkar (ND)	Rajendra Dharkar	Digambar Gangaram	Bashir Mansuri	Ujagarsingh
Kanchanlal Dhruve	Bolumal Khemchand	Dodchand Jain (K-M)	S. N. Kelkar	Kishanlal Chaudhuri	Ramprasad Manoharlal	Govindram Bajaj
Abdul Hafiz Khan	Shivdutt Sood	Komalgiri Goswami (K-M)	(A) Satyabhan Singhal	Bajrangprasad Madhuji	Abdul Quddus	Avinash Zamindar
S. K. Kemkar	Prabhudas Badlani	Govind Deshmukh (ND)		Ishwar Namdeo		Deovrutt Sharma
M. R. Khutal	Shankerlal Joshi	Morulal Yadav (ND)		Gandharve Guru		(A) Yugydutt Sharma
Chandraprabhash Shekhr	(N. K. Shukla, since 1967)	Gayadin Hardiya (ND)		Durgadin Sukhram		(A) Saraswatidevi Sharma (K-M)
Ramkripal Sharma	Saryuprasad Sharma	Vijaysingh Chauhan (ND)		Namdeo Shravan		
Sitaram Koshal	Mahesh Joshi	Chandmal Gupta (ND)		(A) Taracland		
(A) L. S. Chauhan	Kripashanker Shukla	Amarsingh Ramsingh (ND)				
(A) Khushiram Somani		(A) S. K. Kaul (ND)				
(A) Kailash Agarwal						

(A) Purshottam Vijay
(A) Hastimal Jain
(A) Munnibai Chauhan
(A) Nirmalarani Potdar

(A) = Alderman, nominated by the government.
(ND) = Nai Duniya group sympathizer.

(K-M) = Khadiwala-Mishra group sympathizer.

same faction. It reflects what tended to be true of the Khadiwala faction in the city all along—that it was, at the elite level, a coalition of Hindi-speaking Brahmans and some Hindu Baniyas (particularly Agarwals and Khandelwals).

An important and new characteristic of this Council was that of intergenerational change, for it contained a substantial number of representatives from highly politicized student background of recent vintage. The generation of students active in the Indore agitation of 1954 was represented in the Congress party by Suresh Seth and N. K. Shukla, and similarly in the opposition by Yugydutt Sharma and Kalyan Jain. Each of these comparatively young men ran in the 1967 general elections for MLA seats, Sharma against Shukla and Suresh Seth against Kalyan Jain. In both cases the opposition candidate won, immensely increasing their individual importance in the Corporation. An even younger generation of students was represented by Mahesh Joshi, Shivdutt Sood, Kripashanker Shukla (Khadiwala–Mishra group), and Chandraprabhash Shekhr and Ramkripal Sharma (Nai Duniya group), all in Congress, and one in the Communist opposition, Vasant Sanvatsar. Most of these young Councillors looked hopefully on municipal politics as a ladder to higher office—and for the first time since the Holkar state era, this appeared in 1967 to be a realistic possibility.

The slightly larger number of Nai Duniya group supporters, including INTUC group allies, made it possible for a Nai Duniya coalition to seize the chief elected offices for the first year of the Council. Laxman Singh Chauhan, the chief Nai Duniya contender, was in the hospital recovering from a heart attack, but Hiralal Dixit and M. R. Khutal successfully canvassed support in the municipal Congress party for his election as Mayor. Hiralal Dixit himself won election as Chairman of the Standing Committee, but the composition of the Committee included equal numbers from the two main factions plus two members of the opposition—giving the opposition a potential opportunity to arbitrate differences within the Congress. The position of Deputy Mayor went to Komalgiri Goswami, an INTUC member who leaned toward the Khadiwala–Mishra group. But the more important Chairmanship of the Public Works Committee went to Madhavrao Khutal, a supporter of the Nai Duniya group and a close friend of Laxman Singh Chauhan. In 1965 this coalition held together fairly well. But 1965 was the first year of real shortage in rainfall, and by March of the following year—the time of mayoral elections—the situation had become critical. The water problem remained severe from the spring of 1966 to the summer of 1967, when a more adequate rainfall brought some relief.

The timing is quite important. The water problem became urgent just one year before the general election of 1967, and D. P. Mishra's efforts through the state government in 1966 must be viewed in the light of his ambition to make the local Mishra faction successful in the MLA contests. He could hope to do this only if the state government made substantial efforts to alleviate the problem, efforts that could reasonably be interpreted by the people of the city as Mishra's actions to help the city. Mishra's election aims, as it turned out, were not realized, but the city and the Corporation did benefit from state government patronage on an unusual scale. The politics of the water problem are dealt with in more detail in the next chapter. For the moment, the factional outcome in the Corporation is the main concern.

If the state government was to delegate substantial sums of money and other assistance to the Corporation, Mishra intended to see that the Corporation was supervised by someone dependent on himself personally. His chosen instrument for this purpose was Lakshmi Shankar Shukla, a Kanyakubja Brahman and a relative through marriage.[37] Just before the mayoral election in 1966, Mishra had the Governor issue an ordinance amending the Municipal Corporation statute to permit the election of an "outsider" as Mayor by the Council.[38] Working again through the President of the City Congress, Joharilal Jhanjhariya, Mishra imposed Lakshmi Shanker Shukla on the municipal Congress party and instructed that he be nominated and supported unanimously by the Congress Councillors. This was made possible by the fluidity of factional membership or the gravitation of certain Nai Duniya supporters toward the Khadiwala–Mishra

---

[37] L. S. Shukla's role in Indore labor politics is treated in some detail in chapter 10 on the labor arena. Shukla is a leading criminal lawyer in Indore. He was once in the Congress party in Mhow before merger, and joined the Congress again in 1966 in response to Mishra's promise of support. Shukla's niece was married to one of Mishra's sons.

[38] Shukla was not among the elected Councillors or Aldermen. He was, of course, a registered voter and qualified to stand for election in the city.

group. In this process the desire for MLA tickets in the coming general election, and the expectation that Mishra would play a key role in state-level politics for the indefinite future, were crucial.

Laxman Singh Chauhan was never happier than when President or Mayor of the municipality, and he was again a candidate for Mayor in 1966. But he also desired an MLA ticket. Having been denied this aspiration by his own group, who found him indispensable at the municipal level, Chauhan felt that Mishra might fulfill this longstanding desire. Moreover, once Shukla's candidacy for Mayor became clear, Chauhan realized he could not keep *that* position. In March 1966 the Nai Duniya coalition had the edge over the Khadiwala–Mishra coalition, but only by one member. At that point L. S. Chauhan defected to the Khadiwala–Mishra coalition, breaking promises to members of his group, and shifted the balance to the side of Mishra and L. S. Shukla. Chauhan's reward was his election as Chairman of the Standing Committee. Shukla duly became Mayor, and Dr. Kaul (Nai Duniya–INTUC) was made Deputy Mayor. But in the following year's election of officers, Chauhan was left completely isolated. Controversy over administrative appointments, which brought their differences to the surface, had made it impossible for Chauhan to ingratiate himself to the Khadiwala–Mishra faction. Moreover, Hiralal Dixit and Gayadin Hardiya, two of his closest supporters before, now deliberately crossed over to the Mishra group to repay Chauhan for his betrayal the year before, as well as to benefit themselves from the new alignment. Under these circumstances L. S. Shukla was returned to the position of Mayor, Purshottam Vijay became Chairman of the Standing Committee, and Hiralal Dixit was made Deputy Mayor.

The Politics of Supersession, 1967–1968

D. P. Mishra's hopes of dominating Indore city politics through the election in 1967 of MLA's of his choice were disappointed. His penetration of city politics succeeded to the extent of determining several of the party's nominations, but it was not sufficient to guarantee the election of his protégés. Not long after the fourth general election, defections by Mishra's opponents from the Congress majority in the Madhya Pradesh *Vidhan Sabha* (Legislative Assembly) toppled the Mishra government in July 1967. The defectors, together with leaders of the opposition parties, formed a coalition known as the

Sanyukt Vidhayak Dal, and assumed power as an alternative government. Three of the Indore MLA's, who had defeated Congress candidates in the 1967 election, belonged to the Socialist or Independent components of the SVD coalition. And two of these MLA's, Yugydutt Sharma (Independent) and Kalyan Jain (SSP), were also sitting as Municipal Councillors.

The influence of Sharma and Jain in the Council was greatly enhanced by their newfound support from the SVD government in Bhopal. They and their municipal colleagues in the opposition now began a campaign of harassment which ultimately brought down the elected Congress officers of the Corporation. Their campaign also laid the groundwork for the supersession of the Corporation, the dissolution of its elected body, and direct administrative rule by the state in the municipal arena. The municipal opposition, however, did not achieve this result alone, but did so with the tacit assistance of the Nai Duniya faction and other Congress councillors who opposed Mishra and sympathized with the position of the Congress defectors. The SVD government, after all, was headed by Govind Narain Singh, a former Congressman. But the subversive role of the anti-Mishra forces in the Corporation was on the whole covert, for they had little need to risk public exposure and eventual party displeasure when Sharma and Jain were ready and willing to launch a noisy and vigorous attack on their own initiative. Thus, opposition politics in general concealed in the politics of supersession what was at bottom an intraparty struggle.

The Congress defectors in the SVD coalition government represented the dissident factions of Chhattisgarh and Madhya Bharat and the Rajput faction of Vindhya Pradesh. Chief Minister Govind Narain Singh had a cordial relationship with Babulal Patodi of Indore and was supported within Madhya Bharat by the Nai Duniya–Takhtmal Jain network and within Chhattisgarh by the allied Deshlehra faction. The SVD Minister for Local Self-Government (Urban) from mid-1967 through 1968 was Sharad Chandra Tiwari of Raipur.[39] Both

---

[39] Tiwari had formerly been active in the municipal politics of Raipur and thoroughly understood how state government statutory and bureaucratic power could be used to harness the municipal arena for political purposes. Although of the same caste as Mishra, Tiwari belonged to a different region. Tiwari was aligned with the Deshlehra faction based in Durg district, neighboring Raipur.

had left the Congress in opposition to D. P. Mishra, and both worked to undermine the pro-Mishra group in Indore and elsewhere.

Without the patronage of D. P. Mishra for support, and with the Nai Duniya group once again under the guidance of Laxman Singh Chauhan, tacitly supporting the opposition Councillors, Mayor Shukla and the Khadiwala–Mishra group were increasingly isolated. The crucial challenge was not long in coming. In August 1967 the opposition led by Yugydutt Sharma sponsored a motion of "no confidence" against Shukla. With the Deputy Mayor presiding, a secret ballot was taken. There were 22 votes from the opposition and 7 from Congress against Shukla, and 29 Congress votes against the motion (favoring Shukla), resulting in a tie. The Deputy Mayor, as is customary, gave his vote to the man in office. The motion failed, as a two-thirds majority is required to remove an elected officer.

Within a few days, however, the opposition brought forward a second motion of "no confidence." At the meeting scheduled for the vote a special scenario was prepared. The challenge to Shukla had been widely advertised by the opposition and about 3,000 spectators had gathered, filling the none-too-spacious public galleries and overflowing into the verandahs and hallways around the Council room and onto the open space around the Corporation building. Among these spectators were a large group of students and Youth Congress workers who had been mobilized by Mahesh Joshi, Kripashanker Shukla, and Shivdutt Sood. Agitational tactics were to be introduced into the Council room.

Under these tense conditions, Hiralal Dixit, presiding again, proposed that the meeting be closed to the public. Laxman Singh Chauhan objected, insisting that the meeting remain open as is customary. It was not clear at this point which group might benefit most from the presence of the crowd, as it consisted of supporters of every group. The meeting remained open, but when Yugydutt Sharma rose to speak for the motion he was almost immediately bombarded with a volley of slogans and the crowd broke into an uproar. Sharma was flustered and his speech halted, but he pressed for an immediate vote (secret ballot). The Deputy Mayor directed the ballot to be taken, but before more than twenty ballots had been deposited in the box—none by opposition members—the opposition leaders interrupted the voting and demanded that they be given protection to leave the premises.

Again an uproar broke out in the crowd, and this time the students recruited by Joshi, Shukla, and Sood broke into the Council room, berating the opposition. Some began to overturn furniture, and some articles were thrown across the room. The opposition demanded police protection to leave the premises, and the police did eventually arrive on the scene. But Dixit adjourned the meeting and the vote was frustrated.

It is not clear whether Lakshmi Shanker Shukla directly instigated this scenario or whether the youthful invaders merely got carried away with their own enthusiasm. But they certainly were tagged as supporters of the Mishra group; and the Mayor well realized that once agitational tactics had been introduced on his behalf in the Council, he would now be unable to face the opposition, who could easily use similar tactics and in any case would lose no opportunity to harass him. So Mayor Shukla attended the All-India Mayors Conference at Trivandrum at municipal expense, returned to Indore, and promptly submitted his resignation.

Hiralal Dixit automatically became Acting Mayor for a few weeks. At the end of September, just before the election of a new Mayor, Rammanohar Lohia, leader of the SSP, died. Dixit, with the agreement of the opposition, postponed the Mayoral election for ten days as a sign of respect. November 6 was the date proposed by the Congress majority; but the opposition objected, probably suspecting that time would be valuable to Hiralal Dixit in canvassing support to get himself elected Mayor or at least unite the Congress members around another nominee, and demanded an immediate election. When Dixit resisted, Yugydutt Sharma initiated a hot exchange and Dixit threatened to have him removed for obstructing orderly procedure. Sharma was offended and brought a motion of "no confidence" against Dixit on November 4. Dixit scheduled the vote on this motion for November 10, hoping that the intervening mayoral election would unite the Congress membership.

Chandmal Gupta was selected by the municipal Congress for Mayor as a compromise candidate. Chandmal had been an ally of Laxman Singh Chauhan, and by supporting him Hiralal Dixit and the Mishra group hoped to patch up the factional schism. But this did not work for Hiralal Dixit in his personal trial. In the "no confidence" vote Dixit got 25 Congress votes, but 10 Congress votes went with the opposition for an almost even split. Although technically the motion failed for lack of a two-thirds majority, Dixit resigned.

This left the Standing Committee, however, under the control of Purshottam Vijay (Chairman) and the Mishra group. The Chairman, unlike the Mayor and Deputy Mayor, could not be unseated from his office by a "no confidence" vote in the Council. He could be removed by a similar vote within the Standing Committee, but unless members of his own group turned against Purshottam Vijay this would not be possible, and the Mishra group members on the Committee were firm. It was possible, however, for either two-thirds of the total membership of the Council or the state government to remove any Councillor from the Corporation altogether after showing cause why he should be removed.[40] The opposition supported by Chauhan and the Nai Duniya group chose to proceed by the avenue of state government removal.

The first problem was to expose Purshottam Vijay's irregular use of his powers. Apparently Vijay was none too circumspect on this point. In January 1968 the Revenue Officer, Murlidhar Chauhan— one of the veteran municipal bureaucrats who owed his original appointment and advancement in the administration to the Nai Duniya group—discovered that the Indore Printery (Vijay's press) had paid *octroi* on only part of a shipment of newsprint imported into the city. He fined Indore Printery, according to procedure, ten times the *octroi* due on the evaded portion. Vijay retaliated immediately. The Standing Committee under his direction transferred Murlidhar Chauhan from the position of Revenue Officer to that of Secretary of the Corporation—a comparatively innocuous position. It was reported that other transfers within the Revenue Department occurred at the same time.[41]

Opposition Councillors wrote to the state government alleging that Vijay grossly misused his powers. S. C. Tiwari, the SVD Minister of

[40]Article 19 of the *Madhya Pradesh Municipal Corporations Act* (1956). The state government had the further power to bar the charged person for up to four years from the Corporation.

[41] *Swadesh*, February 2, 1968. Murlidhar Chauhan was hurt too in this process. About one year from the stipulated age of retirement, he could now no longer expect an extension of his tenure in office from the Standing Committee. But moving Chauhan could not stop the exposure or the machinery that was now set in motion.

Local Self-Government (Urban), directed the Revenue Commissioner to conduct an inquiry into the charges.[42] Following the inquiry and report, the government on March 27 sent a "show cause notice" to Vijay asking him to explain within fifteen days why he should not be removed from the Council for having misused his office.[43]

Vijay did not send his reply until April 21, more than a week past the deadline. He was aware that his reply would be of no immediate use but should go on the record for the future. The following day the Municipal Commissioner was instructed that Vijay was formally removed from the Council and disqualified for the next three years from being seated on the Council.[44] On the next day the Corporation was superseded.

The supersession of the Corporation was essentially a political decision. The charges made in the "show cause" notice may have been partly true, but similar charges could have been leveled at other points in municipal history with equal validity, yet were not. Between 1965 and 1968 the Corporation had been run neither better nor worse than before. The main difference after the summer of 1967 was the incompatibility of the coalition in power on the state level and the Mishra group in power in the Corporation. Previously, except for the period from 1958 to 1960, the group or groups in power in the municipal arena were acceptable, if not intimately linked, to those in power on the state level—and even when the *Nagrik Samiti* took over, the municipal administration remained in state hands. The main political objective of the advocates of supersession was to undermine the political base of the Mishra group in the municipal arena in Indore and to prepare for new elections in which ward boundaries and other factors could be adjusted to facilitate the entry of anti-Mishra members into the next Council.

---

[42] There is reason to believe that S. C. Tiwari had his own scores to settle. *Indore Samachar* had been less than cautious in its criticism of individual Congress defectors.

The Revenue Commissioner was M. P. Srivastava, from the Vindhya Pradesh region, and an ally of Govind Narain Singh, the Chief Minister.

[43] The notice specifically listed charges that Vijay (and the Modern Printery) had benefited irregularly from an enormous number of municipal printing contracts and had deliberately evaded the payment of *octroi* on the imported rotary machine. It even noted that allegations had been made that Vijay had sold privileged information concerning Standing Committee proceedings to newspapers, and demanded an explanation. *Nai Duniya,* March 28, 1969.

[44] *Ibid.*

The problem of supersession for its advocates was that they were a mixed sort with competing aims, and it was probably unclear who would gain most. The Nai Duniya group had in common with the SVD coalition and the municipal opposition the desire to weaken the Mishra group, but each group wanted to strengthen itself at the expense of the others. The advocates of supersession, therefore, had mixed feelings regarding it, and it was not clear until mid-April that it was certain to occur.

The Nai Duniya group may actually have been in the strongest position to benefit from supersession. The administration of the municipality was still fairly well packed with pro-Nai Duniya bureaucrats, and the SVD Chief Minister and Minister of Local Self-Government (Urban) were both more sympathetic to the Nai Duniya group and Congressmen than anti-Congress parties. On the other hand, the MLA links between the city and the government after 1967 were largely in the hands of the SVD and the local opposition. Yugy-dutt Sharma, as a leading member of the Lok Sevak Dal, the largest constituent in the SVD coalition, would certainly be able to bring considerable pressure to bear on the City Administrator, the Collector, and other officials involved in the preparation and supervision of new elections. Furthermore, the Home Minister, Virendra Kumar Saklecha, was a Jan Sangh leader in a strategic position in relation to police administration—formerly a major asset of the Mishra regime. There seems to have been a strong possibility that the various advocates of supersession would indeed reduce Mishra group influence, but beyond that they would probably veto each other's efforts to profit further from the situation. This was apparently better than nothing and supersession ultimately came, but not without ambivalence and hesitancy.

By November 1967 there were rumors that supersession was likely in Indore (one reason few seriously contested the election of Chandmal Gupta as Mayor), following a state-wide pattern.[45] The formal preliminary, a "show cause" notice from the government to the Cor-

---

[45] By February 1968, 95 municipalities in 32 districts of Madhya Pradesh had been superseded, including those of Dewas, Jhabua, Ratlam, Ujjain, Khargone, Mandsaur, Shahjahpur, Bhilsa, Rajgarh, Gunah, Morena, and Bhind. *Nai Duniya*, Feb. 9, 1968. The other City Corporations, Bhopal, Gwalior, Jabalpur, and Raipur, had already been superseded, some by the Mishra regime.

poration, was finally delivered on December 20.[46] The notice charged the Councillors with misconduct on three counts. The government charged that the disorderly Council meeting of August 29, when the motion against Mayor Shukla was considered and the police were called, was a disgrace and a violation of Corporation procedures and standards of conduct; that the Councillors had disrupted the functions of the Corporation by delaying consideration of the budget beyond the statutory time limits; and that the Corporation spent more than 5,500,000 rupees on the water problem in 1966, but that much of that amount (about 2,000,000) was misspent or could not be accounted for properly.[47]

The Council established a special "answering committee" of seven members to answer the "show cause" notice. The committee consisted of Chandmal Gupta (Mayor), Purshottam Vijay (Chairman of Standing Committee), Deochand Jain and N. K. Shukla from the Congress, and Yugydutt Sharma, Abdul Quddus, and Rajendra Dharkar from the opposition. The committee was badly divided from the outset, the opposition members demanding the resignation or removal of Vijay and an acceptance of the government's charges. They quickly resigned when their demands were not met, and were replaced by three Congress members, including Chironjilal Gupta, buttressing the Mishra group viewpoint. The committee formulated its answer to the charges and forwarded it to the government on January 9.[48]

A month later the government directed that the preparations for the regular municipal election, due at the end of February, be stopped pending government action.[49] The public attack on the Mishra group was continued. The Assistant Examiner of Local Fund Accounts, Rikhande, sent a report to the government on Mayor Shukla's trip

[46] *Indore Samachar,* Dec. 21, 1967.
[47] *Nai Duniya,* Jan. 10, 1968.
[48] *Ibid.* There were internal differences within the municipal Congress party over how "hard" the reply should be. The final draft was nonprovocative in that the charges were met with sober explanations. The committee argued that the disorder in the August Council meeting was caused not by Councillors but by spectators, and that calm had been restored before the arrival of the police without serious injury to anyone; that the budget had been late in every previous year except 1966, and that the government had always before permitted an extension of the deadline; and that more than half the money sepnt on the water problem was accounted for in permanent fixtures, and the rest was accounted for in an itemized statement appended to the answer.
[49] *Nai Duniya,* Feb. 9, 1968.

to the All-India Mayor's Conference, noting that he visited not only Trivandrum but also Mysore, Bangalore, Rameshwaram, and Hyderabad—all at Corporation expense. The government report implied that Shukla had taken a private vacation at the expense of the taxpayers of Indore.[50]

Not long before supersession, Mayor Gupta, Purshottam Vijay, and the Indore M. P., Prakash Chand Sethi, went to Delhi, ostensibly to confer with the Prime Minister and Minister of Railways about the projected Siaganj railway overbridge, but apparently also to try to secure high command intervention to block the impending supersession.[51] The effort was in vain. On April 23, following the removal of Vijay and on the eve of the election of a new slate of officers, the Council was dissolved for a stated period of one year.[52] The Municipal Commissioner became the City Administrator of the municipality, responsible now in theory as well as fact to the government. There were a few desultory protests against the state's action by local politicians, but there was remarkably little resentment on the part of the populace against supersession. The impression that the move was on the whole welcomed by the articulate middle class of Indore was unmistakable. The state government for the first time in Indore had played its strongest hand against the Corporation (short of its statutory abolition) and made it temporarily an arm of state administration.[53] The subservience of the city to state politics could hardly have been made more obvious.

The microanalyses of municipal politics in this chapter have been designed to serve a number of related purposes. They have made it possible to get a more detailed picture of the ascriptive and economic bases of political factions in the local Congress and opposition parties participating in the municipal arena. For example, the affiliation of Maharashtrian Brahmans with the Nai Duniya faction in the early years, and the tendency for them to support the Jan Sangh in later years, was documented. It was also possible to show the affiliation of

---

[50] *Nai Duniya,* March 28, 1968.

[51] *Nai Duniya,* April 4, 1968.

[52] *Nai Duniya,* April 24, 1968.

[53] The Administrator, K. G. Telang, was pliable but had little initiative for the purposes of the state politicians. He was eventually replaced by P. K. Dixit, an officer with previous experience only up to the level of Deputy Collector but whose credentials included birth and service in Vindhya Pradesh and the capacity for vigorous action.

Agarwal and Khandelwal Baniyas with the Khadiwala and Mishra groups, an affiliation that could not be so clearly delineated in city-wide general electoral politics. The factional analysis of competition and outcomes revealed shifts in the strengths of Congress factions in municipal politics. The early hold of the Nai Duniya faction of elected positions and their residual leverage in municipal administration even after their municipal electoral strength declined, the take-over of elected positions by the INTUC group in 1955, the opposition electoral victory in 1958 followed by Congress indirect rule, the dominance of the Mishra group from 1965 to 1967, and the supersession of the Corporation by the SVD government in 1968 were the main changes. The role of external conditioning factors at the state level and the lack of municipal autonomy were apparent in almost every case.

Emphasis was placed on the potential rewards of participation in the municipal arena. It is apparent that the status of elected positions in the Corporation has great appeal to certain segments of the population. The tangible rewards available, the small stipends for Council and committee membership, the patronage of advertisements in newspapers, the capacity to influence building regulations, and the rigor with which tax laws are enforced helped explain the particular motives for many individuals for participating competitively in the municipal arena, despite the limited scope and power of the municipal government. The location of material rewards in municipal administrative jurisdictions revealed the extent to which bureaucrats, and especially engineers, become key political participants in the municipal process, building their own constituencies and bases of factional support.

The analysis strengthens the thesis that the keys to governance of the city, as well as the municipal arena, lie at higher levels of politics. The centrality of vertical political and bureaucratic linkages was manifested by the collaboration of V. V. Dravid, the Labour Minister, and Ramsingh Verma to enlarge municipal electoral boundaries and increase the number of labor wards, enabling the INTUC group to seize control of municipal resources and divert a larger proportion of them to the labor area. Similarly, Congress control of the state government ensured that the *Nagrik Samiti* coalition in the Corporation could be manipulated indirectly by the local Congress through a strategy of divide and rule and utilizing informal influence in the municipal administration. The vertical influence of Mishra during the water crisis was demonstrated by his imposition of a protégé Mayor and Alderman (by amending ordinances), and his cultivation of a subordinate faction in the Council from 1963 to 1967. Finally, the extent to which the rules of the municipal game are set from above was confirmed once again by the supersession of the Corporation, precipitated by opposing groups on the municipal and state levels.

Central to the analysis are the weakness of the municipal government and the predominance of vertical political and bureaucratic linkages. The manipulation of municipal politics by extra-local forces was complemented by the tendency to slice away the powers and functions of the municipality, putting them instead under state-level bureaucracies and insulating them from local electoral accountability. The jurisdictional invasions of municipal competence have led to bureaucratic agency conflict with the municipal government and progressively reduced the opportunities for elected local representatives to build durable political constituencies in the municipal arena. These factors have contributed to the functional fragmentation of urban politics and the impotence of the municipal government. On the other hand, the vertical political and bureaucratic linkages have been primary factors in the integration of Indore city, governmentally under the state capital, and politically under the influence of chieftains and factions operating on the state level of politics.

8

THE POLITICS OF THE WATER
CRISIS: JURISDICTIONAL CONFLICT

Until the general election of February 1967 and the fall from power of D. P. Mishra soon after, the main preoccupation of the city of Indore, as well as of the Corporation, was the critical water shortage that developed. The politics of the water problem deserves separate treatment because of the generality of its impact on the city. It provided an opportunity for a variety of political actors to become involved, revealing not only the impingement of extramunicipal bureaucratic actors on the municipal jurisdiction, but also a special case of the impingement of municipal actors, with help from above, on other bureaucratic arenas in the city. The crisis conditions and the resulting intensity of political competition brought into clearer prominence some of the political linkage patterns that it is the purpose of this work to chart out and explain.

While every major political actor in the city was involved at some level or point in time in the politics of water, special attention should be focused on several of them, notably the state government, particularly the Chief Minister, D. P. Mishra; the Minister for Local Self-Government (Urban); the state and district levels of the Public Health Department (Engineering); the Revenue Commissioner; the Collector; foreign missionaries; the Corporation; and the Mayor. The central-government-level actors were less visible in the local political process but helped set the conditions by which the problem of Indore's water supply may be resolved in the long run.

The purpose of this part of the study is to illustrate: (1) the inter-play of political actors on different levels, and the outcomes of their competition; (2) the manner in which the state Public Health De-partment (Engineering) competes as an institutional actor, how it preempts the political constituency of the Corporation within the municipal arena, and how it constrains the jurisdictional boundaries of the Corporation from without; (3) the opportunities that arose for the Mayor and the Corporation to shove more centrally into the city arena of politics, albeit temporarily, because of the nature of the crisis and the determination of Mishra to build his own political ma-chinery in Indore; (4) how the bureaucratic engineers preside over the flow of expenditures (patronage) used for construction and develop-ment; (5) the outlines of bureaucrat-faction linkages caused by, or conducive to, the horizontal and vertical political penetration of the bureaucratic machinery; and (6) the ultimate predominance of ver-tical bureaucratic and political relationships in city politics.

To put the critical nature of the water problem in relief, some factual background will be helpful. It will also serve to introduce the structural conditions of Corporation and Public Health Depart-ment competition in the city. Indore's antiquated water supply system was inherited from the Holkar state. It consists of a group of reser-voirs, filtration equipment, and pumping stations, main conduits bringing the water into the city, and a system of underground mains for distribution of the water in the city. The older reservoirs, the Bilaoli, Sirpur, and Residency "tanks," are small and date back to the late nineteenth and early twentieth century. Following a drought and water famine in 1925–26, the Holkar state planned and constructed a larger reservoir called the Yeshwant Sagar on the Gambhir River catchment area. Completed in 1938, the Yeshwant Sagar reservoir was designed to supply a population of 150,000 with 30 gallons a day per person. The system was enlarged to supply 234,000 persons, with the expectation that the population would not reach that level until 1961, but the limit was surpassed as early as 1945. The flow from the Gam-bhir was augmented between 1950 and 1960 by the expansion of the filtration and pumping machinery—but at the risk of depleting the reservoir resources more rapidly than they could be replenished by rainfall, which comes mainly in the summer between June and the end of August. Meanwhile the population continued to expand to about 350,000 in 1955 and an estimated 500,000 in 1967.

In the early 1960's the total daily supply of water reached a level of about 11.5 million gallons per day. The Yeshwant Sagar provided the bulk of this, approximately 9 million gallons per day. The Bilaoli, Sirpur, and Residency sources added 2, 0.4, and 0.1 million gallons per day, respectively. At best, in relation to population estimates, the supply had dropped from the desired 30 gallons to 20–23 gallons a day per person. But the actual situation was more complicated, for only about 70 percent, or a little more than 7 million gallons per day, reached domestic consumers through private metered connections or public taps. The rest went into industrial consumption (10 percent, or a little over 1 million gallons per day) or was lost through leakage (20 percent, or a little more than 2 million gallons per day).[1] Before 1965 conditions did not reach a crisis point because of the numerous wells scattered throughout the city on which many localities rely.

The crisis developed in 1965 and reached its peak in the summer of 1966, remained severe until the summer rains of 1967, and subsided to some extent thereafter. In 1965, the worst drought year, only 15.8 inches of rain fell (against the normal figure of slightly over 33 inches). 1966 was nearly as bad, with 22 inches, and 1967 brought only 28 inches. The main reservoir did not refill in 1965 and 1966, the small ones dried up completely, and with these depleted conditions it was possible to supply only about 4 million gallons per day in the summer of 1966. The situation was exacerbated by the fact that many of the wells in the city had dried up or run frighteningly low, as ground water levels fell. The sanitation functions of the Corporation were impaired and the risks of an epidemic increased. It had clearly become an emergency, and contingency plans for evacuation of the city were drawn up.

Under these circumstances the friction always present between the Corporation and the Public Health Department (Engineering) became pronounced. The tendency toward conflict was built into the situation whereby the main reservoirs and waterworks, possibly be-

---

[1] The high losses due to leakage are said to be due to the frequent breaks in pipes resulting from the expansion and contraction of the area's compacted "black cotton soil."

cause of their rural location, were placed under the state Public Health Department by the Holkar government, and were transferred to its counterpart in the Madhya Bharat period. This meant that the gross supply of water was controlled by the Public Health Engineers. The Municipality, or Corporation, was left with control only over how that water was then distributed and allocated within the city. This meant that the Corporation decided who would receive new private water connections or in what areas public taps might be installed, but even this power was severely limited by the low net supply of water entering the city mains from the Public Health Department's conduits. The net supply of water, of course, became dangerously low in 1965, 1966, and 1967, and was the occasion for increasingly intense bickering. The Corporation was subjected to public pressure when the diminished supply in the mains resulted in low water pressure. This meant some elevated locations and those furthest from the inputs received no water at all, until it was decided to phase distribution in sections of the city so that adequate pressure could be maintained for one or two hours a day in each section. But this meant great inconvenience, and not infrequently real distress. The Corporation, reflecting public pressures, turned its ire on the Public Health Engineers.

The conflict was essentially one of jurisdiction. The Corporation was the focus of public pressure for action but lacked the power to act on the crux of the problem, the expansion of water resources. But friction also focused on certain more specific issues: (1) the Corporation was required to pay the Public Health Department a fixed rate for the bulk supply of water, but the determination of how much the daily supply came to was made by the Public Health Engineers who controlled meters on the conduits leaving the pumping and filtration works. The Councillors suspected, and probably correctly, that the net supply entering city mains was lower than what the meters showed or what they were being charged for. Various proposals were put forth to resolve this problem, but without success. (2) The officials of the Department seldom felt it necessary to inform the Corporation when temporary shutdowns of the water supply for repairs to pipes affected sections of the city. The Councillors resented the humiliation of always having to seek out such information after receiving complaints from their constituents, rather than being informed beforehand.

There were additional factors in the situation. By 1968, under the SVD government, an offer was made to transfer the waterworks from the Department to the Corporation at a cost to the latter of 10 million rupees, and probably on condition that the Corporation not resist a large (but not inequitable) increase in the water rates. The Corporation wanted control of the waterworks free of payment, contending that the machinery was antiquated and the supply inadequate, implying that the state government was trying to sell the system only after it had become a liability.

Rates should have been progressively increased. The rates were set low in 1938 to encourage the use of reservoir water[2] and had never been raised. The Corporation paid the Public Health Department 25 *naya paisa* (comparable to cents, a new form of currency),[3] for each 1,000 gallons of water,[4] and charged citizens with private connections only 37 n.p. per 1,000 gallons. Others using public taps pay a low annual flat rate collected with property tax. Both the Corporation and the Public Health Department operate the water system at a deficit.[5] The SVD government attempted to raise income by tripling the existing rates—though still a moderate level by comparison with other Indian cities, and even others in Madhya Pradesh—but the action was resisted by city politicians.[6] The latter hoped to continue to tap state revenue for the deficits incurred by the Public Health Department as long as possible.

One might ask whether the water crisis was anticipated and whether any measures had been taken in advance to deal with it. The problem was indeed recognized early, and there was a good deal of thinking, but little concrete action. The rapid increase of population and increase of private water connections—which were granted long after it had become technically undesirable to do so—put strains on the facilities in the best rainfall years. Ameliatory measures had been

---

[2] There was some fear that citizens would avoid using public water because of the fear of pollution from leather washers in the water mains or the employment in the water works of low-caste attendants.

[3] The equivalent of less than four cents in a U. S. dollar.

[4] Slightly less above a certain level. The Department recently raised its charge to 37 *naya paisa*, about five cents, but the Corporation refused to pay the new rate and is now officially in arrears.

[5] Corporation expenses run approximately twice as much as income from water rates.

[6] The issue remained unresolved while this research was being conducted.

taken between 1950 and 1960. In 1961 the Madhya Pradesh government prepared the so-called "Kalaria scheme" for the construction of a new reservoir near Indore at a then-projected cost of 16.7 million rupees. The scheme was forwarded to the central government for consideration.[7] The leisurely pace is indicative. In 1964 the Deputy Director General of Health Services (G.O.I.) visited Bhopal to confer with state officials on this scheme, among other things. A revised Kalaria scheme at a projected cost of 32.9 million rupees was subsequently submitted to the center. In the midst of the Indore crisis, the Kalaria scheme was dropped as inadequate.

Attention shifted to two larger, long-term projects known as the Chambal scheme and the Narmada scheme. The hope was that the Indore water problem could be solved for some time into the future through one or the other of these schemes. The Chambal scheme proposed construction of a dam to catch the water in the Chambal river basin, forming a reservoir about twelve miles long with an average depth of eight feet. It would require bringing water from a distance of thirty miles (or twelve miles beyond the Gambhir waterworks in the same direction) and lifting it about 150 feet to the elevation of the city. Its advantages were that it would provide about 20 million gallons per day, nearly double Indore's existing water supply, at an initial cost of about 60 million rupees and at a lower annual operating cost than the Narmada scheme projections. Its disadvantages were that it would be a more rapidly depreciating asset than the Narmada alternative, because the reservoir would silt up at a calculable annual rate, diminishing the storage capacity. Moreover, it too would be vulnerable to drought, like the Yeshwant Sagar. Finally, it would be politically problematic because it would require the condemnation and submergence of good agricultural land.[8]

The Narmada scheme proposed to tap the permanent flow of the Narmada River about 30 miles from Indore near Barwaha. The major advantages of this scheme were that it would provide a theoretically

---

[7] Central legislation authorizes the development of urban water resources under an arrangement for sharing the financial burden—the center paying 50 percent, the state 30 percent, and the local government 20 percent. This provision practically ensures that the center will determine the timing and basic shape of any scheme.

[8] The local engineers favored the Chambal scheme, the given reason being the lower annual operating costs. But an additional incentive may have been the projected need to construct a dam on the Chambal, which would have permitted the engineers to dispense numerous contracts.

permanent and unlimited supply of water to the city at an initial cost of about 70 million rupees, and would not require construction of a dam or submergence of agricultural land. Its disadvantages were that water would have to be lifted to the Malwa plateau from the Narmada valley, a difference in elevation of about 1540 feet, requiring a series of pumping stations and entailing a higher annual operating cost.[9]

The near water famine in Indore served as a stimulus to the research and reports underlying the Chambal and Narmada schemes, but the central government did not reach a decision before the urgency had passed for the time being, and the advent and final collapse of the twenty-month SVD regime in Madhya Pradesh contributed to withholding of a final determination on the issue. Pending resolution of this issue, the politics of the water problem in Indore centered between 1965 and 1968 on stop-gap solutions.

The Corporation attempted to step into the center of the picture during the crisis. Under the leadership of Laxman Singh Chauhan and Hiralal Dixit, the Corporation sought state financial assistance from D. P. Mishra. The state government authorized loans before March 1966 totalling about 1.5 million rupees, but under Chauhan the Corporation was prevented by the internal opposition of the Mishra group in the Council from drawing this sum for actual use. Despite this handicap, a look at budgetary expenditures, particularly the proportion sanctioned for use by the Corporation Public Works Department (i.e., the Engineers of the Corporation), is indicative of the total effort envisaged by the actors in the municipal arena and provides startling evidence of the strategic position of the bureaucrat-Engineers over very substantial financial resources.

As Table 29 shows, the proportion of municipal expenditures over which the PWD Engineers technically presided rose from under one-fourth to over one-half within a decade. The absolute increase in PWD expenditures was equally impressive, from about 1.5 million

---

[9] To the consumer the cost of 1,000 gallons of water under the Chambal and Narmada schemes would come to about 1.60 and 2.50 rupees respectively—largely from annual operating costs. This would mean to the consumer an increase from 1967 rates of about 3.2 or 5.6 times, respectively. As a result the city politicians tended to favor the Chambal scheme for its lower projected rates to the consumer. The interstate disputes between Gujarat, Maharashtra, and Madhya Pradesh over the use of the Narmada scheme also introduced uncertainties and the prospect of longer central delays, and this may also have acted in the favor of the Chambal option from the vantage point of local politicians.

TABLE 29. PWD Expenditures in Corporation Budget, 1952–1968

Year	Budgetary Status	PWD Expenditures	PWD Expenditures as Percentage of Total	Total Budgetary Expenditures	Savings (Unspent Income)
1955–56	Actual	989,716	24.0	4,132,277	N.A.
1959–60	Actual	1,982,771	36.6	5,400,109	1,781,888
1964–65	Actual	2,646,360	35.5	7,470,798	3,642,628
1965–66	Sanctioned	6,527,042	50.0	13,177,500	—
1965–66	Actual	3,518,118	41.8	8,434,372	3,596,496
1966–67	Sanctioned	7,310,382	51.4	14,232,400	—
1966–67	Actual	5,653,310	51.0	11,088,204	2,093,328
1967–68	Sanctioned	6,650,800[a]	44.3	15,003,800	—

Sources: the printed *Statements of the Budget*, the Municipality and the Corporation, 1952–53, 1957–58; 1962–63; 1966–67; 1967–68; Indore: the Corporation Office.
[a] Sanctioned: for PWD Staff and Establishment 1,310,910
for PWD Work and Projects   5,339,900

rupees sanctioned for 1956–57 to 5.6 million rupees actually spent in 1966–67. The figures also reveal that in 1965–66 the PWD succeeded in spending only a little more than half the sanctioned amount of 6.5 million, and only 41.8 percent of the total budget, even though the authorized proportion was 50 percent. (The Corporation had an unspent amount of nearly 3.6 million from the sanctioned level of 13.17 million remaining at the end of the same financial year.) But the following year the PWD succeeded in actually using 51 percent of the total Corporation expenditures. Although the PWD and Corporation both fell short of spending the total amounts sanctioned, both consumed much larger proportions as well as greater absolute amounts. PWD actual expenditures rose from 3.5 million in 1965–66 to 5.6 million in 1966–67 as a result of the water crisis.

The apparent reason for the inability of the PWD to claim its full proportion of the budget in 1965–66 and for its comparative success in 1966–67 was the group distribution of power in the Corporation in successive years. As Mayor and Chairman of the Standing Committee in 1965–66, Laxman Singh Chauhan and Hiralal Dixit did not have sufficient political support in the Council or on the state level of politics to carry through their plans regarding the water problem and other municipal works with as much success as they envisaged in the sanctioned estimates. That they were still partly successful and not totally obstructed is indicated by the fact that PWD expenditures rose by nearly 1 million over the previous year, accounting for almost all the increase in total Corporation expenditures. Their partial success seems to be accounted for by the fact that the Nai Duniya group, Chauhan in particular, had its bureaucratic allies in the municipal administration at most key points even as late as 1965.[10] The City Engineer, Ghatpande, as related before, had long been a protégé of the Nai Duniya group, and managed to avoid retiring until December 1966.[11] In 1965 the Assistant Engineer under Ghatpande was the comparatively young S. N. Agal, a close friend of Hiralal Dixit (Nai Duniya faction) and from the same village in Dhar district, near Bagh.

Lakshmi Shanker Shukla became Mayor in March 1966 under much more favorable circumstances for the exercise of informal executive power. Although Chauhan was Chairman of the Standing Committee, its membership supported Mayor Shukla. Moreover, Hiralal Dixit with his special access to the Assistant Engineer had crossed lines and allied himself with the Mishra group.[12] As already shown, Shukla was made Mayor with the support of the Chief Minister, allies in the City Congress, and the now-growing Mishra group on the Council. Mishra bypassed the Municipal Commissioners (S. C. Dube and K. G. Telang) by showering the Mayor with support and state government largesse. In 1966–67, budgetary resources from loans reached an unprecedented 5.78 million, money largely from the state government tagged for use in the water crisis. Under Shukla's auspices in 1966–67 the Corporation sanctioned budget rose to 14.2 million, nearly twice the amount actually spent by the Corporation just two years before. The large amount spent on the water problem between 1965 and 1967, listed as about 5.5 million rupees in the SVD government's "show cause" notice of 1968, was largely spent under Shukla's regime.[13]

---

[10] Chauhan was particularly proud of the fact that in the closing days of his regime he succeeded in clearing the way for the construction of a new and much wider Krishnapura bridge, a serious traffic bottleneck on Mahatma Gandhi road where it crosses the Khan River. The project was inaugurated with much fanfare and newspaper publicity and, although the work was not completed until 1969, Chauhan succeeded in identifying the project with his name.

[11] By contrast, his former deputy, S. V. Dravid—a protégé of the INTUC group —had thrice been denied promotion and finally left the Corporation in 1958.

[12] When Ghatpande retired in December 1966, S. N. Agal took his place operationally as Acting City Engineer.

[13] See Table 29. Under Shukla's regime the Corporation also received extensive material support in the form of well-digging machinery and crews on loan. The machinery and its operation were subsidized by the state government or other sources. Further details on this are given below.

TABLE 30. PWD Selected Comparative Items of Expenditure,
1964–65 to 1966–67

Item	Actual Expenditures		
	1964–65	1965–66	1966–67
Head Office Expenditures:			
"Incidentals"	265,576	211,414	2,010,948[a]
Waterworks Section:			
Pumping Expenses	632,004	527,750	277,158[b]
Pipe-laying Expenses	1,148	977,248	—
"Nonreturnables"	1,000	—	1,231,689[c]
Workshop Expenditures:			
			(for trucks)
"Incidentals"	—	—	199,652

Source: printed *Statement of the Budget, 1967–68*, Indore: the Corporation Office.
[a] Included "Nonreturnables," itemized in the following manner:

"Miscellaneous"	350,000
Modern Market	200,000
Road Construction	599,339
Slum Improvement	400,000
City Improvement	100,000

The balance consisted of a variety of smaller expenditures.
[b] The sanctioned amount under this head for the same year was 700,000.
[c] This large figure was not even itemized in the budget statement. The contrast with previous expenditures under this head is remarkable, as is the comparatively small figure of 175,000 sanctioned for the following year.

Table 30, giving comparative figures of actual PWD expenditures officially recorded in the budgets of 1964–65, 1965–66, and 1966–67, tells remarkably little about how large sums were spent. Specifically, the large sum of 1.23 million rupees under the heading "nonreturnables" in the expenditures of the Waterworks Section—spent under the Shukla Mayoralty—would seem to call for further explanation. Similarly, under Head Office incidental expenditures in 1966–67, the large sum of 350,000 rupees is merely listed as "miscellaneous" expenditures. The comparison of these headings in the different budget years in Table 30 shows striking increases.[14]

The Mayor's power stemmed not only from the disposal of these considerable financial resources but also from the bureaucratic in-

[14] It was undoubtedly these figures that provided the fundamental documentary evidence underlying the charges of the SVD government that excessive sums had been spent on the water problem, and that about 2 million rupees were not properly accounted for.

fluence of the Chief Minister in the state Public Health Department. The district-level Executive Engineers had been under the influence mainly of the Nai Duniya group or its allies (such as V. V. Dravid or K. N. Katju) until 1964, when the appointment of S. C. Sharma, a Mishra protégé, changed the picture. When S. C. Sharma advanced up the ladder to a higher rung (Superintending Engineer, Bhopal) in 1966, he was replaced in Indore by P. L. Gavande, another person depending for his advancement on Mishra. Thus Mayor Shukla could rely in 1966 and 1967 on the support of the engineers in the Public Health Department.[15]

Friction between Mayor Shukla and the Corporation Engineer, G. S. Ghatpande, apparently developed in 1966. Ghatpande, it may be recalled, was a bureaucratic ally of the Nai Duniya group in the municipal administration. His Nai Duniya loyalties and control of the municipal PWD machinery seem to have posed obstacles to Mayor Shukla's attempts to deal with the water problem in his own way. In any case, Ghatpande was due for retirement in December 1966 and the Corporation declined to extend his tenure by special provision. Instead S. N. Agal, an Assistant Engineer who attached himself to the Mishra group in the Corporation, was appointed Acting Corporation Engineer, providing Mayor Shukla with an ally at the head of the municipal PWD. Agal's promotion was at the expense of M. K. Bayas, another Assistant Engineer, who had a slight claim to seniority over Agal but was bypassed because of his links with the Nai Duniya faction and with a number of the opposition Councillors. The selection of Agal over Bayas to replace Ghatpande was indicative of factional preferment and the attempts by Mishra and his protégé-Mayor to establish control of local administrative machinery. Linkages between bureaucratic executives in the state Public Health Department (Engineering) and the municipal PWD and the Chief Minister and Mayor ensured that the resources allocated to deal with the water problem would be used to serve the political interests of Mishra's factional allies in Indore.

Mayor Shukla began by criticizing some of the actions of the previous Corporation regime, such as the large expenditures on metal water storage tanks for slum areas, arguing that this ignored the real

---

[15] With the exception of one dissident Assistant Engineer.

problem of expanding water supplies. "Of what use are tanks when
there is nothing to fill them with?" He proceeded to reformulate existing "temporary schemes" and added his own to meet the emergency.
One problem on which progress was being made was to encourage
the people of the city to clean out and reclaim abandoned wells in
the city, for which they were compensated by the city. Over 300 wells
of varying usefulness were reclaimed this way. Where water from
reclaimed wells was found unfit for drinking purposes, it was used
for sanitation (flushing the gutters, sewage and drainage systems). The
water supply to the industrial area was cut by agreement. The Electricity Board consented to a cut in its city supplies for cooling the
generators and found a way to utilize underground water and seepage
from the river. The city water supplies were cut down to 4 million
gallons per day, and opened for 1.5 hours per day in sections of the
city by rotation. Water-tank trucks were purchased to carry water to
slum areas or places where the pressure was inadequate to reach public
taps.[16]

The "temporary schemes" for the emergency development of new
water supplies were where Shukla concentrated his efforts, and provide
an interesting case where local missionaries became embroiled in municipal politics. The city received on loan or by arrangement with
the state government a number of tube-well drilling machines for
the emergency. In one case, the machine was a giant high-speed boring
machine constructed in Bhilai. It was of considerable public interest
that this "Russian" machine, heralded by great advance publicity, was
almost a total failure.[17] A second large rig was imported under the
auspices of missionaries, the fruit mainly of efforts by Sister Baptista,
a highly respected and energetic mission worker in Indore, who se-

[16] The three-man Water Committee, consisting of Dr. Kaul, V. R. Lokhande,
and Abdul Quddus, handled public complaints, taking pressure off the Commissioner
—who was gratified to be relieved of the onerous executive duty of sorting out
public priorities in a time of crisis—and saved the Mayor time to concentrate on
the development schemes.

In a humorous sidelight on the situation, Mubarak Husain, the Municipal
Waterworks Superintendent, finally received a pass to go abroad on a pilgrimage to
Mecca. The hard-to-get pass came just at the height of the water crisis. Husain went
to Mecca and prayed daily for rain for Indore. On the day of his return to Indore,
summer rains finally began in the city.

[17] Its crew was reported to be lazy if not incompetent, and the drill bits supplied
did not hold up and were continually being sent back to Bhilai for repairs, holding
up progress.

cured financial backing for the machine in Holland. It was brought into India under an agreement between the Food Foundation for India (not to be confused with the Ford Foundation) and the central and Madhya Pradesh governments whereby the machine would be operated privately but under government contracts and supervision. The state government wanted it to be used first in Indore.

Meanwhile the machine came under the operational control of David Eadie, a member of the "Canadian Mission" (United Church of Canada), a one-time carpenter and small businessman now engaged in technical missionary work. Eadie brought the rig into Indore on the authority of a letter from the Mayor waiving *octroi*. The letter was subsequently a cause of trouble, for the Mayor wrote it without official supporting action in the Council. The Mayor has no independent authority over *octroi* regulations.

The rig had been assigned by agreement with the state government to bore ten tube-wells in places designated by the Corporation. The operation of the rig was to be financed under the same agreement, a matter between Eadie and the government. But the Corporation was to pay for the permanent casings and other fittings inserted in the tube-wells. The tangle of lines of accountability probably confused Eadie and caused difficulties in his relations with Mayor Shukla. After the machine arrived, and Eadie had begun work, the Corporation advertised for bids on casings and other fittings, but there was some delay in negotiating contracts and actually getting delivery of the materials. Meanwhile the new machine, which was extraordinarily effective, had finished boring its first well. Eadie became impatient and buttonholed the Mayor, demanding to know why the casings and other materials had not been delivered according to promise. The explanation did not satisfy him, and he allegedly made some slighting remarks about India and inefficiency. The Mayor was understandably indignant at the provocation and thereafter became more assertive on behalf of the Corporation.

The work eventually proceeded, though the Mayor and Eadie avoided crossing paths. The original ten wells were completed, and the Corporation sanctioned five more. When approached, Eadie agreed to do the new work, but only if the Corporation paid 35 rupees per foot for operational expenses as well. This was probably an equitable amount for maintenance from a technical point of view, but Shukla suspected Eadie was trying to make money out of a machine that had been donated for humanitarian purposes. The Mayor started *octroi* recovery proceedings, including the assessment of a fine of ten times the amount due for having brought the machine in without paying *octroi*. When Eadie refused to come to terms, the Mayor prepared a long cable relating to the Foundation in Holland how Eadie was improperly utilizing the machine they had sent. The cable was sent from Indore and a copy was forwarded to Sister Baptista "for information."

Sister Baptista phoned the Revenue Commissioner (Mahavir Prasad Srivastava) and the Collector (Kapur). These authorities stopped the cable in Bombay prior to its transmission overseas. A meeting was held in the presence of the Revenue Commissioner with the Collector, Sister Baptista, the Roman Catholic Bishop of Indore, David Eadie, and the Mayor present. Eadie agreed to do five more wells for the Corporation under the original terms, and the *octroi* proceedings were withdrawn by the Mayor. Three more wells were actually completed for the Corporation under these terms, and subsequently the "Holland machine" worked on contract under the Public Health Department to dig 23 tube-wells on the Fort and Sawer roads for the city water supply.

This case study of the politics of the water problem in Indore illustrates several points. First, and most important, the water crisis brought municipal actors temporarily to the center of city politics, but revealed once again their subordinacy to political forces operating at the state level. Secondly, the water shortage was a nonpartisan problem affecting the bulk of the citizens of the city in the most direct way, but the provision and distribution of resources to deal with the problem were conditioned by partisan and factional interests operating externally and internally. D. P. Mishra, the Chief Minister, provided the Corporation with substantial emergency funds to alleviate the water shortage, but used formal and informal powers to determine the distribution of those resources through the Corporation and other bureaucratic line agencies in the city. By positioning subordinate bureaucratic allies in the state Public Health Department and in the municipal Public Works Department, and by imposing his own protégé as Mayor on the Corporation, he was able to use the water problem to influence political processes in the city that had a bearing on the selection of electoral candidates for the approaching general elections.

Normally the Public Health Department (Engineering), because of its control over the city waterworks and water supply, tends to come into conflict with, and to undermine the powers of, the Corporation. Normally, too, the Mayor and the Corporation are neither central to urban politics nor particularly powerful. But in these emergency conditions, and given the external political support of the Chief Minister, the Mayor briefly became a powerful actor with considerable resources at his disposal and had the capacity to command the cooperation of the usually autonomous Executive Engineer of Public Health. Mayor Shukla appeared to be in the process of establishing an executive-centered coalition, moving the Corporation onto center-stage in the politics of the city, until the collapse of the Mishra regime eliminated his external sources of support and made him vulnerable to factional opponents in the Municipal Council. Without any real formal authority inherent in his position of Mayor, Shukla's dependence on the informal power of the Chief Minister revealed the primacy of vertical political linkages and external power sources.

PART FOUR

POLITICAL ARENAS
IN THE CITY

9

THE POLITICS OF TOWN PLANNING: BUREAUCRATIC AGENCY COMPETITION

The arena of town planning and improvement politics reveals prime examples of the political and bureaucratic linkages between political actors on the state level and those in the city, and the manner in which those linkages are used by state-level actors to build constituencies in the city. The central bureaucratic and institutional focus of the town planning arena within the city is the Indore Town Improvement Trust. Although the Trust is the institutional focus, other institutional or bureaucratic actors become involved, both as allies and competitors, in the politics of town planning. The more important of these are the Chief Town Planner's Office (Bhopal), the district Public Health Department (Engineering), the district Public Works Department (PWD), the Collector, the Courts, and the Corporation (or municipal government). Other institutional actors that become involved less frequently are the Housing Department, the district Nazul Office, the Public Health Department (Medical), the Revenue Commissioner's Office, and the Police Department.

At the state level the most important political actors include the Chief Minister and the Minister of Local Self-Government (Urban), along with their bureaucratic subordinates, but Ministers with other portfolios, particularly Development and Planning, Labour, Housing, Public Health, and PWD, among others, may become involved from time to time, especially when the holders of the portfolios happen to be politicians elected from Indore. On the local level, politicians active in the Congress party organization, the municipal arena, the improvement arena, and other political arenas in the city obtain access to Trust and other agency activities through representation on the Trust or through political linkages with prominent city politicians in the state Cabinet or Legislature.

The first strong impression the observer receives of the Trust is its high degree of statutory dependence on the state government. The primary channel of dependence consists of the requirement that the main policies of the Trust, which consist of formulation and implementation of "improvement schemes," must be sanctioned at prescribed stages by the state government (the Department of Local Self-Government, Urban) and may be overruled or halted at any point or in any detail by the state government. The dependent relationship is reinforced by controls enforced through appointment powers and financial provisions.

In structure the Trust is characterized by autocratic and bureaucratic features which confirm the primacy of vertical statutory, bureaucratic, and political linkages, and strictly limit the accountability of the Trust to the ordinary citizens of Indore. The executive officer (Chairman) of the Trust is appointed by the state government. The body of Trustees also consists in part of bureaucrats who become Trustees *ex officio* by virtue of another position they hold (e.g., Chief Town Planning Officer or the Municipal Commissioner) or are directly appointed as Trustees by the government. The Trust tends toward bureaucratic dominance, but there have been trends toward increasing the weight of political representatives on the Trust, elected from the Municipal Council or chosen by other means explained below.

In practice the autocratic and bureaucratic features of the Trust are moderated, on one hand, by the pluralism of functional and political interests differentiating those bureaucrats who sit on the Trust —a result of their linkages with politicians, factions, or other clients who seek to benefit from Trust projects or the departmental powers of the bureaucrats in their primary jurisdictions—and on the other hand by political pressures transmitted through organizational and personal channels from local interest groups or influentials to allied

state-level politicians that ultimately feed back through the bureaucratic chains of command to the Trust itself. For those with seriously
limited political access, there remains access to the courts for stay
orders, injunctions, and other judicial means of delaying or blocking
Trust actions.

The statutory linkages and structure of the Trust, however, favor
those individuals or groups who have ready access at the state level
of politics, making the vertical linkages, political and bureaucratic,
clearly predominant for the arena of town planning and improvement
policies. Local horizontal linkages remain important in the day-to-day
exploitation of patronage opportunities that arise from the ongoing
work of the Trust.

In this chapter the linkage structure of the town planning arena
will be explored to show how the Trust operates both as a political
actor in its own right and as an instrument of the state (or state-level
politicians). The main contention is that the cumulative effect of the
political activity of the Trust, both as an instrument of higher political forces and as an institution protecting and enlarging its own
domain through building clienteles or constituencies, is to invade and
undermine the jurisdiction and powers of the Municipal Government
and of the associated political actors in the municipal arena. The
political behavior of the Trust will be analyzed through brief case
studies of selected improvement schemes.

Before turning to the cases, however, it is worth outlining the
statutory constitution of the Trust, to set down the formal powers of
the constituent elements of the Trust and to demonstrate the state-
level constraints on the Trust. The constitution in turn is related to
the actual composition of the Trust, the changing distribution of
bureaucrats and politicians, variations in the seating on the Trust of
different departments of government, the distribution of factional
representatives, and bureaucrat–faction linkages.

Constitution and Functions of the Trust

In the early twentieth century the European model of the city
improvement agency was being adopted in certain cities of India.
Sensitive to currents of governmental reorganization in British India,
the Holkar State established the Indore Town Improvement Trust as

early as 1924.[1] The essential assumption underlying the constitution
of the Trust is that town planning should be entrusted to administrators who are effectively insulated from political pressures so that
they can conduct their work according to rational principles and
objective information. The interesting thing is that after independence the popular governments of Madhya Bharat and Madhya Pradesh
largely accepted and perpetuated an instrument designed more for
control than representation—that is, an essentially "colonial" bureaucratic pattern—and preserved the myths of rationalism and administrative superiority as a camouflage for the use of the Trust as a
political instrument in the city.[2]

The Indore Trust constitution, originally borrowing from all-
India models, was easily integrated along with counterparts in other
cities into state-wide legislation.[3] The Trust consists of a body of
Trustees, the bureaucratic establishment—most of whom were recruited under the Holkar regime and persisted as part of the princely
heritage in the city—and the Chairman, who presides over the Trustees as the executive officer. There is also a Tribunal with limited
powers of judicial review over questions of compensation raised
against the Trust.

The Trustees serve as the governing body of the Trust, exercising
the policy-initiating powers of the Trust to formulate "improvement
schemes." The number of Trustees has varied, but was fixed at nine
in the Act of 1960. The Chairman of the Trust is the first Trustee and
presides over all meetings of the Trust at which he may be present.
The incumbent Mayor (or President) of the municipal government
automatically becomes a Trustee. Two other Trustees may be elected

---

[1] Patrick Geddes, the famous town planning expert, had been invited to Indore
in 1916 to survey the city and draw up guidelines for the development of the city
according to a coherent scheme. In his report Geddes advised against the adoption
of an improvement trust in Indore. His experience suggested that such agencies
were unsatisfactory if not counterproductive. See his *Town Planning Towards City
Development: A Report to the Durbar of Indore,* Vol. II, pp. 103–104.

[2] This does not mean that the Trust was not used in a similar way by the
Holkar officials, but then the Holkar government made little pretense of being a
popularly representative government. Moreover, the politicians in state power after
independence were increasingly drawn from classes of people not actively participant
before nor publicly committed to princely or colonial government machinery.

[3] The Holkar State Act of 1924 was modified by the Madhya Pradesh Town Improvement Act (1960). The following descriptions are based primarily on the latter
document.

by the Municipal Council from among its members. A fourth elective politician may be appointed by the state government from among the sitting MLA's whose constituencies fall wholly or partly in the city. The Chief Town Planning Officer (Bhopal), or his delegate, is *ex officio* a Trustee. The three remaining slots are filled by state government appointments. Two administrative officers are customarily selected from government departments in the city, but the third must be a private citizen of the city. The normal term for a Trustee is four years.[4]

The Trustees, except for the Chairman, do not receive salaries for their service on the Trust. But the 1960 Act under Article 9 permits the Trust to give "allowances" to Trustees to compensate them for time spent in meetings. The allowance for Trust meetings is now 15 rupees, and a smaller allowance is given similarly for committee meetings authorized by the Trust. This allowance may be significant supplementary income for the representatives of the Municipal Council.

The Act lays down certain rules of procedures. The Trust is required to meet once a month, but may meet oftener as the Chairman sees fit. Two or more Trustees may by written request get the Chairman to hold a special meeting at short notice. A quorum requires the presence of only three Trustees. Questions are decided by a majority of those present and voting, though the Chairman or Trustee presiding may vote only to break a tie. The Trustees may form committees and delegate to them specific duties, but no committee resolution may be implemented unless confirmed by the Trust. The opportunity for limited forms of patronage and representation of special interests is provided under Article 17: the Trust may "associate" with itself, temporarily and subject to specified regulations, "any person or persons whose assistance or advice it may desire in carrying out any of the provisions of this Act." [5]

---

[4] This is not applicable to the Chairman or the Town Planning Officer. Furthermore, Trustees may be removed by the government for cause. The Mayor, Municipal Councillors, or the MLA cease to be Trustees if they lose their elected positions outside the Trust or otherwise become disqualified.

[5] Such an "associate" is, of course, not deemed a Trustee and has no voting rights. The provision is probably designed to permit the Trust easy access to advice from bureaucratic and other technical experts. But it is also clear that an "associate" sitting in meetings may garner advance information about Trust plans that could

The powers of the Trustees (collectively) are of two kinds, those over the internal establishment and those over the "improvement schemes." Both sets of powers are narrowly constrained by the overriding powers of the state government. The Trust may fix the number and salaries of its permanent employees, subject to state civil service regulations. The Chairman's official powers of supervision over his staff are so limited as to bar almost all patronage considerations except where he might have the personal support of a sufficient number of Trustees. The Chairman may advance or punish only those Trust employees whose salaries fall *under* 150 rupees per month.[6] Otherwise the employees, excepting the Chairman himself, may be promoted or punished by the Trust.

The more substantive powers of the Trust, as will become clear through the cases, are those over the formulation and implementation of "improvement schemes." The reason is that such schemes almost invariably affect the possession or value of private land and building properties—fundamental stakes in Indian politics. Subject to the explicit approval of the state government,[7] the Trust may draw up and implement "improvement schemes" that entail the acquisition of privately held or government property; the payment of compensation; the lease or sale of acquired property; the closing of roads and traffic in the scheme area; the demolition of buildings or obstructions to the scheme; the alteration of buildings or construction of new buildings, roads, bridges, etc.; the definition of future land use in a scheme area; the provision of sanitary or drainage facilities, means for water supply, electric connections, and lighting, and measures to prevent pollution of rivers and water sources; the accommodation of any class of inhabitants; the imposition of new building regulations; the as-

---

be of economic or political value. Where an "associate" has special interests of his own, he might informally be in a position to affect the application of Trust schemes. The exercise of such influence need not be invidious, but the point is that access is not equal to all, but discretionary and under the control of a small group of Trustees.

[6] This is one example of where bureaucratic executive power has been eroded by forces beyond bureaucratic control. Before independence almost all the employees of the Trust—including office supervisors—drew salaries below this level. But with the devaluation of the currency and rising salary levels for Class II and Class III employees, the Chairman has been priced out of his statutory power. Politicians have made no haste to help the bureaucrat here with legislative amendments.

[7] Under Articles 44, 51–52, 65, 70, and 83.

sumption of jurisdiction over municipal properties and the exercise of municipal authority in the scheme area; the negotiation and entering of contracts; the direction of the municipal authorities to resume charge over an improved area; the raising of loans in the open market; and the collection of "betterment contributions" from property-owners whose property values have appreciated as a result of the scheme.

When the state government sanctions a scheme it may in the process authorize the use of several or all of these powers. But there are a series of procedural limitations on the Trust's moves that may allow affected persons to delay or effect modifications in the scheme. Once a scheme has been systematically drawn up, the Trust must publish notices announcing the purpose of the scheme and the areas to be affected. Property-owners likely to be affected must also be notified individually. The Mayor must be informed. The Trust is then required to submit detailed information upon request and give applicants reasonable opportunities to present objections or requests for modifications. The Trust may then forward the scheme, with or without modifications, accompanied by reasons in either case, to the state government.[8]

The government may reject the scheme, return it for reconsideration, or sanction the scheme with or without modifications. Once sanction takes effect through publication in the government *Gazette,* the Trust is obliged to proceed expeditiously to its implementation. But implementation may be delayed or modified by the further requirements that the Trust compensate the municipal authorities for municipal properties taken over in a scheme, and that the Trust notify property-owners of intent to acquire property, consider their written objections and give them a hearing, and compensate them for their losses.[9]

The powers of the state government over the Trust are comprehensive and formally decisive. The government may repeal the statute and abolish the Trust, though such action is improbable. The appointment and removal powers of the government give it some meas-

---

[8] The channel normally runs through the Office of the Chief Town Planner for his comments and then up to the Department of Local Self Government (Urban).

[9] Records of sale and transfer of land frequently understate actual values to evade taxation. Consequently, there is a tendency for compensation to be set too low to satisfy the owner. When agreement between the Trust and the injured party is not reached, the matter is referred to the Tribunal, or on appeal to a court of law.

ure of control over all the Trustees and potentially decisive control over the bureaucratic complement.[10] The Trust is obliged to keep the government closely informed of its activities and to immediately forward any documents or information requested by the government. The government may decide disputes between the Trust and the municipal or other local authorities, and has broad powers to review the activities of the Trust and "direct" it in the "proper performance" of its duties.

It is ironic that one of the political resources of the Trust is its statutory opportunity, if not compulsion, to act autonomously in the financial sphere. The state government and Corporation each give equal annual grants to the Indore Trust.[11] These grants together total 88,000 rupees, and are earmarked for the recurring costs of the Trust establishment. But the fact that rising costs in salaries, "dearness allowance" (salary supplement geared to increases in cost of living), and other establishment costs have outstripped the annual grants,[12] and the fact that development schemes must be financed by other means, have worked together to encourage the Chairman of the Trust to try to make the institution financially self-sufficient. Funds are provided by the state and central governments for specific types of schemes such as "slum clearance and re-housing schemes," but the Trust most frequently initiates profitable or self-supporting "housing colony schemes." The acquisition of undeveloped land is made at low rates, the land is partially developed, and then sold to private parties or building contractors at a profit that at least covers the Trust investments and as often as not provides a surplus that may at some point be applied to "deficit schemes." The development of housing colonies also allows the Trust as an institution and the Trustees as individuals to build their own constituencies among entrepreneurs who are also in a position to profit from land transactions. The same schemes are useful for the same reasons to state-level politicians, so

---

[10] Article 10 empowers the government to remove any Trustee who "misconducts himself" or who "abuses his position as a Trustee, and in the opinion of the State Government his continuance as Trustee is detrimental to the public interest."

[11] Fixed according to the population of the city as given in the decennial census.

[12] The Trust expenditures on establishment were originally below the 88,000 rupees fixed on the basis of the 1961 Census, but by 1967–68 the same expenditures had risen to about 100,000 rupees a year.

the process does not interrupt the linkages between the Trust and the state government. But there is a certain pressure toward financial self-sufficiency and institutional autonomy, as long as it is consonant with the political objectives of allied state and local politicians.

The Trust operates within the municipal territorial jurisdiction. It can and does undertake schemes that have the effect of suspending municipal authority (e.g., the collection of taxes or enforcement of building by-laws) in scheme areas and undermining the competence of the municipal government to conduct its own plans for improvement. Both agencies have functionally overlapping statutory powers, so that the potentiality for institutional rivalry and conflict is ever present. The statutory powers of the Trust to invade municipal jurisdiction are limited by the requirement that it communicate with municipal authorities. This requirement added to the representation of Municipal Councillors, the Mayor, and at one time the Municipal Commissioner, constitute the formal or institutionalized linkages between the two agencies.

Once a scheme gets government sanction, the Trust may take over municipal functions in a scheme area and require the Mayor or Commissioner to provide the necessary information, such as property assessment lists, on which municipal taxation is based. When a scheme is completed, the Trust may by written notice direct the Corporation to resume its jurisdiction. Resumption of jurisdiction, as seen from the Jawaharmarg case below, can be a point of contention between the two agencies.

Bureaucratic and Political Composition of the Trust

The analysis that follows, of the changing composition of Trustees, distinguishes the "bureaucrats," who are not only permanent administrative employees of the state government but usually also line agency executives of certain state government departments in the city, from those who are (usually) "politicians," and who become Trustees by government nomination, by election from the Municipal Council, or by virtue of holding the elective post of President or Mayor of the municipal government. (See Table 31.) The analysis provides insight into the special roles of the designated line agency executives in the arena of improvement politics, especially as they

TABLE 31. TRUST COMPOSITION: BUREAUCRATS AND POLITICIANS, 1947–1969

Year	Bureaucrats	Political Representatives	Trustees	Composition
1947–48	4	2	6	Chairman, Munic. Commiss., DPHS, Engr. PHD, 2 Councillors.
1948–49	3	3	6	Chairman, Munic. Commiss., DPHS, President, 2 Councillors.
1949–50	4	3	7	Chairman, Munic. Commiss., DPHS, HDC, President, 1 Councillor, 1 GN.
1950–51	3	4	7	Chairman, Munic. Commiss., DPHS, HDC, President, 1 Councillor, 1 GN.
1951–52	5	4	9	Chairman, Munic. Commiss., ADPHS, President, 2 Councillors, 1 GN.
1952–53	5	4	9	Chairman, Munic. Commiss., ADPHS, DI, Engr. PWD, President, 2 Councillors, 1 GN.
1953–54	4	5	9	Chairman, Munic. Commiss., ADPHS, DI, Engr. PWD, President, 2 Councillors, 1 GN.
1954–55	4	5	9	Chairman, Munic. Commiss., ADPHS, Engr. PWD, President, 2 Councillors, 2 GN.
1955–56	4	5	9	Chairman, Munic. Commiss., ADPHS, Engr. PWD, President, 2 Councillors, 2 GN.
1956–57	4	5	9	Chairman, Munic. Commiss., ADPHS, Engr. PHD, President, 2 Councillors, 2 GN.
1957–58	2	5	7	Chairman, Engr. PHD, Mayor, 2 Councillors, 2 GN.
1958–59	2	5	7	Chairman, Engr. PHD, Mayor, 2 Councillors, 2 GN.
1959–60	2	5	7	Chairman, Engr. PHD, Mayor, 2 Councillors, 2 GN.
1960–61	2	4	6	Chairman, Engr. PHD, Mayor, 1 Councillor, 2 GN.
1961–62	3	6	9*	Chairman, Engr. PHD, CTP, Mayor, 2 Councillors, 2 GN.
1962–63	3	6	9*	Chairman, Engr. PHD, CTP, Mayor, 2 Councillors, 2 GN.
1963–64	3	6	9	Chairman, Engr. PHD, CTP, Mayor, 2 Councillors, 2 GN, 1 MLA.
1964–65	3	6	9	Chairman, Engr. PHD, CTP, Mayor, 2 Councillors, 1 GN, 1 MLA.
1965–66	3	6	9	Chairman, Engr. PHD, CTP, Mayor, 3 Councillors, 1 GN, 1 MLA.
1966–67	3	5	8	Chairman, Engr. PHD, CTP, Mayor, 2 Councillors, 1 GN, 1 MLA.
1967–68	4	5	9*	Chairman, Engr. PWD, CTP, Nazul Officer, Mayor, 2 Councillors, 1 GN.
1968–69	5	2	7	Chairman, CTP, Nazul Officer, Collector, Administrator of the Corporation, 1 GN, 1 MLA.

* One post actually vacant. Delay in appointing MLA under statutory provisions occurred.

DPHS = Director of Public Health and Sanitation
PHD = Public Health Department
HDC = Housing and Development Commissioner
PWD = Public Works Department
CTP = Chief town Planner
ADPHS = Assistant Director of Public Health and Sanitation
DI = Director of Industries
GN = Government Nominee
MLA = Member of Legislative Assembly

contribute to collaboration or competition among various departments of the state government in urban politics. It also provides a
basis for tracing political linkages between bureaucrats and politicians
(or the factions they represent) and for displaying shifts in the factional composition of the Trustees.[13]

A feature of improvement politics, even more striking than in
municipal politics, is the presence in key positions of bureaucrats who
are trained as civil engineers. Engineers are the executive officers of
the government in the administration of public housing, the construction of public works such as roads, railways, and communication
facilities, and the administration of public health—insofar as it includes the construction and operation of waterworks and drainage
facilities. When engineers are not merely technical advisors but are
actual executives, their opportunities to exploit the patronage inherent in construction and development are enormous. Consequently
they can and do to a great extent usurp the power of elected politicians and insulate technical work from electoral accountability.[14]

Bureaucrat-engineers have invariably been well-represented on the
Trust. (See Table 31.) In fact, the Chairmen of the Trust until 1956
were themselves engineers. Before 1963 the Chairman of the Trust
was usually a government servant wearing two or more hats; his primary responsibilities lay elsewhere, and the Trust Chairmanship was
only a part-time job. Under the Holkar State, the Trust Chairman
usually held the more important position of Chief Executive Engineer
of the state government concurrently. And in the Madhya Bharat
period, the pattern differed only slightly; Chairman Premnath Bhalla
(1948–50) was also the Superintending Engineer of the Southern Circle
of Indore in the state of Madhya Bharat. V. G. Apte, a former official

---

[13] The discussion that follows is based on tabular data regarding the official
composition of the Trust, and can be obtained from my "Area, Power and Linkage
in Indore," pp. 367–368.

[14] A particularly important power is formally delegated to the Executive Engineer (district level) of the Public Works Department to draw up the schedules of
"government-approved" contractors. This consists of investigating the competence
and financial solvency of applicants, and sending the recommended schedules to
the state level. Only contractors included on these schedules may present bids for
government works. The Executive Engineer, of course, does not have exclusive power
in determining the schedule, but he has the initiating power, which means that
applicant contractors first deal with him.

of the Holkar State, was both Chairman of the Trust and the Executive Engineer, at the district level, of the Public Health Department (Engineering) until 1956.[15]

When Apte retired, the Trust Chairmanship passed out of the hands of engineers and into the hands of the Collector, bringing the agency more explicitly under district administrative supervision. But even when the Chairman was not an engineer, the other bureaucratic Trustees frequently were. In all but three years since 1948, either the Public Health or PWD Executive Engineers have been Trustees. Before the Municipality became a Corporation in 1957, it seems to have been a convention to have the PWD Engineer on the Trust. Similarly after 1956 the convention applied to the Public Health Engineer.[16] The Department of Public Health has been more continuously represented on the Trust than any other. The representation of the engineering section in 1947–48 and from 1956 to 1967 was functionally important to the Trust because of the engineers' control over the city waterworks, frequently a major element in housing schemes. Other engineers represented on the Trust have been the Housing and Development Commissioner (1949–50) and G. S. Ghatpande (1955–57), then Acting Municipal Commissioner but normally the Chief Engineer of the Municipality.

The presence of a high proportion of civil servants on the Trust has given the institution a predominantly bureaucratic complexion, especially when there have been long periods of uninterrupted bureaucratic representation, either of individual administrative officers (e.g., V. G. Apte, whose tenure lasted eight years), or of particular departments (e.g., the Public Health Department was represented on the Trust by at least one officer for an unbroken period of twenty years, from 1947 to 1967). There have also been shifts in the composition of the Trust that have tended to reduce the proportion of

---

[15] At the same time, V. G. Apte was a government-nominated Alderman on the Municipal Council (from 1945–50 and 1950–52), thus personally linking three of the agencies most important in city politics. Apte's role as a protector of Maharashtrian (and Holkar) civil service employees in the Public Health office was noted in Chapter 3.

[16] The convention was interrupted in 1967 when P. L. Gavande, who had been on the Trust the previous year, was removed from the Trust. The action came not long after the SVD came to power on the state level.

bureaucrats in favor of politicians, shifts that have been brought about by the desires of state-level chieftains and allied local politicians to assert a greater measure of political control over the operations of the Trust. The size of the Trust has fluctuated, though its normal size was increased from 6 to 9 Trustees in 1951–52, and the expansion was advantageous to politicians over the long haul. (See Table 31.) Whereas in 1947–48 bureaucrats outweighed politicians 4 to 2, by 1952–53 the balance favored politicians by 5 to 4, and by 1960–61 the normal proportions were stabilized for five years at 6 politicians to 3 bureaucrats. In 1968–69, however, because of the supersession of the Municipal Corporation, the Trust passed back into the hands mainly of bureaucrats.

The shifts occurred in the following way: before the Municipality became a Corporation (in 1957), the rule was that the Municipal Commissioner and either the Director or Assistant Director of Public Health and Sanitation would be on the Trust. Both of these officers were dropped from the Trust in 1957, though the Executive Engineer of Public Health replaced the latter. And, at the same time, the PWD Engineer was dropped from the Trust for several years. The number of Trustees fell from 9 to 7, automatically increasing the proportion of politicians. Even after the number of Trustees reverted to 9, the number of bureaucratic representatives increased by only 1, so that the balance remained in favor of politicians. Somewhat earlier, in 1949–50, the government began the practice of nominating a "non-official," supposedly an ordinary citizen of the city, but in fact usually one with political aspirations if not extensive political involvement. The first so named was Purshottam Vijay, the editor of *Indore Samachar,* who depended for this appointment on the Khadiwala faction which briefly held power in Madhya Bharat under Chief Minister Liladhar Joshi, a Hindi-speaking Brahman from Gwalior. Vijay defected from the Congress in 1952 when the Cabinet came under Jain and Nai Duniya dominance. In 1953 the pressure for increased political representation on the Trust led to the appointment of Hastimal Jain, who owed this favor to a Jain political associate, Mishrilal Gangwal, who had become Chief Minister the previous year. Hastimal Jain is one of the few politicians from his religious community in Indore who have close ties with the Khadiwala faction, though he, like Gangwal, has sought to keep some reputation for neutrality.[17] After 1963 the government ceased appointing one of the two "non-official," at-large representatives from the city, and began appointing instead one of the MLA's elected from the city, as provided for under the Act of 1960.

Although politicians have sought to increase political control over bureaucrats, the dominant theme of Trust politics is not so much one of role conflict between bureaucrats and politicians as one of mutual cooperation to exploit the political constituency-building and patron-age opportunities offered by the Trust. Where cleavages exist they are more of a factional nature than of a bureaucrat-versus-politician na-ture. The factions are most easily traced among the politicians on the Trust. Less can be said about bureaucrats, except that those formerly in the Holkar administrative service were prone to cooperate closely with Indore city politicians, most frequently with those of the Nai Duniya or INTUC groups, or with Mishrilal Gangwal, V. V. Dravid, and Manoharsingh Mehta—the "big three" Indore politicians in the Madhya Bharat cabinet. Bureaucrats who had been recruited outside the Holkar service, in one or another part of Madhya Bharat or Madhya Pradesh, were more usually allied with politicians from their respective regions or former princely state areas.

The factional distribution of politicians on the Trust reflects sev-

---

[17] Hastimal Jain held this nominated post for a total of ten years, from 1953 to 1955 and from 1959 to 1967. He has also been elected to the Trust from the Municipal Council for four additional years as Trustee. Jain is certainly the most experienced politician of the Trust, an expert broker in the politics of the im-provement arena.

Hastimal Jain was one of the most successful agents in representing private in-terests' claims for exemption from the application of schemes. For example, under Scheme 59 (Pipliarao), plans were formulated to develop an essentially rural area within municipal limits. In this area there were properties belonging to members of the former royal family (daughters of Tukoji Rao), a former Sardar of the Holkar Court (Bolia), and a temple supervised by a priest (S. B. Joshi). Jain was ex-tremely interested in obtaining exemptions for these properties, and it is not unlikely, according to the former Trust Chairman, that he was well rewarded for pressing for the desired modifications. In these cases, it was practical for the Trust to avoid acquiring expensive residences and a religious property (normally exempt in any case), but exemptions for one lead to claims by others and make it difficult to maintain impartiality. Jain's personal exploitation of these and similar circum-stances, however, led the Chairman to object to his renomination to the Trust. The Chairman's recommendation of Zutshi, the Principal of Daly College, was accepted instead (see Table 32).

eral factors, but especially the representation of faction chieftains on the state Cabinet, and the balance of power among Congress factions in the City Congress party and in the Municipal Council. On occasion, opposition party leaders too arrive on the Trust, reflecting their successes in the Municipal Council elections or general elections, and shifts at the state level. (See Table 32.) The municipal President or Mayor, as the case might be, was usually a leader of the faction or coalition then dominant in the Municipal Council. In the early years, between 1947 and 1955, the dominant faction on the Trust was Nai Duniya, for it had at least two political representatives on the Trust (and better access to the bureaucratic Trustees), while other factions had only one, or were entirely unrepresented. But as we saw earlier in surveying the municipal arena, the principal Council factions before 1955 were personalist factions, headed on one side by V. V. Sarvate and Tarashanker Pathak, and on the other by Laxman Singh Chauhan. This rivalry was conveyed to the Trust as the municipal position of the two factions alternated. The Jains on the Trust in this period (Hastimal Jain, Pukhraj Bahen, and Hirabai Bordiya), irrespective of their connections with the Khadiwala or Nai Duniya factions, were supportive of Laxman Singh Chauhan, as was D. S. Patil, the INTUC representative, who became a Trustee in 1953. Consequently, even before 1955, the power on the Trust was that of Nai Duniya, but of the business-labor coalition *within* Nai Duniya that linked it with the INTUC faction as well.

The composition of the Municipal Council in 1955 changed, following new elections, and brought an influx of INTUC representatives into the municipal arena. Although Babulal Patodi, a Nai Duniya faction chieftain, served briefly as Mayor and as a Trustee, he was the sole Nai Duniya Trustee, and following his departure in 1957 there was a hiatus in Nai Duniya membership on the Trust. At the same time, the Khadiwala group also went unrepresented for some three years, until Hastimal Jain reappeared on the Trust in 1960–61. Most of the politicians on the Trust from 1955 to 1958, whether government nominees or Municipal Councillors, were from the INTUC faction, and it was during this period that the use of the Improvement Trust's jurisdiction to provide amenities in the labor area reached its peak. D. S. Patil, who had been on the Trust as

TABLE 32. FACTIONAL DISTRIBUTION OF POLITICIANS ON THE IMPROVEMENT TRUST [a]

Year	Nai Duniya Faction	INTUC Faction	Khadiwala (Mishra) Faction	Opposition and Independents
1947–48	V. V. Sarvate (P)		Hastimal Jain (C)	
1948–49	V. V. Sarvate (P) N. G. Kothari (C)		Hastimal Jain (C)	
1949–50	Bhanudas Shah (P) Narendra Tiwari (C)		Purshottam Vijay (C)	
1950–51	V. V. Sarvate (P) T. Pathak (C)		Pukhraj Bahen (C)	Purshottam Vijay (N)
1951–52	T. Pathak (P) V. V. Sarvate (C)		Pukhraj Bahen (C)	Purshottam Vijay (N)
1952–53	L. S. Chauhan (P) V. V. Sarvate (C)		Pukhraj Bahen (C)	Purshottam Vijay (N)
1953–54	L. S. Chauhan (P) Hirabai Bordiya (C)	D. S. Patil (C)	Hastimal Jain (N)	Purshottam Vijay (N)
1954–55	V. V. Sarvate (P) T. Pathak (P) Hirabai Bordiya (C)	D. S. Patil (C)	Hastimal Jain (N) Chotilal Gupta (C)	Purshottam Vijay (N)
1955–56	T. Pathak (P) B. Patodi (P)	D. S. Patil (C) M. Sharma (C) Natwarlal Shah (N)	Chotilal Gupta (C) Hastimal Jain (C)	
1956–57	B. Patodi (P)	M. Sharma (C) C. Katariya (C) Natwarlal Shah (N) D. S. Patil (N)	Hastimal Jain (C)	
1957–58		I. C. Jain (M) C. Katariya (C) M. Sharma (C) D. S. Patil (N) Natwarlal Shah (N)		

1958–59	Suresh Seth (C)	D. S. Patil (N) Natwarlal Shah (N)		Purshottam Vijay (M) R. M. Bhandari (C)
1959–60	Suresh Seth (C)	D. S. Patil (N) Natwarlal Shah (N)		Balkrishna Gohar (M) R. M. Bhandari (C)
1960–61	Suresh Seth (C)	Natwarlal Shah (N)	Hastimal Jain (N)	Shersingh (M)
1961–62	Suresh Seth (C) V. V. Sarvate (C)	Natwarlal Shah (N)	Hastimal Jain (N)	B. Purohit (M)
1962–63	Suresh Seth (C) V. V. Sarvate (C)	Natwarlal Shah (N)	Hastimal Jain (N)	R. N. Zutshi (M)
1963–64	M. Khutal (C) M. S. Mehta (N)	G. Tiwari (MLA)	N. K. Shukla (M) Hastimal Jain (N)	Yugydutt Sharma (C)
1964–65	B. S. Bhandari (M) M. Khutal (C)	G. Tiwari (MLA)	Hastimal Jain (N)	Yugydutt Sharma (C)
1965–66	L. S. Chauhan (M) M. Khutal (C)	G. Tiwari (MLA) Chandmal Gupta (C)	Hastimal Jain (N)	Yugydutt Sharma (C)
1966–67		G. Tiwari (MLA) Chandmal Gupta (C)	L. S. Shukla (M) Hastimal Jain (N)	Yugydutt Sharma (C)
1967–68		Chandmal Gupta (C)	L. S. Shukla (M)	Yugydutt Sharma (C) R. N. Zutshi (N)
1968–69		Chandmal Gupta (M)		Yugydutt Sharma (C) Kalyan Jain (MLA) R. N. Zutshi (N)

(P) = President of Municipality.
(M) = Mayor of Municipal Corporation.
(C) = Municipal Councillor, delegate.
(N) = Government Nominee.
(MLA) = Member of Legislative Assembly (also a government nominee).

[a] This table lists all of the non-bureaucratic Trustees (mostly politicians) who appeared on the Trust in a given year, but at some cost in precision, for not all of those listed for a particular year, especially in the period between 1954 and 1958, were on the Trust simultaneously. Some replaced others. In 1956–57, for example, Ishwar Chand Jain succeeded Babulal Patodi on the Trust in mid-year, by virtue of having been elected municipal President. Because charting such mid-term shifts would make the table inordinately complex, they have been omitted. Even so, the changing factional distribution is discernible.

early as 1953, was a particularly important instrument of Labour
Minister Dravid's power over policy initiatives in the arena of improvement politics.[18]

In the 1958 municipal election, all three Congress factions were
weakened by the combined opposition of the *Nagrik Samiti*. As a result, the opposition gained a significant level of representation on
the Trust for the first time in 1958–59. But as we saw in municipal
politics, the *Nagrik Samiti* was a fragile coalition which succumbed to
municipal Congress party efforts to divide and undermine it, leading
to Congress' indirect rule in the Council. And the Trust, therefore,
was really controlled in the 1958 to 1967 period by Congress forces.
The Nai Duniya faction by 1961 had regained Trust representation
and even an edge over the two rival Congress factions, though each
was represented. The *Nagrik Samiti*, however, had to be content with
only one Trustee.[19] The instrument of government nomination was
used to strengthen Congress representation exclusively, but it is also
significant that it was used (with only one exception, Manoharsingh
Mehta of Nai Duniya) to place INTUC or Khadiwala faction members on the Trust.

After D. P. Mishra emerged as the principal leader of the Madhya
Pradesh Congress, and became Chief Minister in 1963, his magnetic
appeal drew certain members of the *Nagrik Samiti*, especially Hindi-
speaking Brahmans such as N. K. Shukla and Lakshmi Shanker
Shukla, earlier defectors from Congress such as Purshottam Vijay, and
existing members of the Congress such as Suresh Seth, into one common group. The first MLA to become a Trustee, Gangaram Tiwari,
the Hindi-speaking Brahman opponent of Ramsingh in labor politics,
and an ally of Mishra, was nominated to the Trust when Ramsingh's
power in the labor arena had been broken. By 1966–67, the Mishra
group on the Trust had become dominant in the persons of L. S.
Shukla, Gangaram Tiwari, and Hastimal Jain. In the years that followed, the Nai Duniya faction went unrepresented altogether, the
victim of the growing strength of the Hindi-speaking Brahman faction
at the state and local levels. But the Mishra faction in turn was in-

---

[18] After INTUC lost control of the Municipal Council, D. S. Patil remained on
the Trust as a nominated member until 1960.

[19] This was made possible by the rule that election of Trustees from the Council is by single non-transferrable votes and results in proportional representation.

jured by the state-level takeover of the opposition under the SVD government coalition in July, 1967.[20]

Over the two-decade period, the real casualty with respect to influence on the Trust was the Nai Duniya group. Because of the early affinity of the Nai Duniya group for the Holkar regime, the Nai Duniya politicians were able to establish an early hold on the Trust. They were able to work closely and productively with the bureaucrats, nine of whom, in the first decade (1947–1957), were former Holkar administrators. Since the INTUC faction under V. V. Dravid's guidance was usually an ally of the Nai Duniya group, the real assault on the Nai Duniya group came from the Hindi-speaking Brahman faction—identified first with Khadiwala (an insider) and later with Mishra (an outsider). The bureaucrats on the Trust who leaned toward the Hindi-speaking Brahman group were rare before 1956, in the Madhya Bharat period, but more common afterward. Pushkarnath Kazi (a Katju man), and S. C. Sharma and P. L. Gavande (Mishra supporters) were those who could be so identified.

The factional coloration of the Trust reflects, often belatedly, shifts in the factional or party balance of power in other arenas or on other levels of politics. The factions are the same as those operating throughout the city. But the Trust presents special problems for those politicians, even on the state level, who seek to control it. The increase in the proportion of local political representatives has made it more difficult for Cabinet politicians to control the Trust. The politician Trustees (except the Mayor) are usually in for four-year terms. And even when their terms expire it is difficult for state-level politicians to determine all their replacements. (The state politicians may choose one from among the elected city MLA's, a limited selection. There remains one non-bureaucrat, over whom state politicians may exercise complete choice.) On the other hand, state-level politicians can gradually alter the bureaucrats on the Trust to bring in

[20] After the failure of Mishrilal Gangwal to win reelection, the Chairman felt it safe to block Hastimal Jain's renomination to the Trust by sending an unfavorable report. Mishra did not have sufficient time to nominate an MLA to the Trust in 1967 before his government fell. The SVD government solicited advice from the Chairman and Yugydutt Sharma, who was already a Trustee. One Indore MLA, Arif Beg, was a Minister and therefore excluded from consideration. That left one SVD MLA, Kalyan Jain. Yugydutt Sharma and the Trust Chairman both recommended that the lone Congress MLA from the city be nominated. The government ultimately overrode this advice and nominated Kalyan Jain.

men of another persuasion. But it takes time. Local politicians cannot easily prevent such changes unless they also have powerful state-level allies. Without factional coherence in both the bureaucratic and political complements of the Trust—if each is oriented to a different group—the bureaucrats may veto the political representatives and vice versa. There may have been a tendency for this to take place in 1966–67, when L. S. Shukla was Mayor and Gangaram Tiwari was still on the Trust. At the same time the Mishra group could count on the support of P. L. Gavande, but not on the Chairman, S. C. Dube.[21]

The three case studies below clearly illustrate that the formulation and implementation of the improvement schemes is a political process, though couched in ostensibly impartial administrative procedure. The "power to improve" embodies the power to demolish or take away what some participants possess and value as well as the power to give what others desire—the power to harm and the power to gratify. The cases demonstrate how the Trust or Trustees build political constituencies (residential colony development) or aid politicians in building constituencies (labor area improvement); how the Trust may be used in an attempt to deny constituencies to one group of politicians by another; and how the Trust as a political actor competes with and undermines the municipal government (Jawaharmarg case).[22]

The Politics of Housing Colony Development

Since Independence, perhaps the greatest economic change affecting the appearance of Indore city is the proliferation of new housing colonies on the outskirts of older parts of the city. Money made and

---

[21] Dube belonged to Mishra's caste, but his primary orientation was to Indore and his closest ties were with Indore politicians of the Nai Duniya group.

It should be pointed out that the Trust was not central to Mishra's drive to build support in Indore. If he succeeded in other arenas—labor and municipal, for example—control of the Trust would be attained as a matter of course. And in any case, control of the Trust was less salient than MLA loyalty, Mishra's prime concern.

[22] Three additional cases—concerning town planning and encroachment in the rural areas, the political and administrative problems for the Trust of a squatter settlement, and the use of the Trust by state politicians as an instrument of attack on the holdings of a large landlord (Niranjan C. Zamindar) in Champabagh—have been omitted here, but are included in my "Area, Linkage and Power in Indore," pp. 380ff.

saved in the city was frequently invested in land and suburban homes. Sometimes the younger members of families have moved out into these new houses, but newly acquired property has often merely been rented out to new residents of the city as reliable long-term sources of income. Residential construction has stimulated supporting industries, brick-making, lumber contracting, cement production, pipe manufacturing, and small-scale industries in hardware, paint, water meters, water pumps, and other equipment. Almost all the real growth in small industries in Indore in recent years is related to such construction.

It is probably in the development of land for housing colonies that the Improvement Trust finds its greatest patronage potentials. The development of housing is a business, and the Trust involvement in this kind of business naturally brings it into contact if not competition with businessmen—land speculators and financiers, and construction contractors.

In the development process, the Trust frequently comes into contact with other government agencies, especially the Public Health Department (Engineering) because of its concern with waterworks, and also with the Nazul and Revenue officers over questions of land ownership and value, and with the Engineers of the state Public Works Department over questions concerning government buildings and state roads that are present in scheme areas. As a result of their legal involvement in matters that affect the Trust and private colonizers, bureaucrats in each of these agencies get opportunities to build constituencies of their own.

Probably the most difficult problem in the effective planning of a residential colony in Indore is the provision of an adequate and reliable water supply. Water is scarce. Private developers frequently attempt to bore wells and set up storage tanks for an individual housing colony, but this is an expensive process and risky because the return on the investment is likely to be slow. Consequently, private developers often seek government assistance on water supply. In such cases they must partly work with or through Public Health engineers. Because the city water supplies are limited and subject to seasonal fluctuations, the Public Health Department is bound to scrutinize requests for permanent water connections to new housing colonies very carefully, and the opportunity to use the power to establish water connections as a form of patronage becomes virtually irresistible.[23]

The predisposition of the Trust to concentrate on financially profitable or self-supporting schemes pulls in the direction of housing colony "development schemes" rather than "improvement schemes" as such, as the latter are likely to be deficit in nature.[24] Developed land can be sold or leased at rates that cover the cost of acquisition and development. As a result, the Trust is as interested as any private developer in permanent water connections and, by its nature as a quasi-governmental agency, it tends to assume that it has a prior claim on the water resources controlled by the Public Health Department. The bureaucratic linkage established by the customary presence of the Public Health Engineer on the Trust is undoubtedly an advantage for the Trust in that the commitment of the Public Health Department to support Trust schemes can be obtained in advance. But even the Trust cannot take the support of the Engineer for granted. His support must be won in some manner or other, through pressure at other points in the bureaucratic machinery or through inducements. The Engineer of Public Health has opportunities to bargain that may be used in a variety of ways to favor private clients.[25] In effect, then,

---

[23] The Public Health Department does not have exclusive power over all questions concerning water supply. As described in the chapter on the municipal arena, the Corporation plays a role on questions of distribution of water, and over new connections. For example, with respect to private housing colonies developed outside municipal limits, the Corporation can indefinitely postpone their incorporation, prior to which no municipal water mains can be connected with the colony. Moreover, the municipality may refuse to assume maintenance responsibility for the roads and drainage systems of privately developed colonies where the works do not come up to specifications in municipal by-laws and building regulations. Those concerned with housing colonies are frequently forced, therefore, to deal with the municipality, not only with the Trust or the Public Health Department. But the scope of the municipal government, and its corresponding capacity to build constituencies in this area, is limited by pressures from the Trust or the veto powers of the Public Health engineers.

[24] Shying from deficit projects is a common characteristic of urban special authorities in the United States also. See Sayre and Kaufman, *Governing New York City*, pp. 320ff.

[25] Such favors, of course, must be granted circumspectly. Favoring private interests can be most dangerous when doing so is in conflict with such regulations as do exist and when the interests of persons who have their own connections with the administration or key politicians are adversely affected. One such case arose when S. C. Dube was Chairman of the Trust and P. L. Gavande was the Executive Engineer of Public Health and a Trustee, in 1967.

Surendranath Dube, the father of S. C. Dube, a retired but influential former official of the Holkar state, had developed a small housing colony near Manik

the Trust becomes a competitor with private interests in the area of urban development.

Private builders have to compete with the Trust not only for water but also for land and on costs. The acquisitions by the Trust may preempt desirable land and send the costs of land higher than they would be otherwise. At the same time, advance or confidential knowledge concerning Trust plans can be of advantage to one builder in competition with others. For example, if one builder knows where the Trust intends to locate a scheme, he can conceivably purchase adjacent property, speculating that such land will naturally appreciate if a Trust development takes place nearby. Furthermore, if water mains are to be laid for the Trust development, it could be easier for the private builder to get them extended just a little further for use in his property.

Even more useful than advance knowledge, however, is having a man on the Trust who can exercise favorable influence for the private builder on Trust decisions. Not only may there be a regular flow of confidential information to the builder concerned, but he may be able to dissuade the Trust from acquisitions that would hurt his existing interests. Moreover, builders are faced with an array of permits that must be acquired, and approvals that must be obtained at different levels of government, for colony development. An agent on the Trust can help turn the Trust into an ally for obtaining clearances at other levels on questions that affect urban planning.

There are two politician–Trustees who have clearly played the

Bagh Palace. He had been careful to develop it in accordance with building regulations regarding the placement of roads, in order to have them connect properly along north–south axes with main roads. (The regulations were designed to ensure that the system of roads through adjacent privately developed colonies would be regular and facilitate movement.) The developers of the adjacent Jaishri Colony attempted to violate this pattern by placing more houses closer together and reducing the amount of land in roads, so as to maximize their profits. (Road land, according to the regulations, cannot be transferred to the municipal authority at a profit.)

The older Dube contested the Jaishri plans through administrative channels, and the case came before the Trust for resolution. The younger Dube, as Chairman, declined to decide the case because of his family connection and presumable interest. He turned the case over to Gavande. As a senior official on the Trust, Gavande could be expected to decide the matter in accordance with the building regulations governing Trust actions. Instead, he gave the Jaishri colonisers permission to go ahead with their plans. The Chairman referred the matter to the government with a complaint, and the government ordered the work in Jaishri colony stopped. Gavande was suspended from the Trust and the following year he was not reappointed.

agent's role on the Trust. The first is Hastimal Jain, mentioned before, who has represented a wide variety of private interests including
the "colonizers' lobby." [26] The second is Suresh Seth, the agent of a
particular colonizing firm—the Indore Land and Finance Company
owned by the Kalani (Jain) family.[27]

Although businessmen like Kalani may be able to establish a
regularized influence on the Trust, the linkage is not merely one-way,
but also operates to make such businessmen supportive constituents
of the Trust's operation and jurisdiction, especially where the institutional interests of the Trust coincide with the interests of particular
businessmen. Whereas Kalani, for example, may find it possible to
have some regulation bent in his favor, it may serve his purpose
equally well to ensure that such regulations are not bent in favor of
his private competitors. This supports the regularized operation and
protects the reputation of the Trust.

Although such special access may not be easy to achieve, it is in
one sense economical—achieved through one or two key representatives—and has the advantages that it is not easily eroded (because of
the four-year term) and not subject to public scrutiny in the same
way as municipal access usually is. Manipulation can be more effectively screened from public view among the small number of Trustees
than among Municipal Councillors. Consequently, those with special
access in the Trust are usually predisposed to support the jurisdiction
and powers of the Trust over questions of urban development against
invasion by the municipal government.

The bureaucratic agency chiefs who sit on the Trust or participate
in the development of housing colonies may be jealous and protective
of their individual powers and jurisdictions. But when the Trust is
confronted by a challenge from the elected Municipal Council, the

---

[26] Among the more important of a large number of colonizers, the names of
Palshikar, Berathi, and Kalani stand out.

[27] The Kalanis have interests in numerous enterprises in Indore, including spun
pipe and pottery factories. Suresh Seth and his brother, Sohan Mehra, are both
employees of Kalani. Mehra is involved in the managment of the Land and
Finance Company, and shuns electoral politics. Suresh Seth puts some time in the
manager's office of the Saurabh Potteries and Ceramics, Ltd., but spends most of
his time in active politics in the Congress organization and the municipal arena,
and in the affairs of the Improvement Trust.

Some of the more important colonies developed by the Kalani firm are Srinagar,
Indrapuri, Kalaninagar, and Radhanagar.

bureaucrats tend to team up against the encroachment. Bureaucrats seek to preserve the shielded decision-making process in the Trust as it affords themselves some protection against public scrutiny. To this extent, these bureaucrats become supportive constituents of the Trust also against the municipal government.

The central point is that an important functional jurisdiction—the power to develop, and regulate the development of, housing colonies —is kept out of the municipal arena, except to the extent that this may be qualified by the presence of representatives of the municipal government on the Trust. The powers of patronage and opportunities to build institutional and political constituencies among those actively interested in the development of housing colonies is largely denied to the municipal government or to its elected representatives. Though the Trust is not immune to local political penetration, such penetration is highly selective and usually depends on vertical linkages with state level politicians—a result of the pattern of state and bureaucratic dominance of the Trust.

The Politics of Labor Area Improvement

This case shows how certain arenas of city politics—labor, municipal, and improvement—can be made to overlap through the concerted use of key vertical linkages by a Cabinet Minister with an armful of portfolios affecting the urban area. The Minister in question, V. V. Dravid, arrived on the Madhya Bharat Cabinet in 1952 after the first general elections. In addition to the Labour portfolio, he also held at various times the portfolios of Development (1952–55), Local Self-Government, Urban (1952–53), Public Health (Engineering), Housing Department, and Town Improvement (1954–57). While in charge of these portfolios, the Labour Minister was able to work simultaneously through the local PWD, PHD, and Housing Department engineers, as well as those of the Improvement Trust and the Municipal Government.

It will be recalled that the INTUC group allied itself with the Chauhan group on the Municipal Council in 1952, resulting in the election of D. S. Patil of the INTUC group to the Trust in 1953. He held this elected position until 1956 and was thereafter a nominated Trustee until 1960. Patil acted as Dravid's primary political agent on the Trust to supervise its activities affecting the labor area.

Prior to 1954, parts of the labor area remained outside municipal boundaries. The INTUC group in the 1950–55 Council pressed for the incorporation of these areas, but were successfully resisted until 1954 by the city-oriented Councillors such as V. V. Sarvate, who feared that the incorporation of such areas would put a heavy financial burden on the Municipal Government—i.e., on the middle-class property-owners and taxpayers of the city. There were the added potential threats of INTUC dominance of the City Congress and the municipal arena. But in 1954 and 1955 the INTUC group won out in the municipal arena, and those parts of the labor area were duly incorporated.

At the same time, the Labour Minister was interested in improving the living conditions of the laborers, to give them an opportunity to participate in and benefit from the municipal arena and also to strengthen his political hold among the labor class by using the powers of his ministerial position in concrete and visible ways. In 1954 Dravid succeeded in getting budgetary sanction of 230,000 rupees for the "development" of Pardesipura and neighboring areas. He used this sum, through the engineers, to put roads, water wells, and storage tanks in the labor area. D. S. Patil and Natwarlal Shah—an INTUC sympathizer—supervised these activities from their vantage point on the Trust, as did Ishwar Chand Jain, Mathuralal Sharma and Chhaganlal Katariya both on the Trust and in the municipal government.

During this same period, under the Madhya Bharat government, the key officials in the Secretariat who were concerned with "development" were either protégés of Dravid or at least former Holkar state officials—who relied for protection in the Madhya Bharat service primarily on Indore politicians in the Cabinet. For example, L. O. Joshi was Development Secretary from 1954–57, S. S. Joshi was Deputy-Secretary of Labour in 1954–55 and Labour Commissioner from 1955–57, Masood Quli Khan was Inspector-General of Municipalities in 1954–55, B. M. Joshi was Inspector-General of Municipalities in 1956–57, P. S. Bapna was Development Commissioner in 1956–57, P. N. Bhalla was Superintending Engineer of Public Health in 1956–57—all former Holkar civil servants.

While development was underway in Pardesipura, the boundaries of the Municipality were extended to include much of the labor area by an act of the state government in 1954, prior to the holding of municipal elections early in 1955. The municipal area of about six square miles was nearly doubled to about eleven square miles. The number of municipal wards was increased from 22 to 35, with reserved seats in the five double-member constituencies. Part of the success of the INTUC group's gaining control of the Municipal Council in 1955 was due to the creation of a half-dozen new seats in the labor area itself.

This case further amplifies the observations on politics in the labor arena concerning the predominance of vertical political and bureaucratic linkages. Dravid successfully combined INTUC local power with his ministerial power and the aid of strategically placed bureaucrats at state and local levels,[28] for the benefit of his labor constituency in the city.

The Politics of Street Planning and Development

The Jawaharmarg project is the most ambitious of the completed schemes of the Indore Trust. In its implementation it has been the most controversial scheme of all, and because of its scope it brought the Trust into direct confrontation with the municipal government. The disputes between the Trust and the municipal government arising from the project provide the clearest illustration of how the Trust operates according to institutional interests that conflict with those of the municipal authority, by saddling the latter with liabilities that are not of its own choosing. On the other hand, the Jawaharmarg project is an example of real city improvement resulting in far-ranging economic and civic benefits that the municipal government, under its present constitutional arrangements and with its present powers, could probably never have brought to fruition on its own. The case also serves to show further the political implications of the linkages between the main institutional actors involved in the controversy—the state government, the municipal government, and the Trust—and the implications of their linkages with special constituencies, particularly the merchants of the central part of the city.

The need for a main traffic-bearing route on an east–west axis through the city had become urgent in the 1930's as a consequence of Indore's growth as a commercial center. The one more or less straight

---

[28] As was noted in Chapter 7 on municipal politics, the first Assistant Engineer who became Acting City Engineer was S. V. Dravid, the Labour Minister's brother.

route running west from the Bombay–Agra trunk road through Indore in the direction of Depalpur on the other side of the city, now known as Mahatma Gandhi road, was too narrow to carry the growing traffic through the city and between the center of the city and the periphery. A second parallel route a little to the south was conceived by the Improvement Trust as a necessary improvement. The existing road running from the Siaganj area through the densely populated center of the city was irregular and winding until its final exit near Raj Mohalla in the direction of Dhar. But it provided a basic route that might be widened, straightened, and improved to facilitate the movement of commercial traffic into the central city and out to Dhar.

The real beneficiaries of such an improvement, however, were to be the commercial communities, particularly the Jain Baniyas who controlled the Cloth Market and were interested in freer movement of manufactured cloth from the industrial area to their wholesale storage points, and from there to markets elsewhere in the Malwa region. The sections of the merchant community that controlled Malharganj and its associated grain market would also profit from better connections with the Bombay–Agra highway. The main moving force for this improvement, therefore, was—not surprisingly—the Nai Duniya group, because of its intimate relationship with the Jain Cloth Market Association and other Jain and Hindu Baniya interests in Sitlamata Bazaar, Subhas Chowk, and Malharganj. The scheme also contained benefits for the Gujarati and Bohra merchant communities, because of their special interests in wholesale distribution of hardware and other merchandise in the Siaganj area on the eastern part of the scheme axis.[29]

The ambitiousness of the scheme stemmed partly from the fact that many semi-permanent brick buildings and shops had to be demolished in order to make room for a wide and relatively straight avenue. Moreover, those who owned the land over which the road would pass would lose the future potential of their investments, as the land would not be directly recoverable for other purposes. As a result considerable opposition to the scheme from individual property-owners could be expected. Their political affiliations, however, were too diverse to enable them to form a combined front of opposition of sufficient strength to block the

[29] Natwarlal Shah, a political representative nominated to the Trust by the government from 1955 to 1962, was there to voice Gujarati merchant interests on how the scheme should be implemented in Siaganj.

scheme. The number and influence of those who would benefit from the scheme was overwhelming. The second factor making the scheme ambitious was the size and cost of the project. Initially it was necessary for the government to bear the lion's share of the expense.[30]

The scheme was prepared between 1943 and 1946, and divided into two portions, eastern and western. The western portion was by far the longest section. The land that had to be acquired for it was divided among numerous small holders, and it was believed that the process of acquisition would not be insuperably difficult. But the priority given to the western section is explained by the fact that here the new road ran adjacent to or nearby the main Jain commercial and residential areas in the heart of Indore. The implementation of the western portion of the scheme began in 1946, and construction was completed between 1952 and 1953 at a cost of 277,000 rupees for the roadway and 1,500,000 rupees for compensation of property-owners.

The eastern and shorter segment of the scheme fell into the Siaganj area across the river from Juni Indore. Most of the land to be acquired in this section belonged to the senior branch of the Zamindar family, and despite their opposition the second portion of the scheme was begun in 1953 and construction was completed in 1957. The cost of the road in the eastern portion came to 1,100,000 rupees and the sum of 420,000 rupees was awarded to property-owners as compensation.[31]

On completion of the road construction in the western portion of the scheme in 1953, an obstacle arose over the fact that a considerable portion of the government loan remained to be paid. The Trust had

---

[30] The beginnings of the scheme in the 1940's were financed by a loan of 800,000 rupees from the Holkar government, and after merger, by a loan of 500,000 rupees from the Madhya Bharat government. The Trust also received "contributions" from the municipal government totaling 525,000 rupees. The municipal government was ordered by the Holkar government in 1943 to pay 325,000 rupees to the Trust, as well as such other contributions as the government might determine. The Madhya Bharat government succeeded to the outstanding loans due to the Holkar government and to the statutory powers of the Holkar government. Accordingly, in September 1952 the Madhya Bharat government ordered the municipal government to contribute an additional 200,000 rupees to the Trust for this scheme. As long as the Nai Duniya faction controlled both the Municipal Council and the non-official positions on the Trust (even the supporters of the Khadiwala faction, Hastimal Jain and Pukhraj Bahen, both Jains, strongly supported the Jain commercial interests on this question), it was not difficult to secure municipal financial cooperation for the scheme.

[31] Zamindar received about 80,000 rupees for his land, and most of the balance went to the owners of buildings which were demolished to make room for the road.

begun repaying the loan from income derived from "lease rents" on cleared property adjacent to the new road that had been let out to private entrepreneurs for the construction of office and commercial buildings.[32] But a substantial part of the debt remained outstanding. Normally the Trust was expected to transfer completed scheme areas back to the Municipality promptly, but with the debt outstanding the Trust was naturally reluctant to transfer the lease rents and the income yet to be derived from them. On the other hand, there was considerable pressure to open the new road. But the Trust had no funds to maintain the road in good repair.

To resolve the dilemma, the Trust sought to effectuate a partial transfer of the western part of the scheme in 1953. The Trust requested the Municipality to take over the scheme, including maintenance of the road, but not including the lease rents except on condition that the municipal authority simultaneously accept the liability of loan repayments. The Trust made a strategic error by opening the road to traffic before obtaining a guarantee from the municipal authority that the road would be maintained.[33] The opening of the road lifted one source of pressure for the municipal government to accept transfer of the scheme. At the same time, the Municipality had been collecting house and property tax from property owners in the scheme area throughout the period of implementation of the scheme. Thus the Municipality had the benefits without the liabilities of the scheme. Consequently there was little incentive to induce it to accept transfer of the scheme area. While the Municipality delayed, indicating its unwillingness to accept the transfer, over two years passed and the condition of the road deteriorated under heavy traffic.

The Trust, according to its rules, passed the matter on to the state government, which finally acted in September 1955. An order was sent

---

[32] The annual income from lease rents in the western section was about 20,000 rupees. The typical lease was for ninety-nine years, but there was a provision that the land under lease could in effect be sold to the lessee for a lump sum equal to twenty times the annual rent. The receipt of lump sums for some of the land made it possible for the Trust to reduce some of the debt more quickly than would otherwise have been possible.

[33] The Chairman at this time, V. G. Apte, had been an Alderman on the Municipal Council as well as Engineer of the Public Health Department. He seems to have been following pro forma the requirements of his Trust office. But this seems to have assisted the Nai Duniya group in the Council to evade the liabilities of the scheme.

to the Trust directing it to effect the transfer of the scheme and requiring the Municipality to accept the tranfer of jurisdiction along with all the "assets and liabilities" of the scheme. The Trust was thereby relieved of financial responsibility for the western portion of the scheme. The municipal government had no choice now other than to accept transfer, and so assumed responsibility for maintenance of the road in the western section; but at the same time it refused to accept responsibility for loan repayment, contending that the term "liabilities" did not include the loans outstanding. On the face of it, there could be no legal grounds for such an argument, but the effect of refusal to pay the loan was to throw the matter back into the hands of the government. If the government let the matter rest, the loans ultimately would be repaid by the government from revenues. In other words, some of the people of Indore would have succeeded in getting a road paid for in part by taxpayers outside Indore. There the matter lay for a few years.

Meanwhile, the eastern portion of the scheme neared completion. The new road in Siaganj was finished about 1957 and again the Trust, responding to local business interests, unwisely opened the eastern segment of Jawaharmarg before the Trust had made ready to transfer the scheme to the Corporation.[34] It was not until December 1961 that the Trust finally requested the Corporation to take charge of the eastern portion of the scheme. In the intervening years the road surface had suffered badly.

Again the Corporation objected to transfer of the scheme, this time on the ground that the road had not been built properly, and that the condition of the road was not worthy of an "improvement" scheme.[35] The Corporation indicated that it would, however, accept transfer of the scheme on condition that the Trust first resurface the road with asphalt. The Trust refused, contending that it had no responsibility

----

[34] A later Chairman, Mr. S. C. Dube, who had the reputation of being a model administrator, followed a different strategy in a similar case, albeit one less politically controversial. In the Shankerbagh scheme (no. 31), the Trust built a road as part of a plan for development. The road was completed in May 1966 but closed by the Chairman (with the Trust's approval) to traffic. The Corporation was requested to assume transfer of the road, and when the Corporation refused, the Chairman referred the matter to the government. The government instructed the Corporation to assume responsibility, but the instruction was ignored. Finally in 1967 the government issued a decree vesting the road in the Corporation. At this point, the Chairman opened the road and washed his hands of responsibility for it.

[35] This assessment was made by the Public Works Committee of the Corporation.

for maintenance or repairs. Finding the matter deadlocked, the Trust referred the matter in January 1963 to the government.

In the meantime, some progress was finally made on the loan repayment issue during the course of 1962. Since 1955 the unpaid portion of the loan had been in two parts, one of 480,000 rupees and the other of 460,000 rupees. As a result of negotiations with the government, the Corporation now agreed to pay the second part of the loan according to a schedule that was worked out. But the issue of repayment on the first part of the loan was left up in the air. In August 1965, the government issued an order to the Corporation to abide by previous government instructions on this matter and specifically mentioned repayment of the loan, but until 1968 this order remained unenforced.

In May 1963 the government called a meeting of Trust and Corporation representatives to deal with the problem of transfer of the eastern portion. After hearing both sides, the government authorized the Revenue Commissioner of Indore Division, M. P. Srivastava, to hold another hearing and settle the matter. Some months later, in November 1963, the government issued new orders, pursuant to the Commissioner's advice, that the Trust turn the eastern portion of the scheme over to the Corporation after making the necessary "repairs" to the road. The Trust followed these instructions by interpreting "repairs" to mean patching up the potholes that had appeared in the asphalt surface.

Toward the end of 1964 the political campaign began in anticipation of the municipal elections to be held in January 1965. Without consulting the Trust, the Corporation repaved the road on its own initiative just before the election, as a vote-getting tactic. All the parties represented on the Corporation were equally interested in this action, each believing it could be exploited to its own advantage. Subsequently the Corporation presented the repair bill of 80,000 rupees to the Trust for payment. The Trust, as was to be expected, objected, and the matter was again deadlocked. The case was referred back to the government in September 1965.

The government Secretary for Local Self-Government (Urban) pointed out that Section 415 of the Municipal Corporation Act of 1956 provided for arbitration in disputes between the Corporation and semi-governmental bodies such as the Trust. On this basis the government appointed Mr. Aramadhu, the Executive Engineer of the state Public

Works Department in Indore, as arbitrator for the dispute. The dispute at this point boiled down to what "repairs" meant. The Corporation was not satisfied with the patching of the roads, and interpreted "repairs" to mean a complete resurfacing of the road. Aramadhu's decision, coming in December 1966, was a compromise that leaned in favor of the Trust. The Trust was instructed to pay the Corporation only 15,433 rupees, and the Corporation was ordered to assume charge of the road immediately. Accordingly, the Corporation resumed jurisdiction of the eastern part of Jawaharmarg at the end of 1966. As no loan was taken for the eastern portion of the scheme, the only outstanding issue arising from the Jawaharmarg scheme remains repayment of part of the earlier loan.

This study of the Improvement Trust provides strong evidence of the recurrent pattern of bureaucratic dominance in urban political arenas, and of the salience of vertical political and bureaucratic linkages in determining political outcomes within those arenas. Despite the trend toward a modicum of popular and local accountability in the Trust, it is characteristically dominated by bureaucrats. Prominent among the bureaucratic Trustees are engineers who frequently preside over local bureaucratic jurisdictions in other arenas as well. The statutory basis of the Trust makes it primarily accountable to the state government, giving state-level politicians and their local allies excellent opportunities to direct the activities of the Trust in construction and improvement schemes. The improvement powers of the Trust can be manipulated in a variety of ways to produce patronage for political constituency-building efforts by those allied politicians at both levels and to offer substantial profit-making opportunities for those contractors and private developers who have good access to the controlling faction or coalition. Thus the Trust becomes an instrument of political chieftains working through the bureaucratic structure, confirming the proposition of the predominance of vertical political and bureaucratic linkages.

The Trust is not only an instrument of external political forces but, because of its statutory obligations to be financially self-supporting, it tends to operate as a political actor in its own right, undertaking schemes that assure a profitable return on its investment. Such schemes frequently include the development of housing colonies, bringing the

Trust into competition with private political and business actors. The powers to acquire land, condemn property, and appropriate jurisdiction over scheme areas within the municipality tend to bring the Trust into conflict and competition with the municipal government. A recurring feature of Trust operations is the invasion of municipal jurisdictions in the issue area of town planning and improvement, the effect of which is to further reduce the powers and scope for political constituency building of municipal political actors. Thus the Trust contributes to the fragmentation of urban politics within distinct bureaucratic arenas, one of the major factors accounting for the political weakness of Indore city in state politics.

10

THE LABOR ARENA IN CITY POLITICS: WORKERS, MACHINE POLITICS, AND THE STRUGGLE FOR POWER

Of the several political arenas embedded in Indore city politics, that of industrial labor politics is especially prominent and sharply defined, and because of its distinctive organizational participants it is relatively autonomous as well, not from vertical influence, but from pressures elsewhere in local politics. This chapter deals primarily with the politics of labor union organization and conflict in a setting of government regulation, and it focuses on several sets of relationships—between the millowners and the organized work force; between government agencies on one hand and the millowners and unions on the other; between unions themselves as rivals for worker support and political power; and between rival forces within the dominant pro-Congress union that strive for control over the organization. Labor unions possess a distinctive occupational concern based on the interests of factory workers, and their primary goals might therefore be expected to consist of gaining benefits in wages and working conditions for their members, but their goals in Indore are, in fact, as much political as economic or occupational in nature. The reasons for this need not preoccupy us here save to say that the conditions of nationalist politics fused the objectives of the Indian labor movement with those of protest organizations and political mobilization generally; the politicization of labor contributed to, and was further reinforced by, government intervention in industrial relations, so that economic goals were most likely to be

furthered by union political activity.[1] Similar conditions came to prevail in the capital of the Holkar princely state.

The politicization of labor in Indore, as well as elsewhere in India,
had two effects relevant to the deeper concerns of this study. First, because union politicization led to organizational fragmentation, sharp
ideological divisions, and bitter interorganizational conflict, there has
been a pronounced tendency toward radicalism and violent agitation
in labor politics. Second, labor politicization brought unions and trade
union federations into close, and usually subordinate, relationships
with political parties, but these relationships have also been marked by
friction over the respective roles of the two types of organizations in
electoral politics. Political party organizations have been loath to see
their principal functions of nominating candidates and mobilizing the
voters usurped by unions. And unions, though their clienteles are predominantly working class in composition, have organizational capabilities which lend themselves not only to bargaining with employers but
to campaigning for electoral candidates as well. Consequently, politicized unions have a tendency to challenge political parties for preeminence, especially in electoral constituencies where laborers are numerically important. While the labor arena, analytically speaking, is
the domain in which unions, industrial employers and the relevant
government agencies interact, because labor unions in Indore tend to
invade also the spheres of city-wide electoral politics and other urban
political arenas, and because they like political parties seek to share
control over the representative and bureaucratic hierarchies that impinge on the city, this chapter also deals with the political impact of
labor arena forces on other aspects of urban politics. It focuses in this
connection principally on the relationships between the dominant pro-
Congress union (the INTUC faction base) and the City Congress party
organization, and on the interaction of factions and primordial groups
within and between the two organizations.

This chapter is divided for convenience into three main sections.
The first section, "Organizing Labor Power," deals with the labor
arena properly speaking; it describes the basic features of the social

---

[1] These tendencies were by no means peculiar to labor in Indian politics, but
have been the general rule in formerly colonized developing countries. For a good
introduction, see Bruce H. Millen, *The Political Role of Labor in Developing
Countries.* For the background on India, see also Charles A. Myers, *Labor Problems
in the Industrialization of India.*

and industrial environment within which unions operate; traces the background of the Indore labor movement in the princely state period; and explains the organizational success and machine attributes of the dominant union in terms of factors of leadership, government power, and financial resources. Section two, "Unions and Electoral Competition," focuses on the electoral roles of union candidates and on union-party relationships of cooperation and conflict in the electoral arena. And the third section, "Union Bosses and the Struggle for Machine Power," consists of a case study which uncovers the dynamics of intra-organizational and factional conflict, and the structure of political linkages, in the open battle for control of the INTUC union, as it surfaced in 1963 and shook the machine's grip over textile workers. Taken together, these sections shed light on the vertical pattern of political and bureaucratic linkages which introduce a measure of centralization into labor politics—especially when local actors become deadlocked—and contribute to the definition of the labor arena as a sphere of organizational activity, points which are expanded upon in the conclusions of this chapter.

I. Organizing Labor Power

Social and Historical Background

This account deals primarily with the *organized* laborers of the textile industry of Indore, because they are the principal (unionized) participants in the arena of labor politics. But it is well to bear in mind that perhaps two-thirds of those who would be classified as "laborers" (*mazdoor* or *shramik*) in Indore are unorganized by trade unions and are distributed among a large variety of occupations ranging from small-scale factories and household industries (workshops, garages, printeries, lumber yards) to *coolies* (burden-carriers and loaders in the commercial and transport sectors), construction workers, scavengers, menial servants, and so on. Unfortunately, the census categories do not lend themselves readily to discovering the proportions of laborers categorized in these terms.[2] Although it is with the textile workers, most

---

[2] What they do show, for the *urban areas of Indore district* in 1961, is the following (see Table 1, p. 31): there were some 119,000 "workers" (income-earners) of all kinds, nearly one-third in "services" (about 39,000), over one-fifth in "trade and commerce" (about 25,000), less than 5 percent (about 5,000) in "construction," nearly

of whom are union members, that we are chiefly concerned, the float-
ing pool of unorganized labor is still relevant as a background factor
in electoral politics.

The number of textile workers—the base of industrial unions in
Indore—has been shrinking, not just in relation to the continued
growth of the city's population, but in absolute terms. As early as 1948,
the Indore textile industry had virtually stopped growing, having
reached a level of 214,000 spindles and 6,300 looms. Since then, without the protective barriers of the princely state, the industry had suffered from the competition of more vigorous textile industries, especially in Ahmedabad and Bombay. Textile employment reached its
peak at a level of 26,000 blue-collar workers (on all shifts) during the
Second World War, but because of work load rationalization and employee retrenchment it has since tapered down to an estimated 19,000
in 1968, a decline of nearly 25 percent.[3] The population of the city,
by contrast, had nearly doubled in the same period, from about 265,-
000 in 1946 to about 500,000 in 1968. By inference, the proportion of
textile workers among potential voters must have declined by more
than half. Of the 19,000 textile workers in Indore in 1968, about 3,000
were *badli* workers, or daily wage workers, who come to the mills and
are hired on an ad hoc basis to fill in for absentees or to take up the
slack when production rises temporarily to a peak. And about 1,000
of the textile workers were white-collar clerical and office employees.

The *labor area* consists of the northeast quadrant of Indore (see
chapter 2), where the major textile mills are located, and it is segre-

---

7 percent (about 8,000) in "transport, storage, and communications," and slightly
more than one-third (about 42,000) in "manufacturing" of all kinds. It is the last
category that contains most industrial workers, and those in the textile industry
(27,081 were recorded) made up nearly 23 percent of the work force. Because these
are not simply Indore city but rather Indore district urban area figures, the number of textile workers is inflated, but its proportion is probably not far off the
mark, even for Indore city. Apart from those figures on workers in "manufacturing,"
most of whom would be classified as "industrial laborers," the figures are not very
helpful in estimating the proportions of non-industrial workers. The figures are also
difficult to use because they do not distinguish employers from employees, white-
collar from blue-collar workers, or public from private employees, within each
category.

[3] The average number of textile mill employees in Indore city was given as
24,809 in 1950; 22,304 in 1955; 19,511 in 1960; 20,271 in 1963; and 19,000 in 1968.
There was some fluctuation, but, over the long term, a general decline. Madhya
Pradesh, Directorate of Economics and Statistics, *Pocket Compendium of District
Statistics,* Indore, 1963.

gated from the heart of Indore city by the railway line. The "labor area," though it should not be confused with the "labor arena" (an analytical construct), is the territorial focus for much that transpires in the arena of labor politics. That is mainly because many of the textile workers have constructed and settled in densely-populated shanty-towns, in buildings which are often of makeshift construction, but which are within earshot of their places of work. While not all mill employees live in the labor area, it is quite homogeneous from an occupational standpoint (unlike most other sections of the city) because the bulk of its residents do work in the mills. Consequently, the settlement clusters of the labor area, and the mill premises themselves, are the union domain—the principal focal points of constituency-building and recruitment by rival unions. The remainder of the labor area residents consist mainly of shopkeepers, merchants, and small-scale landowners or building proprietors who derive their incomes from selling, renting, or providing other services to the laboring population. Some of these businessmen and rentiers develop patron-client relationships (through moneylending, the extension of credit, or through the power to evict tenants from rented shacks) which sometimes become useful points of pressure in union membership drives, and which offer these patrons opportunities to become involved in politics. Others of the labor force live outside the labor area, and are scattered throughout the *mohallas* of the denser parts of the city. The concentration of laborers in the labor area, all of which falls within (but does not totally comprise) one MLA constituency, the "labor seat," virtually dictates that candidates for this seat, whatever party puts them up, will be political leaders with established connections and a following among the workers. Most usually such candidates have established their labor following through union organizational activities. But wherever laborers live in the city, their aggregate voting power, especially when it is combined with that of other members of their households, is substantial, and can affect the balance in close contests. This factor has been a key incentive in the expansion of union political activities outside of the labor area and within the central city.[4]

The arena of labor politics in Indore crystallized in the 1920's,

---

[4] See chapters 4, 7, and 9, and in this chapter, section two.

following establishment of the major textile mills between 1915 and 1922. The work force of "outsiders" that came into existence retained their ascriptive bases of identification. The primacy of ascriptive identifications has not prevented the organization of textile workers in permanent unions, but it has encouraged the pluralization of unions, factional conflict within unions, and the development of diffuse political linkages cross-cutting and obscuring potential class cleavages.[5] Although class conflict is not the prevailing condition of local labor politics, the labor arena more than any other in Indore is pervaded by a sense of potential conflict or expectation of violence, and the use of physical force and severe sanctions is comparatively common and visible.

Certain enduring linkage patterns among the political actors of the labor arena were formed in the period of princely politics, before 1948, and these ties are essential to understanding labor politics since that time. Figure 1 shows the linkage pattern as it has been reconstructed for the princely period. The chief labor organizations then were two rival unions—the pro-Congress Textile Labour Association (which was renamed the *Indore Mill Mazdoor Sangh*, or Indore Mill Workers Union, in 1941) and the Communist-led *Indore Mill Mazdoor Sabha* (Indore Mill Workers Association). In addition to the unions, several other political actors were involved in the labor arena, the textile millowners and managers, the Holkar government (especially its Labour Department), the British authorities in Indore, the local leaders of the Indore Praja Mandal and of the Congress branch organization, and the national leaderships of the Congress-oriented trade union movement (then based in Ahmedabad of Gujarat) and the Indian National Congress (Delhi).

The linkage structure is complex, for it contains internal (Holkar state) and external (British Indian) dimensions, and there are linkages of several kinds—between governmental and non-governmental actors, between political interest groups and popular political organizations, and between factions, primordial elites, and leading personalities. In-

---

[5] The origins of the local trade union movement are briefly reviewed in A. S. Banawalikar, *A Study of Industrial Dissatisfactions* (hereafter known as the *Banawalikar Report*); and V. V. Dravid, *Labour, Labour Movement and Labour Legislation in Madhya Pradesh.*

For the principal caste groups, and their regions of origin, in the laboring occupations of Indore city, see Appendix A, Table 1, pp. 381ff.

Figure 1

Linkage Map of Indore Labor Arena with City, State and National Levels of Political Activity — 1947

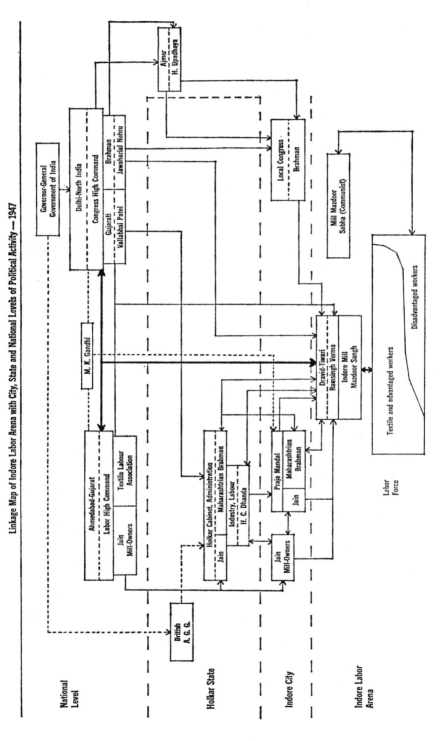

side the princely state, one key set of linkages of reciprocal support was that established between the millowners and the Holkar government, and based on personal and economic ties of long standing. As we saw in chapter 2, four of the private textile mills were started by Jain entrepreneurs, and all six of the mills were obligated to the Holkar government for land, customs exemptions on imported machinery, and a favorable tax climate generally. In the interwar period, the Prime Minister (Siremal Bapna) and several other high government officials were Jains, so that the government-millowner linkage consisted of personal access, reinforced by traditional community ties.

A second important set of political linkages was that between the labor movements, and their respective elites, of Indore and Ahmedabad. Located just 200 miles to the west of Indore, in Gujarat, the textile center of Ahmedabad was not only an important center of national political leadership (Sardar Patel and Morarji Desai, among others) but it had a pioneering role in the formation of the Congress policy on labor issues, primarily because of the successful efforts by Mahatma Gandhi to build an effective union (the Textile Labour Association of Ahmedabad), and to guide it into moderate but fruitful bargaining relations with the Gujarati (and predominantly Jain) millowners of that city. The informal ties that existed between the Jain millowners of both cities helped to make those in Indore receptive to the Gandhian pattern of industrial relations worked out in Ahmedabad. Thus, beginning in the 1920's, Gandhian labor leaders from Ahmedabad became sponsors of the labor movement in Indore, applying their approaches now within a princely capital. The interorganizational linkages between the labor movements in both cities were embodied after independence, formally and institutionally, in the Indian National Trade Union Congress (INTUC), the all-India federation of pro-Congress party unions. In fact, because the high command of INTUC was dominated by labor leaders who had served before independence in the Ahmedabad TLA, the informal paternalism (asymmetry) of the Ahmedabad group vis-à-vis labor leadership in Indore continued, but now in a hierarchical form.

A third set of political linkages consisted of those between labor unions and allied political parties. The TLA and Mill Mazdoor Sabha in Indore were closely tied, of course, to the Congress party and the Communist party respectively. But partisan interorganizational linkages were interwoven with factional and primordial linkages as well, especially in the case of the TLA and Congress forces. For the TLA (and its successor, the Indore Mill Mazdoor Sangh), the existence of two rival popular organizations—the Praja Mandal and the Indore branch of the Indian National Congress—posed something of a dilemma. The union desired and received support from both of these organizations. But the TLA developed a more intimate relationship with the Praja Mandal, for these two organizations had more in common with each other, from their Gandhian outlook and similarities in the composition of their core leaders (Marathi-speaking Brahmans and Jains), to greater access to the princely regime, than they had with the Congress branch.

Even so, the TLA was a pluralistic organization and also had its share of Hindi-speaking Brahman leaders who tended to look to the Congress more than the Praja Mandal for support. Although the underlying cleavage between Jains and Hindi-speaking Brahmans was kept under control in the union until well after independence, it did generate tension, and when it finally erupted in 1962 and 1963, it produced a factional division within the union that was congruent in many respects with that between the Nai Duniya and Khadiwala factions of the Congress party. Informal primordial ties between elites of the same communities became evident not just as factions within separate organizations but as interorganizational factional coalitions. Moreover, Jain-Brahman primordial competition, and ascriptive interorganizational linkages, appeared not just at the local level but in the Congress and INTUC organizations at the state and national levels too, and seemed to coincide with rival initiatives from elites based in Ahmedabad and Delhi. Such ascriptively-defined vertical political linkages between local elites and the party and union high commands played a part in surfacing the power struggle that broke out in the arena of labor politics in Indore in 1963.

Labor union organization first appeared in Indore in the postwar business boom of the early 1920's, but the early movement was fragmented among numerous small unions. Not until 1926 were the local unions able to forge a united front, but when they did so they launched the city's first major textile industry strike, in support of demands for a bonus. The ensuing labor-management deadlock stimulated interest by the princely authorities as well as by local labor leaders in outside help, and an appeal was made to the labor movement in Ahmedabad. Gandhi responded by delegating Gulzarilal Nanda, a key leader at the time of the TLA in Ahmedabad, to visit Indore and to use his good offices to promote a solution to the deadlock. Under Nanda's supervision, the Textile Labour Association of Indore was founded (on the Ahmedabad model), and it became the first labor union to receive official recognition in a princely state. At the same time, S. T. Dravid, a Brahman lawyer from a family based in Nagpur, was authorized by the Holkar government to issue an arbitral award, the outcome of which required the millowners to provide a bonus. Shortly thereafter, working hours were reduced from 12 to 10. The TLA was the beneficiary, for by 1930 its estimated membership had risen to three-quarters of the 12,000 workers then in the textile labor force.[6] In the early years, from 1926 to 1933, the TLA was the common representative of radical and moderate labor groups in Indore. The TLA was led after Nanda's departure by N. H. Dravid, a local lawyer, who sought to navigate the union through the tempestuous decade of the 1930's. His nephew (the third Dravid from that Nagpur Brahman family) was also his successor to leadership, as we will see below.

The economic boom of 1926 dropped sharply off into a depression, resulting, in 1931 and 1932, in bitter strikes provoked by wage cuts and fears of retrenchment. A general strike was mounted against the entire textile industry in Indore in 1933. The strike, however, was unsuccessful. During this period, the millowners' interests were paramount in Holkar government labor policy. The government's primary concern was to keep the mills economically viable during the period of economic contraction, and government machinery was used accordingly. Threats of disorder were firmly repressed, and labor was put on the defensive until the outbreak of the Second World War.

By 1939 the political situation had changed considerably. British officials had become extremely sensitive to threats of internal disorder, and their apprehensions affected Holkar government policy. Repression had made some of the labor groups increasingly radical. The defection of radical elements from the TLA reduced its membership and organizational strength after 1933. A militant section of the labor force finally formed a separate union, the Indore Mill Mazdoor

---

[6] *Banawalikar Report*, p. 7.

Sabha (Mill Workers' Association), in May 1939. The new union was dominated by Communist organizers whose tactics were less inhibited by Gandhian ideology. The Communist Mazdoor Sabha concentrated on the widening gap between real wages and rapidly rising wartime prices, and adopted an aggressive strategy leading to street demonstrations, wildcat strikes, and sporadic acts of violence. Escalating pressures finally produced a general strike in 1941 that threatened the entire city with chaos. The ensuing confrontation with the government ended in a police firing, and the deaths of several workers. The Mazdoor Sabha's leaders exulted in the bloodshed as the first signs of revolution, bringing into view their goal of "Lal Indore" (Red Indore). The membership of the Mazdoor Sabha, stimulated by these developments, grew rapidly between 1939 and 1945.

Shaken by the power demonstrated by the Communist union in the streets and fearing the consequences of repeated police firings, the Holkar Cabinet hastily reviewed its labor policy. Several factors converged to bring the Cabinet itself to ask for external assistance. To begin with, the millowners were anxious to curb Communist strength and keep the industrial peace and were ready to support government policies with that objective. H. C. Dhanda, a friend and advisor of Yeshwant Rao and from 1942 to 1947 the Minister of Commerce and Industries, urged that Gulzarilal Nanda be invited to return from Ahmedabad to Indore. The local pro-Congress labor leaders, the local Congress leaders, and most important of all, Sardar Vallabhbhai Patel in the Congress high command, urged the Cabinet in the same direction. Accordingly the Holkar government invited labor "experts" from Ahmedabad to conduct an inquiry into the labor problem of Indore. Implicit in the request was a search for means to block the growing power of the Communist Mazdoor Sabha over the labor force in Indore. Gulzarilal Nanda responded to the request by delegating two junior TLA leaders, V. V. Dravid and Ramsingh Verma, to conduct the inquiry and rebuild Congress strength among the textile workers.

Following the inquiry, Dravid and Ramsingh Verma reestablished the Textile Labour Association as the Indore Mill Mazdoor Sangh (Indore Mill Workers' Union) in December 1941. Before their rebuilding efforts had borne much fruit, however, the "Quit India" movement of 1942 began and the labor leaders of Indore were jailed under the preventive detention clauses of the Defense of India Act. In confinement, Dravid and Ramsingh Verma recruited Gangaram Tiwari, the third member of the Congress labor trio that was to emerge in Indore. The prisoners were finally released in December 1943, and Dravid, Verma and Tiwari went to work to build up the Mazdoor Sangh's strength.

The task was a challenging one. Although Dravid and Ramsingh were able to bring the IMMS membership up from 1,760 in 1943 to about 5,000 in 1945, the Communist leaders attracted nearly 3,000 new members of their own, bringing the total membership of the Mazdoor Sabha to a peak of 6,450.[7] Once the war ended, however, the Communist union rapidly declined in organizational strength, and all except its hard-core members were weaned away to the IMMS. The Mazdoor Sabha was further battered by the legal ban on its existence that went into effect in 1947, right after V. V. Dravid became Minister of Labour in the Holkar government. By 1948 the IMMS, now affiliated with the Indian National Trade Union Congress (INTUC), had become clearly dominant, with approximately half of the textile labor force enrolled as members. In the following years the membership continued to increase, so that from the mid-1950's on the IMMS could claim a membership fluctuating between 80 and 90 percent of the employed textile workers. Congress (IMMS) dominance in Indore labor politics lasted effectively from 1948 to 1964, and formally from 1964 to the present, a total of over twenty years. It is appropriate at this point to take a closer look at the IMMS leaders who brought off this achievement, for part of the explanation of their initial success lies in the quality of their leadership and working relationships.

INTUC Labor Leadership in Indore

Vyankatesh Vishnu Dravid comes from a traditionally orthodox but modernizing family of South Indian Brahmans who were based in Nagpur and had assimilated the ambience and culture of their Marathi-speaking surroundings. His maternal uncle, N. H. Dravid, a protégé of Gulzarilal Nanda and Kandubhai Desai, had helped lay the pro-Congress foundation in the Indore labor arena as the leader of the TLA, and his contacts with North Indian politicians and labor

---

[7] Figures are reported in the *Banawalikar Report*.

leaders of national stature were converted into similar assets for the younger Dravid. V. V. Dravid got his college education in the natural sciences at Gwalior, and he continued for some postgraduate work in economics before his restlessness in the nationalist environment drew him off into active work. At his uncle's suggestion, he went to Ahmedabad in 1937 for a political apprenticeship in the labor movement there, and worked for about five years under the tutelage of Gulzarilal Nanda before returning to Indore on his official mission in 1941 at the age of 28.

Ramsingh Verma's background was quite different. His father, a *Jadon* Rajput, was by occupation a *shikari* (hunter's guide) in Kotah, one of the southernmost princely states of Rajputana. According to his own account, Ramsingh was enrolled in a state school, something like a military academy, for the sons of Rajput military men and gentry until the age of 16. His formal education was then abruptly terminated because of his interest in nationalist politics, and he was briefly confined to prison by the princely government. Managing to escape, he rode the Frontier Mail (ticketless) to Ahmedabad and joined Gandhi's *Sabarmati Ashram* (a social work center on the banks of the Sabarmati River) for two years. In 1930, at the age of 18, he became an active worker in *satyagraha* (Gandhian nonviolent) movements and was jailed for short periods in Delhi and Agra. After joining the Indian National Congress in 1934, he began labor organizational work under Gulzarilal Nanda and Kandubhai Desai in the Ahmedabad Textile Labour Association. During his years in the labor movement there, he proved his value as a popular organizer. Ramsingh*bhai* (or "Brother" Ramsingh, as he became known in Gujarat) was subsequently selected to accompany Dravid to Indore as a lieutenant. He was 29 and married at the time.

Dravid and Ramsinghbhai evolved an intimate partnership, with an intelligent division of responsibilities and spheres of action, that enabled them together to dominate the arena of labor politics and participate as chieftains in Indore city politics until 1963. As long as they supported each other firmly, their position in the labor arena was impregnable. The durability of their partnership, which lasted from 1941 to 1962, is surprising, however, in view of the differences in their social origins, leadership styles, and personalities. Dravid fits the *pundit* (priestly) stereotype—a high-status Brahman, a bachelor, learned, intelligent, devotional and restrained in manner, simple in dress, and disciplined in his habits. He spends much of his leisure time reading, writing, and in meditation. He has little enthusiasm for barnstorming or public speaking campaigns, and apparently has a Gandhian aversion to open violence. His personal support among laborers derives to a considerable extent from his Gandhian style, his devotion to the laborers' welfare, and his personal austerity.[8] Dravid's contribution to the partnership has been intellectual (that of a legal strategist), symbolic (high status and Gandhian style), and most important of all, his links with extra-local sources of power and authority: his regular position as Cabinet minister in the state government, and his ties with the Brahman leaders in the Congress high command and the national leadership of INTUC. Dravid's primary spheres of action between 1948 and 1964 were outside Indore, on the state and national levels of politics. He used his interest in designing and implementing labor legislation shrewdly from his position in the state government to build INTUC strength among industrial laborers not only in Indore but also in Ujjain, Gwalior, and elsewhere in Madhya Pradesh.

If Dravid may be regarded as the extra-local mind of the IMMS (as well as of the state-wide INTUC organization), Ramsinghbhai Verma has been the local right arm, the master of organization and tactics in Indore city. Without as much formal education, Ramsingh (the abbreviated first name will be used for convenience) is nevertheless Dravid's equal in native intelligence and possibly his superior in shrewdness. What Dravid designed, Ramsingh operationalized in practical politics. Dravid's reserve contrasts with Ramsingh's platform presence, penchant for oratory, and enthusiasm for labor processions and demonstrations. Although Dravid has an underlying steel-like quality, Ramsingh comes closer to the Machiavellian stereotype— ruthless, daring, cunning, and politically well-informed.

At the height of this partnership, the skills of each member com-

---

[8] Of course, there are other ways to view these attributes. As a South Indian Brahman, as long as he maintains the expected *pundit* role, he can take status for granted, and publicity has always come easily as a result of his established political connections. Without a wife and children, he has less incentive to hoard materially for the future, and in the meantime the union provides him with spacious, comfortable—almost grand—quarters in the Shram Shivir, and a car and servants at his beck and call. By Indian standards Dravid lives well, though the style is austere.

plemented those of the other. Dravid's high-status and extra-local ties facilitated his inclusion in the Holkar and Madhya Bharat Cabinets and gave him easy access to the officials and mill owners with whom negotiations were necessary to win concessions for labor. Ramsingh's organizational talents were indispensable to Dravid in bridging the gap of communication with the labor constituencies and in mobilizing widespread labor support for Dravid's labor policies, giving him the local bargaining power he needed to win concessions and implement policies. Ramsingh and his lieutenants fulfilled the practical role of allocating political rewards and economic benefits differentially among laborers in return for organizational membership and loyalty, a role for which Dravid was tempermentally unsuited. Dravid might have found other hatchet men, but not likely one so adept at using the carrot and the stick as Ramsingh.

The division of authority, responsibilities, and spheres of action tended to give Ramsingh freedom of action in Indore but included the expectation that he would confine his activities primarily to Indore —something he was, not unnaturally, loath to do. Ramsingh acquired certain assets that were integral to his organizational success in Indore, but vulnerable once he moved outside the labor arena too aggressively. The main assets were his own supportive linkages with the local Jain political forces and with similar forces in the industrial labor arena at Ahmedabad. The Jains in Indore as well as elsewhere have consistently sought alternatives to Brahman dominance, and the division of responsibilities in Indore, with Ramsingh rather than a Brahman as local potentate in the labor arena, was supported by the Nai Duniya group (and millowners) as long as Ramsingh did not threaten Jain strongholds outside the labor area. Thus Ramsingh had sources of support independent of Dravid; but the linkages, unlike Dravid's, were more vulnerable precisely because they were not inherently ascriptive—that is, Ramsingh was not himself a Jain.

The second-level leadership of the IMMS tended to be largely a coalition of Jains and Hindi-speaking Brahmans, filling the administrative, office, and publishing positions of the organization, or holding strategic positions as mill employees: accountants, office supervisors, labor officers, or similar positions as union-employed "inspectors" and "labor officers," authorized to supervise, influence, and report on the behavior of union members within the mills. Among the

more prominent and active Jain functionaries were Ishwar Chand
Jain, chief editor and managing director of *Jagran* (the INTUC daily
newspaper of Indore), Motilal Jain, for a number of years the influential Secretary of the IMMS, and Chhaganlal Katariya, formerly
head clerk in the Hukumchand Mills. The Brahmans were chiefly
represented by Gangaram Tiwari and Mathuralal Sharma (Rajasthani)
the latter the chief accountant of the Malwa Mills and the President
of the Textile Clerks' Association. As will be seen later, when the
1963 power struggle developed the key Jain labor leaders tended to
support Ramsingh, and the Brahmans fell in line behind Dravid.

The most important of the second-level leaders in the long run
turned out to be Gangaram Tiwari. A Kanyakubja Brahman of Uttar
Pradesh, Tiwari came from a family of *kathavachaks*—popular musi-
cians who sing *bhajans* (hymns) and musical stories from the religious
traditions. Tiwari was able to adapt the traditional role of actor,
musician, and entertainer to the political role of platform performer
—an asset of some importance among the laborers, who have a strong
appreciation for campaign humor. Tiwari had little opportunity to
get a formal education in his boyhood—he was still a nonmatriculate
when defeated in an MLA contest by Homi Daji (Independent–
Communist) in 1957—but he has recently distinguished himself by
completing high school and college credits and earned an M.A. degree in Hindi literature from the University of Indore. He has contributed fundamentally to the success of the IMMS by his earnestness
and capacity for hard work, assisting Ramsingh in political education
and field work among the laborers. Since 1963 he has come into the
foreground of Indore labor politics as a protégé of Dwarka Prasad
Mishra (also a Kanyakubja Brahman), the former Chief Minister of
Madhya Pradesh.

Government Power and the Representative Union Issue

The working relationships and complementary skills of Dravid
and Ramsingh, backed by dedicated second-level leaders like Tiwari,
provide part of the answer to how the IMMS so quickly became dominant and remained so in Indore, but other factors were more important. Some have already been alluded to. Dravid and Ramsingh's
work was supported at the outset by external political forces, the
national figures of the Congress and related labor organization in

Ahmedabad, as well as by the local Praja Mandal and Congress leaderships. But equally important were the collaboration and support of Holkar government officials and the millowners, both desiring labor tranquility. On one hand, Holkar officials mediated between the millowners and the IMMS leaders, frequently interceding on behalf of labor demands in the interests of maintaining order, and using the government machinery to repress only the Communist union, leaving the IMMS leaders free scope for organizational activity. On the other hand, the millowners, fearful of Communist disruption of textile production, were predisposed to cooperate with Holkar officials and to concede the demands of the IMMS leaders so that the comparatively moderate union would get credit for successfully representing labor demands and win the support of laborers accordingly. The millowners, moreover, cooperated with IMMS functionaries in the mills to put pressure on recalcitrant laborers to join the IMMS and to maintain discipline among those who were already members. Crucial to the success of Dravid and Ramsingh, therefore, was the support received from princely government machinery and the millowners who used economic sanctions within their own domains.

Following the release of political leaders from jail in 1943, Dravid cultivated a close working relationship with the Holkar officials, particularly with H. C. Dhanda (Punjabi), who was in charge of labor and industrial affairs in the war period, and with K. A. Chitale (Maharashtrian Brahman), a legal advisor to Yeshwant Rao (as well as the Praja Mandal and IMMS) and the Commerce and Finance Minister in the Holkar government in 1948. Through personal access of this kind, Dravid was able to get Dhanda to put pressure on the millowners to agree to an increase in the "dearness allowance" (wage supplement geared to changes in the cost of living) of the workers in 1944, bringing the local rates into line with those already in effect in Bombay and Ahmedabad. Similarly in 1946, the IMMS obtained its demand for a reduction from ten to nine working hours.[9] The consolidation of IMMS strength was aided by Dravid's becoming the Holkar State Labour Minister himself in the 1947 and 1948 Cabinets.[10]

---

[9] About the same time, basic wages in relation to types of work were standardized in the Bombay–Ahmedabad pattern. *Banawalikar Report*. Working hours were subsequently reduced from nine to eight. The IMMS took credit for winning a bonus for the workers almost every year.

[10] See Chapter 3, p. 64.

Supplementing the carrot with the stick, he imposed a ban on the Mazdoor Sabha in 1947, forcing it underground.

When merger occurred in June 1948, an interim government of Madhya Bharat was established and the leading position of Indore as an industrial-labor center was acknowledged by giving the Labour portfolio in the Cabinet to Indore politicians D. M. Parulkar (Maharashtrian Brahman) and Manoharsingh Mehta (Jain), Praja Mandal leaders close to Dravid, and—from 1952 on—Dravid himself. Through Dravid's influence, the Holkar ban on the Communist union was continued under the interim government of Madhya Bharat, one of the few states in the Indian Union in which such a ban existed. In the meantime, Dravid had begun preparing labor legislation following precedents in the Bombay Industrial Disputes Act of 1938 and the Bombay Industrial Relations Act of 1947.[11] The Bombay statutes, inspired by Gulzarilal Nanda, contained a set of special provisions for the specification of a "representative union" for a given industry in a given location. The "representative union," once recognized as such by the Registrar of Trade Unions, had the power to accept or deny "change" in the industry. Should a textile employer in Indore, for example, wish to alter the "standing orders" posted in the mill defining rules of discipline and work practice, or to cut back wages or increase work load, constituting a "change" in the textile industry, he could do so only after entering into an agreement with the "representative union." The "representative union," in other words, had the legal power to hold the status quo regardless of the employers' wishes. Once the "Bombay model" was adopted and put in force in Madhya Bharat by Dravid, as one observer put it, "it forced the mill-

---

[11] The *Banawalikar Report*, inspired by Dravid, contains a detailed set of proposals based on the Bombay model. The Report was used as a "white paper," or supporting document, for the labor policy of the Madhya Bharat government. Madhya Bharat statutes, with slight modifications, became operative in 1956 in the new Madhya Pradesh as the Madhya Pradesh Industrial Relations Act, the Madhya Pradesh Industrial Employment (Standing Orders) Act, and the Trade Unions (Madhya Pradesh Amendment) Act. Dravid, *Labour, Labour Movement and Labour Legislation,* pp. 32ff.

For an excellent historical review of the evolution of Bombay labor statutes and a description of their key provisions, see Morris David Morris, *The Emergence of an Industrial Labor Force in India: A Study of the Bombay Cotton Mills, 1854–1947,* especially pp. 107–128. The standard general source on Indian labor is Myers, *Labor Problems in the Industrialization of India.*

owners to come to Ramsinghbhai as supplicants rather than the other way around."

The Madhya Bharat and succeeding Madhya Pradesh legislation required that a given union in order to be recognized as the representative union, must have at least 15 percent of the workers of the industry as its members, as well as a plurality of the total number of registered union members in the industry. Only one representative union in a given location and industry is permitted under the terms of this law, so that, while other unions may function, enroll members, and seek to bargain with the employers, only the representative union has the power to accept or deny "change" in the industry and to enforce agreements in the Industrial Court. The legislation, in effect, encourages a form of organizational monopoly.

The Registrar of Trade Unions holds the authority to determine whether a union fulfills the statutory membership requirements to be recognized as "representative." As the Registrar is a part of the state government administrative machinery, responsible to the Labour Minister, he cannot help but be influenced by the indicated desires of the Labour Minister when the interpretation and implementation of the statute is in question. Disputes regarding membership, and appeals against the Registrar's decisions, can be taken to the Industrial Court, which is formally a separate judicial system, but the Court itself is dependent on administrative sources (the Labour Department and Registrar's Office) for most documentary information, including such things as membership figures, on which its judicial findings are based. Consequently, the recognition of "representative unions" by the state government tends to be a political act, for there is typically a correspondence between the party or group in government power and the union that is recognized as representative; it becomes extremely difficult to dislodge it from that position except by capturing control of the state government, and even that may not be sufficient in the short run. The power of the representative union to deny "change" is an asset that can be transformed into powerful constituency supports.

The justification of the Bombay model is usually based on two major arguments. First, without constraints imposed by the government, and under conditions of free labor competition, there is a tend-

ency toward union fragmentation, a condition which is easily exploited by management and which has adverse effects on the interests
of industrial workers. Second, union fragmentation encourages the
political radicalization of workers, and an economically poor country
such as India can ill afford extremist tendencies in its industrial areas.
The Bombay model is a potential solution to these problems, it is
argued, for it discourages union proliferation and labor militancy by
making it more profitable for workers to seek remedies through a single channel. The implementation of this model in Indore placed a
new handicap on the Communist labor leaders, adding to the burden
they already faced from the legal ban on their organizational activity.
By the time that ban was finally lifted, in December 1951, just before
the first general elections, Dravid and Ramsingh had had sufficient
time to consolidate their power and to be certain of winning the
Indore labor seats in the 1952 elections.

The growing power of the IMMS in Indore did not go unchal-
lenged, however, for while the Mazdoor Sabha was under the ban, the
Socialist leaders seized the opportunity to try to establish a base in
Indore by capturing Communist constituencies. The center of this
move in Indore was Lakshmi Shanker Shukla (Kanyakubja Brahman),
then a young advocate, who subsequently built up a thriving practice
in criminal law. Shukla was in his early 30's when he began his law
practice in Mhow and joined the local unit of the Congress party
that was formed there about the time of Independence. According to
one story, he was snubbed by local Congress leaders and forced out
of the party (his "counter" or primary membership form was "mis-
placed" in office records). Shukla then joined the Socialist party. Encouraged by Jayaprakash Narayan and Ashok Mehta on the national
level, he started the Mazdoor Panchayat, a local affiliate of the Socialist Hind Mazdoor Sabha. Shukla became President, and Goverdhanlal Ojha (Sanadya Brahman) became the General Secretary of
the Socialist Union. The Mazdoor Panchayat was the main rival of
the IMMS between 1948 and 1951. Shukla and Ojha attracted a substantial following from among the Kanyakubja Brahman and Chamar
communities in the Malwa Mill compound, Pardesipura, and Patnipura.[12] He claims that by 1949 the Panchayat had captured about

---

[12] Shukla's family came from Hamirpur, south of Kanpur, in Uttar Pradesh.
His grandfather was a *vaidya* (ayurvedic physician) who had acquired something of

10,000 of the 25,000 textile workers as its members. On this basis, the Mazdoor Panchayat challenged the "representativeness" of the IMMS, both before the Registrar of Trade Unions and in the Industrial Court in 1949. The challenge was ultimately unsuccessful, but in the course of it Shukla was gratified that the Court acknowledged the *locus standi* of the Mazdoor Panchayat. The demonstration effect of the ruling, that a nonrepresentative union could challenge the representative union (and implicitly the government) in Court, according to Shukla, brought the Mazdoor Panchayat membership up to 13,000 within a month.

Ramsingh and the IMMS counterattacked in August 1950, about a year and a half before the first general elections. The IMMS drive began with a manufactured incident that escalated into a riot in the premises of the Malwa Mill, the location of the Mazdoor Panchayat's greatest strength. Ramsingh hoped to capitalize on the incident with the help of the local authorities by weakening the Mazdoor Panchayat and drawing away most of its following. The Malwa Mill was at the time in a state of tension. Once owned by Bohras, it had been the largest employer of Muslim workers before 1947. But the emigration of Muslims before and after independence had been the cause of considerable bitterness. A number of minor but threatening incidents led the police to station themselves in considerable numbers around the mill premises on this occasion. Ramsingh knew that if there were an outbreak of major violence, the police would round up and arrest the main labor leaders in the mill, most of whom belonged to the Mazdoor Panchayat, and subsequent prosecution could be used to harass those leaders and intimidate their followers in the mill. Opponents of Ramsingh have alleged that there was direct collusion between Ramsingh and the police, that the police were expecting

---

a saintly reputation and was venerated by the common people. Many of the Chamars of Indore migrated from the same area, enabling Shukla to capitalize on the memory of his grandfather as a basis of identification linking these people to his union. Shukla also had the support of a number of poorer Kanyakubja Brahmans who live in the same labor settlements, supplementing their wages as mill-hands with small incomes from makeshift temples or shrines, in which they officiate as priests, and small *paan,* cigarette, and tea-shop businesses. Some rent small bits of land or huts to other laborers and develop patron–client relationships that serve also as machinery for mobilizing votes and other forms of support. Ram Prasad Tiwari of Patnipura is a middleman of this sort, and personally loyal to Shukla.

trouble and had instructions to intervene only when doing so could be turned to the advantage of the IMMS.

The IMMS helped to set the stage by encouraging women workers, led by one named Ukiabai, to hold a procession protesting their grievances. Once the demonstration had begun to attract attention from bystanders and the police, a stone was thrown from somewhere and the cry was raised that the women were being beaten. Workers in the mill poured out into the yard, causing a good deal of commotion. The police reacted with a "*lathi*-charge" (police on riot-detail are often armed with heavy bamboo canes, and the cane is called a *lathi*). In the resulting confusion, Joshi, a Deputy-Superintendent of Police, was struck on the head with a piece of wood and mortally wounded. In the aftermath 165 active members of the Mazdoor Panchayat were arrested and held in jail pending judicial action.

The city police officials were incensed by what they called the "murder" of a senior colleague and were determined to prosecute the case with a vengeance. Fifteen persons were singled out from among those arrested and charged with rioting and murder under Section 302 of the Criminal Code. The remaining 150 persons were charged merely with rioting. In the trial court, two workers, Babulal Tendwah and another Babulal, were sentenced to death, and their conviction was upheld in appeals all the way to the Supreme Court. Lakshmi Shanker Shukla then approached Jayaprakash Narayan, whose influence, he felt, might bring the President of India to pardon the two prisoners or at least reduce their sentences. Ramsingh's reputation had suffered in the labor area because of widespread allegations of his covert role in the riot. He was smarting under the accusation that he had demanded the stiffest penalties for the rioters and wished to see the two prisoners hanged, confirmation to some that he was indeed an instigator of the incident. He saw an opportunity to outflank Shukla and protect his own reputation. Ramsingh went to see the two prisoners in jail while Shukla's clemency petition was still being prepared and persuaded the two workers to sign a petition, which he promised them he would use to obtain their pardon with the help of the Labour Minister. Dravid used his influence to have the Governor reduce the sentence to life imprisonment (effectively, fourteen years), while Ramsingh paraded this humanitarian gesture in the labor area as his doing.

The judicial proceedings in this case were remarkable in that all of the accused were members of the Mazdoor Panchayat, and almost all of the eyewitnesses for the prosecution were members of the IMMS. The testimony of an assistant manager of the Malwa Mills that Babulal Tendwah was in the manager's office at the time of the assault on Joshi, although recorded in the police diary, was not admitted as evidence in the court. The assistant manager was transferred to Bombay.[13] The cards were apparently stacked against the accused because of the political competition underlying the case. Had the defense been able to obtain the acquittal of the Mazdoor Panchayat members, it would have greatly bolstered the morale of the Socialist union members.

As it turned out, the results were a grave setback for the Mazdoor Panchayat and in the months that followed the riot, IMMS functionaries in the mills, "inspectors" and "labor officers," compiled the names of the more active and visible Mazdoor Panchayat workers. The key leaders were sorted out from the lists, and the IMMS leaders used their special relationships with the mill managements to dismiss the Panchayat leaders on some pretext or other from their jobs in the mills—a method that the IMMS has ruthlessly employed on various occasions. The Socialist leaders, with no base in the government or administrative machinery, were unable to thwart this attack. As a result, Mazdoor Panchayat members were intimidated and forced to the sidelines, or forced to become nominal members of the IMMS in self-defense. The loss of the court case combined with this harassment damaged the Mazdoor Panchayat financially and politically beyond real recovery. Committed Socialists had no recourse but to link up with the Communist union when it legally reentered the labor arena in 1951. Shukla himself left the Mazdoor Panchayat, for all practical purposes, in 1955. The organization was taken over by Prabhakar Adsule (a Maharashtrian Brahman), a political and legal entrepreneur aligned with Homi Daji and the Communist party. The Mazdoor Panchayat was finally merged, just before the 1957 general election,

---

[13] The ownership of the Malwa Mills had been acquired by the Sakseria (Marwari) interests, who were easily able to find alternative employment for the assistant manager in one of their Bombay enterprises. The actual management was in the hands of Chandan Singh Bharkatiya, an employee of Sakseria enterprises and a Rajasthani Jain.

with the Mazdoor Sabha, to form the new Communist-dominated Mill Mazdoor Union.

Organizational Power and Union Financial Structure

The importance of the Nanda–Dravid (Bombay model) labor legislation has already been explained by showing how the prescription of a "representative union" gives structural opportunities to that union closely linked to the party or group in power. The "representative union" in the Indore textile industry has from the beginning been the IMMS, the local affiliate of INTUC. As Madhya Bharat was governed by the Congress party, dominated a large part of the time by chieftains from Indore, including V. V. Dravid, the intimate relationship between the IMMS and the Madhya Bharat government was obvious. That the IMMS should successfully claim recognition as the "representative union," while the Mazdoor Sabha was under a ban and before the Mazdoor Panchayat had gotten off the ground, hardly requires more explanation. But it is useful to see how the "representative union" maintained its claim to representativeness without special assistance from the Registrar of Trade Unions. In doing so, the role of the millowners in supporting Congress dominance in the labor arena will become clearer.

The legislative criterion of a union's representativeness is based on "membership," as ascertained and verified by the Registrar of Trade Unions, but the criterion of membership in turn is based on periodic evidence of financial subscriptions to a given union. Consequently, the question of representativeness (and of political power) becomes entwined with the finances of the unions. The financial resources and modes of collection also reveal something about the internal distribution of power and relationship of organization leaders to their clienteles within the Congress union.

When the IMMS was first established, it received financial support mainly from the Ahmedabad Textile Labour Association. In 1946 and 1947 the Holkar government granted the IMMS 10,000 rupees for "labor welfare," underlining the government objective of building up the IMMS as a check against the Communist union. The annual grant was continued by the Madhya Bharat government and raised to 16,000 rupees annually, reflecting the influence of Dravid as Labour Minister. Moreover, the Jivan Vikas Sangh, or youth wing of the

IMMS, was given an annual grant of 2,500 rupees by the Holkar and Madhya Bharat governments for its so-called *sharab-bandi* (prohibition) work. In 1946 the IMMS began to seek financial self-sufficiency by the collection of voluntary subscriptions from the workers. It is doubtful that the workers had much faith, or much reason to have faith, in this method of collection where there was ample opportunity for "leakage." The amounts collected were small, ranging between 500 and 1,000 rupees a month. By 1954 the amounts had reached only about 2,000 rupees a month.

In 1954 the method of collection was revised. IMMS members were given "union books" and their names were entered in a register along with a notation when they paid their dues. They were periodically reminded to pay their dues when they omitted to do so. The assessment varied from four annas to two rupees, depending on the size of the income of the worker. Through this new system the monthly collection had been raised to about 11,000 rupees by 1957. The success of this system was due to the fact that the IMMS leadership were quick to help those laborers in difficulties who could demonstrate that they had paid their dues regularly, signifying their loyalty to the union. Faced with the prospect of retrenchment, displacement, or harassment, a worker who paid his dues was prudent. At the same time there was some check on the leadership, for workers who felt strongly enough to withhold dues were likely to be listened to, providing leaders with clues to grievances and political undercurrents in the labor area. The system also had the advantage that the IMMS could show its registers to the Registrar of Trade Unions and claim with some plausibility that each dues-payer recorded was a full member of the IMMS. In lieu of some better method of verification, financial contributions were the most positive evidence to come before the Registrar in routine fashion.

The "union book" scheme of 1954 worked successfully until the general election of 1957 when, much to the surprise of almost everyone, the young Communist leader, Homi Daji, defeated Gangaram Tiwari in the MLA seat identified with the labor area. The election results seem to have had a direct effect on IMMS collections, as the monthly total dropped almost immediately from 11,000 to 3,000 rupees per month. The Congress defeat may have suggested to the ordinary IMMS dues-payer that the power of the IMMS was waning and that it was no longer imperative to support the IMMS. There was also a growing resentment over the allegedly autocratic practices of Ramsingh and some of his colleagues in the IMMS. There were growing doubts as to the appropriateness of IMMS budgetary expenditures,[14] and a probably well-justified suspicion that there were numerous irregular expenditures and incomplete accounting of subscriptions collected from the workers. The drastic fall in collections was a serious matter, because it threatened to undermine the credibility of the IMMS's claim to representativeness by making it impossible to supply the Registrar with convincing membership figures.

Motilal Jain, then Secretary of the IMMS, proposed as a solution to the problem the "yearly advance subscription scheme," based on a dues "check-off" procedure. The scheme—requiring the cooperation of the millowners, which was obtained through an agreement—called for the employers to advance a sum larger than the annual subscription of each IMMS member, in addition to his monthly wages, at the beginning of the year. When the worker called at the cashier's window for his wages on that particular payday, an IMMS "inspector" was invariably present to collect the subscription on behalf of the IMMS. The worker was asked to sign a waiver authorizing the annual subscription amount to be made over to the IMMS and a statement indicating that he had received his monthly wages and the yearly advance in full from his employer. Once his signature or thumbprint was recorded, the worker received his wages, what was left of the yearly advance, and usually a receipt for having paid his subscription. For employer purposes, the advance was subsequently deducted by management in installments from the worker's monthly wages during the course of the year.

The yearly advance subscription scheme greatly simplified the IMMS's problem of collections, confining it to one short period at

---

[14] It is an interesting sidelight on Indore city politics that a substantial number of the leadership of the IMMS, including V. V. Dravid, Ramsingh Verma, Gangaram Tiwari, Mathuralal Sharma, Pratap Sinha, Motilal Jain, Chhaganlal Katariya, Ishwar Chand Jain, Dattatrey Patil, Nand Kishore Bhatt, Kanhaiyalal Yadav, and others have traveled abroad in Europe or the United States as members of delegations, but not one Indore Congress politician outside the IMMS has had a similar experience. Foreign travel was one INTUC attraction to middle-income white-collar clerks and accountants to join the IMMS, a form of patronage for which Dravid could take most of the credit. Travel abroad was probably financed from sources other than labor subscriptions, but the contributing workers could be persuaded otherwise.

the beginning of the year. The scheme, moreover, simplified planning and budgeting for the entire year, since the total annual income from subscriptions was known immediately after collection. And finally, the scheme was far more efficient, for it brought the income from subscriptions up from its previous best level of about 130,000 rupees, in 1956, to a new annual level of about 250,000 rupees in 1958. The scheme also put the Communist Mazdoor Union at a great disadvantage, as its methods of collection were essentially voluntary in nature and Communist support came generally from the poorest laborers, those least capable of paying any subscriptions at all. There were very few textile workers who refused to become nominal members of the INTUC affiliate under this scheme. Their subscriptions were in effect insurance premiums against removal or harassment. The irony is that many Communist, Socialist, and anti-Congress workers were involuntarily subsidizing their political enemy, compelled by IMMS–millowner collaboration. The millowners in turn were virtually compelled by the power of the "representative union" to collaborate, despite the fact that by so doing they were perpetuating the monopolistic power of that union.

The long-run disadvantage of this scheme was that it tended to reduce the financial accountability and responsiveness of the union leadership to its constituents. Alternative sanctions could be applied (theoretically) through the system of representation within the IMMS, where the Working Committee (executive officers) formally depended on a supporting majority in the *Sanyukt Pratinidhi Mandal* (United Representatives' Council), and the Mandal members in turn had to win election from local labor communities or constituencies. But this system became in practice more an instrument of manipulation and elite domination than a responsive system of representation. The only action workers could take secretly against the IMMS, without fear of detection and retaliation, was to vote against the IMMS candidates in the general elections or in municipal elections, but these were not effective sanctions as they could not by themselves have much effect on government policy through the administrative machinery or the state-wide organizational power of INTUC; and without turning out the government, the dominance of the IMMS could not easily be challenged. As a result, the IMMS lost its responsiveness to the textile workers as a whole.

The new financial structure was obtained in part because of Ramsingh's established power, and its introduction enhanced his personal control and freedom of maneuver in the IMMS. Ramsingh and certain of the other IMMS leaders are said to have developed a mutually profitable relationship with the millowners that depended on the IMMS leaders' being able to control decisions in the organization without having to worry about adverse repercussions on the financial resources of the union. Under these circumstances the chief IMMS leaders made a variety of agreements with the millowners regarding "changes" in the industry, especially in work-load, entailing retrenchment, against the general wishes of the union's membership; yet that membership as well as all the other workers were bound to accept these changes, as they had been officially sanctioned by the "representative union."

In return for these agreements and enforcing labor discipline, the millowners were obliged to follow Ramsingh's bidding when he or one of his agents—a "labor officer" or "inspector"—demanded the dismissal of one or another worker from his job on a union-generated charge, or the reward and promotion of Ramsingh's supporters. Based on this power, Ramsingh assumed virtually dictatorial control over the ordinary members of the IMMS, and workers everywhere feared to oppose him openly. For many years he had the labor population intimidated. It is also widely alleged that Ramsingh and some of the clerical and administrative employees of the IMMS benefited financially—receiving handsome sums from the millowners—for acquiescing in "sweetheart contracts" or concealing illegal or questionable financial practices of the millowners within their own operations.

II. UNIONS AND ELECTORAL COMPETITION

The election history of the MLA seat in the labor area in Indore provides an opportunity to account for the changing fortunes of the rival labor organizations and their candidates. A peculiarity of the "labor seat" is that in two out of four general elections the outcomes have run counter to the general pattern in the city: in 1957 a Communist candidate (running as an Independent) won in the labor area while the other Indore seats went to Congress, and in 1967 a Congressman won the labor seat, while opposition candidates defeated Con-

gressmen in each of the other three MLA seats in the city, and an opposition candidate ran ahead of the Congress candidate in the Indore
city portion of the parliamentary constituency. The electoral individu-
ality of the labor seat is no accident but reflects the comparative autonomy of the arena of labor politics from influence by other political
actors in the city. The reverse is not the case, however. The other city
MLA constituencies, and the municipal wards, contain substantial
numbers of labor-class voters. As a result, what happens in these constituencies may be and often is affected by political outcomes in the
labor arena. In taking account of the electoral outcomes of labor politics, attention is given, therefore, not only to the labor seat but also to
contests where labor leaders have run in other constituencies, or contests in which labor votes may have been decisive.

In the first general election of February 1952, the IMMS claimed
Congress party nominations for two MLA seats. The comparative affluence of the IMMS, combined with abundant support by the millowners who not only contributed money but vehicles, drivers, and campaign workers from among mill-hands temporarily released for this
purpose from their normal jobs, ensured that the IMMS claim would
be recognized. Ramsingh received the nomination for the MLA constituency spanning most of the labor area, and Dravid was allocated
the "safe" south seat falling outside of most of the labor area, conform-
ing to their division of spheres of responsibility—Ramsingh being the
local organization boss, or the insider, and Dravid being the state
leader, outside the local labor arena. The two IMMS leaders, together
with the other Congress candidates in the city, swept to easy victories.[15]
Yet there were portents of weakness evident in the labor area results.

Despite the impressive array of resources the Congress forces brought
to bear on the election, and despite Ramsingh's control of the Mazdoor
Sangh, Ramsingh won by only a plurality (49 percent), a poor showing
by contrast with the other Congress candidates, who all won by clear
majorities. Even more significant as an indicator of the real loyalties of
the labor force was the fact that in those polling areas that were predominantly labor in composition,[16] the combined vote of the opposi-

---

[15] For the lists of candidates and election outcomes in this section, see Appendix
B, Tables 1–3, pp. 385ff.

[16] Based on my analysis of returns by polling booth, obtained from the Elections
Officer of the Collectorate, Indore.

tion candidates was 8,209 to Ramsingh's 6,058. This indicates that
Ramsingh ran a weaker race in what was regarded as his stronghold,
making up for it elsewhere in the city—where the support of the Nai
Duniya (Jain) faction may have counted in middle-class and commercial communities—and in rural Khajrana.[17] Had the Communist and
Socialist parties put up a common candidate, and if the votes their
candidates did receive were transferable, they might have drawn 6,643
votes (the sum of Ojha's and Khandkar's returns), still short of Ramsingh's total but a substantial number nonetheless. The opposition
drew a lesson from this for the next election.

V. V. Dravid and Homi Daji (a Parsi Communist leader) stood
against each other from the south constituency. The seat was predominantly nonlabor in composition, but contained pockets of laborers and
lower-class and lower-caste families in Gadi Ada and the Harijan colony of Juni Indore. The area also contained sizable concentrations of
Muslims in Ranipura, and Malwi and Maharashtrian Brahmans in
Juni Indore and Harsiddhi. The constituency enclosed the commercial
area of Chowni and the adjacent Sanyogitaganj market, areas with
heavy Hindu Baniya concentrations, and stretched out to include the
Residency area and the rural fringes of Indore in the south. Dravid got
a much larger proportion (68 percent) of the votes cast in his race than
Ramsingh got in the labor seat, despite the fact that another of Dravid's opponents was G. V. Oke, a Maharashtrian Brahman and respected local leader of the Hindu Mahasabha. Homi Daji, standing for
the first and only time formally as a "Communist," was then only 26
years old and practically unknown outside of Communist organizational circles, but he scored more votes than Oke. Oke's main support
came from his own community and Sindhi refugees. Daji's strongholds
were Muslim mohallas and Harijan and low-caste communities such as
Gadi Ada.

Between 1952 and 1957 the organizational power of the IMMS was

---

[17] Nandlal Joshi (Malwi Brahman), the Khadiwala faction parliamentary candidate, although his primary base of support was in the rural areas, ran ahead of
Ramsingh in each of the 24 predominantly labor polling areas and scored significantly
higher (twenty votes or more) in 16 of the 24. Joshi's cumulative vote in the labor
area was 7,043, or about 14 percent higher than Ramsingh's. Joshi achieved this
result despite the fact that he was opposed by two other Brahmans, Lakshmi Shanker
Shukla and Narayan Waman Pantvaidya, a Marathi-speaking office manager in the
Hukumchand Mills at that time. Joshi, however, had only two opponents, so there
was less tendency in his case for the vote to be fragmented.

expanded outside the labor area and within the city. The IMMS set up a parallel and rival Congress party organization in the city, utilizing the labor residents (including clerical employees of the mills) scattered in practically every mohalla throughout the city. The parallel organization consisted of a network of *Mohalla Sudhar* (Improvement) Committees. These committees were used to enroll primary members in the Congress party, intensively in 1952 and 1953, in order to capture majority representation in the *Mandal* or local Congress committees. The Mandal committees, of which there are about 16 in Indore, collectively determine the composition of the City Congress representative body and the executive committee and play a key role in selecting nominees for the municipal elections. As a result, the IMMS—or, as it was known in the city, the "INTUC group"—secured a majority of municipal tickets for the 1955 municipal elections and returned a larger number of Councillors to the municipal body than either of the rival factions (Nai Duniya and Khadiwala). From 1955 to 1957 the "INTUC group," with the help of a few members of the other factions, dominated the Municipal Council. But this expansion of INTUC power into the city, the domain of the Nai Duniya and Khadiwala groups, was not sympathetically received by the Jain leadership of the Nai Duniya group or the Brahman and Hindu Baniya leaders of the Khadiwala group. Consequently the two city factions teamed up against the "INTUC group" in 1956, prior to the approaching general elections, in an effort to regain control of the City Congress organization.

In the 1952 elections the IMMS had been satisfied with two of the Indore tickets, but in 1957 the INTUC group felt powerful enough to demand three tickets. Dravid wanted to reward Gangaram Tiwari with an MLA seat. Ramsingh was willing to give up his MLA seat to run for the more glamorous Lok Sabha (parliamentary) seat. It was this move that Kanhaiyalal Khadiwala (with Nai Duniya support) was able to block by securing the Indore Lok Sabha ticket for himself. The Congress high command arbitrated the ticket dispute and offered Ramsingh the Nimar (Khargone) Lok Sabha ticket instead. The effect of the decision was to blunt the expansion of the INTUC group into the city, but it provided the local INTUC leadership with the opportunity to retain two seats in the state legislative assembly and also have a lobbyist at the Prime Minister's doorstep in New Delhi, or at least that is how it appeared before the election.

The INTUC group got its lobbyist in Delhi, and Dravid retained his seat in the state Legislative Assembly, but Gangaram Tiwari failed to live up to Dravid's expectations. Tiwari's defeat by Homi Daji, the young Parsi leader of the local Communist party and Mazdoor Sabha, was a major blow to the IMMS and a serious symbolic challenge to its power. (It will be recalled how hard this election hit the collection of subscriptions by the IMMS.) Tiwari's defeat was a surprise and deserves explanation. He was not personally encumbered with the accusations made against Ramsingh in the Malwa Mills episode. Moreover, a substantial amount of patronage had been going into the labor area through administrative and INTUC channels. The demonstration effects of the Congress Session in the city boosted the other Congress candidates, and it seems strange that those effects did not spill over more effectively into the labor area.

Tiwari lost because there was a united opposition—the opposition candidate being a singularly effective mass leader—and possibly because of electoral sabotage by Ramsingh supporters in the labor arena.[18] There were additional reasons of less importance, especially the selectivity of Congress patronage in the labor area and uneasiness about the value of the return to the textile workers for their financial contributions to the IMMS. The election results indicated that nominal membership in the IMMS, based on financial contributions, was not a reliable guide to the degree of voting support for Congress labor candidates running in the labor area. The election implicitly denied the representativeness of the recognized union, even in the textile labor area.

The key to the election, from the point of view of the opposition, was the concentration of their efforts so as to maximize and unite anti-Congress voting support. In the 1952 election there had been 24 candidates in the four MLA constituencies. In 1957 there were only 10. The leftist leaders united, despite the fact that among them were aspirants who would not have an opportunity to stand for election. The Socialist and Communist unions were merged to form the united Mazdoor Union, under the leadership at that time of Prabhakar Adsule. Lakshmi Shanker Shukla and Goverdhanlal Ojha gave their combined support in the labor area to Homi Daji, on the condition that he stand

---

[18] Although Ramsingh would appear to gain by Tiwari's defeat, interviews did not turn up evidence supporting this conclusion firmly.

as an Independent—a condition that was duly authorized by the Central Committee of the Communist party. In this election Daji also got the support of Abdul Quddus and Bashir Mansoori, and therefore did well among Muslim laborers.

Although little-known outside the labor area, Daji had the admiration and respect of many of the workers. Articulate in Hindi and a more effective public speaker even than Ramsingh, he was at his best when focusing on the discrepancies between the promises and performance of the IMMS and the Congress government. Gangaram Tiwari was no match for Daji's public image or campaign intelligence. In spite of the assets of the IMMS and the financial support of the millowners, Tiwari lost by a substantial margin of 5,799, or about 21 percent of the total vote. Daji won just over 60 percent of the vote. He ran ahead in 39 out of 58 polling stations, and his strength was approximately equal in both labor and nonlabor areas, indicating the broad nature of Daji's appeal to middle-class and professional voters as well as laborers. Daji ran far ahead of Tiwari in the city in Murai and Kacchi Mohallas, settlements of occupationally fragmented labor. Within the labor area, Communist strength was especially visible in Shilnath Camp and Kulkarni Bhatta, and the lopsided, high poll in Bhindiko (Sivajinagar) suggests that Daji received the lion's share of the vote of Marathi-speakers.

V. V. Dravid won his contest in the inappropriately designated "Indore" constituency. The constituency boundaries in Indore were relocated for the 1957 elections, so that only three seats covered most of the urban area of Indore. Instead of running in the south seat (Juni Indore, Chowni, and Residency areas—in 1957, part of the Indore city west constituency), Dravid got the ticket for the fourth seat that fell outside the city in the rural areas to the east of the labor area, including Khajrana, Khajrani, Piplia Hana, Musakhedi, Harsola, Kampel, and other villages. He was not opposed by a labor candidate. By running in the rural area, however, he avoided friction with the City Congress leaders of the Nai Duniya and Khadiwala factions who wished to run in those parts of the city where they had special community support, but still assured himself of a place in the government.

When the 1962 elections approached, the INTUC group in Indore renewed their attempt to secure three of the five tickets and this time they succeeded, but not without central intervention and intense bitter-

ness within the City Congress. Ramsingh wanted very much to run in
the Indore parliamentary constituency, where he anticipated no great
risks as long as he had central endorsement by the Congress high command. He had not nursed his Nimar (Khargone) constituency and
would have been on the defensive there. Consequently, with the support of Dravid, Ramsingh got the Congress high command to override
Khadiwala's claim for the ticket (as the sitting member) and it was
given to Ramsingh instead.[19]

Despite his defeat in 1957, Gangaram Tiwari still appeared to be
the strongest alternative candidate of the IMMS in the labor area, so
he received that ticket, and Dravid was nominated to run again in the
rural Indore seat to the east of the labor area.

Once Ramsingh's candidacy for the parliamentary seat was assured,
Homi Daji took on the role of giant-killer. There was little he could
lose. As a Communist and opposition leader there was not much in the
way of patronage for him in the Vidhan Sabha, and so it was not hard
to give up the MLA seat.[20] It was what he might gain by defeating
Ramsingh that was decisive. If Ramsingh were squarely defeated by
Daji, it would be a great symbolic blow to the power of the INTUC
organization in Indore and a concrete blow to the personal prestige
and power of Ramsingh. It would demonstrate the vulnerability of the
most powerful organization man, the linchpin, of the IMMS in the
labor arena.[21] It would be subsequently more difficult for Ramsingh to
overawe the workers. Under new circumstances of this sort, the
Mazdoor Union and Communist party would have more scope for political growth and maneuver.

In a more personal sense also, if Daji were successful, he would immensely increase his own prestige in the city and partly defuse the
stigma attached to Communism. Daji had become better known as a
result of his victory in 1957, but until now he was still regarded as a
lawyer, a civil rights and labor area worker, and an intellectual. Defeating Ramsingh in a parliamentary constituency would make him a na-

---

[19] Khadiwala was shunted off to the Nimar (Khargone) seat that Ramsingh was
so glad to get off his hands. Khadiwala was badly defeated in the election, despite
his personal ties with *adivasi* (tribal) political leaders in that area.

[20] Technically, Daji could have run for two seats simultaneously, later resigning
one if he won in both. But the claims of other leftist aspirants negated this option.

[21] It is said that Ramsingh boasted in his campaign of Nehru's remark that
"There are two Congress leaders who could win from any constituency. They are the
Maharani of Gwalior and Ramsingh Verma."

tional figure. And it would make him the single most important "Communist" leader in all of Madhya Pradesh. The attractions, therefore, were compelling.

In addition, Homi Daji was probably more aware than anyone else of Ramsingh's electoral vulnerability in the city. The nomination of Ramsingh imposed on the City Congress brought organizational rivalries to the foreground, alienating the Nai Duniya and Khadiwala groups in the city from the IMMS, and especially from Ramsingh personally. Daji was shrewdly conscious of the opportunity lying in this latent division within the City Congress. He knew too, better even than Ramsingh, how vulnerable the latter was in the labor area itself. Yet despite these factors, Daji was to all outward appearances the underdog. He had to overcome the stigma of his known Communist affiliation and the massive advantage that any Congress nominee would have in the rural areas.

The first requirement was to forge again a united leftist opposition and if possible work out some form of cooperation with the Jan Sangh. The Jan Sangh leadership was determined to run their own nominees against Ramsingh and Babulal Patodi, but they did not set up candidates in the labor area, or Dravid's seat, or against Mishrilal Gangwal. This was partly to Daji's advantage, as the Jan Sangh parliamentary candidate would draw votes away from the Congress more than a Communist candidate in the rural areas. Lakshmi Shanker Shukla and Prabhakar Adsule made agreements of mutual support with Daji and mounted a combined leftist offensive in the labor arena, Adsule running against Gangaram Tiwari, and Shukla against Dravid. All three ran as Independents.[22]

Homi Daji campaigned vigorously and won the parliamentary election, while his colleagues each went down in defeat.[23] The fundamental

[22] The leftist opposition was not solid because of internal rivalries within the Socialist party. Baleshwardayal ran as a Socialist in the parliamentary contest, and nominally Socialist candidates stood in all of the MLA constituencies except Gangwal's. None of the Socialist MLA candidates won significant numbers of votes except perhaps in the Tiwari-Adsule race, where getting the mere 555 votes that went to the nominal Socialist would have enabled Adsule to defeat Tiwari by an exceedingly narrow margin of 102 votes. See Appendix B, Table 3.

[23] The incongruity of the victory of a known Communist in a parliamentary constituency where 7 out of 8 MLA contests were won by Congress was so unusual an outcome that it was selected for a case study by Wayne Wilcox. "Trade Unions, the Middle-Class Intelligentsia and a Communist M.P.: The Indore Parliamentary Election of 1962."

reason for his victory, as Daji himself admits, was Ramsingh's "unpopularity," particularly in Indore city. This is, of course, really a simplified statement of several factors. Ramsingh was certainly personally unpopular among large numbers of labor voters, whether in the labor area or in the heart of the city.[24] Even more fundamentally, Ramsingh was personally repugnant to many of the nonlabor City Congress leaders as a result of his social origins and style. There was also the organizational rivalry for control of the City Congress, the city leaders of the Nai Duniya and Khadiwala factions being determined to thwart the penetration of INTUC group influence outside the labor arena. Despite the relatively powerful electoral oppositions to Babulal Patodi and Mishrilal Gangwal, Ramsingh polled consistently fewer votes than either Congress MLA candidate in their respective areas. This tends to support Ramsingh's contention that Patodi and Gangwal (Jain leaders) sabotaged his potential support in their constituencies,[25] their efforts being designed to reverse the trend toward INTUC dominance in the City Congress. Ramsingh believed also that Sajjan Singh Vishnar, a member of the Khadiwala faction and the leading scheduled caste politician in the Indore area, worked against Ramsingh in the Sawer MLA portion of the parliamentary seat.

Finally, according to Wayne Wilcox's theory,[26] the "middle class" played a major role in the parliamentary contest, especially within the urban area. In a negative sense, the urban middle class, not self-consciously but as a layered collection of professional, business, and clerical groups expressing common preferences of style and taste, were repelled by Ramsingh's unlettered and sometimes crude approach. Homi Daji, by contrast, is a product of the middle class, college-educated with a law degree, intellectually well-informed, and sophisticated in his appeal to the clerical, government servant, and professional layers. In addition, Daji's reputation on financial matters has been almost impeccable (he has no immovable property, and manages on a modest income), and his tireless service to the labor and lower-class elements was

---

[24] My survey of the polling station returns of the labor seat showed that Gangaram Tiwari ran consistently ahead of Ramsingh, and Daji consistently ahead of Adsule.

[25] Patodi denied this allegation, pointing to how Ramsingh had alienated himself, by his ruthless methods and arrogance, from the working-class voters interspersed throughout the city, and arguing that this accounted sufficiently for the disparity.

[26] Wilcox, "Trade Unions."

a well-established and admired fact. His attacks on Ramsingh and the Congress party on these themes were particularly hard-hitting as well as humorous, and struck a sympathetic note among the middle and lower middle classes. Daji's style fitted congruently with the values of disparate groups in the Indore middle class.

Daji carried the city of Indore with 58,359 votes against 41,809 for Ramsingh, offsetting the latter's advantage in the rural areas.[27] Although none of Daji's Indore collaborators won (Adsule came very close),[28] the long-run consequences of Ramsingh's defeat seriously weakened the INTUC leadership internally and undermined the formerly almost impregnable hold of the IMMS in the labor area of Indore.

The labor seat in the 1962 election was carried successfully by Gangaram Tiwari, bringing him for the first time into the limelight as an electorally successful politician. Though he won, he polled fewer votes than Daji in the labor area but more than his opponent, Adsule. Thus the IMMS's electoral hold on the labor area recovered from the 1957 defeat, strengthening the position of Dravid and Tiwari against Ramsingh. Tiwari's electoral success was an important asset for the anti-Ramsingh forces in the approaching power struggle for control of the IMMS. Dravid successfully held on to his rural Indore seat in 1962 but for the first time failed to win a clear majority of the vote.

Ramsingh's defeat destroyed the myth of his invincibility. It was a shock to his expansive ego and aroused his suspicion of his partner and patron, V. V. Dravid, and of his junior subordinate, Gangaram Tiwari.

---

[27] Ramsingh's rural total was 47,444 to Daji's 37,256. It is interesting that Daji could do so well in the rural areas, starting as he did with an urban-labor base and without much in the way of rural party organization. In Dravid's constituency, of course, he benefited from the support of Lakshmi Shanker Shukla. In Dhar, a portion of the parliamentary constituency, there was no leftist MLA candidate at all for Daji to get help from.

[28] Shukla had an unexpected handicap. Jagannath Bhagwan, an unknown candidate, was encouraged to stand with the hope of drawing votes away from Shukla. Daji's symbol was the "bicycle." Shukla expected to get the same symbol, but Bhagwan applied for it also. In the casting of lots to decide the issue, Bhagwan got the "bicycle" and Shukla was allotted a "flower" (rose) symbol. Many uneducated voters, identifying the bicycle with Daji, voted unwittingly for Bhagwan on the MLA ballot, or marked both the bicycle and flower symbols on the MLA ballots, making them invalid. This explains Bhagwan's inordinately large total of votes. It is possible that Shukla could have defeated Dravid had he won all the votes that went to Bhagwan and about 700 votes from among those that were invalid. See Appendix B, Table 3.

He sensed the polarization of the Brahman labor leaders against him, viewing them as contributors to his electoral defeat, paving the way to his ouster from the labor organization. He recognized, too, that he had forfeited to a large extent the former support he received from the Nai Duniya group by insisting on his own parliamentary candidacy in Indore. To compensate for his setbacks and reconsolidate his position, Ramsingh tried to tighten his grip on the IMMS and the labor area through his resources as the current President of both the local IMMS and the Madhya Pradesh INTUC organization. If his position as boss of the local organization were secured, Dravid would be forced to continue to deal with Ramsingh as a partner, giving him future opportunities to stage an electoral comeback.

But Ramsingh's move to consolidate his hold on the IMMS was countered by resistance deriving strength from his electoral defeat and shattered prestige. Dravid for the first time listened receptively to complaints and criticisms about Ramsingh's autocratic demeanor and intemperate behavior, criticisms that he had formerly appeared to ignore or dismissed as irrelevant or motivated by spite and jealousy. Dravid accordingly sought to put restraints on Ramsingh, interfering with his formerly autonomous day-to-day control of organizational affairs. Ramsingh refused to accept these new elements of subordination, so the conditions were set for a power struggle within the IMMS that was ultimately to weaken INTUC dominance in Indore labor politics.

III. UNION BOSSES AND THE STRUGGLE FOR MACHINE POWER

At the core of the struggle was the issue of who would command the Congress labor forces in Indore, whether Ramsingh would continue to be the supreme local boss or be swept aside in favor of fresh leadership. The tension following Ramsingh's election defeat in the spring of 1962 mounted and finally became public about a year later. The period of open conflict lasted from June 1963 to January 1964, at which time Ramsingh was effectively removed from his positions of organizational power. This case study of the high points of that period of struggle provides a vivid picture of the interplay of actors and the linkages of power and influence at different levels of INTUC politics. The struggle was from beginning to end organizational in focus, key resources being the support of industrial workers in Indore (and to some extent the support of leaders and workers in other industrial centers in the state) and the alternate linkages of support that Ramsingh and Dravid had with the national leaders of INTUC and the Congress high command in Ahmedabad and Delhi, and Dravid's superior access to the bureaucratic machinery of the Labour Department through his official position as Labour Minister on the state level. Tiwari, then allied with Dravid, also received support from the new Chief Minister, D. P. Mishra, who came into power in 1963.

The immediate cause of the struggle's coming into the open was the dispute over the introduction of the "four-loom" system in the Rajkumar Mills. The "four-loom" system entailed an increase in the work-load of loom operators, from running two looms to handling four simultaneously.[29] Ramsingh had a close relationship with Rustamji Cowasji Jall, the Parsi owner of the Rajkumar Mills and the chief manager of the Kalyanmal Mills, a relationship built up through mutual support and cooperation in the postwar years.[30] Now the Rajku-

---

[29] According to informants, the "four-loom" system had been in unofficial operation in all the mills for nearly a decade during the hot months of the year (March to June) when the flow of workers, especially *badli* workers, to the agricultural areas for the harvest and planting season (preceding the monsoon) caused a temporary annual shortage of labor. The representative union under Ramsingh had unregistered agreements to this effect with the millowners, and before 1963, Dravid and Tiwari had invariably acquiesced. In 1963, the issue concerned the official introduction of the system on a year-round basis, requiring an agreement or series of agreements to be registered in the office of the Registrar of Trade Unions.

The increased work-load was one that younger workers could handle, but it put a heavy strain on older workers. Part of the political division in 1963 may have been based on age, younger workers supporting the system because they could earn about 40 percent higher wages for operating four looms. Obviously the increase in work-load for younger workers would entail retrenchment of older workers.

[30] R. C. Jall is an interesting actor on another level of politics in the industrial arena in Indore, the level of millowner and manager (or capitalist) politics. The millowners are typically concerned with national legislation, taxation, and price controls that affect profits and the ability of the mills to remain economically viable. The millowners' linkages with particular parties and politicians, and their internal family and financial rivalries, are important in Indore city politics. Unfortunately, research limitations of time and resources did not permit an extensive exploration of this subject.

R. C. Jall is of special interest because of his rise from an ordinary middle class background (legal education) to the level of a capitalist and millowner. He was originally the managerial employee of the Hukumchand family, and became the chief manager of the Hukumchand, Kalyanmal, and Rajkumar Mills of Indore and the Hira Mills of Ujjain, holding all four posts simultaneously. His managerial salaries from four plants, combined with financial manipulation of the mills' buying and marketing activities, provided him with a fortune sufficient to buy out the Rajkumar Mills entirely when it got into apparently desperate financial troubles

mar Mills was in financial trouble (so were the Swadeshi and Malwa Mills), and R. C. Jall wanted Ramsingh's support in establishing the official introduction of the "four-loom" system on a year-round basis.[31] Jall was in turn supported by the other millowners and managers, because an agreement concerning one mill would be the thin edge of the wedge, a precedent, for bringing the system into all the Indore mills later.

Ramsingh, as President of the IMMS, apparently made a secret agreement with Jall some time in the spring of 1963, committing the IMMS to the introduction of the "four-loom" system on a permanent basis, the idea being that Ramsingh would maneuver the agreement through the IMMS ratifying process at some convenient time and then have it officially registered by the administrative authorities. It was not to be so. Before Ramsingh had time to bring the agreement before the Working Committee (executive body) or the Sanyukt Pratinidhi Mandal (representative organ) of the IMMS, his political opponents brought the matter out into the open, the Labour Minister immediately registering his strong disapproval of the agreement.[32]

(under his own management), making him one of the millowners in his own right. His success was due in large part to the cooperation of Ramsinghbhai, who was privy to much confidential financial information and who could maintain labor discipline or allow strikes that seriously affected the short-run production and financial viability of the mills.

R. C. Jall has been the Congress legislative representative from the nearby safe seat of Mhow, elected four times successively from 1952 to 1967. He has been one of the major allies of the Nai Duniya group and a representative of millowner interests in the state government.

[31] One informed INTUC respondent estimated that the regularization of the "four-loom" system would bring a monthly saving of 500,000 rupees, or an annual saving of 6,000,000 rupees, to the millowners, even after paying higher wages to the operators of the four looms. On all shifts, it would have meant the retrenchment of about 3,000 permanent employees.

[32] Sputnik, a leftist weekly paper, on June 10, 1963, reported that on hearing about the agreement, Dravid "broke into tears."

An additional dimension of the struggle was precipitated in the labor area, causing Ramsingh embarrassment and undoubtedly adding unusual heat to his subsequent actions. Among the complaints made against him of the abuse of his powers and lack of real concern for workers' interests was that he had an inordinate interest in an exhibition given by the Mahila Vikas Mandir (Women's Development Association—an extension of INTUC social work among the women in the labor area). It was alleged that he spent a large part of each day with the association, ostensibly helping prepare the exhibit, but at the cost of organizational and field work for the IMMS.

Tiwari denounced Ramsingh's behavior in connection with the Mahila Vikas Mandir exhibition, provoking a fierce round of public meetings in the labor area,

Ramsingh responded by engineering the expulsion of Gangaram Tiwari from the office of Secretary of the IMMS. Ramsingh's first step was to hold an urgent meeting of the IMMS Working Committee on June 5 when, in Tiwari's presence, he tried to ram through a motion of "no confidence" in the Secretary. The effort failed on this occasion, but Ramsingh then appointed a committee of five of his own supporters to inquire into four charges leveled against Tiwari, to the effect that he was sabotaging the work of the IMMS.[33]

In the meantime, Ramsingh found a new grievance. As a result of the impending switch-over to the "four-loom" system in the Rajkumar Mills, there were violent disturbances on the mill premises. Four laborers (members of IMMS) were punished, two with dismissal and two with suspension. Normally such disciplinary actions in Indore do not take place against IMMS workers without the tacit concurrence of the IMMS. Normally also, workers with such problems must seek help from the representative union and it, if it so desires, can take the case to the Industrial Court for a judicial finding. Ramsingh was uninterested in helping these workers, but Tiwari and Dravid came to their aid. Tiwari sought legal assistance for the workers in filing a case before the Industrial Court in spite of Ramsingh's instruction that he refrain from doing so.

At the same time, behind the scenes, Dravid, the Labour Minister, prepared an ordinance which the Governor duly promulgated on June 19.[34] The ordinance, called the Madhya Pradesh Industrial Relations (Amending) Ordinance of 1963, qualified the provision in the Industrial Relations Act that required workers to take grievances to court exclusively through the agency of the representative union, by permitting workers for the first time to seek relief in the Industrial Court as

---

where Ramsingh attacked Tiwari's reputation—laying the foundation for Tiwari's expulsion from the Secretaryship of the IMMS. See *Nai Duniya*, June 25, 1963, for a colorful review of events in the spring, and *Sputnik*, June 3, 1963, for a pungent account of Ramsingh's platform tactics.

[33] The charges against Tiwari were that: (a) he had not contributed his Vidhan Sabha allowance to the IMMS; (b) he had close ties with Babusingh Dingar, Satyanarayan Bajpai, Sardar Labhsingh, Babulal Bisrua, and 62 other Communists, or fellow-travelers; (c) he was expounding on the Gita (relating religion to politics and Ramsingh's morality) after he had been instructed not to by Ramsingh; and (d) he had contrived to smear Ramsingh's reputation, by alleging that Ramsingh had consorted with the girls in Mahila Vikas Mandir, and by encouraging *Sputnik*, through Dingar and Bajpai, to print these matters. *Sputnik*, June 10, 1963.

[34] *Nai Duniya*, June 21, 1963; *Sputnik*, June 24, 1963.

individuals in their own right. The implication was clear. Dravid and Tiwari had moved to bypass one of Ramsingh's more important legal resources, the exclusive intermediary power of the IMMS in seeking relief for its members in the courts. With Tiwari's help, the injured laborers filed their own case against the management of the Rajkumar Mills. Now workers displaced by the introduction of the "four-loom" system could challenge it in the Court themselves.

Dravid, from his position as Labour Minister astride the administrative machinery, was initially confident of his independent ability to wear down Ramsingh's resistance. Being weak at the state level, Ramsingh countered by appealing to the INTUC high command to intervene on his behalf, but their initial response was ambivalent. The high command communication consisted of an even-handed rebuke to both Ramsingh and Dravid, ordering that the Mahila Vikas (women's development) center be closed to access by any IMMS male member and instructing Dravid to concentrate on his ministerial responsibilities. The "four-looms" agreement was suspended, pending the search for new information. It was clear that the INTUC high command was divided, one group supporting Dravid and the other favoring Ramsingh.[35] The factional division in the high command, and the support for Dravid of Congress Brahmans in Delhi, prevented decisive external intervention in Indore for eight months while Dravid strove to achieve his objectives through the state government machinery and Tiwari cooperated locally to undermine Ramsingh's control of the organized workers.

On June 23, Ramsingh again called a meeting of the Pratinidhi Mandal to oust Tiwari from the office of Secretary, but he sent notices of the meeting only to his own supporters among the members of that council. Tiwari himself was allowed into the meeting, but many of the council members known to be supporters of Tiwari were forcibly barred from entering the meeting by strong-arm men posted at the entrance. In the meeting, fourteen charges were read out against Tiwari, some based on brief quotations from his private diary;[36] and without giving Tiwari a chance to answer the charges, a motion to expel Tiwari from his position in the IMMS was put and carried.[37] Tiwari there-

---

[35] *Nai Duniya*, June 25, 1963.

[36] Tiwari's diary had been stolen from his desk the previous day and found its way into Ramsingh's hands. Tiwari was charged with having written things against the IMMS in it. *Nai Duniya*, June 25, 1963.

[37] *Ibid.*

upon filed a petition in the Industrial Court against this move, charging that his removal was illegal.[38] The magistrate issued a "stay order" against the removal, and served Ramsingh and Kanhaiyalal Yadav (an IMMS lawyer, then supporting Ramsingh) with a "show cause" notice asking why Tiwari's petition should not be granted. Pending a judicial decision, Tiwari was to remain legally Secretary of the IMMS.

Ramsingh's strategy was to move simultaneously on two fronts. On one hand, he attempted to obtain a complete monopoly on all the positions of power in the union organization. He had already caused the disruption of sales of the *Mazdoor Sandesh* (an IMMS weekly paper) and forced the resignation of its pro-Dravid editor, Ladli Prasad Sethi. By removing Tiwari from the position of Secretary, Ramsingh hoped to replace him with one of his own right-hand men, Kanhaiyalal Yadav. Ramsingh had already filled a number of other key positions with loyal supporters. Ishwar Chand Jain, one of Ramsingh's most intelligent and influential backers, was chief editor and managing director of the INTUC daily newspaper, *Jagran*. Chhaganlal Katariya, another middle-class Jain, had been promoted from an ordinary clerk to the position of head clerk in the Hukumchand Mills, with a salary of about 700 rupees per month.[39] Mathuralal Sharma (Rajasthani Brahman), the chief accountant in the Malwa Mills,[40] had been elevated to the positions of President of the City Congress and President of the Textile Clerks' Association through Ramsingh's influence.[41] The government-appointed "labour officers"—who are charged with representing within

---

[38] In the petition it was noted that: (a) Tiwari and other Mandal members were not notified of the meeting; (b) no agenda of the meeting was posted; (c) numerous Mandal members were forcibly prevented from entering the meeting; (d) no previous inquiry was made into the charges against Tiwari by any legally constituted body, nor was he informed of the charges against him before the meeting, nor given a hearing before the meeting; and (e) even in the meeting, he was given no opportunity to reply to the charges made against him. Thus procedure was violated in a variety of ways; the meeting was "packed" with Ramsingh supporters and the action was entirely illegal and unconstitutional. *Nai Duniya*, June 30, 1963.

[39] *Sputnik*, June 24, 1963.

[40] It was through linkages of this sort with the clerical and financial staffs of the mills that Ramsingh was able to collect accurate information about the financial operations of the mills, giving him knowledge that could be used damagingly against the millowners, one more resource that induced the millowners to cooperate with him most of the time.

[41] Sharma, however, unlike I. C. Jain and Katariya, was not entirely dependent on Ramsingh and maintained good relations with Dravid and Tiwari. He attempted to reconcile Dravid and Ramsingh and, when this failed, gravitated toward the winning side. Katariya had his eye on Sharma's position at the head of the Clerks' Association.

the mills the day-to-day grievances of workers before management, and who are in powerful positions to influence recruitment, dismissal, and punishment of workers in the mills—were predominantly Ramsingh's men. Likewise the "inspectors," paid officials of the IMMS who were supposed to act as intermediaries in resolving workers' problems in the mills, were almost all acting as Ramsingh's agents.

By monopolizing the IMMS organization and its instruments of power, Ramsingh hoped, on the second front, to retain firm control of the bulk of the textile workers so that, should the INTUC high command ultimately settle the dispute, they would be forced by a demonstration of Ramsingh's preponderant local power to settle it in his favor. Holding large public meetings in the labor area was an integral part of this strategy of demonstrating numerical support. At the same time, Ramsingh put on public record very early that he would abide by the decisions of his *gurujans* (elders) in the high command.[42]

The competition between Ramsingh and Tiwari for numerical support in the labor area factionalized the workers, forcing them to take sides. The intimidation and pressures involved in this process and in the rounds of public meetings resulted in numerous outbreaks of violence within and outside the mills. In the summer months the police responded in a fairly nonpartisan way, arresting the more troublesome leaders and rabble-rousers of both factions.[43]

By the first week of July, the INTUC high command again considered intervention to reconcile the estranged parties in the IMMS in Indore. The national INTUC Working Committee was scheduled to meet in Delhi on July 9. Word began to filter down that the high command was generally displeased with Ramsingh's behavior, and there were rumors that some were in favor of transferring Ramsingh to Kanpur.[44] Ramsingh drew in his horns somewhat and publicly described the dispute as merely a "family quarrel" not requiring high command intervention.[45] Various other proposals were in the air, that Ramsingh be made to step aside, that he be instructed to obey high command instructions to the letter, that a trial of strength be staged through a secret ballot in the Pratinidhi Mandal and, if worst came

[42] *Nai Duniya,* June 26, 1963.
[43] *Nai Duniya,* June 30, 1963.
[44] *Sputnik,* June 17, 1963.
[45] *Nai Duniya,* July 7, 1963.

to worst, a complete secret ballot of the 18,000 workers officially belonging to the IMMS.[46]

The Working Committee held its meeting but instead of considering the dispute in detail decided, at the urging of Gulzarilal Nanda (the Union Home Minister and an ally of Dravid), to allow Kandubhai Desai, then the national Secretary of INTUC, to seek a compromise and reconciliation through private meetings in Delhi with Ramsingh and Dravid.[47] Desai announced after two days that progress had been made and that he was confident the problem would soon be resolved.[48]

Dravid got the better of this first round, evidenced by the fact that Ramsingh returned to Indore chastened and unusually restrained. He announced that his senior leaders had ended the dispute and he was now ready to cooperate again with Dravid.[49] He responded to press questions about Tiwari's removal by indicating that the IMMS was now powerless in the matter. He assumed that the case would either be appealed to the high command or settled in the courts, and the IMMS would abide by the decision. Dravid had remained in Delhi for further INTUC Working Committee meetings, but when he returned he was even more emphatic. He informed the press that the dispute had been resolved, but the high command had unequivocally instructed Ramsingh to follow his (Dravid's) guidance.[50]

Another important development occurred at this stage. Nai Duniya and City Congress leaders took advantage of the fact that Ramsingh was under attack to get a high command decision, tacitly supported by Dravid, on a local party organizational matter, while the INTUC meetings were going on in Delhi.[51] The *Mohalla Sudhar* Committee structure, one of the major means by which Ramsingh exerted influence in the city and in the City Congress, was abolished by fiat of

---

[46] *Nai Duniya*, July 9, 1963.

[47] *Nai Duniya*, July 11, 1963.

[48] *Nai Duniya* and *Indore Samachar*, July 12, 1963. Abid Ali, the Election Officer of the Madhya Pradesh Congress party, announced that the dispute was only a "family quarrel" and was practically over.

[49] *Nai Duniya*, July 13, 1963.

[50] *Nai Duniya*, July 21, 1963.

[51] The All-India Congress Committee criticized the INTUC dispute and asked the Madhya Pradesh Congress to submit a report on the labor problem. Rameshwar Dayal Totla, whose main ties have been with the Nai Duniya group in Indore, was Chairman of the committee requested to make the report. *Nai Duniya*, July 13, 1963.

the IMMS in the third week of July.[52] Evidently Ramsingh had returned from Delhi with specific orders to terminate the Mohalla committee system.

The pacification efforts of Gulzarilal Nanda and Kandubhai Desai had little enduring effect. Conflict ensued anew a few days later when the Labour Department under Dravid's direction rejected two amendments proposed by the IMMS which would have given Ramsingh and the union powers to discourage defection of union members.[53] In August, Tiwari used a *raksha bandan* celebration gathering outside the Malwa Mills to attack Ramsingh's dictatorial practices.[54] And at the annual *Ganpati* festival celebrated in Indore with large processions of textile workers, complete with floats and decorations paid for by the millowners, the usual harmony of INTUC forces was disrupted by clashes between the opposing factions.[55] Almost simultaneously the dispute was carried into the state-wide arena by Ramsingh, who used his presiding position at the annual Working Committee meeting of the Madhya Pradesh INTUC organization as a platform for a public attack on Dravid and the state Labour Department.[56]

As the situation deteriorated again, the district authorities intervened. The Collector advised Tiwari and Ramsingh by letter not to hold any more meetings or demonstrations in the mill area for a month.[57] The two leaders ceased to attend such meetings personally, but their lieutenants continued to hold them. Two days later the Collector warned that conditions in the mill area were threatening the peace of the whole city, and he sent a confidential report to the government on the situation. Police were stationed at key points in

---

[52] Editorial entitled, "Mohalla Committees, INTUC and Congress," *Nai Duniya*, July 18, 1963. The only reason given in the announcement of abolition was that the committees were not authorized by the IMMS constitution or INTUC regulations and were, therefore, illegal. The editorial writer pointedly asked how it was that these "illegal committees" could have been allowed to exist without INTUC repudiation for over ten years, in spite of repeated complaints by non-INTUC Congress leaders in the city. The complaints belatedly bore fruit when the INTUC and Congress high command (Brahman group) finally decided it was necessary to bridle Ramsingh by, among other things, severing one of his institutional bases of power in the city.

[53] *Indore Samachar*, July 24, 1963.

[54] *Nai Duniya*, August 8, 1963.

[55] *Nai Duniya*, September 6, 1963.

[56] *Ibid.*

[57] *Nai Duniya*, September 12, 1963.

the labor area and in front of Shram Shivir, the IMMS office head-quarters,[58] to the disadvantage of Ramsingh.[59] It was perhaps more than coincidental that about this same time D. P. Mishra was winning his battle for supremacy in the Madhya Pradesh Congress organization, to become Chief Minister of the state government on September 24, 1963. His support was extended to Tiwari in Indore. A significant proportion of the high-level police officers in Indore, as well as in Madhya Pradesh as a whole, have been Brahmans from the Hindi-speaking north, so it was no surprise after September 1963 to see the police restrict Ramsingh's scope for action.

It was learned in September that the INTUC high command had once again decided to intervene in the Indore dispute, on this occasion by sending S. R. Vasavada, a member of the "Ahmedabad group" sympathetic to Ramsingh, to investigate and report on the conflict. Tiwari and Ramsingh each sought in his own manner to prepare for Vasavada's arrival the following month. On September 17, Gangaram Tiwari publicly attacked the IMMS mill "inspectors" and the mill-owners. He accused them of collaborating to exacerbate conflict among the workers and to intimidate those who declined to support Ramsingh. Tiwari proposed a "secret ballot" of the IMMS ordinary membership to solve the dispute.[60] He reiterated and amplified his proposal in a speech before a crowd of about 15,000 persons in *junta chowk* (the public square in the heart of Indore) on September 22. His strategy was to gain public support for a referendum by the 18,000 common members of the IMMS on the question of the removal of Ramsingh from his official position at the head of the union prior to Vasavada's arrival.[61]

Ramsingh's counter-strategy was to obtain a vote of confidence from the Pratinidhi Mandal (representative body), to invest his leadership with legitimacy by ostensibly normal procedures. He assumed that a referendum would be difficult to stage, and calculated that Vasavada would be predisposed to endorse the outcome of a Pra-

[58] *Nai Duniya*, September 14, 1963.

[59] *Nai Duniya*, September 18, 1963. Tiwari supported and Ramsingh opposed the deployment of police in these locations. There were indications reported in the papers that the factional competition for support in the Madhya Pradesh INTUC organization had spread to other labor centers in Ujjain, Nagda, and Kemur.

[60] *Nai Duniya*, September 18, 1963.

[61] *Nai Duniya*, September 23, 1963.

tinidhi Mandal confidence vote. The sticky part was to mobilize an
overwhelming vote of confidence, not just a bare majority, for Ramsingh's grip on the organization was under erosion. The resulting
tactics were transparently intimidatory. A subcommittee of the IMMS
had met under Ramsingh's direction to formulate charges of indisci-
pline against 85 pro-Tiwari members of the Pratinidhi Mandal, and,
on October 10, Ramsingh scheduled a Mandal meeting for the following day. The 85 Tiwari supporters were instructed to appear at Shram
Shivir (the IMMS headquarters) to answer the charges. But when they
assembled in the garden in front of the building, instead of being
admitted to the Mandal meeting as a body, they were informed that
they would be required to enter the meeting one at a time to hear
the charges and face disciplinary action. The 85 refused to cooperate,
however, and demanded that the meeting be held in the open where
they would have strength in numbers and the benefit of publicity.
When his plan broke down, Ramsingh held the Mandal meeting without the 85 members present and the Mandal expelled them from the
organization for five years. When the meeting ended and those inside
came out, a violent clash erupted in the garden and the police stationed nearby intervened to disperse both parties.[62]

On Vasavada's second day in Indore, Dravid addressed a meeting
of about 10,000 workers in the labor area, some of whom had been
mobilized to form a massive demonstration against Ramsingh in
front of Shram Shivir.[63] Labor absenteeism caused the mills to be
effectively shut down for the day. Meanwhile, Ramsingh had again
called a meeting of the now purged Pratinidhi Mandal in Shram
Shivir, at which Vasavada was present. Without a pass issued by the
IMMS, no one was allowed to enter Shram Shivir. In the Mandal
meeting, Ramsingh's vote of confidence was duly elicited by an overwhelming majority of 579 to 54. Vasavada was, as expected, impressed
and announced afterward that the result must have been genuine
because the vote had been by secret ballot.[64] Vasavada also announced

---

[62] *Nai Duniya,* October 12, 1963.

[63] *Nai Duniya,* October 25, 1963.

[64] *Ibid.* There was an unmistakable irony in this situation, however, as thousands
of workers gathered outside Shram Shivir compound were enthusiastically and almost uniformly shouting for Ramsingh's removal, and Vasavada could hardly be
unaware of the discrepancy between the overwhelming vote of confidence on one

that Tiwari and Dravid had only just agreed to arbitration of the dispute, while Ramsingh had accepted arbitration in writing some time ago. The dispute would, therefore, be decided by an arbitrator appointed by the high command. He informed the press that there were charges against both Tiwari and Ramsingh that would have to be looked into.[65] A meeting of the national INTUC Working Committee to appoint the arbitrator was set for October 31.[66]

Vasavada's confidential analysis of the problem along with recommendations was submitted to the high command at the meeting in Delhi. It was reported that Vasavada had panned Homi Daji's proposal for a public inquiry into Ramsingh's property holdings, and that he laid much of the blame for the dispute on the shoulders of the Labour Minister. Vasavada apparently recommended that Dravid be invited to give up his ministerial position and return to work directly in Indore,[67] probably out of the belief that Dravid would be unwilling to do so. The following day, the Working Committee formally approved the proposal for arbitration and appointed Ambekar the arbitrator.

---

hand and the opposed feelings of a substantial part of the textile labor force on the other.

The Labour Minister publicly charged that the Mandal vote, according to participants, had been far from secret. It was reported that open cards (rather than sealed ballots) had been distributed, that one pencil had been circulated for marking ballots, and that each card had been individually collected as soon as it was marked. Dravid also noted that the meeting had been illegally packed with Ramsingh's supporters by the device of substituting non-elected Mandal members for those legally elected in 1962. He charged that three different Mandal membership lists existed, the first and official list published in *Mazdoor Sandesh* in June 1962, a second list used by Ramsingh in the Tiwari removal case before the Industrial Court, and the third list used for the present Mandal meeting. See *Nai Duniya*, October 25, 27, and 30, 1963.

[65] In response to press questions, he elaborated that the charges against Ramsingh were that: (a) he had made a number of agreements with the millowners without placing them before the Working Committee or Pratinidhi Mandal of the IMMS; (b) he had a "vindictive" nature; (c) he harassed and victimized workers in various ways; and (d) he had violated the rules and procedures of the IMMS. Against Tiwari the charges were that: (a) he had conspired against the IMMS, and (b) he had taken union matters into the courts. Vasavada indicated that the high command would also consider allegations that the Labour Department had interfered in internal union affairs, that the removal of Tiwari from the Secretaryship and certain other members from the Mandal was illegal and in violation of the IMMS constitutional procedure, and that the composition of the Pratinidhi Mandal was unrepresentative. *Nai Duniya*, October 25, 1963.

[66] *Nai Duniya*, October 24, 1963.

[67] *Nai Duniya*, November 1, 1963.

In this second intervention by the high command, Ramsingh came
off a little better than Dravid and Tiwari. Ramsingh had convinced
the visiting INTUC leader that his position was organizationally
sound by the vote of confidence, and the arbitration decision, even
if it split the differences in the dispute, would leave Ramsingh in his
positions of power and possibly stronger than he had been before
the removal of Tiwari. Vasavada and others among the high command who sympathized with Ramsingh knew that, whatever his faults,
the field work successes of the INTUC organization in Indore were
in large part his work, and that Dravid by himself would be far from
an adequate substitute.

With arbitration imminent, however, violence in the labor arena
escalated again, as both parties sought to impress the arbitrator with
their strength. Despite the official ban on meetings and demonstrations in the mill area imposed all through November and December,
they continued unabated. On November 18 the intensive collections
of contributions for a "welcome" of Ramsingh in the Malwa Mills
led to open fighting between members of the two factions. A riot
appeared likely. Supporters of Ramsingh were allegedly extorting
money from 77 shopkeepers outside the mill. Police intervention resulted in the arrest of 78 persons.[68] There were also indications that
the police administration was being penetrated by the division in the
labor area. A deputation of Tiwari's supporters filed a complaint with
the Collector that the *thanedar* (police station official) of Pardesipura
was taking sides in clashes by arresting supporters of Tiwari and ig-
noring violent provocations by Ramsingh workers.[69]

But time seemed to be on the side of Tiwari in his effort to gradually win over sheer numbers in the struggle. On December 14, Tiwari
was able to mobilize a demonstration of 5,000 workers, under his
leadership, to demand a bonus.[70] The large procession moved from
the labor area to in front of Shram Shivir, shouting slogans against
Ramsingh, and ended up at the office of the government Conciliation
Officer. This officer, Mr. Khaurannekar, met the workers outside, and
his statement suggests that he was coached or at least aware of what

---

[68] *Nai Duniya,* November 19, 1963.

[69] *Nai Duniya,* December 5, 1963.

[70] In early November the 200,000 textile workers in Bombay had won a bonus
of 5 to 25 percent of their basic wages through an agreement between the INTUC
leaders and the local millowners. *Nai Duniya,* November 6, 1963.

was coming. He said that he had seen the balance sheets of the mills and that all except the Swadeshi and Malwa Mills made substantial profits, so that a bonus was well within the realm of possibility. He indicated that if necessary the bonus demand would be taken to court by the Labour Department on behalf of the workers. He informed them that the millowners had agreed that wages which had been withheld for some time due to supposed financial difficulties would be forthcoming on the 23rd of December.[71]

An even more significant development had occurred a few days before this demonstration, when it was announced that the Sanyukt Pratinidhi Mandal had met and by a two-thirds majority vote, under Section 10(2) of the IMMS constitution, had removed 373 members of the Mandal, and their replacements had been elected in the labor area. In addition the Mandal sent a letter to the Registrar informing him of the action, and a letter to Ramsingh instructing him to hold a meeting of the Mandal by December 16 to elect new officers of the IMMS. Borrowing Ramsingh's tactics, the rump of Tiwari's supporters in the Mandal, including those who had been expelled, had set themselves up as the true representative body.[72] They were relying on a growing sense of assertiveness and confidence among workers that Ramsingh's power was being steadily eroded and that his days were numbered.[73]

Instead of calling a meeting of the Pratinidhi Mandal, as was demanded, Ramsingh went to Hyderabad to confer with Ambekar, the arbitrator, who had been unable to travel himself because of poor health. At the same time, Ishwar Chand Jain and Chhaganlal Katariya (Ramsingh's Jain lieutenants) went to Ahmedabad to speak with

[71] In response to charges by demonstration leaders that there were gross irregularities and various forms of corruption in the Badli Control office, resulting from Ramsingh's residual influence in the administration, the Conciliation Officer announced that a reform in the direction of the "Kanpur system" was under consideration by the government. He also indicated that the charges of intimidation and oppression by the "inspectors" was being inquired into, and strong action would be taken by the Labour Department. *Nai Duniya,* December 15, 1963.

[72] *Nai Duniya,* December 12, 1963.

[73] A further indication of this was that Ramsingh, driving his jeep in the labor area, was stopped by a group of workers and freely abused by them within earshot of the Pardesipura *thana.* Ramsingh is reported to have driven angrily to the police station, burst in, and according to the new thanedar—who had the courage to report the matter to the City Superintendent of Police—Ramsingh had shouted at him, "You are not doing a damn thing! Just give me the word and I'll put these guys in the cooler myself." *Nai Duniya,* December 18, 1963.

Vasavada, probably hoping to get an order from the INTUC high command to Tiwari blocking the Pratinidhi Mandal meeting that he had himself called for December 22 (in lieu of Ramsingh's own refusal to hold such a meeting).[74] The meeting, however, was held as scheduled, in Sonarvada (Jail Road), as Shram Shivir was not opened by Ramsingh's followers. The basic outcome of the meeting was that a motion of "no confidence" against Ramsingh was put and carried, and he was declared removed from all of his positions of power and authority in the IMMS. Ladli Prasad Sethi, a dependent ally of Dravid's, was declared elected as the new President of the IMMS with all the powers inherent in that position, and a notice to this effect was dispatched to the Registrar of Trade Unions, requesting him to act accordingly.[75]

Although Ramsingh attacked the new developments as illegal, and claimed that he had a wire from Ambekar instructing him to continue in his capacity as President, the Registrar of Trade Unions instructed the banks holding IMMS deposits to disregard instructions from Ramsingh and honor only the signature of Ladli Prasad Sethi. By this one stroke, Ramsingh's financial powers were paralyzed and his position was now clearly in jeopardy.[76] Ladli Prasad Sethi published an advertisement in his capacity as President informing the millowners that henceforth any agreements made with Ramsingh would be illegal and not binding on the IMMS.[77]

Within a few days the new Pratinidhi Mandal met again to round out its attacks on Ramsingh's local sources of power. Gayadin Morya and Ramrao Dube, pro-Ramsingh office-holders in the IMMS, were declared removed. Jaisingh Verma, the "leader" of the Mazdoor Seva

---

[74] *Nai Duniya*, December 20, 1963.

[75] The resolution noted that Ramsingh had been served with a charge sheet on December 20, but had made no reply nor presented himself before the Mandal to answer charges. It ordered Ramsingh to turn over all the office files, papers, records, check and bank books, and all other IMMS office properties in his possession to Ladli Prasad Sethi. Of the 740 members of the Pratinidhi Mandal, about 540 were reported to have taken part. Of these, approximately 343 were new and 197 old members. *Nai Duniya*, December 23, 1963.

[76] In a lengthy news conference, Ramsingh anounced that he had given his acceptance of an arbitral agreement in advance to Kashinath Pande, the President of the national INTUC, who had assumed the powers of arbitrator when Ambekar's illness made it impossible for him to carry out this responsibility. *Nai Duniya*, December 28, 1963.

[77] *Ibid.*

Dal (worker's service organization), was declared removed, and Ramgopal Salvi was appointed in his place. Jagdish Vyas was elected Vice President of the IMMS. The positions of "inspectors" were declared abolished, and a decision was made to substitute *shramik sevakon*[78] to help workers with their grievances in the mills. Ishwar Chand Jain and Chhaganlal Katariya, two of Ramsingh's key supporters, were declared removed from all their positions in the IMMS.

At this juncture the Communist leaders moved to take advantage of the opportunity presented by the bonus issue. Harisingh, the Secretary of the Mill Mazdoor Union, announced that, since the bonus scheduled for 1962 had not been received even a year later, the Union would call for a strike unless the bonus was paid within fifteen days. Notice to this effect had been delivered to the millowners and the government on December 21. The Union Council in its meeting of the 27th formally requested the government for permission to hold meetings and demonstrations in the mill area, in view of the ban still in effect.[79] Homi Daji, now a Member of Parliament, explained that a strike had become necessary because the millowners were profiting from the predicament of the now paralyzed IMMS, and Ramsingh's dependence on the millowners, to put off paying the bonus indefinitely. He felt that Ramsingh had obfuscated the bonus issue and that Dravid (who presumably would inherit millowner support) would only "get caught up in legal circles for three years without resolving the problem." [80] He proposed that the Chief Minister take personal charge of the bonus matter, realizing shrewdly that Mishra personally had little warmth for the Indore millowners, and impose a decision as had occurred in Bombay. By coming out in support of the bonus demand, the Communist leaders were indirectly reinforcing the momentum of the Dravid–Tiwari group in the struggle against Ramsingh.

The irony of the situation was that the tables had been turned on Ramsingh. For the last 22 years he had been the most uncompromising and effective opponent of Communist power in Indore, and now his world was crumbling about him with the Communists contributing, however marginally, to the process. He attacked the Com-

---

[78] *Shramik sevakon* means servants of labor. The new appointees were all supporters of Tiwari and Dravid, and opponents of Ramsingh. *Nai Duniya,* January 1, 1964.

[79] *Nai Duniya,* December 28, 1963.

[80] *Ibid.*

munist party for supporting Tiwari, alleging that it was the official
policy of the local Communist Central Committee. Daji replied that
the Communist leaders did not deign to participate in internal
INTUC quarrels, but he admitted that wherever any political boss
("malik") makes himself an "object of worship," the Communists
would invariably be part of the movement to tear him down.[81] The
Communist leaders were delighted by the erosion of Ramsingh's
power, and pointed to Daji's victory in 1962 as the fundamental blow
initiating Ramsingh's spiralling decline. But actually the Communist
leadership and organizations were a negligible quantity in deciding
the power struggle within the IMMS. In this sense, Daji's disclaimer
was quite true and Ramsingh's indictment of the Communists a sign
of his desperation.

But Ramsingh was never ready to acknowledge complete defeat,
and he still had a chance to pick up the pieces through arbitration.
He sent his "inspectors" back into the mills to try to reassert their
authority and control despite the fact that they had been declared
removed by the Tiwari-controlled Pratinidhi Mandal. This time the
"inspectors" met resistance, and trouble broke out in the Malwa,
Kalyanmal, and Rajkumar Mills controlled by Chandan Singh Bharkatiya and R. C. Jall. The entry of "inspectors" caused the workers
in parts of the Malwa and Kalyanmal Mills to shut down operations
in wildcat strikes until the "inspectors" were ordered back out. Coun-
terdemonstrations by Ramsingh supporters brought violent clashes
and fresh police intervention. Those arrested, however, were largely
from among the Tiwari faction, as the reports to the police were
made by the "labour officers," still under the control of Ramsingh and
the millowners.[82]

Meanwhile the machinery of government continued to roll ponder-
ously on. The Registrar served Ramsingh on January 4 with a "show-

---

[81] *Ibid.*

[82] *The Hindustan Times,* January 6, 1964. Homi Daji alleged that in this series
of incidents the Collector and Police were acting in league with Ramsingh and the
millowners, contrary to the interests of the workers. He sent a formal protest to
G. Nanda, the Union Home Minister, and detailed his criticism of the Collector.
Nai Duniya, January 4, 1964.

Daji's complaint was followed by a deputation from the Madhya Pradesh Mill-
Owners Association to the Home Minister, to inform him that production was suffering because of the political unrest. Nanda assured them that there would be an
early solution to the problem in Indore. *The Hindustan Times,* January 8, 1964.

cause" notice, asking him to present his reasons why he should not be regarded as effectively removed from the position of President of the IMMS.[83] Not long after Daji's complaint to the Home Minister, the Collector imposed Section 144 on the mill area of Indore, prohibiting all public meetings, assemblies, processions, demonstrations, sloganeering, and propaganda for one month. The same day, Ramsingh submitted his answer to the "show cause notice", and the Registrar forwarded the reply to Ladli Prasad Sethi for his counter-statement.[84] On the 8th of January, Ramsingh gave his revolver up to the safekeeping of the Collector, as the central Home Affairs Department had revoked his license for three months.[85]

Just before the arrival of Kashinath Pande (Brahman), the new arbitrator, it appeared as if Ramsingh might win a reprieve. The central office of INTUC strongly criticized the formation of a rival Pratinidhi Mandal by the Dravid–Tiwari group, indicating that the act had not been canvassed or approved outside of Madhya Pradesh. The General Secretary, Vasavada, sent a message to Ramsingh urging him to be patient and to await the arbitral award.

A meeting of the Pratinidhi Mandal (Ramsingh section) was called for January 19, the day of Kashinath Pande's expected arrival. But before Pande had even been met at the railroad station, Tiwari had begun to assemble the largest purely labor demonstration yet in this struggle. Workers began to gather in front of Shram Shivir early in the morning until by 9 a.m. about 7,000 were present in a crowd that filled the cross-road and blocked traffic. Police reinforcements were moved in and an attempt was made to persuade the crowd to move to Chiman Bagh maidan (open space) nearby, but the workers refused. They were determined to confront Pande with their demands for the removal of Ramsingh. Their new slogan was, *"Aya hai chownsat ka sal, Ramsingh ko diya nikal!,"* or "Now that 1964 is here, remove Ramsingh!" The police finally gave in and turned their efforts to preventing an outbreak of violence. They halted 100 of Ramsingh's

---

[83] *Nai Duniya,* January 5, 1964.

[84] Ramsingh argued, among other things, that the Registrar had no authority to decide on the issue before him. It was properly, in his view, under the exclusive jurisdiction of the Industrial Court. *Nai Duniya,* January 7, 1964.

[85] *Ibid.* On the same day it was reported that the Sugar Mill Mazdoor Sangh of Jaora had registered a complaint with the Labour Commissioner that Ramsingh had taken possession of 4,000 rupees of the Sangh's funds without authorization, and that he had ignored repeated requests to return it.

supporters, who were on their way to Shram Shivir, in Sneheletaganj.

A rumor began to circulate that Pande had entered Shram Shivir from a rear door, and the slogan-shouting was coordinated and raised to an intense level. Pande emerged from the front door with Dravid after a few minutes and climbed on a police vehicle to address the crowd. As he did so, Tiwari and Vyas welcomed him with flowers. Pande informed the workers that his authority was limited for the moment to investigating the situation. He was interrupted by repeated demands to order Ramsingh to step down. Unable to speak, Pande stopped and Dravid climbed on the vehicle and requested the workers for discipline. He thanked them for their support and enthusiasm but suggested that the central INTUC leadership be given another chance to resolve the problem.

Pande then retired into Shram Shivir with Tiwari, and after a few minutes called Ladli Prasad Sethi and Vyas inside. He asked Tiwari to disperse the crowd, and Tiwari went outside to do so. The crowd obeyed, but not without grumbling. With the crowd gone, Ramsingh was finally free to bring some of his supporters into Shram Shivir and Pande gave them a hearing. The substance of the conferences in Shram Shivir was not reported, but the outcome was soon obvious. Ramsingh announced his resignation from the Presidency of the IMMS.[86] The pro-Dravid, Brahman group in the INTUC high command, supported by allies in the Congress and central government, had finally asserted supremacy, ending Ramsingh's local control of the labor arena.

The following day Ramsingh went a step further, announcing in a press conference that he would not contest any election of the IMMS. Pande's statement in *Jagran* published the same day informed the people of Indore that within fifteen days an "outsider" would arrive in Indore to take up the interim leadership of the IMMS. His own primary responsibility would be to arrange for new elections

---

[86] Ramsingh attempted to cushion the impact of his resignation by informing the press that he had actually submitted a written resignation a full month ago to Vasavada, and sent copies to Shankerlalbhai, Kandubhai Desai, and the Prime Minister, implying they had not then accepted his resignation. He made clear, however, that his resignation contained a condition that the Presidency of the IMMS be held by an "outsider" not party to the conflict in Indore. Introducing an "outsider" was, in any case, part of the plan at this time of the high command. *Nai Duniya,* January 20, 1964.

by June of 1964. In the meantime, as arbitrator and as President of the central INTUC organization, he had relieved Ramsingh, at his request, of his responsibilities, and was assuming personal charge of the IMMS.[87] On January 22, the Registrar of Trade Unions accepted the substance of Ladli Prasad Sethi's petition, and recognized him as President of the IMMS in place of Ramsingh. Sethi first acknowledged the Registrar's action and then announced his own resignation the following day.[88]

Ramsingh's resignation did not entirely resolve the problem. A decision still had to be made regarding the leadership of the IMMS prior to new elections. V. V. Dravid knew that if an "outsider" were sent, it could do irreparable damage to his own influence in Indore and give Ramsingh new opportunities to rebuild his power. Dravid went personally to Delhi again to try to persuade the high command of a different solution. Ramsingh's sympathizers in the national organization, especially Vasavada, Manohar Mehta, and others of the Jain group in Ahmedabad, were firmly opposed to Dravid. Dravid's position with the Chief Minister of Madhya Pradesh was shaky, and what support there was depended primarily on his cooperation with Gangaram Tiwari. But Dravid had a close personal relationship with the Union Home Minister, Gulzarilal Nanda, dating back to the 1930's, and support from a number of other influential senior INTUC leaders, including Kashinath Pande, Kanti Mehta, Ramanujan, and N. K. Bhatt. Moreover, Dravid seems to have been supported by Indira Gandhi, on whom Prime Minister Nehru tended to rely once his health declined, as well as other Brahmans in the Congress high command. Dravid still had enough influence to obtain an audience for his proposals, but insufficient influence to get agreement. The factionally divided high command proposed to Dravid that he give

---

[87] He indicated also that on the 19th, Tiwari and Dravid had orally accepted his authority as arbitrator. In response to a press question whether he recognized Sethi as the President of the IMMS, he indicated that such recognition was precluded by his acceptance of the President's (i.e., Ramsingh's) resignation. He also seemed to feel that it was now too late to try to reconcile Ramsingh with Dravid and Tiwari. *Nai Duniya, The Hindustan Times,* and *Indian Express,* January 21, 1964.

[88] *Nai Duniya,* January 24, 1964. He was apparently acting in accordance with the outcome of a conference between Dravid and the Governor. Sethi's resignation removed the friction that might otherwise have developed with the high command had he retained the position.

up his Ministership and return to Indore to supervise the IMMS personally. This was apparently a bargaining ploy forced by Dravid's opponents, but not one that they genuinely believed in. Much to their surprise, Dravid agreed, throwing his opponents off balance. Out of sheer exasperation, this way out of the deadlock was then ratified by the Working Committee.

The Madhya Pradesh INTUC and IMMS governing bodies were dissolved in February 1964, terminating Ramsingh's state-wide position. Dravid resigned from the Labour Ministership and the high command appointed him "convenor" of an ad hoc committee that would govern the Madhya Pradesh INTUC in the interim while arranging for the promised elections. In the elections, V. V. Dravid became President of the Madhya Pradesh organization and Gangaram Tiwari the President of the IMMS. True to his word, Dravid returned to live and spend most of his time in Indore, working to restore the strength of the IMMS.

Ramsingh had been defeated decisively by a combination of forces. The initial blow to his prestige came from losing the 1962 election, which signified the defection of previous supporters. He could not ultimately fend off the apparatus of government mobilized against him by the Labour Minister and the new Chief Minister. His overthrow was confirmed by opponents in the high command who felt Ramsingh's behavior was an embarrassment to the labor movement. Losing his grip on the local textile workers, who sought to free themselves of the suffocating machinery that Ramsingh had built up, forced even Ramsingh's supporters in the high command to recognize that his leadership was no longer legitimate in Indore. Ramsingh's organizational power, the support of the millowners, and the sympathy of some of the members of the INTUC high command were not sufficient to withstand the coalition of forces built up against him.

Yet in spite of the impressive numerical displays on the local level, the textile workers were mobilized *against* Ramsingh more than they were organized in united support of alternative leaders, such as Dravid, Tiwari, or others. This fact accounts for the persisting weakness of the IMMS under Dravid and Tiwari's leadership in the last five years. Until this struggle for power began, Ramsingh had held the IMMS together as an effective organizational instrument. Dravid and Tiwari alone were unable to duplicate this achievement. Ramsingh's success, however, relied on government power channeled by Dravid through the apparatus of the Labour Department. Once he resigned from the Cabinet, Dravid had no strong state ministerial and government support for his work in Indore. In fact, Dravid's efforts were undermined by Mishra's regime. D. P. Mishra supported Dravid only to bring down Ramsingh, not because he desired to build up Dravid any further. After Ramsingh's defeat, Mishra worked constantly to build Tiwari up as a labor leader independent of Dravid, with his own political following. As a result, by the 1967 general elections the pro-Congress textile workers in Indore had been divided into three factions, or followings, the smallest still identified with Ramsingh[89] and the rest divided about evenly between Dravid and Tiwari.

In the distribution of 1967 election tickets, D. P. Mishra's influence was clearly visible. Dravid declined even to stand for election. Against Dravid's wishes, Gangaram Tiwari was given the ticket for the labor seat and Dravid's candidate, Mathuralal Sharma, was denied a ticket altogether. This setback reflected the diminished power of the IMMS in the city. Instead of the customary two or three city nominations, in 1967 the IMMS only secured one. The results of the 1967 general election were, in Indore at least, a rebuff to Mishra, for two of his candidates lost.[90] Gangaram Tiwari won in the labor area, defeating a formidable opponent—the young and popular Harisingh, Secretary of the Mill Mazdoor Union. But Tiwari might have been defeated had there been a united opposition as there had been in 1957. Tiwari's proportion of the total vote was just under 44 percent. His major opponent accumulated 41.3 percent of the vote. Ramsingh, in an effort to draw potential Congress support away from Tiwari in the hopes of seeing him defeated, encouraged his friend, Morulal Yadav, to run as an Independent. Yadav got about 5.3 percent of the total vote, reflecting support mainly from his community (Bairwa) and from Ramsingh's supporters. The Jan Sangh nominee obtained about 7.6 percent of the total vote, reflecting their recent efforts to take advantage of IMMS factionalism in the labor area.

Homi Daji stood again for the parliamentary seat, but this time

---

[89] Ramsingh's hard-core (Bairwa) supporters, numbering perhaps 500, followed him out of the IMMS altogether in 1964 in an unsuccessful effort to set up a rival organization.

[90] See Appendix B, Table 4, and Chapter 4, pp. 91–92.

he did not have Ramsingh's unpopularity to focus on and the City and Madhya Pradesh Congress organizations were more united in their support of the Congress parliamentary nominee. Daji suffered slightly also from the general Communist embarrassment following the Chinese invasion of October 1962. Furthermore, the Jan Sangh drew opposition votes away from Daji more effectively in 1967 than in 1962 in the city and rural areas both.[91] Despite these facts, Daji was clearly the front-runner in the city of Indore area itself, but lost more decisively in the rural areas than he had in 1962.[92] The defeats of Daji and Harisingh, therefore, were setbacks for the leftist labor opposition leaders in Indore, showing that they had not gained in voting strength in the labor area merely because the IMMS had been weakened organizationally. Furthermore, there was a defection from the ranks of the united leftist opposition in the labor area. Lakshmi Shanker Shukla, of the same caste as D. P. Mishra, had not long before defected from the Socialist party to Congress. In the 1967 election, Shukla worked directly against Daji, partly out of resentment at his defeat in the 1962 election, which he attributed to sabotage by the Communist leaders.[93]

This chapter on labor politics in Indore has sought to illuminate the processes of political competition—the stakes and rewards that motivate competition, the political actors and their social constituencies, the legal and administrative sanctions available to successful political actors, and the distribution of economic and political power in the labor arena. It has depicted the strategies of Congress labor leaders who established INTUC dominance in Indore, and explored the reasons both for the outbreak of the power struggle within the IMMS and the outcomes of that struggle. The study has also made it possible to demonstrate the variety and basis of political linkages, and

---

[91] In 1962 the Jan Sangh parliamentary candidate obtained only 8.68 percent of the votes (or 11.72 percent, if Hindu Mahasabha votes are added), but in 1967 the Jan Sangh candidate secured nearly 21 percent of the total votes, a substantial increase.

[92] Daji accumulated 74,573 votes in the four Indore city constituencies, as against 67,382 for Sethi.

[93] Shukla suspected that voter confusion over his symbol was caused by careless Communist election instructions to the voters in the urban corner of his constituency on how to vote. See Footnote 28, Chapter 10.

to show to what extent vertical and horizontal linkages are salient in political outcomes, in the Indore labor arena.

The major conclusions bearing on the larger map of Indore city politics are: (1) the predominance of vertical political and bureaucratic linkages in defining the arena of labor politics and affecting the shape of political outcomes—or, in other words, the dependence of local labor politics on higher levels of politics external to the city; (2) the relative distinctiveness and autonomy of the local arena of labor politics as a self-contained sphere of political competition embedded within the larger arena of city politics, and the comparative weakness of local horizontal linkages; and (3) the political salience of caste and other ascriptive bases of identification and mutual support in determining the structure of factions and factional competition apart from formal linkages inherent in organizations (unions, political parties) and the administrative structure of government.

The predominance of vertical political and bureaucratic linkages refers to the central role played by political actors outside Indore city and by those who controlled the instruments of state (not the local) government in determining political outcomes in the Indore labor arena. The role of "outsiders" has invariably been important in Indore labor politics, possible partly because a large part of the labor force are immigrants to the city from northern and western India and naturally responsive to leaders from the same regions. The top leadership of Congress labor in Indore has generally come from outside, N. H. Dravid and V. V. Dravid from Nagpur, Gangaram Tiwari from Uttar Pradesh, Ramsinghbhai Verma and Mathuralal Sharma from Rajasthan, and the Jain secondary leaders also from families that migrated to Indore from Rajasthan, though not as recently.

The key Congress labor leaders, N. H. Dravid, V. V. Dravid, and Ramsingh, were protégés of national-level labor and party leaders of Ahmedabad and north India. Gulzarilal Nanda, Kandubhai Desai, and S. R. Vasavada visited Indore and encouraged local leaders to found the Textile Labour Association and assisted the TLA in bargaining with the Holkar government and the millowners in the princely state period. V. V. Dravid and Ramsingh were sent by the Ahmedabad labor high command to restore Congress control in Indore from the Communists seven years before the princely state came to an end. The national-level leaders of Congress labor and the

Indian National Congress itself have invariably been strong arms of support for the "outsiders" delegated to Indore, constituting external and vertical political linkages between local and national organizations.

V. V. Dravid's high status, from a dignified South Indian Brahman family with a Maharashtrian cultural overlay, combined with the backing of Gulzarilal Nanda (Punjabi) and national Brahman leaders, gave him easy access to H. C. Dhanda (Punjabi), K. A. Chitale (Maharashtrian Brahman) and the other high Brahman and Jain officials of the Holkar government, so that the government machinery, the efforts of the millowners, and the work of Dravid and Ramsingh could be coordinated to build up the Indore Mill Mazdoor Sangh as the dominant organization. It was the same extra-local, national-linkage support that ensured that Dravid would become Labour Minister in the first representative Holkar government. It gave him a chance to lay the groundwork for new legislation through the *Banawalikar Report,* to place a legal ban on Communist organizations that continued into Madhya Bharat until 1951, and to step into the Labour Ministry of the Madhya Bharat and Madhya Pradesh governments, holding that position from early 1952 through early 1964.

The control of the Labour portfolio, in conjunction with other portfolios and with supportive bureaucratic allies, made it possible for Dravid to introduce the Nanda-inspired "Bombay model" of labor legislation in Madhya Bharat and Madhya Pradesh. The Bombay model statutes authorized the recognition by government of "representative unions" as the official bargaining agent of workers with the industry. The corresponding control of government machinery (the Labour Department and the Registrar of the Trade Unions) ensured that INTUC affiliates would almost invariably be recognized, giving Dravid a considerable degree of control of political outcomes in local labor arenas from outside, on the state level of politics. Thus vertical political linkages—between Dravid and Ramsingh on the state and local levels, and the high commands of INTUC and the Congress on the national level—and political linkages—between Dravid as Labour Minister and Ramsingh as the local organizational boss, supported by bureaucratic linkages (government machinery) between Dravid and the local labor arena—played the crucial roles in furthering and maintaining INTUC dominance in the Indore labor arena after 1948.

Finally, vertical political linkages of a personal and ascriptive nature divided the Congress and INTUC organizations from top to bottom. At the top the main rivalry and political cleavage were between groups identified with Ahmedabad (Jain) and Delhi (Brahman), the rival groups penetrating both the INTUC and Congress high commands. In Indore a similar cleavage obtained. On one side was Ramsingh, externally supported by Ahmedabad Jain millowners and by non-Brahman labor organization leaders, and locally supported by Jain millowners or their agents and by the Jain city politicians of the Nai Duniya faction. On the other side were V. V. Dravid and Gangaram Tiwari, externally supported by Brahman chieftains of INTUC and the Congress high commands, and locally supported by those Maharashtrian Brahmans identified with the princely state, and to some extent by the Khadiwala faction.

Until 1962 Dravid and Ramsingh collaborated successfully to dominate the Indore labor arena, but in 1962 Ramsingh alienated some of his local Jain supporters by standing for the Indore parliamentary seat, threatening the entire city with INTUC organizational dominance, and Dravid and Tiwari seized the opportunity to remove Ramsingh altogether from his position of power. This detailed study of the power struggle revealed the reliance of both Dravid and Ramsingh on external supporters, with those opposed to Ramsingh obtaining his removal from state and local positions of power, and those against Dravid obtaining his removal from state cabinet and governmental power to confinement (thus far) within the INTUC organization. Thus the basic outlines of labor politics in Indore have been determined by vertical linkages, between national and local labor leaders and organizations and between the state government and local labor administration, indicating a centralization of local labor politics through vertical political and bureaucratic linkages, with competition between ascriptively based factions occurring at each level: local, state, and national.

The distinctiveness and autonomy of local labor politics as an arena within city politics is due to the functional division of administrative jurisdictions as well as to the predominance of "outsiders" in the labor force and among the labor leaders. To the extent that many of the textile workers from Uttar Pradesh and elsewhere were temporary migrants—as many were, leaving relatives and property behind

to which they return upon retiring or losing work opportunities—
they were concerned primarily with the industrial work opportunities
in Indore, and less with other aspects of city politics. Moreover, Dravid
and Ramsingh, coming into Indore in 1941 as "outsiders," were viewed
to some extent by the city leaders of the Praja Mandal (Nai Duniya)
and Hindi-speaking Brahman (Khadiwala) factions as rivals independent of their control.

Ramsingh, as an effective organizer and political boss, was regarded
as the most serious threat, as a result of his *Mohalla Sudhar* Committee network (from 1952) and his preemption of the Indore parliamentary ticket in 1962—as his defeat in 1962 and his organizational
downfall in 1963 indicated. Ramsingh was tolerated as long as he confined himself primarily to the labor arena and relied on the support of
city politicians outside, but when his activity involved aggrandizement
and penetration outside the labor arena, opposing coalitions became
effective. Within the labor arena, however, he was secure as long as
Dravid and Nai Duniya chieftains in the Cabinet supported him vertically. As "outsiders" in control of the Indore labor arena, Dravid and
Ramsingh tended to control it apart from the city leaders or organization of the local Congress. INTUC penetration of the spheres of Nai
Duniya and Khadiwala factional dominance was more likely than the
reverse. Labor politics tended more to impinge on the rest of Indore
city politics than vice versa, but INTUC dominance of city politics
outside the labor arena was invariably resisted by political leaders in
the city, helping contain labor politics as a separate sphere of political
action.

The functional organization of state government bureaucracies
impinging on the city tends to produce distinct clienteles surrounding
each agency. The picture is particularly clear in the case of the Labour
Department and Registrar of Trade Unions, where the millowners
and labor unions become political actors spending much of their time
attempting to influence the administrative implementation of labor
statutes and regulations. That most of these actors, particularly the
labor unions, are confined primarily to political problems surrounding
industrial and labor issues tends to give the arena of labor politics ex-
ceptionally clear boundaries. Thus the vertically organized labor bureaucracies help define the arena of labor politics and maintain the
vertically separated compartments of city politics.

Vertical political (factional, ascriptive), organizational (INTUC, Congress), and bureaucratic (government machinery) linkages provide the major parameters of Indore labor politics, are predominant in that sense, and reveal the high degree of centralization of arenas of local politics (see Figure 2). This tends to insulate one local arena from penetration by political actors based in another, preventing the establishment of strong, durable horizontal linkages that generally characterize the areal (territorial) organization of politics. In Indore horizontal linkages and the areal organization of city politics are weak.

Figure 2
Ascriptive Linkages of Indore Labor Politics

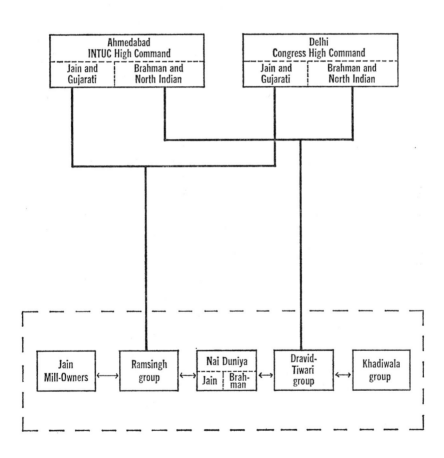

Horizontal linkages between the labor and other arenas are almost invariably of secondary and subordinate importance when compared with the predominant vertical linkages. Yet horizontal linkages do exist, and cannot be discounted altogether.

The strongest horizontal linkages are generally ascriptive in nature, based on caste, community or regional identification—reinforcing the centrality of vertical ascriptive linkages. Ramsingh's success in making the IMMS a machine under his personal control depended not only on Dravid's support, the "Bombay model" of labor legislation, and local access to government machinery, but also on his personal linkages with Jain millowners or their agents in Indore. To check Brahman dominance of organized labor, Jain businessmen and political leaders, both in Ahmedabad and Indore, gave special opportunities to non-Brahman labor leaders. Hence Ramsingh was tacitly supported in Indore at least until 1962 by the Jain chieftains of the Nai Duniya group (Ramsingh, a Rajput, corresponded to Laxman Singh Chauhan, the Rajput mass mobilizer of the Nai Duniya group in the municipal arena), and by the Jains who were dominant in all but the Swadeshi Mills from 1947 to about 1964 (when an Agarwal group took over the Hukumchand Mills), either as millowners (the Bhandaris and Hukumchand-Kasliwals) or as Managing Directors (Chandan Singh Bharkatiya of the Malwa Mills, until 1968). Ramsingh was supported especially firmly by R. C. Jall, the agent-manager for the Hukumchands of the Kalyanmal, Hukumchand, Rajkumar, and Hira Mills (Ujjain), and himself the owner of the Rajkumar Mills since about 1960. These horizontal linkages of support were of great utility to Ramsingh in ensuring control of the textile work force through the organizational machinery of mill "inspectors" and "labor officers."

Similarly, Dravid and Tiwari had ascriptive, horizontal ties of mutual support with Brahmans in the Nai Duniya group (Narendra Tiwari of *Nai Duniya,* V. S. Sarvate, V. V. Sarvate, and others such as K. A. Chitale who were sympathetic to Nai Duniya group interests) and with the Khadiwala group, including not only Brahmans but the chief Harijan leader of Indore district, Sajjan Singh Vishnar.

The horizontal, primarily ascriptively based linkages, were relatively weak because of organizational rivalries and the threat of INTUC penetration outside the labor area, with the attendant possibility of INTUC control of the city and district Congress organizations. INTUC penetration of the city outside the labor area was not a threat to be viewed lightly, because of the residential scattering of textile white-collar workers and laborers throughout most of the densely-populated *mohallas* of the city, the coherence and size of the IMMS electoral machinery—an asset when used on behalf of city leaders, but a formidable instrument when used against them—and the affluence of the IMMS as a dues-collecting organization. When INTUC and city leaders cooperated as they did in 1952 and for the most part in 1957, Congress electoral success was almost assured in every seat. But when city leaders felt obliged to resist INTUC invasions of the city, Congress candidates were weakened correspondingly. The factional division of the INTUC group itself in 1963 helps explain the weakness of Congress candidates in the city in the 1967 general election.

This study of labor politics in Indore thus supports the characterization of city politics as the aggregate of political activities in several quite distinct political arenas, each shaped by predominant vertical political and bureaucratic linkages and influenced secondarily by subordinate horizontal linkages passing through arena boundaries, bridging them areally, but not subjecting them together to a single, local center of political control.

11

OTHER POLITICAL ARENAS: THE FRAGMENTATION OF URBAN POLITICS

Besides the municipal, labor, and improvement arenas explored in earlier chapters, there are a number of other political arenas in Indore city that contribute to fragmentation of urban politics along functional and vertical lines. Among these arenas, not all equally well-defined, are public transportation, commerce, housing colonies, small-scale industries, agricultural produce markets and cooperatives, education, public health, public safety, and the underworld. A thorough study of urban politics in Indore would require inclusion of each of these arenas. Although time did not permit a detailed inquiry into these arenas, this chapter provides an introduction to the politics of agricultural markets, education, and the underworld to show how they fit into the system of city politics and reinforce the subordination of urban affairs to governance from higher levels outside the city. As working sketches of politics in each case, they are meant to suggest lines of future research in Indian cities.

The Politics of Agricultural Markets

One of the important areas of inquiry suggested by research on Indore is that of rural–urban linkages, particularly the relationships between agricultural credit and marketing networks and party organizational and electoral behavior. Among the governmental or quasi-governmental agencies that appear to impinge most directly on rural–

urban agricultural linkages are the cooperatives, under the jurisdiction of the state Registrar of Cooperatives, government banking and financial institutions such as the Reserve Bank of India and the Madhya Pradesh Financial Corporation, the state departments of Agriculture, and of Food and Civil Supplies, the state Warehousing Corporation, and the quasi-autonomous Agricultural Produce Market Committees. Each of these agencies tends to generate specialized clienteles in urban or rural areas, so that tracing their impact on politics would throw light on the areal economic and political interdependence of cities and their hinterlands.

Since the 1930's there have been two rival agricultural produce markets in Indore, designated places where farmers come to sell grain and other produce from their fields. The produce is sold by farmers to dealers through brokers (*adath* or *dalal*), who hold a form of auction and collect a commission for their work. The organizers of the urban market usually provide services to the farmers, including storage facilities and loans against the final sale price of their commodities should there be a delay in transactions. The markets are profitable for the brokers and often the dealers with whom they are affiliated, hence the location of a market, or the existence of competing markets, become political concerns of the traders who are affected. The original agricultural market in Indore was located in Malharganj, on the western side of the city, adjacent to the areas where Jain businessmen tend to be concentrated. Not surprisingly, therefore, the Malharganj Grain Merchants Association and the corresponding market were dominated by Jain merchants, affiliated with the Praja Mandal (before 1948) and the Nai Duniya group since merger.

A second market grew up in Sanyogitaganj, part of the Chowni commercial area that once came under the Residency jurisdiction, lying near the Bombay–Agra trunk road in the southeastern part of the city. The Sanyogitaganj market and the Sanyogitaganj Grain Merchants Association were controlled primarily by locally dominant Hindu Baniyas, Agarwals, and Khandelwals, who were affiliated with the local Congress party faction of Hindi-speaking Brahmans and Hindu Baniyas.

Each market had a quasi-autonomous governing body dominated by the locally powerful groups, and each market clique looked upon the existence of the other market as an economic threat. The Jain Nai

Duniya faction was, as we have seen, dominant in the Madhya Bharat government and influential in that of Madhya Pradesh before 1963. The Nai Duniya group sought legislation that would restrict the number of agricultural markets in each city of the state to one, hoping thereby to legally abolish the Sanyogitaganj market. Legislation to this effect, the Madhya Pradesh Agricultural Produce Market Act, was passed in 1960, and rules were elaborated under the Act in 1962. The Act brought into existence a single Agricultural Produce Market (governing) Committee, a quasi-autonomous body of 17 members, to regulate what was supposed to be the single such market in Indore. But the Sanyogitaganj market simply refused to go out of business, and its existence is gradually becoming accepted as an exception to the legislative rule. Consequently the Committee now actually regulates both markets.

The bulk of the members of the Committee are elected from functional constituencies connected with market affairs. Ten members are elected from among "cultivators," but this does not necessarily mean that they are actually villagers. Urban residents who farm land through relatives or tenants qualify as "cultivators," evading the obvious legal intent of this provision and ensuring that the Committee will be dominated by urban commercial, not rural farming, interests. Five other members are elected from among traders or representatives of commercial interests. One member is a delegate from the Municipal Corporation, providing a narrow link with the municipal arena, and another ex officio member is a representative of the state Warehousing Corporation.

As a result of the competition that developed in the 1950's and 1960's, it was recognized by the Malharganj group that they suffered from a lack of space for expansion, while the Sanyogitaganj market, coming into existence more recently in a vacant portion of the city, had acquired far more space. Consequently the Nai Duniya and Jain chieftains, Mishrilal Gangwal and Babulal Patodi, saw to it that the Malharganj traders received an additional area from government lands in Laxmibainagar, allowing for expansion. They also got the government grain purchasing agency, the Apex Cooperative Marketing Society, and the state Warehousing Corporation, located near the Malharganj market in Subhas Chowk, where they remain to this day. Nai Duniya residual influence in the state government bureaucracies has ensured that the Malharganj market not only survives but continues to compete effectively. On the other hand, since Mishra's succession to power in 1963, the regulatory Committee has come under the control of Sanyogitaganj agents, allied with the Mishra faction in state politics.

The arena of agricultural produce market competition is particularly interesting because of how it reveals the summation of areal and ascriptive community cleavages with business and political cleavages within the local Congress party. It further illustrates vertical linkages between allied local and state level political leaders and how government influence is brought to bear in the form of discriminatory legislation and in the location and purchasing practices of bureaucratic agencies. The autonomous governance of the markets is another example of the denial of local jurisdictions and constituencies to the municipal government.

The arena of agricultural markets is also significant as a political base for certain business-cum-political entrepreneurs seeking wider scope for their political influence. One such example is Chironjilal Gupta, a young Khandelwal Baniya educated as a lawyer, who has become a prominent businessman in the Chowni area and the Sanyogitaganj market. Gupta's family is an entrepreneurial family with recent but large economic successes in the oil milling industry.[1] Chironjilal Gupta obtained the concerted support of members of his caste in Chowni and Sanyogitaganj and enrolled them, together with clients and laborers in the market area, as "primary members" of the Congress party. This enabled him to win control of the Sanyogitaganj market area Mandal Congress Committee. As President of the Mandal Congress, he obtained a voice in the allocation by the City Congress of nominations in the city. He failed to obtain an MLA nomination in 1962, but did get a municipal ticket in 1965 and won election to

---

[1] A list of his offices and affiliations is indicative of commercial linkages between ascriptive and functional groups, and of his wide-ranging constituency-building efforts. Gupta in 1968 was simultaneously Secretary of the Indore Grain Merchants Association, Secretary of the Madhya Pradesh Oil Millers Association, Joint Secretary of the Federation of All-India Food Grain Dealers Association, Joint Secretary of the Malwa Chamber of Commerce, President of the Shri Khandelwal Vaisya Panchayati Sabha (Indore region), General Secretary of the Khandelwal Vaisya Mahasabha (Jaipur region), Secretary of the Indore Small Scale Industries Association, President of the Indore Occupational and Citizen's Sangh, President of the Oil Industry Workers Sangh, a member of the Western Railway Advisory Committee (Indore), a member of the Indore Agricultural Produce Market Committee, and the President of the Sanyogitaganj market area Mandal Congress Committee (1961–1968).

the Corporation. He made a strong effort to get the Chowni MLA ticket in 1967, but his claim was denied. The victory of an anti-Congress candidate (Yugydutt Sharma) by a narrow margin of 100 votes may have reflected the chagrin of Gupta and the Chowni Baniyas in being passed over by Mishra for a Brahman candidate (N. K. Shukla).

The Politics of Education

The educational arena is highly politicized, and political competition is more visible than in some of the other arenas. The visibility of competition in the educational arena is due to the breadth and diversity of the educational constituency, drawn not exclusively from specific functional clienteles but rather from all parts and levels of the local society. The politicization of the educational arena, and the intensity of competition, are functions of the extent to which educational qualifications have become primary stakes of socioeconomic competition. Educational qualifications have a crucial bearing on recruitment into the high-status white collar and professional occupations—especially much sought after government service appointments —in a setting of employment scarcity.

There are a variety of important political participants in the educational arena. First of all, there are government bureaucracies, the Department of Education and the quasi-autonomous corporate structure of the Indore University, which administer the educational system and give definition or boundaries to the educational arena (or its sub-arenas, such as university politics). Second, there are the educational institutions that participate in ways varying according to their level in the educational system—primary, secondary, collegiate, and university; according to their function or special character as religious, vocational, technical, or professional institutions; and according to their relationship to the government, as parts of the public school system, as government-aided private institutions, or as entirely privately supported schools. Third, there are the patrons of private schools, many of which serve members of particular language, religious, or caste communities of the city. The patrons are frequently political leaders, or have close ties with political leaders, who are in turn affiliated with political parties and factions, serving as channels through which patrons seek favors or government financial support for their schools. Finally, the teachers and administrators of schools on one hand, and the students of higher schools—particularly those of the colleges and university—on the other, act as political participants, building alliances with political leaders, parties, and factions for support and survival as well as for advancement and favors within the educational arena.

The politics of the educational arena, insofar as it involves taxation for educational purposes, budgetary allocations to the public school system and government-aided private schools, employment in the public school system, the standardization and conduct of examinations, and the standardization of curriculums and required textbooks, is primarily centralized at the state government level in the Department of Education. Thus the keys to the benefits and patronage of the public educational system lie not in the city but rather on the state level of politics, making vertical linkages predominant in the educational arena.

Conceivably, some measure of control of the educational process in Indore, once funds have been allocated, would be local if administration were also local, as it is in the private institutions. But in the public educational system, especially at the collegiate level, the principals, administrators, and teachers are state, not local, employees, and may be transferred from one institution to another or from one part of the state to another. To retain a voice in getting or maintaining jobs in desirable locations, or advancing up the administrative ladder, government employees in the educational system are necessarily most responsive to their bureaucratic superiors and the Cabinet-level politicians, thus reinforcing vertical linkages not only in the budgetary allocation process but also in the day-to-day administration of the public educational system.

The politicization of college and postgraduate students (especially those in the arts, humanities, and law) is a prominent feature of local, state, and national politics. The politicization appears to take place primarily among students who are least capable of occupational or professional advancement on the basis of individual merit or performance. The students of average or below-average performance appear to believe that political affiliations are as important as educational qualifications for employment. Politicization of students is encouraged also by the fact that organized student agitation can affect the costs, standards, and language medium of education. Students in colleges are generally anxious to reduce fees, or prevent them from rising, and to ensure that examination standards will be easily surmountable. In Indore, as elsewhere in Hindi-speaking regions, the bulk of the nontechnical students have increasingly come to support the conversion of the system of higher education to the vernacular language. Student agitation has more often than not brought a favorable response from the government on these questions. Thus for a variety of reasons, most of which have a bearing on their future employment and advancement opportunities, college students have organized into groups and have affiliated themselves with political leaders, parties, and factions for support and for access to policy-making groups on the state level.

The political leaders, parties, and factions have had their own reasons for building clienteles among the student groups. The students, if not already voters, are soon to become so, and electoral support is an ongoing consideration. More important in the short run is that organized student groups, easily rewarded by assorted bits of patronage and recognition, are effective cadres for electoral campaigns, providing energy, enthusiasm, and sufficient skill for a variety of campaign tasks. Students often fill out the ranks of processions and demonstrations, swell the audiences at public speeches—applauding their patrons and heckling opponents with catcalls, disturbances, and other noisy distractions. Students are used to distribute campaign literature, to carry messages, and to infiltrate and spy on the opposition. Beyond elections, when political leaders of a party or faction desire to provoke public resistance to a government action, or in favor of an unfulfilled demand, organized students become the vanguard in enforcing *hartals* (city-wide closing of shops and business activities) or staging protest demonstrations to test the will of the police in the face of prohibitory regulations. Political leaders seek to manipulate students, to use them as instruments in violent or quasi-violent political incidents to affect government policy or embarrass opponents when they themselves wish to avoid implication in those incidents.

The *golikand* (police firing) of 1954 illustrates a number of tendencies in educational politics.[2] The disturbances occurred in the

---

[2] See the *Report on the Causes and Course of the Students' Agitation in Indore, and the Disturbances Resulting Therefrom, Culminating in the Firing on the 21st of July, 1954*, known as the *Wanchoo Commission Report*.

summer of 1954 while the seat of the Madhya Bharat government was in its summer location, Indore city, rather than in Gwalior. Indore city was amply represented in the state Cabinet with the positions of Chief Minister (Mishrilal Gangwal), Home Affairs (Manoharsingh Mehta), and Labour (V. V. Dravid). The portfolio of Education, however, was held by Narsinghrao Dixit, a Hindi-speaking Brahman from Gwalior. The setting for the disturbances was the rivalry between Indore and Gwalior, the two former princely capitals.

Among the numerous problems of integrating princely states into the Madhya Bharat Union was that posed by the fact that most states had public educational institutions in which the teachers and administrators were employees of the several princely governments. As long as the princely states were quite small, people recruited into the education services were usually local or at least capable of establishing local attachments, and the area in which transfer could be made was not so large as to cause great discomfort. At worst, location would be changed, but the state politicians and officials would remain the same. When Madhya Bharat was formed, the princely education services were integrated into a unitary system. Consequently the prospect of transfer entailed the possibility of more severe dislocation, the requirement of establishing attachments in localities falling in different princely state areas and dealing with a new set of local political conditions and political leaders. The *ad hoc* integration of government teachers in 1950–51 in Madhya Bharat was the cause of considerable tension and uneasiness in the service. Final integration was postponed and a so-called "provisional integration" took place in 1954, resulting in the transfers of government school teachers all over Madhya Bharat. The discomfort and sense of uneasiness was transmitted in turn to students in the government colleges, who now were subjected to strange faces and suspicions that they were being deprived of "qualified teachers" (allies?) by the changes in the system. The tension was manifested in concrete form in Indore in 1954.

The immediate issue was the scheduled retirement from the education service of Mr. Ghosh, the Principal of the Holkar College. Ghosh had reached the prescribed age of retirement in the spring of 1954, and his term had been extended by a few months to complete the school year in July. He was to be replaced by a Mr. Bhagwat who had been teaching at the Madhav College in Ujjain, a connection that seems to have identified him with the former Gwalior state and aroused the suspicion that Narsinghrao Dixit was placing one of his own clients in a strategic position of the educational arena in Indore. The leaders of the student organizations and student government in the Holkar College announced their opposition to Ghosh's retirement by the government and demanded that he be given an extension of tenure.

The student leaders and their allies were predisposed to view the retirement of Ghosh, in the light of the Indore–Gwalior rivalry, as a move by the Education Minister from Gwalior to short-change Indore in favor of Gwalior, to replace the lenient and popular Ghosh with one who had a reputation for being a strict disciplinarian. In any case, in the prevailing mood it was easy to make the issue appear to be a conflict between the interests of Indore students and Gwalior politicians. Cases of alleged Gwalior favoritism were collected to show that on several occasions educators and other administrative officials with origins in Gwalior had been given extended tenure beyond the official age of retirement. The failure to extend Ghosh's tenure in the same manner was viewed as discriminatory.

A deputation of Holkar College student leaders had an audience with Dixit on July 5, when they formally presented a demand for Ghosh's retention by special provision according to existing precedents. They were rebuffed, and word was spread that Dixit had been intransigent, abrupt, and arrogant. Pressure mounted with the call for a student strike in the College on July 16. Preparations were made for a procession. Most of the local newspapers, *Jagran* (INTUC), *Nai Duniya,* and *Indore Samachar,* were either sympathetic to the students' position or critical of the government's policy on the question of extension. *Nav Bharat,* a newspaper published by Gwalior businessmen but with a limited circulation in Indore, was supportive of the government policy. Meanwhile, political leaders outside the educational arena became visibly active on the issue, conferring with student leaders and giving them moral support.

On July 19 a procession composed mainly of students, about 300 in number, was formed to march to the Secretariat, then located in Moti Bungalow just off of Topkhana (Mahatma Gandhi Road). The imposition of Section 144, prohibiting assembly, was considered but withheld. When the procession arrived nearby the Secretariat, it was stopped by the police. After some argument, the District Magistrate

(Collector) and the Superintendent of Police accompanied a delegation of about ten students to the Secretariat, where they had an interview with Dixit. The Education Minister informed them that the matter was not open to reconsideration. The deputation leaders were angry, and upon their return stirred up their followers in the procession. The body of students surged forward against the blocking cordon of police. Followed by a warning, the police retaliated with a *lathi* charge, resulting in some injuries but effectively dispersing the procession.

The situation now became highly charged. The students met the same evening to plan a larger demonstration. The Holkar College student leaders sought support from allied groups in other colleges, particularly the Indore Christian College. While until now the students had resisted the advances of city politicians, they now welcomed them even at the risk of confusing the goals of the agitation. Political leaders from the several Congress factions (particularly Laxman Singh Chauhan of Nai Duniya, Gangaram Tiwari of INTUC, and Kanhaiyalal Khadiwala leading his own group), and from the Communist and Socialist parties and related labor organizations, saw opportunities to establish ties of interdependence with student organizations and leaders, to embarrass the government or particular ministers in the government, or to outbid rivals. Again an official decision was made to withhold Section 144. Some interpreted this to signify that the Home Minister, Manoharsingh Mehta (Nai Duniya), secretly supported the students and was not averse to seeing the Education Minister, of the rival faction, put under pressure.

On July 20 the demonstration was much larger, estimated at about 3,000 people, and a large proportion consisted of nonstudents. Again the procession was stopped by the police before it reached the Secretariat, and an order to disperse was read. But the crowd was unruly and belligerent. Instead of dispersing, the crowd began to stone the police and the situation deteriorated into a street brawl. *Lathi* charges were only partially effective. The District Magistrate and the Superintendent of Police sought advice from the Chief Minister, who directed that a delegation of student leaders be formed to consult with him. Despite efforts to restrain the crowd, however, it broke through the police barriers into the Secretariat compound and milled noisily around the building. The Chief Minister and the Labour Minister in

succession attempted to address the crowd but were unable to command attention in the confusion. The crowd erected and burned an
effigy of the Education Minister. Within an hour a procession of mill
workers arrived at the Secretariat and merged with the crowd. Automobiles parked in the grounds were damaged. The Chief Minister
refused to permit a police firing requested by the district authorities,
and patience eventually paid off. Orders to disperse were renewed over
a loudspeaker, and part of the crowd, believed to be mainly students,
did leave the grounds. The remainder, mainly millworkers, were then
effectively dispersed by a *lathi* charge. Some student leaders, including
Yugydutt Sharma, Suresh Seth, and others, were arrested. Their release was later negotiated by local Congress leaders with the Chief
Minister.

The situation, however, continued to escalate, although now the
opposition political leaders (Communist and Socialist) were in the
forefront and the students and their issue were fading from the scene.
On the following morning a crowd consisting primarily of nonstudents
collected in front of the Secretariat and began to throw stones. By
noon the crowd had become large, and it surged into the adjoining
High Court compound and invaded the Court buildings. Some members of the crowd began purposefully burning records, papers, and
furniture. Among the papers burned were records kept by the Food
and Civil Supplies Department concerning food control, records that
involved the prosecution of black marketeers in the grain trade. For
some reason the police did not turn up in force until considerable
destruction had been done. Once the police were organized on the
spot, a firing was finally ordered. About twelve people were killed,
including innocent persons, one merely passing by in a car and another watching the scene from an adjacent building.

Despite the gravity of the disturbances, the students did not obtain
their demand. But the government thereafter was more sensitive and
cautious on questions affecting the integration of the education services. The Education portfolio was returned in 1955 to Manoharsingh
Mehta. The importance of the case, however, is twofold. On the local
level it reveals the tendency for student leaders to establish linkages
of mutual support with political leaders outside the educational arena,
who desire both to build constituencies in the colleges and to use student agitation as a shield for purposes of their own. But more im-

portant, the background of the disturbances in the integration of the education services, the rivalry between Indore and Gwalior, and the focusing of agitation on the state cabinet—where the issue of Ghosh's retention was decided negatively—show that control over outcomes in the public educational system is centralized and resides on the level of state politics.

The Politics of Order and the Underworld

The central actors locally concerned with public safety in the city of Indore are the Collector (or District Magistrate, as he is sometimes called) and the police bureaucracy. The police are employees of the Indian Police Service, a central service, and the higher-level officers are particularly responsible to their superiors in the state capital (the Inspector-General and Deputy Inspectors-General of the IPS) and in Delhi. Within the state the activities of the police are directed by the Chief Minister, Chief Secretary, the Home Affairs Minister, and the Home Affairs Secretary. These officials work partly through the Inspector-General directly, as well as through the Collector locally. The Collector normally holds ultimate responsibility for law and order in the district, and the City Superintendent of Police normally defers to the Collector in critical or politicized situations.

The municipal authorities, as has been pointed out, do not possess a police force but must work for the enforcement of local regulations through the state and centrally controlled police bureaucracy. On minor matters the Municipal Commissioner can usually obtain police cooperation directly or through communication with the Collector. But the major questions of public safety, traffic control, the arrest and prosecution of criminals, and action to forestall or suppress riots or disturbances are not under the jurisdiction of municipal authorities at all. Traffic control is an issue where there tends to be friction between the municipal and police authorities, who hold differing views on the urgency of the problem of crowded streets and the capacity of police to enforce existing regulations.

Public safety is of especially great importance in the labor arena and in the underworld. As was pointed out earlier, there is an expectation of violence that pervades labor politics, and actual violence is a frequent factor. The police bureaucracies, consequently, are important actors, often arbiters, in labor conflicts. Of equal, if not greater, importance is the relationship of the police bureaucracies to the underworld—another arena in which the expectation of violence is constant, and actual violence recurrent.

The underworld as an arena is defined by its illegitimacy. The main actors of the underworld in occupation and habit tend to violate the legal constraints and the prevailing societal codes of morality. The underworld in Indore is primarily engaged in smuggling, gambling, bootlegging, prostitution, and wrestling. All except the last are publicly disapproved of and legally proscribed or regulated in various ways, and even wrestling tends to come under disrepute among the higher-caste communities because of its underworld associations. The boundaries of the underworld encapsulate those elements of society whose main income is derived from these illegitimate activities. Yet the underworld, extensive as it is in Indore, exists because there are steady clienteles and customers paying for its services and because the police and political organizations, despite their official stance, have their own stakes in its survival.

The profitability of underworld activities—particularly in the smuggling of opium from the nearby areas of Neemuch, Mandsaur, and Jhalawer, and its exchange for gold being smuggled into India through Bombay—induces wealthy merchants and entrepreneurs to deal covertly with underworld figures, forging "strong links between the rich and the reckless." [3] The bulk of the underworld is made up of the unemployed and semi-employed idlers of the labor class in Indore, providing both operators of and customers for the *satorias* (gambling dens) and other forms of vice.

The structure of the underworld is divided socially—both between Muslims and Hindus, and among Hindus by caste—and areally, by *mohallas* and sections of the city. The underworld is most frequently found in densely populated *mohallas* where large proportions of the population are from lower income classes. The *mohallas* most notably associated with underworld activities are Lodhipura, Bombay Bazaar, Pinjara Bakhl, Ranipura, and Jinsi, but there are others as well. The surface operators of the underworld are known as *dadas* (toughs) and *pahlwans* (professional wrestlers). Wrestling is a popular sport, especially among the lower classes, so that *akharas* (wrestling rings)

---

[3] *The Hindustan Times,* June 8, 1969.

exist in many parts of the city. Wrestling bouts are well-publicized, well-attended, and profitable for their managers. But the *akharas* and the associated *pahlwans* and *dadas* perform functions other than entertainment. It is they who recruit customers for the other money-making ventures of the underworld, while protecting and enforcing the order of the underworld (as bouncers) within drinking and gambling dens. It is they who negotiate with the police for protection, making it possible for major figures to remain concealed in the background free of public embarrassment. The *dadas* and *pahlwans* transmit protection money to the police, buying off harassment and exposure, but they also perform functions administratively useful to the police.

As local strong men, each with his own turf, the *dadas* terrorize the neighborhood but maintain a kind of order. When the police are investigating a crime, it is usually the *dada* who can provide them with information about the whereabouts of the criminal. The *dadas* also act as informants to some extent regarding the activity of their rivals, providing the police with means of checking the pulse of the underworld. Moreover, the *dadas'* control of densely populated areas leads political party leaders to coopt them as local agents, to mobilize the vote and to intimidate opposition voters. Paid in a variety of informal ways for these services, the *pahlwans* and *dadas* make decent incomes and it is no surprise that there are many of them, perhaps 300 or more in Indore. Prominent among *dadas* and *pahlwans* are Muslims, Rajputs, and Kanyakubja Brahmans. "Karamat pahlwan," the father of Arif Beg, a sitting Muslim MLA, was a prominent figure in the underworld, murdered in 1964 by rivals. Babu Shukla, of the Kanyakubja community, was a well-known underworld boss for many years.

It is from the underworld that communal disturbances arose in Indore in 1969, through the political linkages of the *dadas* and *pahlwans* with political parties and factions. The fact that a power struggle was occurring on the state level in the winter and spring of 1969 gives plausibility to the hypothesis that the communal disturbances were exacerbated by higher-level competitors operating covertly through vertical linkages to manipulate rival communities in the underworld. In the middle of March, the SVD government led by Govind Narian Singh—consisting of a coalition including Congress party defectors, the Rajmata of Gwalior's following, the Jan Sangh, the SSP, and part of the PSP—finally collapsed and the defectors rejoined the Congress party, enabling Shyam Charan Shukla to win election as leader of the Congress legislative party and to form a new government as Chief Minister. The collapse was most bitterly resented by the Jan Sangh component of the SVD coalition, which had possessed the Deputy Chief Ministership and Home Affairs portfolio through V. R. Saklecha, their major representative in the Cabinet, for the preceding twenty months. In that period the Jan Sangh had set about altering the composition of the police bureaucracies at the highest levels, transferring opponents out and bringing sympathizers into strategic spots. A number of high-level police officers had been transferred out of Indore on a single day, an almost unheard-of occurrence.[4] The Muslim population of Indore was reported to be apprehensive about the implications of these changes.

On New Year's Eve, a series of communal incidents broke out. They stemmed from the death of Avantilal Sonkar, a young gambler who together with friends had defeated a number of Muslims in a gambling bout but decided to quit while he was ahead. He was assaulted and knifed by his gambling opponents on December 26, 1968. His death three days later gave rise to communal suspicions and disturbances. The Sonkar community of Rampura, a Muslim and low-caste Hindu *mohalla,* requested permission for a large funeral procession to wind throughout the city. The Collector held a meeting attended by the Superintendent of Police and representatives of all the major political parties in the city. It was agreed by all at the meeting that it would be advisable not to permit such a funeral procession but to cremate the body under direct administrative supervision. The Collector announced that this was the policy he would follow. By the next morning, however, it was clear that the Collector had changed his mind, probably following communications from Bhopal, and the funeral procession was authorized. The Collector allowed a funeral procession provided the Sonkar leaders agreed in writing to follow a prescribed route. As it turned out, however, they deviated from the prescribed route to the burning ghat and passed through parts of Rampura and Daulatganj. Clashes broke out between Hindus in the procession and Muslims in the *mohallas.* The

---

[4] See S. N. Khanna's report, *The Hindustan Times* (overseas airmail weekly edition), July 5, 1969.

incidents caused some injuries, but not widespread destruction and no deaths. They did signify that communal tension had been ignited. Six weeks later the SVD government fell.

In the summer of 1969, as S. C. Shukla was attempting to get his bearings as the youngest Chief Minister of Madhya Pradesh, fresh riots broke out in Indore. The connection with the underworld was even more explicit. The immediate occasion was the procession of welcome given to honor Chandgi Ram, a Punjabi (Hindu) wrestler who had just won the national wrestling championship by defeating Mehar Din, a Muslim. Chandgi Ram and Mehar Din were the national favorites of their respective communities in Indore. Prior to the arrival of Chandgi Ram's procession along Jawaharmarg, Hindu Mahasabha leaders were reported to have penetrated the Muslim *mohalla* of Bombay Bazaar and made provocative speeches, playing up the defeat of Mehar Din and describing him as a "Pakistani wrestler." By the time the procession approached the crossroads of Bombay Bazaar, a belligerent crowd of 200 or more Muslim toughs from the area had gathered. They obstructed the procession and a violent clash broke out, dispersed ultimately by police firing. Trouble then spread throughout the city, to the labor area where Hindu laborers sought to block Muslim workers' access to the mills, and in the form of arson, murders, and rape in such areas as Karabin, Jinsi, Banganga, Juna Pitha, Toda, Daulatganj, Alapura, and Hathipala, most of which contain Muslim elements and underworld networks. Over two dozen persons were officially acknowledged to have been killed, and unofficial estimates run four to five times higher—including all persons unaccounted for. There were hundreds of injuries, extensive property losses, and the police belatedly made arrests totalling 1,614 people. The police failed to arrest known trouble-makers for at least a day after the trouble began, and the Chief Minister replaced several police officials with those "old, tried police officers" whom the Jan Sangh had previously shifted out of Indore.[5] The government ordered a judicial inquiry and placed a ban on the Jan Sangh daily of Indore, *Swadesh,* preventing publication for one month.[6]

---

[5] See *The Hindustan Times* (overseas airmail weekly edition), July 5, 1969, and *Hindustan Times,* July 8, 1969.

[6] *The Hindustan Times,* July 11, 1969.

Although the connections were concealed for obvious reasons, the communal disturbances of July appear to have been stimulated and exploited by state-level political actors interested both in embarrassing the new Congress government and in polarizing the population of Indore along religious community lines.

The cases provided in this chapter give a glimpse into a few of the many corners of city politics in Indore. A comprehensive political map would require the tracing of political linkages between social constituencies, factions, political parties, and leaders in each of these arenas. But the survey here is sufficient to reinforce the assertion that city politics in Indore is fragmented into a variety of political arenas, each of which is predominantly vertically organized, contributing to the weakness of the municipal (or representative) local government. The organization of politics in the multiple local arenas is highly centralized, supporting the view that the governance of the city is essentially state government.

12

AREA, POWER, AND POLICY
IN A PENETRATED SYSTEM

Dimensions of Urban Politics

City politics in Indore is full of energy and drama. Its actors play their parts to the hilt, often with great seriousness but seldom without humor, and occasionally with a tragic note. The quest for power, status, and material gain is sometimes ruthless, sometimes playful, and frequently compassionate. There are several scripts, a multitude of plots and subplots—interwoven and unfolding in many directions —and much improvisation as well. Some rules are handed down from above and others are locally fashioned, but few dictate the entire story, and they are subject to change in any case. The question is, who will be able to make, enforce, and unmake the rules? And who will benefit thereby? There are many claimants, not all equally strong or well-equipped. Some win, some lose. But the game does not end. There is always another contest, a next time. Strength and strategy can be altered. The winners need not always be the same, and in Indore they often are not. Few win big, but many hope to, and their hopes are fed by how many win small.

It is urban politics because the nature of the community makes it so. The population is large and compact, and social heterogeneity is so pronounced as to distinguish it not just in degree but also in kind from the typical rural community. Not only does the correlation of ritual status and subcaste membership remain vital in the city, but the types of relevant cleavage are multiplied. Differences of language and regional origin persist as vertical fissures between groups that may be similar in other respects, by occupation, ritual status, wealth, or political influence. Class differentiation, partially concealed by the more visible primordial affiliations most individuals possess, emerges gradually to cut across those primordial ties and produce affinities based on functional and occupational interests, income levels, and styles of life. It is urban politics not just because participation levels are high, for that may be true in the rural areas as well, but because the forms of participation are more complex and differentiated, the number and variety of associations is greater, and participation is more highly structured by political organizations. It is urban politics, too, because the issues of politics are less concerned with agriculture and land tenure and more with industrial production; large-scale commerce; retailing of many kinds; business in residential land, housing, and offices; the services of banking and transportation; finding jobs in the large blue-collar and white-collar sectors; and influencing densely concentrated government activities in education, public health, licensing, tax collection, law enforcement, municipal services, and the courts.

The unity of urban politics in Indore derives from this areal concentration of peoples, economic functions, and governmental activities, and from the identification of the inhabitants with the socioeconomic boundaries of the city. Indore is a place in people's minds, and a feeling of community is shared. It is but one reference point among many, for the symbols of state and nation have acquired meaning as well, and the parochial identification with communities of religion, caste, and regional origin have, if anything, gained rather than lost strength. In the long run, such parochial groups may be submerged by class change, but in Indore, where modernization has been less than precipitous in rate, there is considerable social stability. The density of settlement and variety of primordial groups produces a wide array of individual and group interactions, which by being as often personal as anonymous in nature have a tendency to intensify the sensation of group differences and to politicize them. Moreover, the inhabitants identify strongly with *mohalla*, neighborhood, and place of work. Such strong ties to locality will eventually be reduced by increasing areal mobility and more frequent changes in residence, some signs of which have appeared in the development of housing colony suburbs on the outskirts of the city; but as yet this has hardly touched the bulk of the city's families. Even neighborhood ties in fact are attachments to the city, and are integrated with the city's political life. Perhaps the strongest factor, however, that gave a sense of political community to the city was its historic role as the center of government of the Holkar princely state. As the focus of government, new forms of political participation and organized demands for access grew up in the city prior to national independence and merger with India. And these budding organizations helped to crystallize political sentiment among the middle and lower strata of the population around the city as a center of political action.

But the features of city politics that stand out in Indore today are more those of external penetration, and internal fragmentation and dependency. Because Indore was the capital of a princely state, and the politics of the capital was the nerve center of politics in the state, the question of the autonomy of urban politics at first did not arise. Indore politics was dominant in state politics. Subsequently, the merger of the Holkar state made Indore but one center of several in a much larger political context. At the outset it held its own against rivals, but over time it was subordinated by the actions of a government responsive to other political forces, resulting in a marked reduction in the autonomy of city politics. Within the city there was no longer a strong and unified institutional base to offset penetration from outside. Instead, sectors of urban politics with specialized interests and clienteles became more prominent, sharply segmenting the urban political system.

Municipal politics is the one institutional arena in Indore city which has city-wide scope, the municipal limits corresponding fairly accurately with the areal boundaries of the urban community. Its elections by wards give it a representative and visible character, and there is a surprisingly high level of participation in municipal affairs. But while the Municipal Corporation straddles the city in areal terms, the scope of its powers are so severely truncated as to make its designation as "local self-government" more for symbolic effect than truly meaningful. There is little that the Corporation governs in the city, from a functional, jurisdictional standpoint. But there is a great deal of government in the city. The difference is that most of that government is part of the state apparatus. As a result, the municipal arena is not the basis of urban politics in Indore. Instead the center of gravity lies elsewhere, in the centralizing structures of the urban political system.

The key to urban politics in Indore is the centralization of political initiatives and decision-making outside the city, beyond its local institutions but still within the reach of influentials who belong to the city. Decision-making takes place at the apex of vertical hierarchies which converge in the state government. These hierarchies are of two kinds. One set is representative in nature, springing from electoral politics and political party competition rooted in the city but becoming focused in the ministerial level of state government, in the state legislature, and to some extent in the state-level headquarters of political parties. The other set is bureaucratic and administrative in nature, linking the cabinet, secretariat and department chiefs in the state capital with the line agencies of state government in the city. Together, these two sets of hierarchies penetrate and give form to local politics. They provide the channels within which power and authority are concentrated and become the center of struggles for position, leverage, and access. Outcomes of these struggles, in turn, have a bearing not only on the selection of candidates and the balance of power among rival factions in the dominant party but also on the content of policy and the implied beneficiaries of policy through the administrative process in the city.

Urban politics in Indore takes place at several levels. First, at the upper levels, national, state, and regional politics impinge on the city from outside, though the arena of crucial importance among these is that of the state. Second, there is the level of city-wide politics in Indore, where the entire city becomes an arena of competition, focused primarily around the electoral competition of city-based political party organizations. Finally, at the base of urban politics are the various distinct political arenas in which specialized sets of political competition takes place. There is, to be sure, considerable interpenetration between levels, so that distinctions cannot be pushed too far. The centrality of the dual sets of hierarchies remains critical at each level, but because the relevant political actors, issues, and pivots of influence vary from one level to another, the ways in which the hierarchies function varies too.

The fact that these hierarchies penetrate the city may handicap but does not necessarily prevent the city becoming an actor in regional and state politics in its own right. It all depends upon who is in the saddle. Urban politics can be extroverted, especially if the key personnel embedded in the dual sets of hierarchies linking the city with the state are partisans of the city. Indore displayed the role of the "city as an actor in politics" most vividly after the merger of the princely states in Madhya Bharat, for its political and bureaucratic chieftains competed self-consciously with those of Gwalior and Ujjain for the key offices in the new state government, for the location in their city of the state capital and its abundance of salaried employees, and for the benefits of large-scale state expenditures on educational institutions, hospitals, and industrial estates. This competition between urban areas was to be expected, given their previous functions as princely state capitals and centers of political organization. But the degree to which each city succeeded in making gains depended not only on the extent to which its partisans dominated the political and bureaucratic hierarchies but also on the extent to which factional rivalries of long standing in the dominant Congress party of each city were subordinated to common ends in the face of external competition. Indore was particularly fortunate in the Madhya Bharat years, both because its political and bureaucratic chieftains captured a disproportionately large share of state government positions and because the leaders of its Congress factions at the state level, principally those of Nai Duniya and INTUC, found more to collaborate about than to fight over. In subsequent years this fortunate combination of factors became unstitched, and the external impact of the city diminished accordingly.

The principal focus of this study, however, is not on Indore's role in state politics as such but rather on the effects of state-level penetration of city politics, both in the arena of urban politics as a whole and in the multiple arenas which divide it at the base. In the arena of city politics, the dual hierarchies are linked with the forces of city-wide political competition. Because there is no unified institutional focus or urban government inside the city itself, apart from the weak and functionally circumscribed municipal authority, the arena of city politics is best defined by the competition among political parties, each seeking to maximize its share of support from strategic interests and from citizens in the urban community at large, to win elected office, and to get access to or influence over the administrative outputs of government.

The most important elections for the arena of city politics are general elections, for it is through them that state-level offices can be won, and it is at the state level that officials, potentially at least, can exercise control over the dual hierarchies in the city. Since the bureaucratic hierarchies fork out among a series of separate functional jurisdictions at the city level, the governance of the city tends to be functionally diffused, except when there is coherent direction and coordination at the top. Electoral outcomes at the base may ultimately interfere not only with the coherence of state level control, but may facilitate or obstruct supervision and coordination of the administrative process locally. Consequently, the more an identity exists between those who win in general elections in the city and those who preside over the vertical hierarchies, and the more cohesion exists among the key actors at both levels, the greater will be the coherence of the governance of the city. An asymmetry of power and authority favors those at the top, but the ease with which their will prevails depends on the degree of support made possible by local electoral outcomes. To understand this interplay, therefore, it is crucial to discover the identities and ties among actors at both levels, in both representative and bureaucratic spheres of operation. Political change over time makes the interplay exceedingly complex.

Several conditions have been of nearly constant importance within the city arena of Indore politics. The local party system has been dominated successfully by the Congress party for most of the period under study, and the opposition has been splintered at both conservative and radical extremes. Congress supremacy, however, has been complicated by vigorous factional warfare. Indeed, the contests among Congress factions are usually just as important as opposition efforts in accounting for the results of elections and changes in policy. Moreover, the personnel of the bureaucratic agencies located in the city have generally had an affinity for the ruling Congress party and in particular for the Nai Duniya faction leaders of the city. Finally, a key factor underlying factional competition within the Congress party, as well as the struggle between the Congress and opposition parties, has been the city's great social heterogeneity, out of which arises competition among ascriptive or primordial groups. This competition has given to city politics an ethnic foundation.

Political Contestants, Primordial Rivalries, and Vertical Linkages

Indore's main primordial and factional rivalries took shape initially in the city's princely setting. The very creation of the Holkar state in a Hindi-speaking region by a Marathi-speaking ruling class introduced tensions between the two peoples. For the administration of the state, the rulers naturally preferred personnel from their own region, and the administratively talented Maharashtrian Brahmans got first place. Maharashtrian Brahmans constituted not only the administrative elite of the city but achieved primacy among its professional, educational, and intellectual elites as well. Only in business and commerce were they without much distinction, for that sphere was dominated chiefly by Jain cotton merchants and industrial magnates, and to a lesser extent by Hindu Baniyas of several kinds. Maharashtrian Brahmans were a key source of inspiration and leadership for the early political movements of the city, from the antecedents of the Hindu Mahasabha to the secular and revolutionary Communist party, cutting across the ideological spectrum. But it was in popular politics that the challenge to their preeminence came, principally from Hindi-speaking Brahmans, who with but a few exceptions were not similarly privileged in Holkar society.

The protest movements that emerged in the early 1920's for the promotion of constitutional reform and redistribution of power in the princely regime became the forerunners not only of the Congress and other political parties in the city but of the major Congress factions as well. Differences in their leadership cores, moreover, reveal the lines of ethnic competition at the elite level. The Indore Praja Mandal was fairly intimately associated with the Holkar government, as it was the least radical of the organizations with a popular base. Its leadership consisted of a coalition of the "entrenched castes"—Maharashtrian Brahmans and Jains. The Praja Mandal clique, operating after 1948 as a faction inside the Congress party, was known as Nai Duniya, after the name of the newspaper which served as its mouthpiece. Its rival was the more militant Indore branch of the Indian National Congress, legal only in the Residency area but organized covertly throughout the city. The Congress chieftains emerged from among two sets of "ascendant castes," both challengers of the princely establishment. One set consisted of Hindi-speaking Brahmans who regarded Maharashtrian Brahman preeminence as their target, and the other comprised Agarwal and Khandelwal businessmen who saw the Jains as their competitors. After 1948, this Congress faction emerged under the name of Khadiwala, then its principal leader. Finally, the INTUC faction embodied the pro-Congress and moderate labor forces, organized in the Indore Textile Labour Association or, as it was known later, the Indore Mill Mazdoor Sangh. Because its leadership was more pluralistic, the INTUC faction was linked both with the Nai Duniya and Khadiwala factions; but like the former, to which it had a stronger affinity in the early years, it was positively oriented toward the Holkar establishment from which it received crucial support in bringing under control the Communist-led radical forces in the labor area.

These factions and leadership groups were the principal contestants in the arena of city politics after the abolition of the princely state. But crucial to urban outcomes in the early years was the manner in which ties and associations formed under princely conditions were reconstructed in Madhya Bharat politics, especially as they were embodied in the political and bureaucratic hierarchies linking state and local political arenas. The political chieftains of the Praja Mandal and the Indore Textile Labour Association were propelled to the forefront of city politics when, as a result of the political reforms of 1947, government representation was broadened and such key figures as V. S. Sarvate, Mishrilal Gangwal, and V. V. Dravid were appointed Cabinet ministers. Even though briefly held, their positions in the government gave them authority and eased the development of working relationships with the predominantly Maharashtrian Brahman and Jain administrative officers of the Holkar state. The same sets of political and bureaucratic chieftains appeared in the Madhya Bharat government in 1948, but now had to compete with other politicians and officials from Gwalior for the key positions of government. Former Holkar politicians looked to former Holkar bureaucrats for support, and vice versa, forming a symbiotic relationship for securing control not only over positions but over the formation and administration of policy in the city.

The chieftains from Indore seated in the state government were fortunate in that the administrative personnel and bureaucratic agencies in the city were for all practical purposes Holkar in origin, for the princely apparatus had been shifted virtually intact from one focus of authority to another. Thus, for each jurisdiction controlled at the apex by Indore politicians, there were responsive administrative allies at the base. The chieftains from Indore at the state level were also fortunate in the size of their share of high-level positions and in the strategic centrality of those positions for urban governance. Mishrilal Gangwal, V. V. Dravid, Manoharsingh Mehta, and others from Indore at the Cabinet level worked through the political and bureaucratic hierarchies to build up their constituencies in Indore city politics. While the Nai Duniya and INTUC factions benefited most, the Khadiwala faction, well-entrenched in the party organization, did not suffer, and factional warfare was comparatively subdued.

Political changes at the state level, however, contributed to the intensification of factional rivalries, eroded the power of Indore politicians and bureaucrats at the apex, and eventually led to the use of the state's penetrative authority by opponents of the Nai Duniya and INTUC leaderships of Indore. The submergence of Madhya Bharat in the much larger area of new Madhya Pradesh in 1956 diluted the influence of Indore officials in an enlarged government. And when D. P. Mishra assumed the Chief Ministership in 1963, he worked through Hindi-speaking Brahman allies and more youthful elites in the Khadiwala and INTUC factions to strengthen the power of the Khadiwala group and to divide and undermine the grip of the INTUC and Nai Duniya factions over their respective clienteles in Indore city politics. Mishra's penetration was at least temporarily aborted, however, by the overthrow of his government in 1967, and younger opposition politicians from Indore, under the auspices of the SVD government, scrambled for control of the bureaucratic hierarchies and strove to displace the Congress-dominated representative network with another of their own making. The enlargement of the government in 1956, the activist constituency-building of Mishra, and the takeover of the government by an opposition coalition contributed to the diminution of former Holkar preeminence in the bureaucratic hierarchies. Power changes at the state level resulted in the transfer of opponents and the substitution of administrative protégés, vastly complicating the available types of ascriptive and partisan linkages in the bureaucratic hierarchies at both state and local levels. The effects of these changes ultimately became visible in the city's electoral politics as well as within the special political arenas of the city.

Indore's political chieftains, most notably Mishrilal Gangwal (who bridged both Khadiwala and Nai Duniya factions), V. V. Dravid (INTUC), and Manoharsingh Mehta (Nai Duniya), came to power at the state level as delegates from the Holkar legislative council to the Madhya Bharat legislative assembly, though unlike his colleagues, Dravid abstained from a ministerial role until after the first general election. But for these figures to continue to preside at the apex after 1951, they had to win elections confirming their roles in the representative hierarchy. This they did, usually in MLA constituencies in Indore city or district. With Mishrilal Gangwal as Chief Minister, these chieftains practically dominated the Madhya Bharat government for its duration, and both Gangwal and Dravid continued to be at the heart of power until after the 1962 elections. They were supported by other key figures in the representative hierarchy and elected from the city, Ramsinghbhai and Gangaram Tiwari of the INTUC faction, and V. S. Sarvate and Babulal Patodi of the Nai Duniya faction.

Although Gangwal was an able conciliator among factions, factional rivalries within the city increased over time, leading to Tiwari's defeat as an MLA candidate in 1957, and that of Ramsingh Verma in the Indore parliamentary election of 1962—defeats administered in each case by Homi Daji, the flamboyant Communist labor leader. But the important point is the record of Congress strength in the city's electoral arena between 1952 and 1962. Of twelve possible MLA wins, Congress got eleven, and it also won two times out of three in the parliamentary seat. The Madhya Bharat chieftains played a major role, guaranteeing their own nominations, steering those of others, and winning strong victories in their own seats. Not only did they return themselves to power, but they assured the Congress of dominance in the city arena. What they could not do was suppress factional rivalry or cope with the new challenge of D. P. Mishra in Madhya Pradesh.

After 1962, Gangwal's ministerial role diminished; he remained in the Cabinet until 1966, but had to give up the key portfolio of Finance for the lesser one of Planning and Development. Dravid left the Cabinet in 1964 when the struggle for power within the Indore

labor arena could only be resolved by his return to the city. As the
1967 election approached, it was obvious that now Mishra, not Indore
chieftains, controlled the representative and bureaucratic hierarchies,
and it was his desires that were most critical in the 1967 Congress
nominations in the city. Three of four Congress MLA nominations
were Mishra protégés, and the last was from Nai Duniya. Mishra
could not, however, control the voters. Congress factions sabotaged
each other's nominees, except in the labor seat, and three opposition
candidates won, breaking for the first time the dominance by Congress
over the electoral arena. Mishra's penetration was of too brief a duration to be decisive, and the same was true for the SVD opposition
in the following eighteen months. But it was sufficiently effective in
Mishra's case to demonstrate the leverage of external actors in setting
the parameters of party nominations in the city. And its effects were
felt even more concretely in policy and administration within the
political arenas of Indore.

Political Fragmentation

The politics of party competition in the arena of city politics
does not center on a local government, because there is not one of
sufficient power to require it. It centers instead on the hierarchies
of power which link the state and the locality, and which produce
most of what government in the city is about. There is no way to
command these hierarchies directly, except at the state level. Not
many can win big that way, but there are sufficient ways to win small,
within various political arenas.

The bureaucratic dependencies of the state government are not
monolithic. They are divided into many subhierarchies, each with its
own functional jurisdiction and its own special responsibilities. The
line agencies of the Departments of Labour, Public Health, Education, Housing, Public Works, Industries, Transportation, Cooperatives, Home Affairs (the Police), and Town Planning (the Improvement Trust) compete with each other and with the quasi-autonomous
Agricultural Produce Market Committee and the Municipal Corporation, snipping away at other jurisdictions wherever the allocation of
responsibility is ambiguous. Jealous of their domains, they are also
frequently eager constituency-builders, especially if engineering and
construction are among their major functions. The substantial regula-

tory, extractive, and expenditure powers which give them the capacity to build or compete for constituencies also produce arenas of political activity. Client political actors and their rivals cluster around agencies, seeking to influence and benefit from government policy within the agencies' jurisdictions. Though major policy decisions are made at the apex of the bureaucratic hierarchies, there is considerable distance and many levels through which policy must pass. Interested actors intervene at the lower levels to exploit bureaucratic discretion and compel accommodation, reshaping and modifying policy to conform to local pressures and needs. Personal, primordial, and factional ties play their part in this local interaction, as does the balance of power among factions within the City Congress, and among political parties, trade unions, and interest groups in the city.

Certain line agencies and local authorities deal with constituencies which are fairly homogeneous in occupational, though not in ascriptive, terms. Chief among these are the Commissioner of Labour and the Registrar of Trade Unions, the Director of Small-Scale Industries and the Agricultural Produce Market Committee. When such is the case the political arena created tends to be quite sharply differentiated within the city by the specialization of the clientele actors and organizations. Around the labor agencies revolve the mill managements and the Millowners Association, and the textile workers themselves, defining the arena of industrial labor politics. Similarly, the Small-Scale Industries arena is primarily concerned with financiers, small business entrepreneurs, and the varieties of business associations they are members of. And the Agricultural Produce Market Committee is oriented toward the brokers, auctioneers, purchasing agents, warehousers, and marketers of grain and other foodstuffs that are brought by farmers from the villages and sold in the city.

The functional concerns of many agencies are sufficiently broad that they overlap with those of others—the Improvement Trust overlapping with the Municipal Corporation and Public Health departments with respect to building regulations and water problems; the Labour Department impinging on the municipality with respect to regulation of shops, and sharing with the Department of Housing a concern for housing development for the working class. One agency, the police, naturally operates everywhere. And political party organizations, labor unions, and interest groups follow these agencies and

local authorities wherever the action requires them to, or is relevant to
their ambitions. Consequently, there is both differentiation among
political arenas and interpenetration as well, the degree varying from
one arena to another. Yet the functional specialization of agencies,
and the corresponding specialization of political clienteles, is so pronounced that it fragments urban politics into a series of spheres, each
of which must be treated in some depth if its place in urban politics
is to be understood.

The fragmentation of politics in multiple arenas means that urban
penetration by newly powerful state-level actors will vary somewhat
from arena to arena. Some arenas take more time to assert influence in
than others, especially if a local electoral, nomination, or appointment
process is involved, as it is in the case of the Municipal Corporation,
the Cooperative Bank, the Improvement Trust, and the Agricultural
Produce Market Committee. Changes of personnel may be necessary
not just in the representative bodies but among the executive staffs
of each agency as well. The Indore chieftains could delay D. P.
Mishra's invasion of their local strongholds after 1963, for example,
because of the pervasive hold by former Holkar administrators of key
positions in the Improvement Trust, the Corporation, and the state
agencies of the city. Each arena is an island of power, a separate battle-
ground of parties or Congress factions. Indeed, particular arenas may
be dominated by a given faction for long periods of time, as was
true of Nai Duniya after 1948 in the municipality and Improvement
Trust, or of INTUC in the labor arena. By contrast, the Nai Duniya
faction was under siege by the Chowni group of the Khadiwala faction in the Agricultural Market arena from the beginning. By 1955
the grip of Nai Duniya on the municipality and the Improvement
Trust was shaken in each case by the INTUC faction, and both Nai
Duniya and INTUC had to contend with the Khadiwala faction's
challenge in these arenas after 1958.

In this fragmented environment, it is extraordinarily difficult for
any one of the factions in Congress, or for the Congress party as a
whole, to make the impact of government in the city coherent. But on
occasion, one or another chieftain has been able to assemble power in
several arenas simultaneously on behalf of special clienteles. The
Labour Minister, V. V. Dravid, succeeded in doing so in the mid-
1950's by combining a virtual empire of portfolios under his control,

in Labour, Development, Housing, Public Health (Engineering), and Town Improvement. At the same time his colleagues in the city, Ramsingh Verma and Gangaram Tiwari, briefly achieved control both of the City Congress party organization and the Municipal Council. By orchestrating the regulatory and patronage powers of the line agencies under his command, together with those of the Trust and municipality, Dravid was in a few short years able to produce an impressive set of concrete improvements on behalf of the textile laborers in the city. The governmental impact in this period on the labor constituency was quite coherent in nature; but even so, it hardly extended to the governance of the rest of the city. For the most part, the fragmentation by arena diffuses urban governance.

Thus urban politics in Indore is penetrated from above, and dominated by representative and bureaucratic sets of hierarchies which link the state with the locality. Major policy decisions are made at the apex of these hierarchies, centralizing power and authority over the city in the hands of political and bureaucratic chieftains. At the level of city politics, because of Congress dominance in the party and electoral system, the City Congress political leaders and organization can function to some degree as a locally integrative force, and serve to focus city politics, by acting as intermediaries between the upper and lower levels of the hierarchies and between the bureaucratic hierarchies and local constituencies.[1] In a qualified way, the City Congress serves as a pale substitute for strong city government. But the extent to which it can do so is greatly limited by its internal factional struggles. Because the dual hierarchies are also complex, divided by party as well as factional and primordial competition on the representative side, and by functional and clientele specialization on the bureaucratic side, much of the city's politics is fragmented in multiple arenas, and by factional rivalries within those arenas. The effect is to make urban politics non-autonomous, and to make its impact on the larger political system weak.

---

[1] As Terry N. Clark observes: "In the United States, the larger cities have been the centers for the development of massive political party machines. While it is possible for these machines to remain decentralized, in many cases where the governmental structures have remained relatively fragmented—Chicago is the archetypical example—the political party has served as the basic integrative structure for decision-making within the community." Clark, ed., *Community Structure and Decision-Making: Comparative Analysis*, p. 99. See also Edward C. Banfield, *Political Influence: A New Theory of Urban Politics*.

Problems of National and Cross-National Comparison

To what extent the Indore pattern of penetration and multiple arenas is a prevalent one in Indian city politics remains to be seen. The work of several others, though it does not focus directly on these dimensions, seems to offer general confirmation.[2] The parallels are very close in the case of "Tezibazar," a small Uttar Pradesh market town of 7,000 inhabitants, described by Richard Fox. While Tezibazar is far smaller and simpler than Indore, and Fox focused primarily on social structure, his finding that social segmentation promotes integration with higher levels of politics, in a setting where the vertical political and bureaucratic linkages are only now in the process of being established, otherwise corresponds to the situation described in this study.[3] In Indore, the penetrative structures are well established now, and the segmentation of city politics is by political arenas as well as social in nature. But the effects of the interplay between the vertical hierarchies and the fragmentation of urban politics in promoting political integration has been striking, especially when viewed against the background of princely state autonomy and the successive mergers in Madhya Bharat and Madhya Pradesh.

By contrast, Myron Weiner's study of the Congress party organization in the metropolis of Calcutta indicates that other patterns are possible in Indian cities, under certain historical and institutional conditions.[4] In this case, the regional and state distribution of power seems to have actually flowed from the city. But there have been key institutional differences between municipal politics in Calcutta and Indore. The functional responsibilities allocated to the Municipal Corporation of Calcutta have been greater in scope, and the elected representatives of the Corporation have had decisive control over ad-

---

[2] See Chapter I, footnote 22.

[3] In "Tezibazar," according to Fox: "Lack of traditional social cohesion and community has promoted the penetration of modern social ideas, the dissolution of local custom and organization and their replacement with new formal structures, and, above all, the increasingly direct merger of the town into a regional and national society. All these changes are evident in the town's reliance on the modern political machinery of the nation-state to establish internal power and status and to arbitrate formerly intracaste and kin disputes. They are also exemplified by the alteration of the significant internal political groups on the basis of regional political organization and national political ideologies." Fox, *From Zamindar to Ballot Box,* p. 5.

[4] Myron Weiner, *Party-Building in a New Nation,* pp. 321 ff.

ministrative processes—so much so, in fact, that Weiner's description
of urban politics in Calcutta resembles the city hall-centered pattern
of many cities in the United States.[5] The key to this state of affairs,
however, was control of the representative hierarchy in West Bengal
by Atulya Ghosh, the "syndicate" chieftain of the Congress party.
Starting from a machine base (the Hooghly group) in Calcutta municipal and district politics, he forged throughout West Bengal the coalition of rural votes and urban financiers which until recently guaranteed Congress power at the state level. The impulses of the Congress
ministers of Bengal, at least insofar as they affected Calcutta municipal
politics, were held hostage to Ghosh's machine-based electoral power.

Yet these conditions are probably exceptional in India, for in no
other major Indian state, with the possible exception of Maharashtra,
is there so clearly a "primate" city, one without significant political
and economic rivals in its region, or one where the metropolitan population is so large in relation to its hinterland. More usual is the
contrary situation which Weiner uncovers in the pre-modern and
smaller city of Madurai.[6] There, as in Indore, state-level chieftains of
Tamilnad intervene in local Congress party affairs and in the governance of the city to break deadlocks and to minimize Communist influence in trade unions. Indeed, Madurai is probably even more subordinate to the impact of the state than Indore.

If centralization by the state and the local fragmentation of urban
politics in Indore is more generally characteristic of city politics in
India, it raises questions about how comparative urban research can
be approached in that setting. It suggests, for example, that the
typical models of urban politics research developed under American
conditions cannot be applied directly in India, at least not without
modifications. The two prominent American conceptual models of
urban political decision-making, the "community power structure"
approach associated with Floyd Hunter, and the "pluralistic" or
"polyarchic" model developed by Robert Dahl, both deal with the
question of who governs the city, but diverge in their major conclu-

---

[5] For a different point of view which stresses governmental fragmentation and
weak performance in Calcutta, however, see Ali Ashraf, *The City Government of
Calcutta: A Study of Inertia.*

[6] Weiner, *Party-Building*, pp. 381–456.

sions.[7] Leaving the methodological disputes aside, both models have serious limitations when related to research on Indian politics. The limitations lie in the unit chosen for primary analysis. For Hunter it is the urban community, and for Dahl it is the city government. Both presume that the locus of major decisions affecting the course of city politics is local. The assumption may be sound in the American context, or even if it be qualified somewhat, an argument can be made for narrowing the focus of urban politics research to local decision-making, viewing higher levels of government as the source of fairly stable constraints that set boundaries to city politics.

This assumption, however, cannot so appropriately be made in the Indian context. The bulk of the important decisions affecting the city's political destiny are made externally, at higher levels of politics. In fact, the governance of the city, to the extent that the Indore pattern is typical, is essentially by the state government. If the keys to power and authority over urban affairs are essentially extra-local, the politics of the Indian city and its various arenas can be understood only by expanding the unit of analysis to encompass those sets of political and bureaucratic linkages which cut through local politics, and this requires analysis of political forces and competition at higher levels of politics.

Otherwise, Dahl's pluralistic model of "dispersed inequalities"—implying several sets of political elites, but endowed differentially with status, wealth, organizational support, and other political resources—has much in common with Indore. The difference lies in the focus. For Dahl, local politicians and the local electorate are central. It is true that the "executive-centered coalition" constructed by Mayor Lee of New Haven had at its disposal incentives made available through federal redevelopment funds, and that these funds were secured by negotiations with federal authorities. But Dahl's focus was not on external linkages, nor in that case did it have to be. By con-

---

[7] See Floyd Hunter, *Community Power Structure: A Study of Decision-Makers*; and Robert Dahl, *Who Governs? Democracy and Power in an American City*. Nelson Polsby reviews the earlier literature in the community power structure tradition (stratification analysis) in *Community Power and Political Theory*. Robert Agger, Daniel Goldrich, and Bert Swanson combine the strengths of both types of analysis and carry the systematization of empirical research further in *The Rulers and the Ruled: Political Power and Impotence in American Communities*.

trast, the state–urban distribution of power and the impact of the
dual hierarchies are critical to the analysis of political outcomes in
Indore. Moreover, while local politicians and the local electorate are
important in Indore politics, bureaucratic participants are equally so.
And, while it is mayoral and municipal elections that count in New
Haven, making its politics introverted, it is general elections that
matter in Indore, making local political and bureaucratic participants
look outward for their cues. Similarly, the political assimilation and
integration detected by Dahl consisted of the attachment of ethnic
groups to one of two integrative parties, and their use of city government patronage to advance themselves socially and economically. Similar behaviors exist in Indore, though the patronage is more likely to
be from the state, the unit of attachment is more likely to be a faction,
and the variety of active ethnic groups is far greater. Finally, the
important integrative forces in New Haven are local, while those of
Indore are between factions, parties and units of government at different levels. Dahl's representation of city politics, in short, is largely
self-contained; Indore politics manifestly is not.[8]

Public Policy and Theory

A multi-centered, externally penetrated system of urban politics
tends to diffuse rather than concentrate policy processes, making them
difficult to grasp and generalize. Where there are many settings for
policy, the content and pattern of policy may vary from one setting
to another. And when major policy decisions are made outside of
the city, at the apex of the dual hierarchies, observations made at the
local level tend to be self-limiting, for they are most likely to center
on the implementation of policy, not its formulation. Yet it is by the
results of political and governmental actions that the effectiveness
and productivity of the system of city governance must be measured
and judged. What gets done in the Indian city, and what does not?
How does it get done, and what difference does it make?

---

[8] Perhaps even in the United States the most fruitful urban research in the
long run will come to be regarded as that based on approaches which do not take
city politics as a self-contained unit but explore instead the interpenetration of different levels of authority. See, for example, Wallace S. Sayre and Herbert Kaufman,
Governing New York City: Politics in the Metropolis; Edward C. Banfield, *Political
Influence*; and Martin Meyerson and Edward C. Banfield, *Politics, Planning, and
the Public Interest*.

Public policy may be defined as a pattern of actions calculated
to achieve a goal, purpose, or program, and carried out by an actor
or agency of government. In ordering data about public policy, this
study has been chiefly concerned with the unit and level of government involved, the structure of decision-making and implementation,
the types of goals sought by policy-makers, the types of clienteles
benefiting from policy, the degree to which the content of policy is
substantive, symbolic, or structural, and the extent to which policy is
areal or segmental in the scope of its impact. A useful way of ordering
policy data analytically so as to consider its theoretical consequences
is that developed by Theodore Lowi and refined somewhat by Robert
H. Salisbury.[9] Dissatisfied with the descriptive or nominalist categories
of policy usually used in American case studies, Lowi developed a
typology of policies distinguished functionally in terms of their impact upon society, as that impact is perceived by political participants.
His three major categories of public policies are "distribution, regulation, and redistribution," with "foreign policy" becoming a fourth
and residual category.[10]

Distributive policies are those that confer direct benefits on specific
individuals and groups, in small increments, and usually in such a
fashion that those who win or lose are not clearly identifiable, so
that conflict occurs more over the distribution of shares than over the
content of legislation. Distributive policies consist mainly of services
and material favors, in such matters as land, housing, education,
health, and ordinary patronage. Redistributive policies both confer
benefits and take them away, affecting large classes of people. Potential
winners and losers perceive the impact of policy more clearly and are
likely to engage in intense conflict over the policy-making process.
Regulatory policies constrain the behavior of particular groups and
open or close opportunities for acquiring benefits in the future. Regulatory policies consist of general rules which must be applied in specific cases. Conflict over regulatory policies is likely to be ambiguous

---

[9] See Lowi, "American Business, Public Policy, Case Studies and Political Theory"; and Salisbury, "The Analysis of Public Policy: A Search for Theories and
Roles."

Other recent sources on policy theory include Thomas R. Dye, *Understanding
Public Policy*; and Robert Lineberry and Ira Sharkansky, *Urban Politics and Public
Policy*.

[10] Lowi, "American Business," p. 689.

and shifting, because general guidelines do not by themselves dictate the specific content and direction of costs and benefits.

For Lowi, the theoretical significance of these types of policy output is that "they constitute real arenas of power. Each arena tends to develop its own characteristic political structure, political process, elites, and group relations." [11] The arena of distributive policy conforms, he argues, to the pluralist structure of decentralized power where policy is the result of compromises among many contending pressure groups, as described by Pendleton Herring, E. E. Schattschneider, and David Truman.[12] The arena of regulatory policies conforms to the polyarchic structure of dispersed inequalities and coalition politics described by Robert Dahl. And the arena of redistributive policy resembles the elitist view of the political process, where power is concentrated in the hands of a few but may be challenged bluntly by nonparticipants. Lowi argues that these types of policies, arenas, and power structures may coexist in the same society and government, but characterize different sectors of it; the tendency in case studies has been to discover one type and generalize from it to the political system as a whole.

Salisbury goes a step further, to a simple systems model for the explanation of the three types of policy, to which he adds a fourth category of "self-regulatory" policy.[13] Self-regulatory policies are like regulatory policies in that they impose constraints upon groups, but they are perceived differently by those groups as increasing rather than diminishing the beneficial options available to them. Self-regulatory policies may involve the delegation of authority to specialized groups in the interpretation of regulatory standards, as in the case of professional licensing or fair trade legislation. When such groups are relatively small, as is true of the legal and medical professions, self-regulatory policies usually occasion little opposition. Salisbury is concerned in his model with an explanation that goes beyond the "systems resources" explanations of levels of policy output to show that "political variables" do account, if not for the *amount* of policy, at least

---

[11] *Ibid.*

[12] E. Pendleton Herring, *Group Representation Before Congress*; E. E. Schattschneider, *Politics, Pressures and the Tariff*; and David B. Truman, *The Governmental Process: Political Interests and Public Opinion.*

[13] Salisbury, "Analysis of Public Policy," p. 158.

for its *functional* type.[14] "While the system resources may determine how much money is spent, the active political system is decisive in determining the kind of policy, including the groups that benefit or suffer, the extent of conflict, [and] the ability to adapt or innovate." [15]

Critical to his argument is a distinction between "demand pattern" and "decisional system," two sets of variables which interact to determine policy type. The demand pattern as well as the decisional system may be either "integrated" or "fragmented." Integration of the demand pattern "is measured by the range, diversity, and compatibility of substantive demands made as well as by the unity or disunity of activity among groups making them." [16] Integration of the decisional structure, though not defined explicitly by Salisbury, is measured by the extent to which decisions are centralized and, once made, are carried out authoritatively and uniformly by a responsive administrative hierarchy. Conversely, fragmented decisional structures may be measured by the number of competing centers of decision and the degree to which each may veto or reverse the decisions of others. Courts are highly integrated decisional structures, while legislatures with committee decentralization typify fragmented decisional structures.

Salisbury's model relates alternative combinations of demand pattern and decisional structure to policy type, to provide a series of fruitful hypotheses. Integrated demand patterns, he suggests, can be expected to produce redistributive policy, particularly when the decisional structure is also integrated. This would be so, for example, in an authoritarian system when excluded groups or a social class exert pressure for a redistribution of benefits away from the privileged sectors of society. When demands are integrated and the decisional system is fragmented, however, the result is likely to be self-regulative policies. The reason for this is that groups making integrated demands

---

[14] "Systems resources" are variables such as wealth, urbanization, and literacy. A growing number of studies have combined systems resource variables with political variables such as legislative apportionment and party competition to show that the former account independently for the levels of policy output in various types of government expenditure, while the latter do not. See, for example, Richard E. Dawson and James A. Robinson, "Inter-party Competition, Economic Variables, and Welfare Policies in the American States"; and Thomas R. Dye, *Politics, Economics, and the Public: Policy Outcomes in the American States.*

[15] Salisbury, "Analysis," p. 165.

[16] *Ibid.*, p. 166.

will seek to avoid the conflict and possible obstruction of their goals implied by redistributive policies in a fragmented decisional system, and will content themselves with less visible and less provocative self-regulatory policies. By contrast, fragmented demand patterns, resulting from a diverse array of groups contending for shares of government output, will ordinarily produce distributive policies, particularly when the decisional system is also fragmented. But when the decisional system is highly integrated, a fragmented demand structure is likely to produce regulatory policies.

This policy typology and model are useful because they permit the inclusion and ordering of complex data in a general form, and permit the testing of hypotheses. The policy categories may be criticized as excessively general, and it is indeed difficult to fit concrete examples of policy into one or another category. The problem with actual policies is that they usually consist of a mixture of functional criteria. But the effort to do so may well be instructive. In general, in Indore, this study has revealed a great deal of distributive and regulatory policy, and comparatively little redistributive or self-regulative policy. Functional policy outputs can be discerned in the various political arenas of the city, but usually as a mixture of types. One type or another may predominate, but the mixture varies, from one arena to another as well as over time.

Distributive Policy and Municipal Politics

In the arena of municipal politics, the policy type is predominantly distributive and fits Salisbury's theory remarkably well, for the demand pattern and decisional structure are normally both fragmented. Predominant in municipal government is the distribution of limited services, ranging from the supply of water, the construction of roads and pavements for pedestrians, the installation of street lights, the provision of sanitary facilities and garbage collection, the organization of public entertainment, and a variety of other seemingly routine activities. Particularistic competition for shares in these benefits is legitimized by the election of Municipal Councillors from numerous individual wards. Because political parties are weakened by internal factional rivalries, representative inputs are poorly integrated and much is left to individual Councillors in pressing for adequate attention to the needs of their wards. A few Councillors achieve promi-

nence in the municipal arena by virtue of important offices in the
Congress party or INTUC organizations, or because they are backed
by business interests or a homogeneous primordial group, and these
may use committee powers and an intimate knowledge of municipal
procedure to serve special interests by discriminating among contractors, bending tax regulations, or by waiving an onerous but seldom
used rule. They can do so because, despite the formal integration of
the decisional structure (the statutory separation of the executive and
administrative powers from the Council), the municipal bureaucrats
in charge of individual departments exercise considerable discretion
over how policies are administered. Since they too acquire personal
and factional ties, and because public knowledge about their past actions is often potentially damaging, the municipal bureaucrats work
symbiotically with the more influential Councillors in distributing
benefits and sharing in side-payments.

Regulatory policies are of somewhat less importance, but should
not be discounted in the municipal arena altogether. Certain municipal functions are more routine than others in their autonomy from
pressure by Councillors or special interests. Irregularities in the collection of *octroi* and administration of building regulations are probably
exaggerated, at least in a statistical sense, and the implementation of
statutes controlling drugs, the cleanliness of food service in hotels
and restaurants, and a variety of other matters, appear to be routinely
regulative in nature. There are also a few areas in which the municipal
government issues self-regulatory policies, as in the case of slaughter
houses or retail markets where the stalls are leased from the municipality.

Under certain circumstances, however, the intervention by actors
at the state level may impose an integrated decisional structure upon
the municipal arena. This occurred in Indore on two separate occasions in quite different ways. D. P. Mishra's penetration of municipal
politics strengthened the regulative outputs of the Corporation by
structuring emergency measures for coping with the water shortage.
The financial powers and political support he showered on Mayor
Shukla, his protégé, temporarily centralized executive authority in a
political rather than bureaucratic figure. The bias in the use of regulative policies, of course, favored the Khadiwala faction and pro-Mishra
politicians of the municipal arena. Subsequently, the supersession of

the Corporation by the state government, then controlled by the SVD
opposition, once again centralized authority in the municipal arena,
but this time under the bureaucratic executive, and for *redistributive*
as well as regulatory purposes. By suspending the elected body, the
state in effect insulated the municipal authority from the normal
fragmented demand pattern, but substituted their own demand pattern from above, integrated around opposition interests defined at
the state level. The ultimate objective was to use municipal patronage
bureaucratically to promote the strength of the opposition parties in
Indore, so that under new elections they would capture a majority in
the Council. This effort to redistribute party power and the benefits
of municipal control, however, was thwarted by the return of a Congress government to power on the state level in 1969.

Regulatory Policy and Improvement Politics

In the arena of town planning and improvement, defined by the
interaction of the Improvement Trust with its clienteles and other
competing agencies, policy is predominantly regulatory in nature,
though there are elements of redistributive policy too. Again, the fit
with Salisbury's theory is good, for these are the types of policy pre-
dicted by the model when the decisional system is integrated but the
demand pattern varies from fragmented to integrated. The structure
of the Trust is conducive to integrated decision-making in several
ways. The Chairman, who presides as the chief executive of the Trust,
is a state appointee from the higher levels of administration. He
generally takes his cues on important policy matters, such as those
affecting the state-designed "masterplan" for the city, from the state's
Chief Town Planning Officer, who is also an ex-officio trustee. Equally
important is the fact that the Trust is small, consisting of nine members—who, because they are drawn from the municipality and from
bureaucratic agencies, fuse together elements of both representative
and bureaucratic hierarchies. Moreover, the Trust's decision-making
process is insulated from electoral accountability and the normal political pressures present in a representative arena. And finally, the
decisions of the Trust may be challenged formally only in the Tribunal or the courts, both highly integrated structures in their own
right. Trust decisions are made by a majority vote among trustees
present, and are not normally delegated to committees. Although the

trustees are frequently divided by factional loyalties, or by their other institutional affiliations and responsibilities, the decisional structure is a relatively integrated one.

The demand patterns impinging on the Trust vary somewhat in composition according to the type of improvement schemes underway at any given time; but whatever the composition, they are usually marked by considerable fragmentation. The interests and clienteles affected by Trust operations include urban landlords and building owners, slum dwellers, construction contractors and laborers, private housing colony land developers (both cooperatives and private firms), shopkeepers, transportation interests, the Municipal Corporation, the engineering section of the state Public Health Department, and a variety of others. These interests may seek access or bring pressure on the Trust through personal, factional, and organizational ties to individual trustees, but in a highly particularistic manner, for the Trust does not operate in an open forum. The pleas and objections of adversely affected interests are considered individually and disposed of, usually, in accordance with formal guidelines. In such a setting, it is difficult to organize coalitions of diverse interests against Trust initiatives. The way in which particular interests are affected does not provide easily identifiable common grounds for joint action. Institutional structure and regulatory procedures favor particularistic rather than integrated demand patterns in the arena of improvement politics.

The powers of the Trust are regulatory, not merely in the sense of perpetuating the status quo among existing interests, but also in ordering the process of physical development of the city. Trust initiatives usually take the form of "improvement schemes," including plans for the permanent development of slum areas and vacant sites according to explicit plans and standards. While development schemes are primarily regulative in nature, because they require appropriating land from some private interests and result in the lease or sale of improved land to other interests, there are also distributive and redistributive dimensions to the Trust's transactions. The best examples of such regulated improvement are the Jawaharmarg road scheme and schemes for housing colony development.

In the Jawaharmarg case, the objective was to build a wide east-west thoroughfare through the city, linking the railway station, truck

terminals, warehouses, and markets of Chowni and Siaganj in the
eastern sections of the city with the densely concentrated and older
financial, mercantile, and cloth market areas to the west. The existing
road was narrow and irregular, creating serious bottlenecks for the
burgeoning motorized traffic of the city. To widen and straighten such
a route, however, required appropriating and demolishing buildings
fronting on the existing route, and imposed hardships on the shopkeepers and residents necessarily displaced by this process. The process
of taking and clearing land, compensating those adversely affected,
and constructing the new avenue was long and tedious, frustrated by
numerous delays and by the jealous obstruction of the Municipal
Corporation. But once accomplished, Jawaharmarg has been a great
asset to the city and to the economic interests now linked between
the city's extremities. The Trust was ultimately successful in producing this valuable artery because the regulatory policy process
moved incrementally, dealing with affected interests one by one,
managing conflict among groups so as to prevent its escalation into
broadly integrated opposition to the venture. The fragmented demand structure slowed the process, but could not prevent its eventual
conclusion.

Housing colony development, which has accelerated in Indore in
recent years, is analogous to suburbanization in that cheap land on
the city's periphery is used by wealthy families to construct new and
more comfortable residences, but different in that it usually takes
place within municipal boundaries so as to take advantage of the
city's water supply and other services. The development of these new
residential settlements is largely by private interests, but the Trust
shares with the Municipal Corporation responsibility for imposing
and supervising uniform standards regulating the layout of streets,
the spacing of buildings, and other factors affecting city design and
public safety. Although this policy process is primarily regulative, it
also takes on self-regulative features. The principal clienteles are land
speculators, builders, and residential cooperatives, who can form an
integrated demand pattern because of their relatively homogeneous
interests. These client groups seek guidelines from the Trust, to be
administered by themselves in a decentralized way, restricting new
competition but enlarging the options available to those already in
the game. The Trust retains regulatory oversight—but, by delegating

some measure of responsibility, builds support groups and allies useful to the Trust elsewhere, when it confronts the Municipal Corporation or other bureaucratic agencies.

Under special conditions, where the decision-making of the Trust is integrated with that of other bureaucratic authorities under the aegis of a state-level chieftain, the policies and powers of the Trust may be used to promote redistribution. Such conditions, complemented by an integrated demand pattern, emerged in the Indore labor arena in the early 1950's. At the local level, the demand pattern on behalf of industrial laborers was integrated by Ramsinghbhai's labor machine, the Indore Mill Mazdoor Sangh. The redistribution sought by the unionized laborers was the use of state government expenditures in a variety of sectors, including that of the Improvement Trust, to build new housing and other residential improvements in the labor area. As Minister of Labour and simultaneously of Development, Local Self-Government, Public Health, Housing, and Town Improvement, V. V. Dravid used the remarkable opportunity at his disposal between 1952 and 1957 to integrate and concentrate efforts under these related jurisdictions to promote a variety of improvements in housing, roads, water supply, and other amenities in the labor area. Other more privileged groups in the city resisted this redistribution, as demonstrated by the Nai Duniya–Khadiwala counterattack in the municipal arena in 1958, and the subsequent erosion of INTUC power both at the state and local levels made it a temporary condition. Nevertheless, it does bear out in a concrete way the functional policy consequences of integrated demand patterns and decisional structure in the arena of improvement politics, and reveals how a regulatory arena can be geared under certain conditions to redistributive purposes.

Policy Mixtures in Labor Politics

A predominant policy type is less easily singled out in the arena of labor politics because government labor policy is functionally overlapping, both as it is perceived by participants and in its impact upon them. The composition of the mix also varies according to shifts over time in the structure of decision-making and the demand pattern. Much of labor policy is regulatory in nature, but it also contains distributive and redistributive features, and occasionally self-regulatory elements as well. Labor unions are organized, in principle, to bring about the redistribution of material benefits in spheres of industrial employment. In other governmental arenas, as has been described earlier for municipal and town improvement politics, labor interests compete directly with upper- and middle-class groups in the city over redistribution of scarce budgetary resources. By contrast, in the relatively autonomous labor arena, the focus of labor demands for redistribution is not on governmental expenditures so much as on the reapportioning of industrial profits, or what might be termed "publicly induced private redistribution."

What is confusing here is not what labor desires but how government policy should be characterized. Is it regulatory or redistributive? The solution is ambiguous, because it is a blend of both. From the perspective of management, the redistributive demands of labor are moderated by government regulatory policy, while from labor's point of view government regulative policy offers both redistributive and distributive opportunities. From the standpoint of most labor administrators, however, labor policy is viewed primarily in regulative terms, for it permits them to arbitrate labor–management conflict.

Labor policies do not conform as neatly to the Salisbury theory as do those of the municipal and town improvement arenas, but the discrepancies are not unduly worrisome. The decisional structure of the labor arena has varied somewhat, but its typical pattern is one of integration, leading one to expect redistributive and regulatory, but not distributive, policies. Under the Holkar regime, at least until the 1940's, labor policy was closely held by the government and attuned primarily to management interests. Thereafter, because of the integration of labor demands under militant and radical unions, the princely government brought moderate labor leaders from outside the city directly into government to coopt the labor movement. V. V. Dravid assumed direct control over Holkar labor policy in 1947 and succeeded in transferring the INTUC-dominated, relatively integrated decisional structure to the government of Madhya Bharat. The formation of Madhya Pradesh in 1956 and the invasion by Mishra's factional protégés of the dual hierarchies resulted in a gradual loosening up of the decisional structure and a degree of fragmentation after 1964. Even so, labor decision-making remains more integrated than fragmented because it is concentrated in the bureaucratic agencies of the Commissioner of Labour, the Registrar of Trade Unions, and Labour Courts —agencies within which hierarchical features predominate and local representative access is procedurally formalized. What complicates the decisional pattern somewhat is the growing tendency for factional sympathies to appear in the bureaucratic hierarchies.

The demand pattern in the labor arena has varied sharply. At the outset management interests were highly integrated, but after 1948 a degree of differentiation made itself felt, partly because the profitability of the industry as a whole declined, and because some firms suffered less than others. On the whole, labor demands were fragmented under the Holkar regime, leading to regulatory policy approaches, but there were periods of both moderate and radical integration of labor demands in the mid-1920's and late 1930's. State-induced redistribution by the textile millowners in the 1940's, eagerly supported by management as long as profits flowed in during the war years, bolstered the leadership of Dravid and Ramsingh, defused labor radicalism, and enabled the INTUC union to become the dominant organization in the labor arena. The demand pattern of labor was never uniformly integrated, because there were substantial grievances for the Socialist and Communist opposition to exploit. The decline of textile industry profitability forced retrenchment, a contraction of job opportunities, and new constituencies for radical unions. Nevertheless, the INTUC union between 1948 and 1963 imposed substantial integration on the demand pattern of labor politics, until the eruption of an internal struggle for power by labor factions caused the labor arena to revert to a highly fragmented demand pattern.

Regulatory and redistributive policies accounted for INTUC's remarkably rapid creation of a strong labor organization and the attraction to its ranks of the majority of the mill employees. Regulatory policies are best exemplified by the Bombay model legislation, which provided for a representative union and fostered a monopoly over labor inputs into labor–management relations by the INTUC union. The regulation of labor–management bargaining was firmly supported by the police and the courts, barring opposition unions from direct access to decisional forums and suppressing their agitational activities, especially when they engendered violence. Regulatory policies thus had their impact in making orderly negotiations possible between management and labor, minimizing the frequency and scope of strikes, and providing means for the prosecution of those leading illegal strikes. INTUC-management collaboration, in the interests of pre-empting labor radicalism, took redistributive form in raising wages, introducing profit-sharing through bonuses, and improving working conditions. The INTUC union cooperated with management in maintaining the discipline of the work force, even under retrenchment conditions.

The interests of the dominant union, however, became increasingly distributive over time, for two reasons. First, and most important, the keys to INTUC power were ultimately electoral in nature, requiring support of Dravid's role at the apex of the representative hierarchy. While INTUC as the representative union possessed an organizational monopoly over labor-management relations, the legitimacy of that role could be seriously undermined by voters showing their sympathies for rival union candidates at the polls, as happened in 1957 when Homi Daji defeated Gangaram Tiwari in the labor seat. Second, because of factionalism within INTUC, and the decline in employment opportunities in the industry, the INTUC union needed distributive capacities both to maintain internal cohesion and to attract voter support back to the fold. Consequently, the INTUC union strategies under Ramsingh Verma became those of a classical political machine, concentrating less on enlarging a pie, which was shrinking anyway, and more on sharing benefits among the diverse labor clienteles to spread satisfaction as broadly as possible. To do so required building up the financial distributive capacity of the union, and this was achieved with management cooperation by the collection of union dues on an annual basis as deductions from the pay of mill employees. The expansion in this manner of the local INTUC budget, together with largesse provided by management at election time in the form of automobiles, excusing of laborers from work, and direct grants, permitted the union to employ resources distributively to secure its electoral base. Given the primordial diversity of the labor force, sharp factional rivalries within the City Congress, and sophisticated opposition under Homi Daji's leadership, what is remarkable about the INTUC role in Indore is not that its dominance was eventually undermined but that it lasted so long and so effectively preempted the growth of potential labor radicalism. Government support through regulatory and redistributive policies were critical at the outset, but distributive processes eventually became essential, and these were fostered by a measure of self-regulatory decentralization, shifting initiative to the partnership between management and Ramsingh's machine, so long as this partnership successfully integrated the demand pattern of labor with the interests of management.

Urban Politics, Policy and Process: An Overview

Urban politics in Indore, viewed as a whole, consists primarily of distributive and regulatory policies and processes. Demand patterns are usually fragmented to a high degree by personal, primordial, and factional rivalries springing from the exceedingly pluralistic social base and ethnic competition of the city. Integration of demands by political parties and unions is shifting and uneven, varying from one arena to another and over time as the composition and sympathies prevailing at the apex of the representative and bureaucratic hierarchies change and alter local access opportunities. Both demand patterns and the decisional structure of urban politics are formally fragmented by the division of power and authority among various functional jurisdictions, resulting in multiple arenas of politics. Informally, a moderate degree of decisional integration is imposed on the arenas of power from above, when the political orientations and relationships among state-level political and bureaucratic chieftains are homogeneous and congruent. But there are built-in tendencies toward the diffusion of bureaucratic power along functional lines, and when factional rivalries erupt at the apex, centralized decisions become less authoritative and more permissive, enabling local actors of differing stripes and persuasions to mitigate regulative policies and expand or diversify their distributive impact.

The decisional structure may become more complex for factional reasons at the apex without necessarily losing its integrated quality within separate bureaucratic hierarchies, however, for much depends on the extent to which state-level political and bureaucratic chieftains can rely upon local political and bureaucratic allies within that particular sphere. Dravid could be denied control over the District Cooperative Bank and lose control over the Improvement Trust, yet continue to be decisive through the Department of Labour in labor politics. Consequently, fragmentation of the decisional structure at the state level as a whole may coexist with decisional integration within sepa-

rate arenas; each must be treated individually, as well as in relation to
the whole.

In the Madhya Bharat period, the effective integration of decisions at the apex by Nai Duniya and INTUC chieftains resulted in the
orchestration of their power simultaneously in the arenas of city politics, assisted at every level in the bureaucratic hierarchies by former
Holkar administrators. As time passed, integration at the apex was
superseded by Cabinet-level factional competition, and integration
shifted to separate arenas, until factional coups eventually followed
there as well. Yet the fragmenting of decisional structures proceeded
slowly, allowing overall dominance in city politics by the Congress
party and INTUC union to continue. In Madhya Pradesh politics,
Mishra attempted to reintegrate the decisional structure of the dual
hierarchies under his command by replacing Indore's political and bureaucratic chieftains with regional and factional allies of his own. His
efforts were of short duration and did not fundamentally alter the
functional pattern of policy. The takeover of state power by the opposition, and the victories of three opposition leaders in the four city
MLA seats in 1967, hinted at the strengthening of redistributive demands and resulted in intensified conflict over policy issues, but efforts
to move in a redistributive direction were aborted by internal opposition rivalries. Managed jointly, regulatory and distributive policies
have on the whole forestalled the sharpening of class-based demands
for redistribution and dampened the radicalization potentials of urban
politics in Indore. But as the decisional structure at the apex has become more pluralized, with successive shifts in the composition of
those in power at the state level, the impact of regulatory policies has
been weakened, and the policy pattern has become more unequivocally
distributive in nature.

Lowi's observations about the correspondence between types of policy and alternative power-structure configurations appears in the main
to be supported by urban politics in Indore. The elitist pattern of a
cohesive power structure beset by demands for redistribution of power
and benefits may have characterized city politics earlier under the
princely regime, but is not present in Indore today. What is present
instead is a polyarchic structure of rival elite coalitions and clienteles,
partly contained within the Congress party and labor organizations in
the form of factional competition, but manifested in interparty compe-

tition as well. Such a structure was preeminent in Indore politics in the Madhya Bharat period, giving rise to regulatory policy patterns. As factional and group competition has intensified, complicating the decisional structure of representative and bureaucratic hierarchies, policy has become more distributive in nature.

The significance of the primacy of distributive and regulatory policies and processes in Indore politics is that it moderates conflict and makes its management easier. Because it takes place in a penetrated system, and the management of conflict is by representative and bureaucratic hierarchies linking the city with the state, the satisfaction of many groups and individuals with small shares of the available resources is both cooptive and integrative in nature. It buys the allegiance of participants in the system, and reorients their loyalties to higher levels of authority at the same time. Their integration in the system is accordingly cemented and legitimized, not just at the local level but beyond—in the broader expanses of state and national politics. The price of this vertical integration is the erosion of local autonomy and the penetration of external authorities, but their intervention is made tolerable by payments in a distributive coin. The disaggregation of urban politics in multiple arenas operates together with traditional social identities to blur perceptions of deprivation—absolute and relative—and impedes the integration horizontally of the unprivileged against the privileged. Those who have less stand to gain in distributive politics, and material progress even in small amounts may count for more than ideological visions of a new order.

Managing conflict and achieving political integration are critical tasks for a new and diverse nation, but success in these two tasks is not sufficient in modern politics over the long run. The problem all too often with distributive and regulative politics is that nothing new gets done. Distributing shares of scarce resources tends to take precedence over creating new ones, because it is consuming in time and energy, and also in resources themselves. It tends to promote not the concentration of power but the diffusion of power, and handicaps those with vision who might otherwise strive to assemble and harness the capabilities of government for developmental and ultimately redistributive tasks.

The picture in Indore is an ambivalent one in this respect, for the centralization of authority over urban affairs by the state is a potential asset for decisive initiatives, but its use thus far has been perfunctory

at best. It augments the opportunities for expanding what Schattschneider calls the "politics of scope," and for shifting the "scale of
conflict" from the local to state and national arenas. The problem of
modern politics is to generate political participation, not so much because that is intrinsically valuable but because it is necessary—necessary for creating public support for effective programs of public action
and essential for "shifting the emphasis from the politics of the distribution of benefits to the politics of the apportionment of burdens." [17] The price of not doing so is entropy. Participation in Indore
politics has grown, but fitfully and hesistantly, for the penetration by
state authorities (the Mishra case excepted) has usually been designed
not to expand the scale of conflict but to contain it. In this, for the
most part, they have succeeded. Loyalty to the larger system has grown,
fed by distributive measures, but the active engagement and support
that would enable the government to apportion burdens has not
grown correspondingly.

The physical amenities for some laborers in Indore have been improved. The opportunities for education have been somewhat enlarged. There are better health services there too. And the caretaker
functions of the municipality and the police are performed routinely
and fairly adequately. But on many of the large issues of public policy
—not the least of which are providing the city with a really adequate
water supply, checking and reversing the slow stagnation of industry,
and expanding the supply of productive jobs to use positively the talents, skills, and available energy, of people in Indore—the picture is
less than bright. Things could be better. They might also be worse.
The public authorities cannot be held responsible for all that must
get done. Individuals by serving themselves can help build society and
the public good as well. And there may be more private innovation
than meets the eye in the course of a year. Still, it is vitally important
that the energies of participation be harnessed, that the risks of greater
turbulence from an expansion of the scale of conflict be faced, and that
efforts be concerted for public policy programs that not only enlarge
available resources but make their growth self-generative.

---

[17] E. E. Schattschneider, *The Semi-Sovereign People: A Realist's View of Democracy in America*, pp. 8–11, 111.

APPENDIX A

TABLE 1. INDORE CITY CASTES BY PROPORTION, REGIONAL ORIGIN, RELIGION, AND OCCUPATION, 1931

Caste and Category	Percentage	Regional Origin	Religion	Occupation
HIGH CASTES				
Brahmans	30.0			
Maharashtrian (Deccani)	18.1	Maharashtra	Hindu	Civil service, professions, clerical
Malwi	8.3	Malwa	Hindu	Priestly, agriculture, professions, clerical
Gujarati	3.4	Gujarat	Hindu	Civil service, clerical
Kanyakubja	0.6	Uttar Pradesh	Hindu	Military, police, clerical, industrial laborers
Bundelkhandi	1.9	Bundelkhand	Hindu	Civil service, clerical, professions
Pallival	1.2	Rajasthan	Hindu	Domestic servants, dairymen
Naramdeo	0.5	South Malwa	Hindu	Priestly, agriculture, clerical
Others	0.2	Various	Hindu	Various
Kayastha	2.0	Uttar Pradesh	Hindu	Civil service, professions, clerical
Baniyas	0.6			
	9.7			
Oswal	1.3	Rajasthan	Jain	Business, professions
Saraogi	1.5	Rajasthan	Jain	Business, professions
Agarwal	2.0	Rajasthan and Uttar Pradesh	Hindu	Business, professions
Porwal	0.5	Rajasthan	Hindu and Jain	Business, professions
Gujarati	0.1	Gujarat	Jain	Business, professions

APPENDIX A, TABLE 1 (continued)

Caste and Category	Percentage	Regional Origin	Religion	Occupation
Neema, Modi	0.8	Rajasthan	Hindu	Business, clerical
Maheshwari	1.3	Malwa	Hindu	Business, agriculture
Khandelwal	0.2	Khandesh	Hindu	Business, agriculture
Others	2.0	Various	Hindu and Jain	Business
Bohra	1.4	Gujarat	Muslim	Business
Khatri	0.2	Punjab	Hindu	Business, professions, clerical
INTERMEDIATE CASTES	56.0			
HIGHER INTERMEDIATE	41.3			
Rajput	5.8	Rajasthan	Hindu	Industrial laborers, civil service, military, police, various others
Sayyad	1.4	Various	Muslim	Business, professions, civil service
Sikh	0.4	Punjab	Sikh	Business, police, clerical
Pathan	4.6	Various	Muslim	Industrial laborers, military
Maratha	4.0	Maharashtra	Hindu	Police, military, civil service, industrial laborers
Sonar	1.2	Rajasthan	Hindu	Business, professions
Teli	1.1	Various	Hindu	Business (vegetable oils)
Sutar	1.0	Various	Hindu	Carpentry
Babaji, Bairagi, Gosain	1.6	Various	Hindu	Mendicants, industrial laborers
Dhangar	2.6	Maharashtra	Hindu	Police, military, civil service, industrial laborers
Jat	0.6	Uttar Pradesh	Hindu	Industrial and common laborers
Ahir	2.6	Rajasthan	Hindu	Industrial and common laborers
Shaikh	6.6	Various	Muslim	Industrial and common laborers
Kulmi, Kunbi, Kurmi, Anjana, Khati, Kumawat	1.2	Gujarat-Malwa	Hindu	Artisans and laborers

Gujar	0.4	Punjab	Hindu	Artisans and laborers
Kacchi	0.8	Uttar Pradesh	Hindu	Industrial laborers
Mali	1.8	Uttar Pradesh	Hindu	Gardeners, industrial laborers
Lodhi	0.9	Uttar Pradesh	Hindu	Industrial and common laborers
Others	3.7	Various	Hindu, Muslim	Artisans and laborers
LOWER INTERMEDIATE				
Bhoi	1.0	Malwa	Hindu	Industrial and common laborers
Gadaria	0.7	Uttar Pradesh	Hindu	Industrial and common laborers
Kumhar	0.9	Uttar Pradesh	Hindu	Artisans and laborers
Lohar	0.8	Various	Hindu	Artisans and laborers
Nai	1.5	Uttar Pradesh	Hindu	Barbers, industrial laborers
Kalal, Kalar	0.3	Uttar Pradesh	Hindu	Distillers, laborers
Tamoli	0.2	Various	Hindu	Paan (betel) sellers
Salvi, Maru	0.1	Rajasthan	Hindu	Industrial and common laborers
Murai	0.5	Uttar Pradesh	Hindu	Industrial and common laborers
Rangara	0.3	Various	Hindu	Dyers, laborers
Momin, Julaha	1.5	Various	Muslim	Industrial and common laborers
Mewati	0.1	Rajasthan	Muslim	Industrial and common laborers
Lunia	0.2	Malwa	Hindu	Salt-producers, laborers
Sonkar	0.1	Central Prov.	Hindu	Industrial and common laborers
Pinjara	0.2	Various	Muslim	Cotton carders, laborers
Bhisti	0.5	Various	Muslim	Water carriers, common laborers
Chhipa	0.3	Various	Hindu and Muslim	Cotton printers, industrial and common laborers
Darzi	0.8	Various	Hindu and Muslim	Tailors, industrial and common laborers
Others	4.7	Various	Hindu and Muslim	Various

APPENDIX A, TABLE 1 (continued)

Caste and Category	Percentage	Regional Origin	Religion	Occupation
DEPRESSED CASTES	13.0			
Dhobi	0.8	Various	Hindu	Washermen, common laborers
Balai	0.5	Malwa	Hindu	Industrial and common laborers
Kosti	0.9	Maharashtra	Hindu	Weavers, industrial laborers
Chamar	4.5	Uttar Pradesh, Rajasthan	Hindu	Leather-workers, industrial and common laborers
Kori	2.7	Uttar Pradesh	Hindu	Weavers, industrial laborers
Bansphor	0.5	Various	Hindu	Bamboo-weavers, artisans
Bhambi	0.5	Malwa	Hindu	Weavers, industrial laborers
Mahar	0.6	Maharashtra	Hindu	Industrial and common laborers
Mang	0.2	Maharashtra	Hindu	Broom-makers, common laborers
Kasai, Khatik	0.4	Various	Muslim	Butchers
Bhangi	1.3	Various	Hindu	Sweepers, industrial and common laborers
Pasi	0.2	Uttar Pradesh	Hindu	Pig-breeders, common laborers

NOTE: Numbers are rounded, accounting for imperfect totals.
SOURCES: *Census, 1931, op. cit.*, vol. one, pp. 243–279, 281; vol. two, pp. 200–201.

APPENDIX B

TABLE 1. 1952 GENERAL ELECTION RESULTS—INDORE

Seat	Candidate	Community	Party	Vote
Indore	Ramsingh Verma	Rajput	Con	10,276
City A	Goverdhanlal Ojha	Hindi-speaking Brahman	Soc	3,805
	Laxman Khandkar	Maharashtrian Brahman	CPI	2,838
	Kishorilal Goyal	Hindu Baniya	JS	1,601
	Gangaram	Harijan	Ind	1,470
	Johrilal Mittal	Baniya	RRP	196
	N. C. Chatterjee	Bengali	Ind	431
	Hemraj Dariavji	N.A.	Ind	332
		(Turnout, or valid votes cast, 48.8 percent)		
Indore	V. V. Dravid	Southern Brahman	Con	13,596
City B	Ganesh V. Oke	Maharashtrian Brahman	HMS	2,036
	Chandrawati Kasarliwal	N.A.	Ind	336
	Gopikrishnan Arjun	N.A.	Ind	857
	Homi Daji	Parsi	CPI	2,185
	Nirmalarani Potdar	Sonar	KMPP	123
	Ramnarain Vyas	Hindi-speaking Brahman	Soc	802
	Harish Chandra Pannalal	N.A.	Ind	121
		(Turnout, 47.5 percent)		
Indore	Manoharsingh Mehta	Jain	Con	15,164
City C	Ram Narain Shastri	Hindi-speaking Brahman	JS	6,371
	Dhannalal	N.A.	Soc	1,152
		(Turnout, 57.0 percent)		
Indore	V. V. Sarvate	Maharashtrian Brahman	Con	12,722
City D	Narayan Waman Pantvaidya	Maharashtrian Brahman	JS	4,760
	Dattatrey Sarmandal	Maharashtrian Brahman	CPI	2,762
	Kundarani Gandhe	Maharashtrian Brahman	Soc	802
	Khemraj Joshi	Hindi-speaking Brahman	Ind	593
		(Turnout, 54.6 percent)		
Indore	Nandlal Joshi	Hindi-speaking Brahman	Con	109,506
Lok	Lakshmi Shanker Shukla	Hindi-speaking Brahman	Soc	22,159
Sabha	Narayan Waman Pantvaidya	Maharashtrian Brahman	JS	46,989
		(Turnout, 46.1 percent)		

SOURCES: Madhya Pradesh Government, Chief Electoral Officer, *Handbook on the General Elections in Madhya Pradesh*, Bhopal, 1967. Community affiliations were determined from interviews.

TABLE 2. 1957 GENERAL ELECTION RESULTS—INDORE

Seat	Candidate	Community	Party	Vote
Indore City Central	Babulal Patodi	Jain	Con	18,338
	Vasudevrao Lokhande	Maharashtrian Brahman	JS	8,002
		(Turnout, 51.5 percent)		
Indore City East	Gangaram Tiwari	Hindi-speaking Brahman	Con	10,903
	Homi Daji	Parsi	Ind	16,702
		(Turnout, 63.2 percent)		
Indore City West	Mishrilal Gangwal	Jain	Con	16,249
	Utsav Chand Jain	Jain	JS	5,712
	Jindal Madanlal	Jain	PSP	2,333
		(Turnout, 53.5 percent)		
Indore	V. V. Dravid	Southern Brahman	Con	11,439
	Umrao Singh	Rajput	Ind	4,299
	Ram Chandra	N.A.	JS	3,195
		(Turnout, 45.7 percent)		
Indore Lok Sabha	Kanhaiyalal Khadiwala	Hindi-speaking Brahman	Con	102,589
	Kishorilal Goyal	Hindu Baniya	JS	42,010
	Shiv Shanker	N.A.	Ind	19,245
		(Turnout, 45.8 percent)		

SOURCES: *Handbook.*

TABLE 3. 1962 GENERAL ELECTION RESULTS—INDORE

Seat	Candidate	Community	Party	Vote
Indore City Central	Babulal Patodi	Jain	Con	16,446
	Rajendra Dharkar	CKP	JS	10,212
	Arif Beg	Muslim	Ind	8,991
	Mohan Singh	N.A.	Soc	677
	Kanhaiyalal Durgashanker	N.A.	HMS	454
	V. V. Vaishampayan	N.A.	Ind	113
	(Turnout, 68.7 percent)			
Indore City East	Gangaram Tiwari	Hindi-speaking Brahman	Con	18,617
	Prabhakar Adsule	Maharashtrian Brahman	Ind	18,164
	Harihar Ganpatlal	N.A.	Ind	815
	Ramai Ram	N.A.	Soc	555
	(Turnout, 71.0 percent)			
Indore City West	Mishrilal Gangwal	Jain	Con	17,598
	Purshottam Vijay	Khandelwal Baniya	Ind	11,863
	Kalyanmal Jain	Jain	Ind	6,744
	Basantsingh	N.A.	HMS	604
	(Turnout, 68.3 percent)			
Indore	V. V. Dravid	Southern Brahman	Con	12,506
	Lakshmi Shanker Shukla	Hindi-speaking Brahman	Ind	7,712
	Jaggannath Bhagwan	Harijan	Ind	4,135
	Surendranath Gupta	Hindu Baniya	Ind	694
	Kalyan Singh	N.A.	Soc	685
	Bhagchand Motilal	Baniya	Ind	401
	Shrikishan Chunnilal	Baniya	HMS	205
	(Turnout, 57.9 percent)			
Indore Lok Sabha	Homi Daji	Parsi	Ind	95,682
	Ramsingh Verma	Rajput	Con	89,389
	Triloknath Bhargava	Kayastha	JS	19,923
	Baleshwardayal	N.A.	Soc	17,538
	Narayansingh Albela	Rajput	HMS	7,014
	(Turnout, 56.6 percent)			

SOURCES: *Handbook.*

TABLE 4. 1967 General Election Results—Indore

Seat	Candidate	Community	Party	Vote
Indore I	Arif Beg	Muslim	SSP	15,748
	Babulal Patodi	Jain	Con	14,739
	Utsavchand Jain	Jain	JS	9,800
		(Turnout, 66.5 percent)		
Indore II	Gangaram Tiwari	Hindi-speaking Brahman	Con	19,735
	Harisingh	Rajput	Ind	18,610
	Madhukar Chandwaskar	Maharashtrian Brahman	JS	3,439
	Morulal Jivan	Bairwa	Ind	2,416
	Bhagwansingh	N.A.	Ind	565
	Shilkumar Nigam	N.A.	PSP	227
		(Turnout, 67.6 percent)		
Indore III	Kalyanmal Jain	Jain	SSP	16,954
	Suresh Seth	Punjabi Khatri	Con	11,576
	Rajendra Dharkar	CKP	JS	11,457
		(Turnout, 66.9 percent)		
Indore IV	Yugydutt Sharma	Hindi-speaking Brahman	Ind	13,371
	N. K. Shukla	Hindi-speaking Brahman	Con	13,271
	Jagdishprasad Vaidik	Hindu Baniya	JS	5,609
	Abdul Quddus	Muslim	Ind	4,557
	Nandram Verma	N.A.	Swa	597
		(Turnout, 63.3 percent)		
Indore Lok Sabha	Prakash Chand Sethi	Jain	Con	134,468
	Homi Daji	Parsi	Ind	100,350
	Satyabhan Singhal	Hindu Baniya	JS	67,557
	Dinesh Awasthi	N.A.	PSP	6,053
		(Turnout, 53.5 percent)		

Sources: *Handbook.*

BIBLIOGRAPHY

BOOKS

Abrams, Charles. *Man's Struggle for Shelter in an Urbanizing World.* Cambridge: M.I.T. Press, 1964.

Agger, Robert, Daniel Goldrich, and Bert Swanson. *The Rulers and the Ruled: Political Power and Impotence in American Communities.* New York: Wiley, 1964.

Argal, R. *Municipal Government in India.* Allahabad: Agarwal Press, 1955.

Ashraf, Ali. *The City Government of Calcutta: A Study of Inertia.* Bombay: Asia Publishing House, 1966.

Bailey, F. G. *Politics and Social Change: Orissa in 1959.* Berkeley and Los Angeles: University of California Press, 1963.

Banfield, Edward C. *The Moral Basis of a Backward Society.* Glencoe, Ill.: Free Press, 1958.

———. *Political Influence: A New Theory of Urban Politics.* New York: Free Press, 1961.

———, and James Q. Wilson. *City Politics.* New York: Knopf, 1963.

Banton, Michael. *West African City: A Study of Tribal Life in Freetown.* London: Oxford University Press, 1957.

Barnabas, A. P. *The Experience of Citizens in Getting Water Connections, A Survey Report on Knowledge, Communication and Corruption.* New Delhi: Indian Institute of Public Administration, 1965.

Bayley, David H. *The Police and Political Development in India.* Princeton, N.J.: Princeton University Press, 1969.

Béteille, André. *Caste, Class, and Power: Changing Patterns of Stratification in a Tanjore Village.* Berkeley and Los Angeles: University of California Press, 1965.

Beyer, Glenn H. (ed.). *The Urban Explosion in Latin America: A Continent in Process of Modernization*. Ithaca, New York: Cornell University Press, 1967.

Bhattacharya, M., M. M. Singh, and Frank J. Tysen. *Government in Metropolitan Calcutta: A Manual*. Bombay: Asia Publishing House, 1965.

Bonjean, Charles M., Terry N. Clark, and Robert L. Lineberry (eds.). *Community Politics: A Behavioral Approach*. New York: Free Press, 1971.

Bose, Ashish. *Urbanization in India: An Inventory of Source Materials*. Bombay: Academic Books, Ltd., 1970.

Brass, Paul. *Factional Politics in an Indian State: The Congress Party in Uttar Pradesh*. Berkeley and Los Angeles: University of California Press, 1965.

Breese, Gerald (ed.). *The City in Newly Developing Countries: Readings on Urbanism and Urbanization*. Englewood Cliffs, N.J.: Prentice-Hall, 1969.
———. *Urbanization in Newly Developing Countries*. Englewood Cliffs, N.J.: Prentice-Hall, 1966.

Bulsara, Jal F. *Problems of Rapid Urbanization in India*. Bombay: Popular Prakashan, 1964.

Carstairs, G. Morris. *The Twice-Born: A Study of a Community of High-Caste Hindus*. Bloomington: Indiana University Press, 1956.

Clark, Terry N. (ed.). *Community Structure and Decision-Making: Comparative Analyses*. San Francisco: Chandler, 1968.

Cohen, Abner. *Custom and Politics in Urban Africa*. Berkeley and Los Angeles: University of California Press, 1969.

Dahl, Robert A. *Who Governs? Democracy and Power in an American City*. New Haven: Yale University Press, 1961.
———. *Modern Political Analysis*. Englewood Cliffs, N.J.: Prentice-Hall, 1963.
———. *A Preface to Democratic Theory*. Chicago: University of Chicago Press, 1956.

Daland, Robert T. (ed.). *Comparative Urban Research: The Administration and Politics of Cities*. Beverly Hills, Calif.: Sage, 1969.

Davis, Kingsley. *World Urbanization 1950–1970: Vol. I: Basic Data for Cities, Countries, and Regions*, Population Monograph Series, No. 4, Institute of International Studies, University of California, Berkeley, 1969.
———. *World Urbanization 1950–1970: Vol. II: Analysis of Trends, Relationships, and Development*, Population Monograph Series, No. 9, Institute of International Studies, University of California, Berkeley, 1972.

Dongerkery, S. R. *University Autonomy in India*. Bombay: Lalvani Publishing House, 1967.

Dube, Surendranath. *Aata hai yad mujhko huzra hua zamana*. Indore: Sarvotam Press, 1967.

Dye, Thomas R. *Politics, Economics, and the Public: Policy Outcomes in the American States*. Chicago: Rand McNally, 1966.
———. *Understanding Public Policy*. Englewood Cliffs, N.J.: Prentice-Hall, 1972.

Eldersveld, Samuel J., V. Jagannadham, and A. P. Barnabas. *The Citizen and the Administrator in a Developing Democracy.* Glenview, Ill.: Scott, Foresman, 1968.

Epstein, A. L. *Politics in an Urban African Community.* Manchester, England: Manchester University Press, 1958.

Erdman, Howard L. *Political Attitudes of Indian Industry: A Case Study of the Baroda Business Elite.* London: University of London, The Athlone Press, 1971.

Forster, E. M. *The Hill of Devi, Being Letters from Dewas State Senior.* London: Edwin, Arnold & Co., 1953.

Fox, Richard G. *From Zamindar to Ballot Box: Community Change in a North Indian Market Town.* Ithaca, N.Y.: Cornell University Press, 1969.

Gans, Herbert J. *The Urban Villagers.* New York: Free Press, 1962.

Geertz, Clifford. *Peddlers and Princes: Social Development and Economic Modernization in Two Indonesian Towns.* Chicago: University of Chicago Press, 1963.

Ghurye, G. S. *Anatomy of a Rururban Community.* Bombay: Popular Prakashan, 1963.

———. *Cities and Civilization.* Bombay: Popular Prakashan, 1962.

Glazer, Nathan, and Daniel Patrick Moynihan. *Beyond the Melting Pot.* Cambridge, Mass.: M.I.T. Press, 1963.

Gosnell, Harold F. *Machine Politics: Chicago Model.* Chicago: University of Chicago Press, 1937.

———. *Negro Politicians: The Rise of Negro Politics in Chicago.* Chicago: University of Chicago Press, 1935.

Greer, Scott, et al. (eds.). *The New Urbanization.* New York: St. Martin's, 1968.

Grodzins, Morton. *The American System.* Chicago: Rand McNally, 1968.

Gurr, Ted Robert. *Why Men Rebel.* Princeton, N.J.: Princeton University Press, 1970.

Hauser, Philip M. (ed.). *Urbanization in Latin America.* New York: International Documents Service, 1961.

———, and Leo F. Schnore (eds.). *The Study of Urbanization.* New York: Wiley, 1965.

Hawley, Willis D., and Frederick M. Wirt (eds.). *The Search for Community Power.* Englewood Cliffs, N.J.: Prentice-Hall, 1968.

Hazelhurst, Leighton. *Entrepreneurship and the Merchant Castes in a Punjabi City.* Durham, N.C.: Duke University Monograph Series, 1966.

Herring, E. Pendleton. *Group Representation Before Congress,* Baltimore: Johns Hopkins Press, 1929.

Hough, E. M. *The Co-operative Movement in India,* rev. ed. London: Oxford University Press, 1966.

Hunter, Floyd. *Community Power Structure: A Study of Decision-Makers.* Chapel Hill: University of North Carolina Press, 1953; New York: Doubleday (Anchor), 1963.

Huntington, Samuel P. *Political Order in Changing Societies.* New Haven: Yale University Press, 1968.

Indian Institute of Public Administration. *Improving City Government.* New Delhi: New India Press, 1958.

Jakobsen, Leo, and Ved Prakash (eds.). *Urbanization and National Development.* Vol. I, South and Southeast Asia Urban Affairs Annuals. Beverly Hills, Calif.: Sage, 1971.

Karve, D. D. *The New Brahmans: Five Maharashtrian Families.* Berkeley and Los Angeles: University of California Press, 1963.

Kesselman, Mark. *The Ambiguous Consensus: A Study of Local Government in France.* New York: Knopf, 1967.

Key, V. O., Jr. *Southern Politics in State and Nation.* New York: Random House (Vintage), 1949.

Khare, R. S. *The Changing Brahmans: Associations and Elites Among the Kanya-Kubjas of North India.* Chicago: University of Chicago Press, 1970.

Kochanek, Stanley A. *The Congress Party of India: The Dynamics of One-Party Democracy.* Princeton, N.J.: Princeton University Press, 1968.

Kornhauser, William. *The Politics of Mass Society.* London: Routledge and Kegan Paul, 1960.

Kothari, Rajni. *Politics in India.* Boston: Little, Brown, 1970.

Kuper, Hilda (ed.). *Urbanization and Migration in West Africa.* Berkeley and Los Angeles: University of California Press, 1965.

Lambert, Richard D. *Workers, Factories, and Social Change in India.* Princeton, N.J.: Princeton University Press, 1963.

Lasswell, Harold. *Politics: Who Gets What, When, How.* New York: McGraw-Hill, 1938; Meridian, 1958.

———, and Abraham Kaplan. *Power and Society: A Framework for Political Inquiry.* New Haven: Yale University Press, 1950.

Lerner, Daniel. *The Passing of Traditional Society.* Glencoe, Ill.: Free Press, 1958.

Lewis, John Wilson (ed.). *The City in Communist China.* Stanford, Calif.: Stanford University Press, 1971.

Lewis, Oscar. *Village Life in Northern India: Studies in a Delhi Village.* New York: Knopf (Vintage), 1958.

Lineberry, Robert L., and Ira Sharkansky. *Urban Politics and Public Policy.* New York: Harper and Row, 1971.

Litt, Edgar. *Ethnic Politics in America.* Glenview, Ill.: Scott, Foresman, 1970.

Little, Kenneth. *West African Urbanization: A Study of Voluntary Associations in Social Change.* Cambridge, England: Cambridge University Press, 1965.

Lynch, Owen M. *The Politics of Untouchability: Social Mobility and Social Change in a City of India.* New York: Columbia University Press, 1969.

Maas, Arthur (ed.). *Area and Power: A Theory of Local Government.* Glencoe, Ill.: Free Press, 1959.

Mabogunje, A. L. *Yoruba Towns.* Ibadan, Nigeria: Ibadan University Press, 1962.

Malcolm, Sir John. *A Memoir of Central India Including Malwa and Adjoining Provinces,* 3rd ed. Two volumes. London: Parbury, Allen & Co., 1832.

Marriot, McKim (ed.). *Village India.* Chicago: University of Chicago Press, 1955.

Mayer, Adrian. *Caste and Kinship in Central India.* London: Routledge and Kegan Paul, 1960.

Menon, V. P. *The Story of the Integration of the Princely States.* Bombay: Orient Longmans, 1961.

Meyerson, Martin, and Edward C. Banfield. *Politics, Planning, and the Public Interest: The Case of Public Housing in Chicago.* New York: Free Press, 1955.

Millen, Bruce H. *The Political Role of Labor in Developing Countries.* Washington, D.C.: Brookings Institution, 1963.

Miller, Delbert C. *International Community Power Structures: Comparative Studies of Four World Cities.* Bloomington: Indiana University Press, 1970.

Miner, Horace (ed.). *The City in Modern Africa.* New York: Praeger, 1967.

Morris, Morris David. *The Emergence of an Industrial Labor Force in India: A Study of the Bombay Cotton Mills, 1854–1947.* Berkeley and Los Angeles: University of California Press, 1965.

Meyers, Charles A. *Labor Problems in the Industrialization of India.* Cambridge, Mass.: Harvard University Press, 1958.

Owen, David Edward. *British Opium Policy in China and India.* New Haven: Yale University Press, 1934.

Phadnis, Urmila. *Towards the Integration of the Princely States, 1919–1947.* New York: Asia Publishing House, 1968.

Polsby, Nelson W. *Community Power and Political Theory.* New Haven: Yale University Press, 1963.

Potter, D. C. *Government in Rural India.* London: G. Bell, 1964.

Pradhan, M. C. *The Political System of the Jats of Northern India.* London: Oxford University Press, 1966.

Prakash, Ved. *New Towns in India.* Durham, N.C.: Duke University, Program in Comparative Studies on Southern Asia, 1969.

Rabinovitz, Francine F., and Felicity M. Trueblood (eds.). *Latin American Urban Research.* Beverly Hills, Calif.: Sage, 1971.

Ranney, Austin (ed.). *Political Science and Public Policy.* Chicago: Markham, 1968.

Rosen, George. *Democracy and Economic Change in India.* Berkeley and Los Angeles: University of California Press, 1966.

Rosenau, James N. (ed.). *Linkage Politics: Essays on the Convergence of National and International Systems.* New York: Free Press, 1969.

Rosenthal, Donald B. *The Limited Elite: Politics and Government in Two Indian Cities.* Chicago: University of Chicago Press, 1970.

Ross, Aileen. *The Hindu Family in Its Urban Setting.* Toronto: University of Toronto Press, 1961.

Rudolph, Lloyd I., and Susanne Hoeber Rudolph. *The Modernity of Tradition: Political Development in India.* Chicago: University of Chicago Press, 1967.

Sayre, Wallace S., and Herbert Kaufman. *Governing New York City: Politics in the Metropolis.* New York: Russell Sage Foundation, 1960; Norton, 1965.

Schattschneider, E. E. *The Semi-Sovereign People: A Realist's View of Democracy in America.* New York: Holt, Rinehart and Winston, 1960.

———. *Politics, Pressures, and the Tariff.* New York: Prentice-Hall, 1935.

Schnore, Leo F., and Henry Fagin. *Urban Research and Policy Planning.* Beverly Hills, Calif.: Sage, 1967.

Scientific American. *Cities.* New York: Knopf, 1965.

Sharma, B. A. V., and R. T. Jangam. *The Bombay Municipal Corporation: An Election Study.* Bombay: Popular Prakashan, 1961.

Singer, Milton B. (ed.). *Traditional India: Structure and Change.* American Folklore Society, 1959.

Sirsikar, V. M. *Political Behaviour in India: A Case Study of the 1962 General Elections.* Bombay: Manaktalas, 1965.

Sisson, Richard. *The Congress Party in Rajasthan: Political Integration and Institution Building in an Indian State.* Berkeley and Los Angeles: University of California Press, 1972.

Sjoberg, Gideon. *The Preindustrial City, Past and Present.* New York: Free Press, 1960.

Sovani, N. V. *Urbanization and Urban India.* Bombay: Asia Publishing House, 1966.

Srivastava, K. L. *The Revolt of 1857 in Central India–Malwa.* Bombay: Allied Publishers, 1966.

Swartz, Marc J. (ed.). *Local-Level Politics: Social and Cultural Perspectives.* Chicago: Aldine, 1968.

Taub, Richard. *Bureaucrats Under Stress: Administrators and Administration in an Indian State.* Berkeley and Los Angeles: University of California Press, 1969.

Tinker, Hugh. *The Foundations of Local Self-Government in India, Pakistan and Burma.* London: University of London, The Athlone Press, 1954.

Truman, David B. *The Governmental Process: Political Interests and Public Opinion.* New York: Knopf, 1951.

Turner, Roy (ed.). *India's Urban Future.* Berkeley and Los Angeles: University of California Press, 1962.

Tysen, Frank J. *District Administration in Metropolitan Calcutta.* Bombay: Asia Publishing House, 1965.

UNESCO. *Social Implications of Industrialization and Urbanization in Africa South of the Sahara*. London: International African Institute, 1956.

Urban Problems and Policies, Social Science Quarterly, Vol. 52, No. 3, special issue, December 1971.

Vidich, Arthur J., and Joseph Bensman. *Small Town in Mass Society: Class, Power, and Religion in a Rural Community*. New York: Doubleday (Anchor), 1960.

Weber, Max. *The City*, ed. and trans. Don Martindale and Gertrud Neuwirth. New York: Free Press, 1958.

Weiner, Myron. *Party-Building in a New Nation: The Indian National Congress*. Chicago: University of Chicago, 1967.

———. *Party Politics in India: The Development of a Multi-Party System*. Princeton, N.J.: Princeton University Press, 1957.

———. *The Politics of Scarcity: Public Pressure and Political Response in India*. Chicago: University of Chicago, 1962.

———. *Political Change in South Asia*. Calcutta: Firma K. L. Mudhopadhyay, 1963.

——— (ed.). *State Politics in India*. Princeton, N.J.: Princeton University Press, 1968.

———, and Rajni Kothari (eds.). *Indian Voting Behaviour: Studies of the 1962 Elections*. Calcutta: Firma K. L. Mukhopadhyay, 1965.

Whitten, Norman E., Jr. *Class, Kinship and Power in an Ecuadorian Town*. Stanford, Calif.: Stanford University Press, 1965.

Williams, Oliver P. *Metropolitan Political Analysis: A Social Access Approach*. New York: Free Press, 1971.

Wilson, James Q. (ed.). *City Politics and Public Policy*. New York: Wiley, 1968.

Wiser, William, and Charlotte Wiser. *Behind Mud Walls, 1930–1960*. Berkeley and Los Angeles: University of California Press, 1967.

Wylie, Laurence. *Village in the Vaucluse: An Account of Life in a French Village*, rev. ed. New York: Harper, 1964.

ARTICLES AND PERIODICALS

Ahmed, Bashiruddin. "Caste and Electoral Politics," *Asian Survey*, November 1970, pp. 979–992.

Alford, Robert. "The Comparative Study of Urban Politics," in Leo F. Schnore and Henry Fagin (eds.), *Urban Research and Policy Planning*, Beverly Hills, Calif.: Sage, 1967, pp. 263–302.

Bachrach, Peter, and Morton S. Baratz. "Decisions and Nondecisions: An Analytic Framework," *American Political Science Review*, Vol. 57, 1963, pp. 641–651.

———. "Two Faces of Power," *American Political Science Review*, Vol. 56, 1962, pp. 947–952.

Banfield, Edward C. "The Political Implications of Urban Growth," *Daedalus,* Vol. 90, 1961, pp. 61–78.

———, and James Q. Wilson. "Public-Regardingness as a Value Premise in Voting Behavior," *American Political Science Review,* Vol. 58, 1964, pp. 876–887.

Barnes, J. A. "Networks and Political Process," in Marc J. Swartz (ed.), *Local-Level Politics: Social and Cultural Perspectives,* Chicago: Aldine, 1968.

Bhatt, G. S. "Urban Impact and Trends of Inter-Caste Solidarity," *Journal of Sociological Research* (Ranchi), March 1962.

Bailey, F. G. "Parapolitical Systems," in Marc J. Swartz (ed.), *Local-Level Politics: Social and Cultural Perspectives,* Chicago: Aldine, 1968.

Berry, Brian J. L. "City Size and Economic Development," in Leo Jakobsen and Ved Prakash (eds.), *Urbanization and National Development.* Vol. I, South and Southeast Asia Urban Affairs Annuals. Beverly Hills, Calif.: Sage, 1971, pp. 111–155.

———, and Howard Spodek. "Comparative Ecologies of Large Indian Cities," *Economic Geography,* Vol. 47, No. 2 (supplement), June 1971, pp. 266–285.

Bose, Ashish. "The Urbanization Process in South and Southeast Asia," in Leo Jakobsen and Ved Prakash (eds.), *Urbanization and National Development.* Vol. I, South and Southeast Asia Urban Affairs Annuals. Beverly Hills, Calif.: Sage, 1971, pp. 81–109.

Brahmananda, P. R. "The Impact on India of Population Transfers in 1947 and After," in Brinley Thomas (ed.), *Economics of International Migration,* London: Macmillan, 1958.

Chauhan, D. S. "Caste and Occupation in Agra City," *Economic Weekly,* July 23, 1960, pp. 1147–1149.

Church, Roderick. "Authority and Influence in Indian Municipal Politics: Administrators and Councillors in Lucknow," *Asian Survey,* April 1973, pp. 421–438.

Cohn, Bernard. "Madhopur Revisited," *Economic Weekly,* July 1959, pp. 963–966.

Cornelius, Wayne A. "The Political Sociology of Cityward Migration in Latin America: Toward Empirical Theory," in Francine F. Rabinovitz and Felicity M. Trueblood (eds.), *Latin American Urban Research.* Beverly Hills, Calif.: Sage, 1971, pp. 95–125.

Crane, Robert. "Urbanism in India," *American Journal of Sociology,* Vol. 60, 1954–55, pp. 463–470.

Dahl, Robert A. "A Critique of the Ruling Elite Model," *American Political Science Review,* Vol. 52, June 1958, pp. 463–469.

Daland, Robert J. "Political Science and the Study of Urbanism," *American Political Science Review,* Vol. 51, June 1957, pp. 491–509.

Davis, Kingsley. "The Origin and Growth of Urbanization in the World," *American Journal of Sociology,* Vol. 60, 1954–55, pp. 429–437.

Dawson, Richard E., and James A. Robinson. "Inter-Party Competition, Economic Variables, and Welfare Policies in American States," *Journal of Politics,* May 1963, pp. 265–289.

Deutsch, Karl W. "Social Mobilization and Political Development," *American Political Science Review,* Vol. 55, No. 3, September 1961, pp. 493–514.

Driver, E. D. "Caste and Occupational Structure in Central India," *Social Forces,* Vol. 41, October 1962, pp. 26–31.

Form, William H., and William V. D'Antonio. "Integration and Cleavage Among Community Influentials in Two Border Cities," *American Sociological Review,* December 1959, pp. 804–814.

Frolic, B. Michael. "Decision Making in Soviet Cities," *American Political Science Review,* Vol. 66, March 1972, pp. 38–52.

Froman, Lewis. "An Analysis of Public Policy in Cities," *Journal of Politics,* February 1967, pp. 94–108.

Godbole, Y. H. "Indreshwar Nagar Ka Itihas," *Nagrik* (bulletin of the Indore City Corporation), July 25, 1963, pp. 7, 38–40.

Handlin, Oscar. "The Social System," *Daedalus,* Vol. 90, 1961, pp. 11–30.

Hanna, William J., and Judith L. Hanna. "The Political Structure of Urban-Centered African Communities," in Horace Miner (ed.), *The City in Modern Africa,* New York: Preager, 1967.

Hart, Henry C. "Bombay Politics: Pluralism or Polarization?" *Journal of Asian Studies,* May 1961, pp. 267–274.

————. "Urban Politics in Bombay: The Meaning of Community," *Economic Weekly,* June 1960, pp. 983–988.

Holmstrom, Mark. "Caste and Status in an Indian City," *Economic and Political Weekly,* Bombay, April 8, 1972, pp. 769–774.

Horowitz, Irving Louis. "Electoral Politics, Urbanization and Social Development in Latin America," in Glenn H. Beyer (ed.), *The Urban Explosion in Latin America,* Ithaca, New York: Cornell University Press, 1967.

Horton, Raymond D. "Municipal Labor Relations: The New York City Experience," *Social Science Quarterly,* December 1971, pp. 680–696.

Hoselitz, Bert F. "The Urban-Rural Contrast as a Factor in Socio-Cultural Change," *Economic Weekly,* January 1960, pp. 145–152.

Jefferson, Mark. "The Law of the Primate Cities," *Geographical Review,* Vol. 29, April 1939, pp. 226–232.

Jones, Rodney W. "Linkage Analysis of Indian Urban Politics," *Economic and Political Weekly,* Bombay, June 17, 1972, pp. 1195–1203.

Joshi, Ram. "The Shiv Sena: A Movement in Search of Legitimacy," *Asian Survey,* November 1970, pp. 967–978.

Katzenstein, Mary F. "Origins of Nativism: The Emergence of Shiv Sena in Bombay," *Asian Survey,* April 1973, pp. 386–399.

Khare, R. S. "The Kanya-Kubja Brahmins and Their Caste Organization," *Southwestern Journal of Anthropology,* Vol. 16, 1960, pp. 348–367.

Kothari, Rajni. "Towards a Political Perspective for the Seventies," *Economic and Political Weekly,* Bombay, January 1970, Annual Number, pp. 111–113.

———, and Ghyansham Shah. "Caste Orientation of Political Factions, Modasa Constituency: A Case Study," *Economic Weekly,* July 1963, pp. 1169–1178.

———, and Rushikesh Maru. "Caste and Secularism in India," *Journal of Asian Studies,* Vol. 25, 1965, pp. 33–50.

Lambert, Richard D. "Factory Workers and the Non-Factory Population in Poona," *Journal of Asian Studies,* Vol. 18, November 1958, pp. 21–42.

Laquian, Aprodicio A. "Slums and Squatters in South and Southeast Asia," in Leo Jakobsen and Ved Prakash (eds.), *Urbanization and National Development.* Vol. I, South and Southeast Asia Urban Affairs Annuals, Beverly Hills, Calif.: Sage, 1971, pp. 183–203.

Lemarchand, Rene. "Political Clientelism and Ethnicity in Tropical Africa: Competing Solidarities in Nation-Building," *American Political Science Review,* Vol. 66, March 1972, pp. 68–90.

Lewis, Oscar. "Urbanization Without Breakdown: A Case Study," *The Scientific Monthly,* Vol. 75, 1952, pp. 31–41.

Long, Norton E. "The Local Community as an Ecology of Games," *American Journal of Sociology,* Vol. 63, November 1958, pp. 251–261.

Lowi, Theodore. "American Business, Public Policy, Case Studies, and Political Theory," *World Politics,* Vol. 16, July 1964, pp. 677–715.

Madsen, Douglas. "Solid Congress Support in 1967: A Statistical Inquiry," *Asian Survey,* November 1970, pp. 1004–1014.

Marvick, Dwaine. "Party Cadres and Receptive Partisan Voters in the 1967 Indian National Elections," *Asian Survey,* November 1970, pp. 949–966.

Mayer, Adrian C. "Municipal Elections: A Central Indian Case Study," in C. H. Philips (ed.), *Politics and Society in India,* London: George Allen and Unwin, 1963.

———. "The Dominant Caste in a Region of Central India," *Southwestern Journal of Anthropology,* Winter 1958, pp. 407–427.

———. "Rural Leaders and the Indian General Election," *Asian Survey,* October 1961, pp. 23–29.

———. "The Significance of Quasi-Groups in the Study of Complex Societies," in Michael Banton (ed.), *The Social Anthropology of Complex Societies,* London: Tavistock, 1966, pp. 97–121.

———. "Some Hierarchical Aspects of Caste," *Southwestern Journal of Anthropology,* Summer 1956, pp. 117–144.

———. "System and Network: An Approach to the Study of Political Process in Dewas," in T. N. Madan and Gopala Sarana (eds.), *Indian Anthropology,* Bombay: Asia Publishing House, 1962.

Mayer, Peter B. "Patterns of Urban Political Culture in India," *Asian Survey,* April 1973, pp. 400–407.

McGee, T. G. "Catalysts or Cancers? The Role of Cities in Asian Society," in Leo Jakobsen and Ved Prakash (eds.), *Urbanization and National De-*

velopment, Vol. I, South and Southeast Urban Affairs Annuals, Beverly Hills, Calif.: Sage, 1971, pp. 157–181.

Miller, Delbert C. "Decision-Making Cliques in Community Power Structure: A Comparative Study of an American and an English City," *American Journal of Sociology,* 64, November 1958, pp. 299–310.

———. "Industry and Community Power Structure: A Comparative Study of an American and an English City," *American Sociological Review,* 23, February 1958, pp. 9–15.

Morris, Morris David. "Caste and the Evolution of the Industrial Work Force in India," *Proceedings of the American Philosophical Society,* Vol. 104, April 1960, pp. 124–133.

———. "Recruitment of an Industrial Labor Force in India, with British and American Comparisons," *Comparative Studies in Society and History,* Vol. II, 1959–60, pp. 305–328.

Morse, Richard. "Urbanization in Latin America," *Latin American Research Review,* Austin, Texas, Vol. I, No. 1, 1965, pp. 35–75.

Nelson, Joan. "The Urban Poor: Disruption or Political Integration in Third World Cities," *World Politics,* Vol. 22, April 1970, pp. 393–414.

Pocock, D. F. "Sociologies: Urban and Rural," *Contributions to Indian Sociology,* No. 4, 1960, pp. 63–81.

Polsby, Nelson W., and Wallace S. Sayre. "American Political Science and the Study of Urbanization," in Philip M. Hauser and Leo F. Schnore (eds.), *The Study of Urbanization,* New York: Wiley, 1965, pp. 115–156.

Portes, Alejandro. "Urbanization and Politics in Latin America," *Social Science Quarterly,* Vol. 52, No. 3, December 1971, pp. 697–720.

Proudfoot, L. "Towards Muslim Solidarity in Freetown," *Africa,* Vol. 31, April 1961, pp. 147–157.

Rabinovitz, Francine F. "Urban Development and Political Development in Latin America," in Robert T. Daland (ed.), *Comparative Urban Research: The Administration and Politics of Cities.* Beverly Hills, Calif.: Sage, 1969, pp. 88–123.

Redfield, Robert, and Milton B. Singer. "The Cultural Role of Cities," *Economic Development and Cultural Change,* Vol. 3, 1954, pp. 53–73.

Rodwin, Lloyd. "Metropolitan Policy for Developing Areas," *Daedalus,* Vol. V, No. 90, 1961, pp. 132–146.

Rosenthal, Donald B. "Administrative Politics in Two Indian Cities," *Asian Survey,* April 1966, pp. 201–215.

———. "Deurbanization, Elite Displacement, and Political Change in India," *Comparative Politics,* Vol. 2, No. 14, January 1970, pp. 169–201.

———. "Factions and Alliances in Indian City Politics," *Midwest Journal of Political Science,* Vol. 10, August 1966, pp. 320–349.

———. "Functions of Urban Political Systems: Comparative Analysis and the Indian Case," in Terry N. Clark (ed.), *Community Structure and Decision-Making.* San Francisco: Chandler, 1968, pp. 269–303.

———. "Symposium on Indian Urban Politics: Introduction," *Asian Survey*, April 1973, pp. 380–385.

Rudolph, Lloyd. "Urban Life and Populist Radicalism: Dravidian Politics in Madras," *Journal of Asian Studies*, Vol. 20, May 1961, pp. 283–297.

Salisbury, Robert H. "The Analysis of Public Policy: A Search for Theories and Roles," in Austin Ranney (ed.), *Political Science and Public Policy*, Chicago: Markham, 1968, pp. 151–175.

Scott, James C. "Corruption, Machine Politics, and Political Change," *American Political Science Review*, December 1969, pp. 1142–1158.

———. "Patron-Client Politics and Political Change in Southeast Asia," *American Political Science Review*, Vol. 66, March 1972, pp. 91–113.

Singer, Milton B. "Urban Politics in a Plural Society: A Symposium," *Journal of Asian Studies*, Vol. 20, May 1961.

Singh, Partap. "Supersession of Municipal Committees," *Economic and Political Weekly*, Bombay, April 8, 1972, p. 747.

Tinker, Hugh. "The City in Asia," *Reorientation: Studies on Asia in Transition*, Oxford, 1965.

Turner, Roy. "The Future of Indian Cities," *Asian Survey*, March 1961, pp. 29–37.

Verma, S. C. "The Changing Role of the District Officer in Madhya Pradesh," in Indian Institute of Public Administration, *The Changing Role of the District Officer*, New Delhi, 1965.

Ward, Barbara. "The Poor World's Cities," *The Economist*, Dec. 6, 1969, pp. 56–70.

Weiner, Myron. "Violence and Politics in Calcutta," *Journal of Asian Studies*, Vol. 20. May 1961, pp. 275–281.

Wilcox, Wayne. "Madhya Pradesh," in Myron Weiner (ed.), *State Politics in India*, Princeton, N.J.: Princeton University Press, 1968.

———. "Politicians, Bureaucrats and Development in India," *Annals of the American Academy of Political and Social Science*, March 1965, pp. 114–122.

———. "Trade Unions, the Middle-Class Intelligentsia, and a Communist M.P.: The Indore Parliamentary Election of 1962," in Myron Weiner and Rajni Kothari (eds.), *Indian Voting Behaviour: Studies of the 1962 General Elections*, Calcutta: Firma K. L. Mukhopdhayay, 1965.

Windmiller, Marshall. "The Politics of State Reorganization in India: The Case of Bombay," *Far Eastern Survey*, September 1956, pp. 129–143.

Wirsing, Robert G. "Associational 'Micro-Arenas' in Indian Urban Politics," *Asian Survey*, April 1973, pp. 408–420.

Wirth, Louis. "Urbanism as a Way of Life," *American Journal of Sociology*, Vol. 44, July 1938.

Wolfinger, Raymond E. "The Development and Persistence of Ethnic Voting," *American Political Science Review*, Vol. 59, December 1965, pp. 896–908.

———. "Reputation and Reality in the Study of Community Power," *American Sociological Review*, Vol. 25, October 1960, pp. 636–644.

REPORTS

Dravid, V. V. *Labour, Labour Movement and Labour Legislation in Madhya Pradesh*. Indore: Mazdoor Press, Shram Shivir, 1966.

National Council of Applied Economic Research, New Delhi. *Techno-Economic Survey of Madhya Pradesh*. Bombay: Asia Publishing House, 1960.

Textile Wage Board Ke Sammukh Shramikon Ka Paksh (The Case of the Laborers Before the Textile Wage Board), presented by Ramsingh Verma, representing the National Labor Congress (M.P.). Indore: Mazdoor Press, Shram Shivir, 1959.

The Mandlik Papers and the Family. Indore: Malav Itihas Mandal, 1946.

UNPUBLISHED MATERIAL

Ahmed, Qazi. Indian Cities: Characteristics and Correlates, Ph.D. dissertation, University of Chicago, 1965.

Church, Roderick. "The Municipal Administrative Process in Lucknow, India." Paper presented at American Political Science Association, Chicago, 1971. (Mimeographed.)

Dube, Sharad Kumari. Municipal Administration at Indore—Evolution and Present Set-Up. Ph.D. dissertation. Ujjain: Vikram University, 1964.

Goldrich, Daniel, Raymond B. Pratt, and C. R. Schuller. "The Political Integration of Lower-Class Urban Settlements in Chile and Peru: A Provisional Inquiry." Paper presented at American Political Science Association, September 1966. (Mimeographed.)

Jones, Rodney W. "Area, Power, and Linkage in Indore: A Political Map of an Indian City." Ph.D. dissertation, Columbia University, 1970.

Kaufman, Clifford. "Mass Support for National Political Institutions: The Lower Class in Mexico City." Paper presented at American Political Science Association, Chicago, 1971. (Mimeographed.)

Leonard, John. "Urban Government Under the Raj: A Case Study of Municipal Administration in Nineteenth-Century South India." Paper, n.d.

Nicholas, Ralph W. "Rules, Resources, and Political Activity." Michigan State University, n.d. (Mimeographed.)

Niehoff, Arthur. "Caste, Class, and Family in an Industrial Community of North India," Ph.D. dissertation, Columbia University, 1957.

Norman, Robert T. "Urban Political Development: India." Paper presented at American Political Science Association, Chicago, 1971. (Mimeographed.)

Oldenburg, Philip. "Indian Urban Politics: Citizen, Administrator and Councillor in Delhi." Paper presented at American Political Science Association, Chicago, 1971. (Mimeographed.)

Owens, Raymond, and Ashish Nandy. "Voluntary Associations in an Industrial Ward of Howrah, West Bengal, India." Paper presented at Association for Asian Studies, Washington, D.C., 1971.

Rosenthal, Donald B. "Deference and Friendship Patterns in Two Indian Municipal Councils." State University of New York at Buffalo, 1966. (Mimeographed.)

Wilcox, Wayne. "Alternative Strategies of Political Elite Survival in South Asia." Paper presented at American Political Science Association, 1966. (Mimeographed.)

Wirsing, Robert. "Socialist Society and Free Enterprise Politics: A Study of the Urban Political Process in Nagpur, India." Ph.D. dissertation, University of Denver, 1971.

————. "Urban Politics in Nagpur, India." Paper presented at American Political Science Association, Chicago, 1971. (Mimeographed.)

GOVERNMENT DOCUMENTS

HOLKAR STATE:

Banawalikar, A. S. *A Study of Industrial Dissatisfactions (Being the Report of an Enquiry)*. Indore: Labour Department, June 1948.

Dhariwal, L. C. *The Indore State Gazetteer*. Four volumes. Indore: Holkar Government Press, 1931.

Dinanath. *A Glimpse Into Holkar State Administration*. Indore: Holkar Government Press, n.d.

Geddes, Patrick. *Town Planning Towards City Development: A Report to the Durbar of Indore*. Two volumes. Indore: Holkar Government Press, 1918.

The Half-Yearly List of Officers of the Holkar State, October, 1947. Indore: Holkar Government Press, 1947.

Hoare, H. J. *Final Report on the Settlement of Indore State*. Indore: Holkar Government Press, 1909.

Index and Classification of Huzur Shree Shanker Orders, 1930–43, 1948, Manik Bagh Reference Library, n.d.

Jevons, H. Stanley. *Report on the Economic Development of the Indore State*. Manik Bagh Reference Library, typescript, 1925.

List of Officers of the Holkar State, 1931 and 1947. Indore: Holkar Government Press, 1931, 1947.

Luard, Lt. Col. C. E. *Central India Census Series, 1921, Vol. I: Holkar State*. Bombay, 1923.

Rashid, Mashir Bahadur M. A. *Census of Central India, 1931, Vol. XVI: Holkar State*. Two Volumes. Indore, 1933.

Reports and Correspondence on Indore City Water Supply and Drainage Schemes, 1927–29. Indore: Holkar Government Press, 1930.

Report on the Administration of Holkar State, 1934, 1943, 1947. Indore: Holkar Government Press.

Sherlekar, A. G. *The Scheme of Cooperative Movement in Holkar State*. Manik Bagh Reference Library, typescript, 1939.

INDIA:

Central Council of Local Government, *Augmentation of Financial Resources of Urban Local Bodies*, Delhi, 1965.

Institute of Local Self Government, *The Directory of Municipal Corporations in India*, Bombay, 1964.

Ministry of Health, *Local Self-Government Administration in States of India*. Simla, 1962.

Ministry of Health, *Report of the Rural-Urban Relationship Committee*. June 1966.

Ministry of Health, *Town and Country Planning in India*. New Delhi, 1962.

INDORE:

Indore City Corporation, *Council Membership Lists*.

Indore City Corporation, *Indore nagar palik nigam varshik—vivaran san* (*Indore Municipal Corporation Annual Review*), 1964–65.

Indore City Corporation, "Madhya Pradesh Municipal Corporations Act, 1956," *Nagrik*, special number, September 15, 1961.

Indore City Corporation, "Nehru Stadium, Rabindra Graha and Mahatma Gandhi Hall Construction Inquiry," Report, 1965.

Indore City Corporation, *Statement of the Budget* for 1952–53, 1955–56, 1966–67, 1967–68.

MADHYA BHARAT:

Census of India, 1951, Volume XV, Madhya Bharat and Bhopal, Gwalior, 1954.

Report on the Causes and Course of the Students' Agitation in Indore, and the Disturbances Resulting Therefrom, Culminating in the Firing on the 21st of July, 1954. Known briefly as the *Wanchoo Commission Report*. Indore: High Court Library, typescript, 1965.

MADHYA PRADESH:

Census of India, 1961, Madhya Pradesh, Census Handbook, Indore District, 1964.

Chief Electoral Officer, *Handbook on the General Elections in Madhya Pradesh*, Bhopal, 1967.

Directorate of Economics and Statistics, *Pocket Compendium of District Statistics*, Indore, 1963.

Directorate of Employment and Training, *Indore Employment Review, March 1961–March 1966*, Jabalpur, mimeographed, 1967.

High Court. "High Court Judgment of the Khadiwala Case," Criminal Revision Nos. 151 and 153 of 1963, *Viswanath vs. Khadiwala*, and *Khadiwala vs. Viswanath*, July 29, 1964. Indore, the High Court Bar Association Library, typescript.

Report of the Christian Missionary Activities Enquiry Committee, 1956, Vol. II. Nagpur: Government Printing, Madhya Pradesh, 1956.

Report of the Christian Missionary Activities Enquiry Committee, 1956, Vol. I. Indore: Government Regional Press, 1957.

Town Planning Department, *Draft Interim Development Plan for Indore*, Bhopal, 1968.

INDEX

Myers, Charles A., 264, n.1, 280, n.11

Nagrik Samiti (Citizens' Committee), 90; internal differences within, 183–192; represented in Trust, 246; role of in opposition politics, 179, 180, 182, 183
Nai Duniya (newspaper), 162; establishment of, 78–79
Nai Duniya faction, 73, 77–78; alliance with Khadiwala group, 87, 179; in Cabinet of Madhya Bharat, 106; as dominant faction on the Trust, 243, 247; compared to Khadiwala faction, 80–81; coalition with, then rivalry with INTUC, 86–87; dominates Council from (1945–1950), 150–152; leaders of, 79–80; as leading faction until (1956), 85; machine characteristics of, 81; opposed by Khadiwala faction, 76; political alignments of, 7, 82; power of, 359; Praja Mandal as forerunner of, 73, 77–78, 80, 85, 94, 151, 353; role of in agricultural markets, 331, 332–333; role of in state-city political linkages, 126, 127; role of in supersession of Corporation, 206; supported by Jains, 109; water shortage crisis and, 219, 221
Nakedars: appointment of, 152; defined 137
Nanda, Gulzarilal: as arbitrator in INTUC factional dispute, 307, 308; role of in labor politics, 272, 273
Narmada scheme, 216
Nav Bharat (newspaper), 338
Nazul land, state vs. municipal administration of, 142
Nelson, Joan, 6, n.9
Newspapers, of Congress party factions, 73
Nominations. *See* Elections.
Non-Maharashtrian Brahmans: increasing administrative activities of, 60–61; represented in municipal councils, 157. *See also* Hindi-speaking Brahmans
Norman, Robert T., 8, n.15

Occupational distribution: and caste system, 38; and political parties in municipal councils, 154–157
Occupations, in Indore, 30–32
Octroi Inquiry Committee, 141
Octroi taxation, 146; attempts to reduce impact of, 167; and authority of Mayor, 223; case against D. Eadie for, 224; defined, 137; irregularities in collection of, 191, 369; revenue from, 141
Official elite: defined, 54; Maharastrian vs. non-Maharashtrian Brahmans in, 56–57
Oke, G. V., 292
Oke, W. V., 113, 125
Opium, 24, 28, n.6, 342
Opposition politics: based in cities, 8; electoral success of in (1965), 193; first opposition Mayor, 182–183; Mishra group and, 192–200; organization of, 179; seizure of power by, 178–192; supersession of Corporation and, 201–210. *See also Nagrik Samiti*
"Outsiders," role of in Indore labor politics, 323–324, 325–326; position of Mayor and, 199
"Overurbanization," 5
Owen, David E., 28, n.6

Pahlwans (professional wrestlers), 79, 342, 343
Panchayat, 19
Panchayati raj system, of district local governments, 8
Pande, Kashinath, as arbitrator in Tiwari-Ramsingh dispute, 317, 318–319
Parasrampuria, Sitaram, 75
Pardesipura, 168; development of, 254
Patel, Kantilal, 166
Pathak, Tarashanker, as Congress party rival in municipal politics, 162–165
Patol, D. S., 165; role of on Trust, 253
Patodi, Babulal, 79, 87–88, 89, 90, 112; becomes President, 175; defeated in 1967 elections, 92
Patronage: centralization of at state-level government, 140; by executive civil engineers, 239; of Improvement Trust, 233, 249, 250, 253; within municipal politics, 136–137, 148–149, 152
Personal Staff, of princely states, 54–55
Phadnis, Urmila, 50, 98
Pluralist model, of urban politics, 362–364
Police department, 137; administration of penetrated by labor factional disputes, 312; anti-Ramsingh in Indore, 309; changes in bureaucracies of, 344; at Malwa Mill riot, 283–284; proportion of Maharashtrian Brahmans in, 57, 58; relation of to underworld, 343; role of in student demonstrations, 336, 339, 340

Political arena: defined, 13; types of in urban politics, 133, 330

Political linkages. *See* Linkages

Political parties: caste distribution and, 158; in cities, 8–9; vs. political role of unions, 264; use of organized student groups by, 336, 339. *See also* Communist party; Congress party; Jan Sangh party; Opposition politics; Socialists

Political radicalization, 6–7. *See also* Violence

Political recruitment. *See* Recruitment

Polsby, Nelson W., 9, n.20, 16, n.36

Polyarchy, 17

Poona, 11

Population of Indore, 22, 29; compared to water supply, 213

Portes, Alejandro, 6, n.11

Praja Mandal, 52; as a coalition of entrenched castes, 353; as forerunner of Nai Duniya faction, 73, 77–78, 80, 85, 94, 151, 353; Gandhian attitude toward, 76–77; as heir of Holkar princely influence, 151; role of in Indore, 76; role of in political linkages of labor politics, 271. *See also* Nai Duniya faction

Prakash, Ved, 4, n.1

President, as term for Mayor, 133

Primate city, 5, 11, n.25

Princely power: continuity of in municipal politics, 150–152, 353–355; decline of, 17; and enduring linkage patterns in labor politics, 268–274; heirs to, 34; persistence of in Madhya Bharat, 97–118; remnants of in Indore, 50–54; vs. nationalism, 76–77

Princely states: administrative recruitment in, 54–63; effects of abolition of, 97; influence of on administration of unified states, 99–103; merger of, 26; nationalist agitation in, 76. *See also* Holkar state

Private schools, patrons of, 334–335

Public educational system, teachers in as state employees, 335. *See also* Education

Public Health Department (Municipal), 135–136

Public Health Department (State), 137; Maharashtrian and non-Maharashtrians in staff of, 68–69; in politics of town planning, 229, 240, 241; water supply and, 213–214, 249–259

Public policy, 364–368; defined, 365; in labor politics, 373–377; process of in Indore, 377–380; typology of, 365–366

Public safety: agencies for, 137; politics of, 341–346

Public Service Commission, 24, 102

Public Works Department (Municipal): Committee of, 163, 164, 165; expenditures of during water crisis, 217–219, 220; expenditures of to benefit labor, 175–177; patronage of, 136–137; position of Chairman of, 166–167

Public Works Department (State): in town planning politics, 229, 240, 241

Purohit, B. B., 188

"Quit India" movement, 273–274

Rabinovitz, Francine F., 4, n.1, 18, n.40

Railroads: economic significance of for Indore, 28; locations of in Indore, 41–42

Rainfall, 212–213

Rajasthan, 35, 38, 75

Rajkumar Mills, 29, 41, 301–302

Rajmata of Gwalior. *See* Scindia

Rajpramukh (Governor): position of given to Gwalior prince, 99; terminated, 122, n.20

Rajputs, 25, 35–36; administrative roles of, 62

Rajya Praja Mandal (States' Peoples' Conference), 76

Ram, Chandgi, 345

Ramchand, Munshi, 57

Ramsingh. *See* Verma, Ramsingh

Rao family of Malwi Brahmans, in early Indore history, 24–25. *See also* Zamindar family

Rashid, M. A., 22, n.1

Rathor, Dr. Prem Singh, 110

Redfield, Robert, 17, n.38

Redistributive public policy, 365; used by Trust, 373

Registrar of Cooperatives, 331

Registrar of Trade Unions, 286; influence of, 326; and issue of "representative unions," 280, 281

Regulatory public policy, 365–366; applied to improvement politics, 370–373; role of in municipal politics, 369, 377, 379

"Representative unions": as bargaining agent of workers, 324; in relation to state government power, 280–286

Reserve Bank of India, 66, 331

Reservoirs, 212–213